THE METROPOLITAN REVOLUTION

THE COLUMBIA HISTORY OF URBAN LIFE

The Columbia History of Urban Life
Kenneth T. Jackson, General Editor

THE METROPOLITAN
REVOLUTION

The Rise of Post-Urban America

Jon C. Teaford

Columbia University Press
New York

Columbia University Press
Publishers Since 1893
New York   Chichester, West Sussex

Library of Congress Cataloging-in-Publication Data
Teaford, Jon C.
  The metropolitan revolution : the rise of
post-urban America / Jon C. Teaford.
      p. cm. — (The Columbia history of urban life)
    Includes bibliographical references and index.
    ISBN 0-231-13372-3 (cloth : alk. paper)
    ISBN 0-231-13373-1 (pbk. : alk. paper)
   1. Metropolitan areas—United States—History—
20th century. 2. Cities and towns—United States—
History—20th century. I. Title.
    HT334.U5T4 2006
    307.76'4'0973—dc22

                                          2005034053

♾
Columbia University Press books are printed on
permanent and durable acid-free paper.
Printed in the United States of America
c 10 9 8 7 6 5 4 3 2 1
p 10 9 8 7 6 5 4 3 2 1

Contents

THE METROPOLITAN REVOLUTION

Introduction:

The Metropolitan Revolution

"We are on the threshold of a crucial era of change in the urban way of life," wrote the respected architect-planner Henry S. Churchill in 1945. "Vast disintegrating and destructive forces are loose on the world," he observed, causing Americans to seek "new physical urban settings" as well as "new social and economic patterns."[1] Although his vision of the future was not perfect, Churchill's sense of impending radical change proved prescient. The American city was indeed on the brink of a revolution that would transform the metropolis and the lifestyle of the nation's residents. During the following half century, traditional notions of the city would become obsolete, and concepts standard to the understanding of urban areas would grow increasingly outmoded. By 2000 changes in metropolitan life would draw into question the meaning of such terms as "urban" and "suburban," as language and notions appropriate to the world of Henry Churchill seemed to fall short of explaining the new reality.

In 1945 the United States was an urban nation, dominated by clearly defined urban places with an anatomy familiar and comprehensible to experts like Churchill as well as city dwellers in general. The metropolis was a place with readily discernible edges, its lifestyle sharply distinguished from that of the rural "rubes" and "hicks," many of whom had obtained the benefits of electricity only a decade before. Cities were in the nation's vanguard, enjoying the latest technology and defining the cutting edge in fashion and culture. They were the centers of commerce, manufacturing, entertainment, and intellect where the luckiest Americans made and spent their fortunes. Manhattan and Chicago were magnets attracting the ambitious and adventurous, those who sought to get ahead and enjoy the best in life. The vast expanses beyond metropolitan America were the "sticks," the home of those who remained behind.

At the core of each of these urban places was a single central business district, the undisputed focus of the metropolitan area. Although segregated by socioeconomic class in different residential zones, all metropolitan Americans recognized the downtown as the center of urban life. It was the unquestioned hub of finance, retailing, office employment, government, and transportation, and Americans viewed the metropolis as radiating from this single preeminent center. Each metropolis had one dominant heart marked by bustling crowds and soaring skyscrapers that was perceived as essential to the urban area's continued existence.

Metropolitan Americans not only perceived a single dominant focus for urban life, but also shared common space. The realities of urban existence forced the diverse elements of the populace to come into contact; it was difficult to escape the various fragments of the metropolitan mosaic. Because of rationing of gasoline and tires during World War II and because few families had more than one automobile, residents relied heavily on public transit. Middle-class men commuted to work on buses or streetcars that passed from middle-class neighborhoods through blue-collar districts, taking on working-class passengers, to the downtown area, a destination for residents from throughout the metropolis. Likewise, middle-class women shoppers traveled to downtown department stores by means of public transit, moving slowly through the various social zones of the city. On reaching downtown, they shared the sidewalks with businessmen, panhandlers, and working-class shoppers.

Metropolitan Americans not only shared common space, but had a common vested interest in urban governmental institutions. Although there were upper-middle-class suburban municipalities, the largest central cities still comprised a full range of neighborhoods from skid row to elite. The central-city government and central-city school administrators had to accommodate a socially and culturally diverse constituency, one that included all elements of the metropolitan social mix. Even residents of independent suburban municipalities generally worked and shopped in the central city, spending much of their lives within its boundaries.

Their safety while shopping or working depended on central-city police and firefighting forces; the viability of their businesses depended on central-city tax rates and regulations. Despite the existence of suburban municipalities, then, the metropolis was to a great extent one city politically. Just as everyone recognized one common hub and shared common space, the overwhelming majority of metropolitan residents realized that the government of the central city affected all their lives and was of significance to the welfare of them all.

Thus in 1945 the great mass of metropolitan Americans still lived an urban existence. Although divided socially, they inhabited a shared metropolis and could not avoid day-to-day contact with one another. They were separated by ethnicity and class, but they lived in the same city. They were different elements of a shared urban world.

Over the course of the following half century, however, the single-focus metropolis disappeared and was replaced by an amorphous sprawl of population without a unifying hub or culture. By the close of the twentieth century, most metropolitan Americans commuted in private automobiles by themselves, or with co-workers of a similar social background, from their homes in one suburb to their jobs in another suburb. If they ever entered the central city, they generally did so along depressed expressways, their vision shielded from the dreary neighborhoods on either side of them. They shopped in enclosed suburban malls that excluded panhandlers and other "undesirables" and insulated them from the social and climatic hardships of the metropolis. The malls catered to the consumption patterns of their social class, and this generally ensured that they would be mixing with people like themselves. An increasing number of Americans were living in gated communities, insulated from those they did not want to see, walled off from the bothersome or threatening elements of the population. Moreover, as residents of suburban municipalities, they did not share a common city government with the less affluent of the central city. And their businesses, jobs, and favorite stores were not in the central city. What happened in central-city government or schools did not personally affect them.

The middle-class Americans who chose to avoid the suburban lifestyle and live in the central city were most often those least dependent on central-city government services. The back-to-the-city movement appealed to childless young professionals who did not suffer personally from the poor quality of inner-city public schools. Central cities attracted these young adults as well as gays and others who did not want to share the American "norm" along the suburban fringe. In other words, by the close of the twentieth century, American metropolitan areas had become spatially and culturally fragmented, with enclaves for the middle-class nuclear family of father, mother, and two children; with special communities for senior citizens, where those over sixty could be isolated from the more youthful; with gentrifying communities for young singles and gays; and with incipient hubs of gentrification inhabited by artists and others who liked to deem themselves bohemian. Because of their poverty, still others were relegated to the areas no one else wanted. Moreover, these disparate groups did not need to mix on a day-to-day basis. Middle-class suburbanites remained in the outlying areas twenty-four hours a day, removed from the other elements of the metropolitan mix.

By the close of the twentieth century, then, the single-focus metropolises had disappeared. Sprawling metropolitan regions, which defied traditional notions of a city, had supplanted them. In Sunbelt Florida, a metropolitan region mushroomed along the Atlantic coast, an unbroken stretch of dense human habitation sprawling over one hundred miles from south of Miami to north of West Palm Beach with two parallel superhighways serving as the regional main streets. Metropolitan development spread over thousands of square miles in southern California, and only a small portion of the residents of the Atlanta metropolitan area actually lived or worked in the city of Atlanta. Across America, new hubs of production and consumption developed around freeway interchanges, and multiple commercial centers dotted metropolitan regions. The central city was no longer central; most Americans lived in regions, not cities.

During the second half of the twentieth century, a revolution in ethnic composition, perception, and politics also transformed metropolitan America. In 1945 and during the following three decades, Americans inhabited black-and-white metropolises. The great ethnic divide that strongly influenced social and political development was between European Americans and African Americans. Other ethnic groups existed, but when Americans discussed the race problem, they meant the troubled relations between blacks and whites. Race was black and white. The black–white division underlay settlement patterns, political debate, and attitudes on schooling and policing. In the black–white city of the post–World War II era, the dilemma of race relations between European Americans and African Americans was an ever-present reality that could not be ignored.

From the 1970s on, however, a new wave of immigration, especially from Latin America and Asia, increasingly complicated the racial picture and transformed the ethnic profile of metropolitan America. By the 1990s, Hispanics outnumbered blacks in many cities, and Asians were a growing presence. In some cities, the percentage of the population that was black actually decreased as newcomers seemed poised to displace African Americans as the preeminent minority group. In Miami, Cuban Americans clashed with African Americans; in Los Angeles, Korean immigrants battled local blacks. Well-to-do Chinese newcomers "invaded" suburban areas, and in sharp contrast to traditional notions of ethnic invasion, they did not depress property values but brought new prosperity to their suburban communities. Asian American physicians, scientists, and engineers joined their European American counterparts in prestigious outlying subdivisions, creating an ethnic diversity at odds with long-standing stereotypes of suburbia.

By 2000, then, Americans inhabited a radically different world from that of 1945. Metropolitan areas sprawled over hundreds of square miles without a distinguishable common center or clear-cut edges. The black–white world had given way to a metropolitan population of every shade, an ethnic world more complex and less sharply defined than in 1945. It was a world that Henry Churchill and his colleagues from 1945 would not have understood, a world that did not conform to their preconceptions of the city.

Although many commentators of the late twentieth century deplored the decentralization of American life while others were wary of the new wave of immigrants, America's metropolitan revolution reflected the felt desires of millions of people who enjoyed unprecedented freedom and mobility. The automobile liberated Americans from dependence on centripetal public transit; federal mortgage guarantees permitted millions of young white couples to escape from tenements or their in-laws' spare room and purchase a house and yard of their own; Social Security and pension plans freed senior citizens from the necessity of living with their children and allowed them to opt for gated communities tailored to their interests; sexual liberation permitted homosexuals to come out of the shadows and openly create enclaves for themselves; and a gender revolution liberated young women from expectations of early marriage and substituted the possibility of a single life in the central city. Meanwhile, liberalized immigration laws unlocked the nation's doors to millions of newcomers from Latin America and Asia, whereas heightened ethnic tolerance and civil rights legislation lowered the barriers to suburbanization for diverse ethnic groups.

Not everyone shared equally in the benefits of prosperity and mobility. Many had no choice but to take the bus and inhabit run-down apartments in crime-ridden neighborhoods. To an unprecedented degree, however, changing technology and increasing wealth enabled metropolitan Americans to pursue different lifestyles and carve spatial niches tailored to their individual preferences. Decentralization and fragmentation undermined prospects for a united metropolitan community. Yet the amorphous pattern of 2000 seemed to reflect the amorphous nature of American life. Metropolitan Americans chose to disperse rather than cluster.

The result was a world that even scholars and journalists of the late twentieth century had a difficult time comprehending. As business moved to the metropolitan edge, they sought to label this new inside-out world in which the center was on the rim and the hub was increasingly peripheral. Some wrote of urban villages, others of edge cities, still others of technoburbs, and some settled for the generic post-suburbia. They knew that they were living in a world in which the traditional labels of urban and suburban no longer exactly fit, but they struggled to conceptualize the strange new environment around them. It simply did not make sense to people unable to escape the concepts of the past. Where did the so-called Philadelphia metropolitan area begin and the New York metropolitan area end? Was Princeton, New Jersey, a satellite orbiting around Philadelphia or New York City? Or was it an independent body, revolving around neither of the historic central cities? Was the larger city of Virginia Beach a suburb of the older city of Norfolk, and what about the populous adjoining municipalities of Chesapeake, Newport News, and Hampton? Was Mesa, Arizona, a city larger than Pittsburgh or Cincinnati, a suburb of Phoenix, and, if so, what made Mesa suburban and Phoenix urban? And what about the adjacent cities of Scottsdale and Glendale, both of which had over 200,000 residents?

Similarly, the experts floundered in their attempts to categorize the new ethnic world. In 1945 the Census Bureau had divided the population into white and nonwhite, the latter consisting primarily of African Americans and a relative small population of East Asians, American Indians, and Pacific Islanders. A Hispanic category did not exist; Mexican Americans were whites. In the racial world of 1945, the categories of white and nonwhite worked. One was either white or not, and that was all that mattered. In 2000, however, the new ethnic world had destroyed the simplicity of past census dichotomies. The 2000 census gave Americans the option of choosing "one or more races" to describe their racial identities. About 6.8 million respondents selected this option, most often identifying themselves as white and some other race. Moreover, more than twice that number passed over white, black, Asian, American Indian, and Pacific Islander categories and identified themselves simply as "some other race," although it was unclear what other races there were. Thus millions of Americans did not conceive of themselves as fitting into the traditional convenient categories of race. In 1945 metropolitan Americans knew quite clearly whether they were black or white, and if anyone had any doubts about racial category, Jim Crow laws in the South and less formal social restraints in the North would make clear their racial place in society. At the beginning of the twenty-first century, the racial picture had become murky, and the validity of racial categorization seemed in question.

The metropolitan revolution of the second half of the twentieth century thus swept away the spatial and racial certainties of the past. The black–white, single-focus metropolis with clearly identifiable central cities and dependent suburbs yielded to a strange new world that traditional thinkers could barely comprehend. This was the world in which Americans of the early twenty-first century would have to live. This was the new scenario with which they would have to come to terms and whose problems they would have to confront.

I 1945

"In the great world drama involving the destiny of civilization which is moving toward a climax, New York has become the center—the core—of the democratic system, carrying in its vitals germs which may threaten social disintegration, but also the seed of larger and better growth."[1] So wrote Cleveland Rodgers, a New York City planning commissioner, in 1943. With London and Berlin in ruins and Paris humiliated and defeated, New York City was the hope of the world, the place where the democratic system would thrive or falter, where social disintegration would destroy civilization or yield to enlightened policy. Moreover, the same could be said of American cities in general. As the United States approached victory in World War II, there was great hope and great trepidation about the future of American cities. The United States was an urban nation, and if triumphant Americans were to succeed in their mission to sell democracy and capitalism to the largely ruined remainder of the world, the cities would have to overcome their problems and demonstrate unquestionably the nation's greatness. With the defeat of European fascism and Japanese imperialism, New York City and its lesser urban compatriots were at the top of the world, but they had to confront their problems and create an even better future.

As war-induced prosperity dispelled the economic depression of the 1930s and American forces triumphed in the battlefield, there was a good deal of optimism that the nation's cities were up to the challenge facing them. Despite concerns about blight and decay in the older cities and racial conflict throughout the nation, urban leaders were drafting realistic plans to remedy metropolitan ills. In a publicity booklet the Bankers Trust Company expressed the mood of 1945 when it presented New Yorkers as a people "to whom nothing is impossible." According to the Wall Street firm, "New York has made up its mind . . . New York won't wait."[2] Neither would Chicago, Saint Louis, Dallas, or Los Angeles. America's cities were poised for action.

Downtown

At the center of the dynamic American cities of 1945 was downtown. Downtown's dominance within the metropolis was universally recognized, and most knowledgeable observers believed that a viable city had to have one command center. A southern California economist wrote in the early 1940s: "Logically, it would seem that every metropolitan organism or area must have a focal government, social, and business center, a heart, a core, a hub from which all or most major functions are directed." Moreover, without a healthy, beating heart, a metropolis, like a human being, would sicken and possibly die. "The degree of success attained by Southern California in economic, social, and political spheres," the economist observed, "is directly dependent upon the soundness and strength of the metropolitan nerve center."[3] Although widespread use of automobiles in the 1920s and 1930s had threatened downtown supremacy and raised the specter of decentralization, the success of a city still seemed to depend on the success of its downtown. In the minds of most urban commentators of the mid-1940s, downtown was the heart of the city, pumping necessary vitality to all the extremities of the metropolitan region.

Basic to the circulatory system of a healthy city was the centripetal transportation system. In 1945 the arteries of transport focused on downtown and funneled millions of Americans to the urban core. Railroads still provided a major share of long-distance intercity transport, and soldiers and sailors coming back from the war generally returned via rail. The rails converged on the urban hub, bringing millions of young veterans to giant downtown terminals from which they would pour into the streets of the central business district. With a soaring vault and noble columns, Pennsylvania Station in midtown Manhattan was patterned after the great Roman Baths of Caracalla and proclaimed to incoming passengers that they had arrived at the imperial city of the Empire State, a metropolis worthy of the corporate caesars of twentieth-century America. Nearby, New York City's Grand Central Terminal became synonymous with the bustling, jostling crowds so characteristic of the dynamic urban core. The Union Stations in Washington, D.C., Chicago, Saint Louis, Los Angeles, and other cities across the nation were likewise monumental midtown structures, great spaces that announced to travelers that they were in the heart of a vibrant metropolis. Although air terminals existed in fringe areas, the downtown rail depots were still the primary front door of the city, the place where wartime Americans arrived and departed from the metropolis.

Public transit lines also converged on the downtown, feeding a mass of humanity into the urban hub. In fact, the concentration of commerce in the downtown area was largely a product of the centripetal transit system that had developed during the century before 1945. The streetcar, subway, elevated rail, and bus lines all led to the central business district, making that area the most accessible to employees and customers dependent on transit and most desirable to businesses dependent on those workers and shoppers. As the number of automobiles soared during the 1920s, reliance on streetcars declined and the prospects for downtown-centered public transit worsened. The economic depression of the 1930s, however, slowed auto sales, and gasoline and tire rationing during World War II forced many Americans back on the trolleys and buses carrying commuters and customers downtown. The number of transit passengers soared from 13 billion in 1940 to over 23 billion in 1945.[4] In 1944 the annual per capita ridership was more than 420 in cities with a population of over 500,000; the figure was 372 for cities in the 250,000 to 500,000 population category.[5] The streetcar or bus was not a little-used alternative to the automobile; it was an everyday necessity. And nowhere was the web of transit lines denser than downtown. The lines were designed to carry as many people as possible to the urban core, and in 1945 they were doing so.

Among the transit passengers were millions of office workers, for downtown was the office district of the metropolis. In fact, downtown was virtually synonymous with office work; all major offices were in the central business district. Every lawyer, accountant, advertising agency, or other business service of any repute had offices downtown. Corporate headquarters clustered downtown, as did all the major banks. The economic depression of the 1930s had reinforced downtown control of finances by eliminating many of the weaker neighborhood financial institutions that had been potential competitors to the central business district banks. Many medical doctors and dentists maintained offices close to their patients in the outlying neighborhoods, but otherwise going to the office meant going downtown. In major cities throughout the nation, gender defined the ranks in the corps of office workers; an army of male managers and professionals and female secretaries migrated each day to the urban core to earn their living.

The preeminent symbols of the office culture were the soaring skyscrapers. These behemoths not only reminded observers of the monumental egos of their builders, but also were tangible evidence of the inflated property values in the urban core. So many people desired to do business in the hub of the metropolis that downtown land values far surpassed those elsewhere in the city. To make a profit from their valuable plots of land, property owners consequently had to build up rather than out. Only layer on layer of rentable space would compensate property owners for their investment in an expensive downtown lot. Vertical growth became a necessity and visibly marked downtown as the real-estate mother lode of the metropolis.

Nowhere were the skyscrapers so tall or so numerous as in New York City. It was the preeminent high-rise metropolis, where vertical movement was as significant as horizontal. In 1945 it could boast of 43,440 elevators, or 20 percent of all those in the nation. They carried 17.5 million passengers each day in trips totaling 125,000 miles, half the distance to the moon. New York's RCA Building claimed to have the fastest elevators in the world, transporting urbanites at the rate of 1,400 feet per minute, or two floors per second.[6] There were as yet no automatic elevators; instead, operators ran each car in the vertical transport system. When the city's elevator operators went on strike for six days in September 1945, New Yorkers became especially aware of the vertical nature of their existence. The strike affected 1,612,000 workers, equal to almost one-quarter of the city's population, most of whom were unable to get to their jobs in the city's multistory structures. Although rain, snow, and sleet could not stay letter carriers from delivery of the mail, flights of stairs could. Thousands of parcels and letters piled up that could not be taken to offices on upper floors.[7] One stenographer expressed the attitude of many when she told her boss: "I'm not going to walk up. It's not good for my constitution."[8] The skyscraper city simply could not exist without the vertical modes of transit.

Surpassing all other office towers in New York City and the world was the Empire State Building, rising 1,250 feet and 102 stories. The Chrysler Building also exceeded the 1,000-foot mark, ranking second among the city's skyscrapers. The most significant high-rise development, however, was Rockefeller Center in midtown Manhattan (figure 1.1). Constructed during the depressed 1930s, this complex of office towers, theaters, stores, and restaurants inspired downtown developers throughout the nation during the half century following World War II. Not only did it offer millions of square feet of leasable commercial space, but its gardens, sculpture, murals, skating rink, and giant Christmas tree display offered an oasis of civilized living in the congested core of the city. It was a landmark that many other cities would attempt to copy when redeveloping their downtowns. Yet none would match the success of Rockefeller Center.

New York City did not have a monopoly on skyscrapers. Each major American metropolis boasted a skyline that proclaimed the city's success and identified to anyone approaching the urban area the location of its

FIGURE 1.1 The vertical city: Rockefeller Center, New York. (Library of Congress)

commercial hub. Clevelanders did not let rivals forget that their 708-foot Terminal Tower was the tallest building outside New York City. At 557 feet, the Penobscot Building was the most prominent skyscraper in Detroit. One block to the south, the exuberant Art Deco Guardian Building rose thirty-six stories, punctuating the Motor City skyline and earning the title of "cathedral of finance."[9] The Foshay Tower, Rand Tower, and Northwestern Bell Telephone Company Building provided Minneapolis with a respectable skyline advertising the city's commercial prominence, and in Kansas City, Missouri, the Power and Light Building and Fidelity Bank and Trust Company proclaimed the metropolitan status of that midland hub. Similarly, Dallas and San Francisco could each boast of two buildings over 400 feet in height, symbols of urbanity in the South and West. Although modest by the standards of the early twenty-first century, the skylines of 1945 were clear indicators that downtown was the single dominant focus of metropolitan life.

Perhaps second only to the office towers as commercial landmarks were the giant downtown department stores. During the 1930s and early 1940s, urbanites bought their groceries and drugs in neighborhood stores, but for department store shopping and the purchase of apparel and accessories, the central business district was the place to go. From 1935 to 1940, downtown Philadelphia accounted for 35 to 36 percent of all retail sales, but in 1935 it held a 72 percent share of the general merchandise category, the merchandise sold at department stores.[10] Downtown had the greatest selection of goods and the latest fashions. For anything but the basics, smart shoppers headed to the center of the city.

Most of these smart shoppers were women. The downtown department store catered to women and did everything possible to attract their patronage. The motto of Chicago's giant Marshall Field store was "Give the Lady What She Wants," but every department store executive in cities across the country shared this attitude.[11] With millions of American men in the military and thus unable to staff the nation's factories and offices, the number of female workers rose markedly during World War II. Yet the traditional, and still significant, economic sphere of women was consumption rather than production. Women were the shoppers, and the downtown department store was their mecca, the place to meet friends over lunch and buy the goods their families needed. This was especially true of middle- and upper-middle-class women who donned their good clothes, complete with requisite hat and gloves, and frequently made the trek to the core of the city. A study from the mid-1930s found that more

than half of the women from Cleveland's upper-middle-class suburb of Shaker Heights went downtown at least once a week to shop.[12] The great downtown department store was to many women what Wall Street was to the stockbroker, a bulwark of their existence. On the day the Japanese bombed Pearl Harbor, a matronly shopper from Chicago reportedly exclaimed: "Nothing is left any more, except, thank God, Marshall Field's."[13]

Marshall Field's, however, was only one of many giant emporiums attracting shoppers to the nation's central business districts. Macy's in New York City was the largest department store in the nation (figure 1.2). On 6 December 1945 it recorded $1.1 million in sales, believed to be the largest amount for one day in any store in the world when there was no special promotion to boost business.[14] Filene's in Boston, Wanamaker's in Philadelphia, and J. L. Hudson Company in Detroit were all renowned as downtown merchandising giants. Cleveland's May Company claimed to be the largest department store in Ohio, with seventeen acres of floor space, although it had a number of downtown competitors, including Higbee's, Halle Brothers, and the Bailey Company. On the West Coast, Bon Marché and Frederick and Nelson vied for business in the center of Seattle, and the Emporium was the largest store in downtown San Francisco. Although offering a more limited range of merchandise than Macy's or Marshall Field's, Neiman-Marcus in downtown Dallas enjoyed an enviable reputation as a purveyor of fashionable apparel and accessories. Each September throughout the war, the elegant retailer drew spectators to its annual Fashion Exposition Show. In September 1944, while American soldiers were marching toward Germany, Neiman-Marcus was informing American women that this was the year of "more hat, less shoe," "tailored gold jewelry," and the "flaring tunic suit."[15]

Women who could not afford gold jewelry would have felt uncomfortable in the precincts of Neiman-Marcus, but most of the largest department stores attempted to cater to a wide range of income levels. The basement store or budget shop offered merchandise for bargain hunters and the less affluent, who could not afford the goods on the higher floors of the emporium. Depending on the store and the locality, African Americans might be excluded or accepted. In a study of racial segregation published in 1943, a black sociologist reported that Atlanta's largest department store had "no restrictions on dealings with Negroes and makes no racial distinctions, except for the special rest room for Negro women which is located in the basement." According to this researcher, "Negroes are allowed credit, may use fitting rooms, and may try on any piece of apparel."[16] Many downtown stores in the South and its border states were not so broadminded. In Baltimore, most of the principal department stores shunned African Americans. Only one downtown department store allowed blacks to try on hats and dresses. Baltimore's May Company channeled all blacks to the basement store, not wanting them to browse or be seen on the upper floors. "I ain't been downtown for over five years," reported one black woman in Baltimore. "I know they don't want Negroes, and I ain't one to push myself on them."[17]

In northern cities, the major department stores generally served African Americans, especially if they appeared able to afford the merchandise. New York City department stores had even begun to hire African American salespeople.[18] In Chicago, however, a campaign in 1943 and 1944 to encourage the downtown department stores to hire black saleswomen proved largely unsuccessful.[19] Throughout the United States, "untidy" women of either race might be discouraged from trying on garments, but generally the largest downtown stores drew on a wide range of clientele from throughout the metropolitan area. Even if one felt excluded and never shopped downtown, the big central stores influenced what one wore and bought. They set the style trends for stores in the neighborhoods as well as in the core. Neiman-Marcus determined what was fashionable even for women who would never enter the store.

Although the downtown giants remained dominant, there was concern about the decentralization of retailing. In the late 1920s, Marshall Field's opened branch stores in the suburbs of Evanston, Oak Park, and Lake Forest.[20] Cleveland's Halle Brothers pioneered the creation of outlying stores, launching five branches in 1929 and 1930. During those same years, a Halle competitor, the Bailey Company, established an East Side store at 101st Street and Euclid Avenue and a West Side branch in the suburb of Lakewood.[21] In the New York region in 1937, Peck and Peck launched a branch in suburban Garden City on Long Island and the next year opened a branch in the elite Connecticut suburb of Greenwich. In 1941 Bonwit Teller expanded into Westchester County, opening a store in White Plains, and the following year Best and Company tapped the increasingly lucrative suburbs with new stores in Manhasset, White Plains, and Bronxville. From 1937 through 1942, New York City retailers opened a total of twenty-four outlying branch stores.[22] Moreover, immediately following the declaration of peace in 1945, Macy's announced plans for branches in White Plains and in Jamaica on Long Island.[23] Explaining these expansion plans in early 1946, the vice president of Macy's observed that "branch units of centrally located department stores are the inevitable result of heavy traffic congestion in downtown shopping areas and the growth of population in the suburbs."[24] Most major downtown department stores had eschewed branch development, believing that branches were a nuisance to manage and only drained business from the downtown flagship store, which was the principal magnet for shoppers because of its unequaled selection of goods. Many retailers in fact were preparing to invest large amounts in their downtown outlets; in its New Year's message for 1946, Neiman-Marcus announced plans for a $1 million expansion of its store in the heart of Dallas.[25] Yet the words of Macy's vice president were ominous for downtown retailing. At the nation's largest department store, executives were aware that the urban core was flawed as a retailing center and that the giant emporiums had to adjust.

Not only was downtown still the place to shop, but it was a destination for millions of entertainment seekers. New York City's Theater District in midtown Manhattan was world famous, with its unequaled cluster of legitimate theaters and movie palaces, including the mammoth Roxy, with over six thousand seats.[26] Other cities could boast of less famous but still significant theater areas in the central business districts. The pride of Cleveland was Playhouse Square, with five theaters built in the early 1920s, four of them showing motion pictures in 1945 and one devoted to legitimate, live theater. In these palatial settings, thousands of Clevelanders enjoyed entertainment fare from Hollywood and Broadway. The State Theater claimed to have the world's largest theater lobby, a gargantuan corridor decorated in a mix of Roman, Greek, and baroque motifs stretching 320 feet and embellished with four allegorical murals representing the four continents of Europe, Asia, Africa, and America. Two marble staircases provided access to the mezzanine, which opened on to the 3,400-seat auditorium. In the Grand Hall of the adjacent Palace Theater, moviegoers were dazzled by the light of Czechoslovakian cut-crystal chandeliers, the richness of golden Carrara marble, and the magnificence of dual white marble staircases. The auditorium, with a seating capacity of over three thousand, was vaguely Chinese in style, the management claiming that it was modeled after the imperial palace garden in Beijing.[27]

Detroit also had its share of exuberant downtown movie palaces. Most notably the Fox Theater, with a seating capacity of more than five thousand, was an incongruous mix of Indian, Siamese, and Byzantine styles with gilded plaster figures of everything from elephants to Hindu goddesses encrusting the interior.[28] In downtown Seattle, the exotic Coliseum and Mayflower theaters demonstrated that the metropolis of the Northwest had its share of cinema palaces. Meanwhile, in Los Angeles the downtown theater district centered on South Broadway, with the Los Angeles, Orpheum, Tower, State, Globe, Pantages, Million Dollar, and Roxie theaters vying for patronage from entertainment-hungry southern Californians.

Many neighborhood movie houses also presented Hollywood's offerings to urbanites throughout the nation. In the largest cities, some of these matched their downtown counterparts in size and elegance. Yet most neighborhood movie houses were modest in comparison with the downtown palaces, and they were generally second-run venues. In other words, the latest offerings from Hollywood showed downtown at first-run theaters, whereas the neighborhood houses exhibited films released a few months earlier that had already played downtown. As in the case of retailing, the latest, biggest, and best were generally found in the central business district. Millions of Americans attended neighborhood theaters because they were conveniently located near their homes. Yet nowhere were there more of the latest film offerings in such a small geographic area as downtown.

Moreover, downtown was the site of the biggest and best in lodging. Tourist courts offered overnight accommodations to auto-borne travelers along the highways leading into the city. But the grim little tourist cabins did not rival the downtown hotels. If one wanted more than simply a bed and a roof over one's head, one had to go downtown. Catering to rail-borne visitors in town to transact business in the metropolis's unquestioned center of commerce, massive downtown hotels arose in every major city during the early twentieth century, the most elegant winning a nationwide reputation. The Waldorf Astoria in New York City, the Palmer House in Chicago, the Peabody in Memphis, the Adolphus in Dallas, and the Brown Palace in Denver were landmarks of the city center and, like the skyscraper and department stores, symbols of downtown's supremacy. Not only did travelers stay in these and hundreds of less distinguished downtown hostelries, but scores of metropolitan organizations held their banquets in the grand hotel ballrooms. The downtown hotels were meeting places as well as shelters for out-of-town visitors. They were places to see others and to be seen.

The downtown hotels were also among the principal entertainment venues of the metropolis. Among their amenities were supper clubs offering big-band music and a variety of other performers. For example, the College Inn in Chicago's Sherman House was the place to enjoy the best in big-band fare. In September and October 1945, it hosted first the Lionel Hampton band, followed by the Les Brown band, with singer Doris Day, and then the Louis Prima orchestra, all among the premier musical groups in the nation. Florian Zabach and his orchestra was playing at the American Room in the nearby LaSalle Hotel, and the posh Empire Room at the Palmer House was presenting its fall revue. If one sought further entertainment, one could try the Mayfair Room at the Blackstone Hotel or go across the street to the Stevens Hotel's Boulevard Room to enjoy its show "Shapes Ahoy!" with Clyde McCoy and his orchestra.[29] That same October, Chicago's Congress Hotel opened its Glass Hat Room; according to a local columnist, it was adorned with a "large glass topper over the bar,

... shimmering spun glass drapes, [and a] fan-shaped glass background for the band, tinted in changing colors by the special lighting system that ostensibly, at least, follows the mood of the music."[30]

With skyscrapers, department stores, movie palaces, and great hotels, downtown was a zone of real-estate riches. The chief source of municipal revenue was the property tax, and in no other area of the metropolis was property so valuable and thus so lucrative to city government. In 1940 the central business district of Philadelphia comprised 0.7 percent of the city's total area yet accounted for 17.4 percent of Philadelphia's assessed value.[31] Likewise, in the late 1930s, downtown Detroit contained 0.4 percent of the city's area but 12.9 percent of its entire assessment.[32] These figures were typical of the situation throughout the nation. With 1 or 2 percent of the land area in the city, the central business district paid anywhere from 12 to 20 percent of the property taxes. Not only was downtown the hub of office work, retailing, and entertainment, but it paid the bills for the city, subsidizing less fortunate areas with low property values. Downtown Saint Louis, for example, paid two and a half times more in municipal taxes than it cost in city services.[33] With the profits from the central business district, Saint Louis city officials could cope with the imbalance between revenues and expenditures in the poorer residential neighborhoods. The single dominant focus of the metropolis, downtown was also the area that ensured the survival of city government. Without the central business district, there could not be a city.

The governmental institutions that benefited from downtown's wealth were appropriately concentrated in the vital hub. County government operated from the centrally located county courthouse, and in the heart of downtown city hall was the command center for the government of the central city. Moreover, in 1945 the central cities of Boston, Philadelphia, Cleveland, Detroit, and their ilk across the nation were clearly the dominant governments of the metropolitan area. Unlike in later years, when the number of people living in suburban cities or towns far exceeded the number in the central city, in the mid-1940s the bulk of the metropolitan population remained within the central-city boundaries. According to the 1940 census, the twenty most populous central cities were home to 63.2 percent of all the residents in their metropolitan areas.[34] Over 80 percent of all people in the Baltimore metropolitan area actually lived in the city of Baltimore, and more than 70 percent of the inhabitants of the Chicago, Detroit, Cleveland, Washington, and Milwaukee metropolitan areas resided within the municipal limits of the central city. In other words, the central-city government was more significant than it would be later in the century. It governed the great majority of metropolitan residents, and downtown's city hall was the preeminent hub of local government.

The metropolitan lifestyle of 1945 had, then, a single focus. The city center dominated work, play, shopping, and government. Even those who could not afford to attend a show at the Empire Room, who felt excluded from Baltimore's department stores because of race, or who did not have a white-collar job in a skyscraper could not escape the influence of the single dominant hub. Its executives dictated corporate policy affecting workers in outlying factories, its city officials determined public policy, and its department stores guided women as to what to wear and what to buy. The critics for the downtown-based metropolitan daily newspapers told urbanites what movies to attend, and the columnists kept them aware of the latest developments in the swank night clubs. Although divided socially, ethnically, and politically, the fragments of America's metropolitan areas were drawn together by their common focus on the preeminent core. They were all satellites orbiting around a common star.

The Black–White City

Despite a common attraction to the dominant hub, metropolitan Americans were far from united. Most notably, they were divided by race. Historically the black population had been concentrated in the rural South. But during the three decades before 1945, an increasing number of African Americans were seeking to better their lot by migrating to cities. In 1940 blacks constituted more than 40 percent of the populations of Memphis and Birmingham, 35 percent of the residents of Atlanta, and 30 percent of the inhabitants of New Orleans. In the North, they were a less formidable contingent of the urban populace, comprising 13 percent of the populations of Philadelphia, Saint Louis, and Indianapolis and between 8 and 10 percent of the inhabitants of Chicago, Detroit, Pittsburgh, and Cleveland.[35]

During World War II, however, the flow of black migrants became a flood as almost 1 million African Americans left farms and small towns for life in industrial centers. With industry operating at full capacity to fill the Allied war needs and millions of men and women serving in the military, urban businesses were desperate for workers. Blacks sought to take advantage of the labor shortage. Between 1940 and 1944, the nonwhite population of the Detroit area increased by 83,000, or 47 percent. An estimated 60,000 to 75,000 African Americans moved to Chicago. On the West Coast, where the black population had been relatively small before the war, the rise was even more spectacular. The number of African Americans rose 78 percent in Los Angeles, 227 percent in the San Francisco Bay area, and 438 percent in metropolitan Portland.[36] In 1944 the Swedish social scientist Gunnar Myrdal titled his study of race in the United States *The American Dilemma*. At the close of World War II, it was becoming more specifically an urban dilemma.

The move to the city, however, did not free African Americans from the long-standing restraints of racial segregation and discrimination. In southern cities, they were required to sit at the back of streetcars and buses, the front being reserved for whites. Railroad stations had separate black and white waiting rooms, and African American children were relegated to separate educational facilities, being forbidden by law to attend school with white students. Cities maintained special African American branches of public libraries, and in Atlanta blacks were not permitted to use any books in the main city library or the other white branches, even through interlibrary loans.[37] The criminal justice system was designed to keep blacks in an inferior position. African Americans generally could not serve on juries, and the white police force reportedly ignored the legal rights of black suspects. According to an African American newspaper editor, "When they arrest a Negro and take him to jail they usually beat him up. It just seems to be a practice here."[38] Houston employed five African American policemen who could hold whites but not arrest them. They were hired to patrol the black neighborhoods that white officers sought to avoid. One black leader explained: "The white police used to run in these Negro sections, but so many of them ran into bullets that they couldn't find who fired, they had to put Negroes out in these places."[39]

Racial segregation was, then, pervasive in the urban South. A 1943 study of segregation stated uncategorically, "No Negroes are accommodated in any hotel in the South that receives white patronage." Similarly, it reported: "Cafes catering to whites frequently have a side or back entrance for Negroes, and they are served at a table in the kitchen."[40] At lunch counters serving whites, blacks could not sit down but could only order food to carry out. In theaters attended by whites, blacks were restricted to seats in the balcony, although by the 1940s there were a number of movie houses catering solely to African Americans. Southern blacks seemed to prefer attending these African American theaters rather than suffer the indignity of a seat in the balcony "crow's roost" of a white movie house. Some Atlanta office buildings had separate elevators for blacks, as did the courthouse in Birmingham.[41]

Segregation was less common in the North, and blacks could sit next to whites on public transit and use the same waiting rooms as whites. In 1945 a study of black life in Chicago reported that "by 1935 discrimination against Negroes in downtown theaters was virtually non-existent and only a few neighborhood houses tried to Jim-Crow Negroes." Yet other businesses did discriminate. The same study found that Chicago's roller-skating rinks, dance halls, and bowling alleys enforced a strict color line, and the city's hotel managers did not "sanction the use of hotel facilities by Negroes, particularly sleeping accommodations."[42] This was true in other cities as well. In 1942 the United Electrical, Radio and Machine Workers Union moved its convention site from Indianapolis to Cleveland because Indianapolis hotels refused to house black union members, and the following year the United Auto Workers Union shifted its annual meeting from Saint Louis to Buffalo because Saint Louis hotels likewise would not accommodate African American delegates.[43] Hotels might make exceptions for distinguished black visitors. In 1943 New York City's Waldorf Astoria made an exception to its usual policy of excluding blacks by accommodating the visiting president of Liberia.[44] The leading hotel in Dayton allowed the famed black concert singer Marian Anderson to stay overnight, but, in the words of the manager, "it was all arranged beforehand, so that when she came in she didn't register or come anywhere near the desk. She went right up the elevator to her room and no one knew she was around."[45]

Especially embarrassing to a nation that lauded freedom and was engaged in mortal combat with racist Nazi Germany was the state of black–white relations in the capital city of Washington, D.C. Blacks were excluded from downtown hotels, restaurants, and theaters.[46] The restaurant in the Capitol was off-limits to African American customers, a fact publicized in 1943 by the ejection of a group of blacks and whites representing the Greater New York Industrial Council.[47] The District Medical Society refused admission to African American physicians, and most hospitals either excluded black patients or restricted them to segregated wards. Most African Americans went to the two public hospitals, the larger of the two being Gallinger Municipal. Yet the conditions at these hospitals were inferior to those at white institutions. According to a national magazine, "Gallinger Municipal Hospital puts the legs of its beds in pans of water to keep the cockroaches from snuggling up to the patients."[48] The public schools were also segregated, and those for blacks were predictably inferior. In 1946 the per-student load for black teachers was 12 to 30 percent higher than for their white counterparts. In the school year 1946/1947, the per-pupil operating expenditure for white schools was $160.21, whereas for black schools it was only $126.52. The two leading universities in the city, George Washington and Georgetown, did not admit blacks.[49]

No aspect of black–white relations, however, was as hotly debated as housing discrimination. Most controversy centered on racial restrictive covenants. These were agreements among homeowners or provisions in deeds that prohibited the sale or lease of property to African Americans. In the mid-1940s, they were most common in middle-income white neighborhoods around existing black areas and in newer subdivisions. Racial covenants were often products of neighborhood improvement or property owners associations dedicated to preserving housing values and the ethnic purity of their area. For example, in 1945 a committee of owners in the North Capitol area of Washington, D.C., warned of the need to adopt restrictive covenants covering all the blocks in the neighborhood so that it could "continue to be the strongest protected white section in the District of Columbia. No section of Washington is as safe from invasion as is your section," the committee told area residents; "let's keep it safe!"[50] In a pamphlet on restrictive covenants published by Chicago's Federation of Neighborhood Associations in 1944, the federation warned that white Chicagoans should not have to explain to returning soldiers that "at the request of a very limited number of people hereabouts, we have altered your home and neighborhood conditions while you were away fighting for America."[51] White soldiers fighting for freedom, the federation believed, should be able to return to the neighborhoods they had left a few years earlier and find them as lily white as ever. Moreover, this was a widely shared belief. In 1944 at least seventy neighborhood associations in Chicago were actively engaged in the preparation and enforcement of racial restrictive convenants.[52]

These associations were ready to resort to legal action to bar blacks from protected neighborhoods. In Los Angeles, suits brought against the well-known black actress Ethel Waters and Academy Award winner Hattie McDaniel publicized the plight of African Americans attempting to move into white areas. Between 1942 and 1946, more than twenty racial covenant suits were initiated in Los Angeles alone, and an estimated sixteen were pending in Chicago at the close of 1945.[53]

Not only did whites oppose blacks moving into existing homes, but they battled any new housing projects that might mark the beginning of an African American invasion. The Seven Mile–Fenelon Improvement Association in Detroit led opposition to black tenancy in the Sojourner Truth public-housing project being built in its area. A neighborhood pastor expressed the views of his parishioners when he told housing officials that the project would mean "utter ruin" for many mortgaged homeowners in the area, "would jeopardize the safety of many of our white girls, . . . [and] would ruin the neighborhood, one that could be built up in a fine residential section."[54] In the minds of many whites, black neighbors meant plummeting property values, a plague of sexual assaults, and doom for neighborhood aspirations. When in February 1942 the first black families moved into the Sojourner Truth project, a riot ensued between blacks and whites, resulting in 220 arrests and leaving 38 hospitalized (figure 1.3).[55]

FIGURE 1.3
Blacks being arrested during the riot at the Sojourner Truth public-housing project, Detroit, February 1942. (Walter P. Reuther Library, Wayne State University)

Elsewhere in the Detroit area, there was resistance to any black projects in white districts. In 1944 suburban Dearborn's white mayor, Orville Hubbard, opposed a project in his municipality, claiming that "housing the Negroes is Detroit's problem." He bluntly proclaimed: "When you remove garbage from your backyard, you don't dump it in your neighbor's." The following year, Detroit's working-class neighborhood of Oakland battled a proposed black public-housing project. One resident told the Detroit city council, "We have established a prior right to a neighborhood which we have built up through the years—a neighborhood which is entirely white and which we want kept white."[56]

Many white New Yorkers shared this devotion to segregated neighborhoods. When in 1943 the Metropolitan Life Insurance Company announced plans for Stuyvesant Town, a giant Manhattan complex of nine thousand apartments, the company's president made it clear that blacks would be excluded from the complex. Responding to criticism of this policy, the following year Metropolitan unveiled plans for a project in black Harlem that would consist of seven thirteen-story buildings, almost all of whose tenants would be African American. In other words, Metropolitan was dedicated to separate but equal housing for New Yorkers rather than racially integrated neighborhoods where blacks and whites might mix.[57]

White resistance to black neighbors and black projects resulted in serious overcrowding and deplorable housing conditions for many African American newcomers to the city. Commenting on his home in a decrepit former saloon, a black worker at one of Detroit's major plants lamented, "It's hell living here," and a journalist wrote of an African American apartment building in the Motor City where the walls were "stuffed with rags and paper to keep out the weather and rodents" and "tin cans are suspended from the ceiling to catch the water that is always coming through."[58] On the West Coast, blacks ironically benefited from racism, for the evacuation and detention of Japanese Americans opened housing to wartime newcomers. Thousands of blacks moved into Los Angeles's Little Tokyo, but the housing proved insufficient. According to one report, "At least 13,700 of these Negro families have had shelter only through doubling up, tripling up or by leading an unhappy existence in abandoned store buildings and in other places never intended for human habitation."[59] In Chicago more than 20 percent of all black households lacked a private flush toilet, and in Saint Louis 40 percent of nonwhite dwellings were without such facilities.[60]

Forced into an overcrowded fragment of the city by white-imposed barriers, blacks had developed communities of their own, subcenters within
the metropolis where African Americans lived, shopped, played, and worshipped. In New York City, Harlem was the preeminent black community,
with 310,000 African American residents; in Chicago, it was South Side
Bronzeville, home to an estimated 250,000 blacks.[61] Paradise Valley was
the principal black neighborhood in Detroit, and Central Avenue the center of black existence in Los Angeles. In these neighborhoods, there were
black churches, black newspapers, and a full range of stores and services
catering to African Americans. This was black territory, and other than the
white merchants operating businesses in the neighborhoods, few whites
frequented these areas. White-dominated downtown was the single dominant focus of the metropolis as a whole, affecting the lives of blacks and
whites alike. Yet for African Americans there were separate communities,
in which they spent most of their hours and to which whites expected
them to remain.

Despite the restraints imposed by whites, in 1945 most blacks probably
believed they never had it so good. This was because World War II opened
unprecedented job opportunities for African Americans and dispelled the
endemic poverty of the economically depressed 1930s. At first, defense industries were reluctant to hire blacks, but as labor shortages developed in
1942 the racial barrier was lowered. In the summer of 1942, only 3 percent of the workers in war industries were black; by September 1944, African Americans constituted 8 percent of war workers. They were especially numerous in the shipbuilding yards, where they made up about
one-eighth of the workforce.[62] The burgeoning aircraft, munitions, and
firearms plants as well as other war industries generally turned to black
males before black females to fill their labor needs. But by 1944, thousands of African American women had left their jobs as domestic servants
and found better-paying factory positions. In 1940 black females constituted 4.7 percent of all women factory operatives; by 1944 the figure was
8.3 percent.[63] The change in black employment was evident in Detroit's
Chrysler plants. Before the war, black men represented 3 percent of the
company's Motor City workforce. Although Chrysler employed more than
six thousand women, not one of them was black. In March 1945, however,
African Americans made up 15 percent of the workforce in Chrysler's Detroit plants, and the five thousand black women workers constituted one
quarter of all female employees.[64]

Blacks not only found factory jobs, but also secured more of the better positions. Whereas before the war African Americans were fortunate if they could obtain the most menial of unskilled factory jobs, between 1942 and 1944 the number of blacks in skilled and semiskilled positions doubled. In 1940, 4.4 percent of black male workers had skilled manufacturing jobs as compared with 7.3 percent in 1944.[65] A leading African American reported that "in World War II, the Negro achieved more industrial and occupational diversification than he had been able to secure in the preceding 75 years."[66] Change was slower and less dramatic in the South, where blacks were more likely to be found in janitorial and maintenance positions at war plants. But for many, the racial barriers in employment seemed to be crumbling.

There was, however, resistance to this change. Before 1941 in most cities, only whites were eligible for employment as bus drivers and streetcar motormen and conductors. Yet serious labor shortages during the war and pressure from the federal government compelled transit authorities to open these positions to African Americans. In some cities such as Chicago and San Francisco, this change occurred without undue delay or much conflict. Elsewhere it was more difficult. In August 1944 in Philadelphia, the proposed hiring of black operators led to an almost weeklong public transit strike by white workers. President Roosevelt authorized the army to take control of the transit system, and five thousand troops were sent to the City of Brotherly Love to force transit employees to return to work.[67] In Los Angeles there were similar problems. When in February 1943 the transit company promoted two blacks to the position of mechanics' helpers at a bus terminal, eighty white employees at the terminal struck, suspending operations until the company rescinded the promotions. Another race-related work stoppage occurred among Los Angeles transit workers a few days later.[68] By 1945 in both Philadelphia and Los Angeles, blacks had won access to the better-paid transit jobs but not without conflict.

Race-related work stoppages also occurred sporadically at war plants. Before the spring of 1943, the Alabama Dry Dock and Shipping Company of Mobile had not placed any African Americans in skilled jobs. In May of that year, however, it attempted to upgrade twelve black workers to welding positions and add them to a previously all-white crew. When white workers heard of this, they went on a rampage, assaulting black workers in the shipyard and injuring an estimated fifty people. Blacks fled from the yard, and peace was restored only when the company agreed to create four separate all-black crews assigned to only the construction of ship hulls. Blacks could move up to welding jobs, but they could weld only with other blacks in segregated, Jim Crow units.[69] The following month, the upgrading of three blacks to skilled positions at Detroit's Packard Motor Company resulted in a short "hate" strike by white workers. And in July 1943 at the Bethlehem Steel Shipbuilding Company near Baltimore, white riveters staged a walkout to protest the training of blacks for skilled jobs.[70] At both Packard and Bethlehem, labor union officials forced the white workers to return to their jobs, but the disruptions in America's wartime industries were symptomatic of deep-seated racial antagonism.

If anyone had any doubts about the existence of such antagonism, Detroit's full-fledged race riot in June 1943 certainly dispelled them (figure 1.4). On a hot Sunday night, fighting broke out between blacks and whites at Belle Isle Park. False rumors spread through the black community that an African American women and her baby had been thrown into the Detroit River, and whites heard tales of a woman raped and killed by blacks.

FIGURE 1.4 Rioters running from tear gas in Detroit during the riot of June 1943. (Walter P. Reuther Library, Wayne State University)

In the early hours of Monday morning, African Americans rampaged through Paradise Valley, looting and wrecking white-owned stores. Meanwhile, white mobs began pelting the automobiles of passing blacks with stones and attacking African Americans as they left all-night movie theaters. As the sun rose on Monday morning, whites and blacks battled at various sites in the city. On Monday afternoon, ten thousand whites congregated in the area of city hall on the northern edge of downtown, attacking any vulnerable black pedestrians and dragging them off streetcars. By midnight Monday, federal troops had been called in, and during the following few days they restored order. Thirty-four people were killed in the riots, 461 were officially reported as injured, and property damage from looting and vandalism amounted to more than $2 million.[71] One nineteen-year-old white expressed the attitude of the Detroit mobs when he exclaimed: "Jesus, but it was a show! We dragged niggers from cars, beat the hell out of them, and lit the sons of bitches' autos. I'm glad I was in it! And those black bastards damn well deserved it."[72] African Americans sharply criticized Detroit's predominantly white police force for its failure to protect blacks adequately and for its seeming reluctance to restrain white rioters. For African Americans, it was one more example that in the black–white city the deck was stacked in favor of whites.

The racial tension in Detroit was not an anomaly. In August 1943, a white New York City policeman shot and superficially wounded a black soldier who had interfered with the arrest of a woman in a Harlem hotel. Amid rumors that the black soldier had been killed, rioting broke out and mobs looted white-owned stores throughout Harlem. In part, this was a reaction to the high prices charged by white merchants. Writing of Harlem, one black observer reported: "For every dollar spent on food, the Negro housewife has to spend at least six cents in excess of what the housewife in any other comparable section is required to pay."[73] Five people were killed in the Harlem riot and approximately five hundred injured. Chicago escaped a full-scale riot, but Chicagoans knew that there was sufficient racial tension to spark a local version of the Detroit melee. At nearby Fort Sheridan, the army commander asked for twelve thousand tear gas and smoke grenades and ten thousand shotgun shells "for use in the event of disorders in Chicago."[74] As blacks prepared to protect themselves, the going price for revolver shells in Bronzeville rose to 12 cents each as opposed to the usual 2 cents. "Occasionally one can see a colored man carrying a rifle or a shot gun wrapped up in a newspaper or a gunny sack," observed a Chicago sociologist during that hot summer of 1943.[75]

Across the country, city leaders were attempting to cool off the racial situation. During the year following the Detroit riot, at least thirty-one cities created municipal commissions to deal with racial questions. Moreover, by the fall of 1945 there were more than two hundred citizens' committees working with these commissions to reduce tensions.[76] In New York City, there was the Mayor's Committee on Unity; in Cleveland, the Community Relations Board; and in Los Angeles, the Committee on Human Relations.[77] Chicago's municipal authorities, however, claimed to have acted first with Mayor Edward Kelly's creation of the Mayor's Committee on Race Relations in July 1943. In its annual report for 1944, the committee acknowledged that Chicago was a black–white city when it recognized "various group conflicts—anti-Semitism, discrimination against Mexicans, Japanese-Americans, and others—" but clearly stated that it had "given its major efforts to Negro-white relationships."[78] The black–white division was the great ethnic problem of the city and the one that demanded immediate official attention. In February 1944, Kelly also called four conferences on race relations, attended by two hundred business and labor leaders, city officials, and social workers. Then in May 1945, with the cooperation of sixty-four civic organizations, Kelly convened the Chicago Conference of Home Front Unity, where blacks and whites again discussed race relations.

Although the Chicago Mayor's Committee claimed some achievements, it also admitted failures. Chicago's public schools in black districts were overcrowded, and the board of education contributed to the racial segregation of the schools by issuing transfer permits to white children living in African American areas. These permits allowed them to attend predominantly white schools outside their neighborhoods. At the close of the conference in 1944, the chair of the Mayor's Committee characterized the schools as "the least satisfactory of the basic city services." A year later, the committee's chair bluntly admitted that his organization's record with regard to the schools was "nearly perfect—a perfect zero."[79] Much talk and mayoral pressure might produce a greater sensitivity to racial issues among city leaders. But the black–white divide was not to close in the mid-1940s.

Chicago-area educators needed to take action, for in the fall of 1945 racial clashes broke out in local high schools. In nearby Gary, Indiana, a fight between African American and white students at a football game led to a two-month strike at Froebel School by white pupils who demanded that all blacks be transferred from the school. Soon afterward, white students walked out of Calumet and Englewood high schools in Chicago to protest the presence of blacks in their institutions.[80] Meanwhile, there was also a growing wave of attacks on blacks who dared to move into Chicago's white neighborhoods. In June 1945 an editorial in the principal African American newspaper in Chicago announced: "Hate-crazed incendiaries carrying the faggots of intolerance have in the past several months attacked some 30 homes occupied by Negroes on the fringes of the black belt, solely because these colored citizens have desperately crossed the unwritten boundary in their search for a hovel to live in." In this racial warfare, buildings had been "set afire, bombed, stoned and razed" and their occupants "shot and slugged." The editorial concluded: "Today racial dynamite is scattered about the South side. It needs but a spark to explode."[81]

Despite the well-meaning rhetoric of mayors' committees and interracial conferences, the sparks of racial hatred were evident everywhere. In both southern and northern cities, the racial chasm seemed unbridgeable. The American metropolis of 1945 was a black–white city, and this fact would be basic to urban life in the decades following World War II. It would determine where and how metropolitan Americans lived. Underlying the metropolitan lifestyle were the fissures of race.

The Suburbs

Underlying the metropolitan lifestyle of 1945 were also the fissures of municipal boundaries. Many people in each major metropolitan area lived in suburban communities outside the central city. They were closely tied to the core municipality, most often working and shopping there. "A night on the town" meant a trip to the central-city downtown, for there were the bright lights and excitement of the metropolis. The outlying municipalities were thus well within the central-city orbit, but they were places apart. They had separate governments that jealously protected their prerogatives and resented the big-city threat to their autonomy. Those who scoffed at the suburbs might claim that the municipal boundaries were artificial and that all metropolitan residents were actually part of one big city. But there was a strong sense of autonomous identity in the outlying municipalities, a sense that the communities were separate entities and wanted to remain such. The suburban municipality was a place where local government could be tailored to the needs and desires of the local populace, where residents were not subject to the amalgamated, insensitive rule of the big city. Although denounced as artificial and parasitical, these suburban municipalities proliferated and survived. Very few ever relinquished their existence and consolidated with the central city. They were a fact of life in 1945 and would become increasingly so in coming decades.

Municipal boundaries did, then, make a difference. The governmental fragmentation of the metropolis placed the imprimatur of the state on the divisions within metropolitan America. It fostered metropolitan divisions along lines of class, ethnicity, and economic interest. And the government boundaries were often insuperable barriers to metropolitan cooperation. Like the fissures of race, the governmental lines were cracks in the single-focused metropolis of 1945. Along these lines the metropolis would divide in future decades as suburban municipalities and their residents grew to feel that the central city's business was none of theirs.

Already in 1945, Americans were aware that the suburbs were of increasing significance in metropolitan life. Whereas in 1910, 76 percent of the inhabitants of the metropolitan areas containing the twenty largest cities lived in the core municipalities, thirty years later the figure was down to 63 percent.[82] During the 1920s and 1930s, millions of Americans moved to the suburbs, and many more seemed poised to make the outward trek once the federal government lifted wartime restrictions on residential construction.

Despite prevailing stereotypes, the satellite communities did not conform to one uniform way of life. There was not, nor would there ever be, a single suburban lifestyle. Some suburbs were upper-class retreats with meticulously manicured estates, and others were industrial communities with factories and working-class ethnic populations. There were suburbs where wives in station wagons met their husbands at the commuter rail station each weekday evening, but there were also communities of modest bungalows or medium-priced neocolonial homes where husbands would rely on the streetcar to take them to their downtown destinations. Those living in fringe communities were a diverse lot, and the outlying municipalities existed for a variety of reasons. What they had in common was political independence from the city and a desire to retain it. Through independence they could pursue their particular diverse destinies, with minimal interference from the central city or from one another.

One of the most famous suburbs, and one that conformed to many people's vision of suburbia, was Scarsdale, New York, a community of thirteen thousand affluent residents. Located in Westchester County nine-teen miles north of Manhattan's Grand Central Terminal, Scarsdale was known as "the richest town in America," its residents having a median annual income in 1949 of $9,580, more than twice that of the nearby suburban communities of Rye and Mamaroneck and more than three times that of Manhattan.[83] Its homes were generally eight- to twelve-room, two-story manses in the fashionable Tudor or colonial-revival styles (figure 1.5). Scarsdale was a community for wealthy commuters to New York City, and its residents wanted it to remain just that.

To preserve their way of life, Scarsdale residents created neighborhood associations. According to one reporter of the local scene, the oldest neighborhood group, the Heathcote Association, was formed in 1904 "so that residents building there would be secure in the ownership of large parcels with a substantial investment in dwellings." The more recently organized Secor Farms Property Owners Association was created "to foster economy and efficiency in government [and] to stimulate public interest in civic affairs" but also "to procure high quality in building construction even to the approval of plans for new houses."[84] Reinforcing the efforts of the Secor Farms group to ensure an upscale residential environment was the village's zoning code. In 1944 a prospective developer sought an

FIGURE 1.5 Home in Scarsdale, New York, in the early 1940s. (Library of Congress)

amendment to the zoning ordinance to build rental units on a twenty-six-acre estate. Numerous residents and neighborhood associations protested this zoning exception, which might open the door to multiple-family dwellings, and the developer withdrew the proposal.[85] The same year, a group of homeowners petitioned the village's governing board to find "some means . . . to protect our section against the creation of low-cost homes."[86] Stirred to action by this potential threat to the Scarsdale way of life, the board embarked on the drafting of a new and more restrictive zoning code.

In this protected world apart, club life flourished. For devotees of patrician sports, the Scarsdale Golf Club and Fox Meadow Tennis Club offered exclusive links and courts. The Woman's Club served female Scarsdale. According to its constitution, this organization sought "to bring together all women interested in the welfare of the village . . . and to foster a general public and democratic spirit" among the affluent few who could afford life in this plutocratic democracy. There were various sections in the club, each catering to some interest of the female population. For example, the American Home Section sought "to bring to its members new and stimulating ideas in the field of home decoration, gracious entertaining and personal grooming."[87]

The pride of both males and females in Scarsdale was the school system. Tailored to suit the class aspirations of upper-crust Scarsdale, the school system prepared its students for a college education, preferably at one of the nation's elite institutions of higher learning. In the early postwar years, over 90 percent of the graduates of Scarsdale High School went on to college. Between 1946 and 1951, twenty-nine Scarsdale graduates went to Cornell, whereas Yale and Dartmouth could each claim twenty-six of the suburb's finest. Among women's colleges, Mount Holyoke led with thirty-four Scarsdale women, and Smith followed with twenty-three.[88] The school system was handsomely funded and offered the best facilities, for it was a vital element in perpetuating the class standing of Scarsdale families from one generation to the next (figure 1.6).

Scarsdale's citizenry was not willing to allow partisan politics to interfere in the governance of their vaunted schools or protected village. Rejecting party contention between Republicans and Democrats such as existed in America's big cities, the suburbanites chose to vest the authority to nominate village board candidates in a nonpartisan committee consisting of the president of the Town Club (the leading civic organization), the president of the Woman's Club, representatives of the neighborhood as-

FIGURE I.6   Schools were the pride of Scarsdale, as is evident in the library of the Quaker Ridge Elementary School. (Library of Congress)

sociations, and some at-large representative citizens. For school board positions, the nominating committee included the president of the Parent-Teacher Council instead of spokespersons for the neighborhood groups. The slate nominated by these committees would run unopposed. Scarsdale residents thus sought to eliminate the unseemly competition of big-city politics and substitute a consensual slate chosen by upstanding civic leaders who nominated only those supposedly best suited for office. One did not run for office; instead, the best citizens were asked to do their civic duty and serve selflessly for the welfare of the community.

Other elite suburbs adopted similar schemes for nonpartisan, consensual rule by the most esteemed citizens. On Long Island, Garden City operated under the "Gentleman's Agreement," which provided that the municipality's four property owners' associations select the nominees for the municipal board. As in Scarsdale, those chosen ran unopposed. "On the theory that municipal housekeeping of a village has nothing to do with political issues," observed the municipal report for 1946, "the nominees usually are chosen from a list of civic-minded men who, regardless of party affiliation, have served their apprenticeship by years of work in the Property Owners' Associations of their sections and who have thereby won the respect and trust of their neighbors." Serving without pay, Garden City's officers could "act with complete disinterestedness for the good of the Village as a whole."[89] A number of suburban communities accepted the reasoning of Garden City's leaders. In nearby Lawrence, New York, the Independent Village Nominating Committee chose the sole slate of candidates appearing on the ballot. Across the Hudson River in suburban Leonia, New Jersey, nonpartisan representatives of civic organizations composed the Civic Conference, which selected the municipal officers.[90] In the Chicago suburb of Hinsdale, the Community Caucus served this function, and beginning in 1944 in nearby Clarendon Hills a similar caucus identified those who were worthy to govern the community, thus saving the citizenry from a contested election.

Residents of Scarsdale and other suburbs were dedicated to preserving their peculiar governmental systems and the prerogatives of their enclaves. Fearing the growing power of Westchester County, in 1940 a Scarsdale defender proclaimed: "We must never lose sight of the fact that in our country we succeed best in government in small units. . . . We must cling to our Scarsdale idea of service by the best people of the Village; we must keep our slogan: The Village that never holds a political election."[91] Scarsdale's cosmopolitan male executives commuted to Manhattan, where they ruled the corporate world and pulled the strings of international finance, but at home they cherished small-town government untarnished by the influences of the big city and based on a simple faith in the wisdom of civic-minded neighbors. Although Scarsdale matrons shopped along Manhattan's Fifth Avenue, kept apace of the world's art and fashions, and prided themselves on a woman's club featuring speakers on world affairs, their ideal community had to remain apart from the sordid realities of urban politics and the bitter socioeconomic and political competition that had plunged the globe into two world wars. Scarsdale was truly a world apart, an insulated enclave where residents had fashioned a better existence.

Few communities could match Scarsdale as upper-crust retreats, but across the nation there were versions of the New York suburb. In the Cleveland area, the elite found solace in Shaker Heights; in metropolitan Saint Louis, there was Ladue; the Miami area boasted of Coral Gables; Dallas's wealthy purchased homes in Highland Park; and southern California's Beverly Hills was known throughout the world. In the late 1930s Shorewood, north of Milwaukee, claimed to be the "Model Twentieth Century Village" where "every foot of land was restricted, either by deed stipulation or village ordinance." A community guide published by Shore-wood's municipal government boasted that the village gave "an impression of shade and affluence," and its school system was "one of the most elaborate in the country for a village of Shorewood's size." A Wisconsin Scarsdale, "the village has no factories and wants none, limits its business area to a small shopping district, and self-consciously devotes its civic energies to making itself a pleasant place in which residents may live and spend their leisure."[92]

Yet not all the communities beyond the central-city boundaries were Scarsdales or Shorewoods. Many were working-class, industrial suburbs that contrasted sharply with the upper-crust retreats but shared with their more affluent counterparts a desire for political autonomy. Few municipalities were more different from Scarsdale than Hamtramck, Michigan. Surrounded by Detroit, although politically independent of the Motor City, Hamtramck was a community of approximately fifty thousand residents, most of them of Polish ancestry. The median family income was about one-third that in Scarsdale, and the homes were primarily one- or two-family frame cottages on narrow lots with small yards. As late as 1950, only 51 percent of the houses in the frigid Michigan suburb had central heating. In 1940 there were sixty-one manufacturing concerns in town, employing 27,434 wage earners.[93] Chief among these factories was the huge Dodge-Chrysler plant along the community's southern boundary.

By the 1940s, Hamtramck's schools were in deplorable condition, owing in part to the corruption of the local school board. At the beginning of the decade, the indignant state superintendent of public instruction felt compelled to withhold any further distribution of state funds to the sorry school system, and the North Central Association of Colleges and Secondary Schools threatened to revoke the high school's accreditation. In 1945 the state audited the school system accounts and found wrongful expenditures of approximately $250,000, including spending for lavish junkets by school board members to Chicago and San Francisco.[94]

The mayor and city council members were even more notorious. During the Prohibition era, their willingness to protect bootleggers, gamblers, and prostitutes was well known, and many ended their terms of office in jail. "Because of chiseling of a few, cheap, grafting politicians, Hamtramck, down the years, has become a by-word of shame and reproach," noted a Detroit observer in 1946. "Smart alecks say, 'The first qualification for public office in Hamtramck is a prison term.'"[95] Detroit journalists delighted in reporting the odious political high jinks of Hamtramck until finally in early 1947 one Detroit newspaper called on its competitors to "Lay Off Hamtramck." "Hamtramck is not spotless, certainly," editorialized the *Detroit Times*, "but neither is it a Gemorrah [*sic*]."[96] Neither was it a Scarsdale.

Hamtramck was not an anomaly. Its counterpart in the Chicago region was Cicero, a suburb with a large eastern European, especially Czechoslovak, population and many industries, including the mammoth Hawthorne Works of Western Electric. During Prohibition, its working-class, ethnic population was more tolerant of alcohol than were the reform-minded do-gooders in the city of Chicago. Consequently, gangster Al Capone took refuge in Cicero, and it became renowned as a place where one could obtain the sinful pleasures forbidden in more reputable communities. Modest one- and two-family homes prevailed, although there were numerous small apartment houses. For those who were a bit more affluent, there was the Chicago suburb of Berwyn, with its acres of look-alike brick bungalows built on small lots in the 1920s. Nearby Elmwood Park offered abundant brick bungalows in a community just one step higher on the economic ladder. In the Chicago region and elsewhere, there were not just rich and poor suburbs but suburbs to serve each gradation of the socioeconomic scale.

This was true in the Los Angeles area, where the community of South Gate housed working-class suburbanites. It consisted of an array of modest frame homes, many of them self-built by their owners, who could not afford professional contractors. In 1940, 64 percent of its employed residents held working-class jobs, as compared with only 34 percent in Beverly Hills. By the late 1930s, the South Gate area had won the appellation "Detroit of the Coast," and many of its residents worked in the nearby General Motors assembly plant or the Firestone tire factory. Among South Gate's recent migrants were many Okies and Arkies, down-at-the-heels newcomers from Oklahoma and Arkansas seeking a decent wage.[97]

Nearby Vernon represented yet another variety of suburb: the community with many factories and few residents. Since the beginning of the twentieth century, there had been a steady migration of heavy industry to outlying sites, and especially favored were municipalities offering low taxes and few restrictions on industries. Among the communities with fewer than one thousand residents and tens of thousands of industrial employees were Vernon, just southeast of Los Angeles; Bedford Park, southwest of Chicago and the site of the giant Clearing Industrial District;

and Cuyahoga Heights, beyond the southern boundary of Cleveland. Just as Scarsdale was tailor-made for upper-crust New Yorkers who wanted the best schools and the most stringent protection for residential property, these enclaves of industry were an ideal fit for manufacturers seeking to escape the exactions and regulations imposed by the big city.

During World War II, the outward migration of heavy industry accelerated with giant war plants proliferating along the metropolitan fringe. Aircraft plants flourished on suburban Long Island, east of New York City, and the Atlanta area's largest defense employer was Bell Aircraft, located not in the city of Atlanta but in outlying Marietta. Chrysler built its great tank works in Warren, immediately north of Detroit, and Henry Ford created his sprawling airplane factory at Willow Run, twenty-five miles west of the Motor City's downtown. In the Chicago area, only three of the eight major war plants were inside the central-city limits.[98] In 1945 many light-manufacturing plants still clustered near the central-city core, but the suburbanization of industry had advanced to the point where millions of metropolitan Americans earned their living beyond the big-city boundaries.

Adding to the variety of suburbs were a few all-black communities. In 1944 Lincoln Heights, north of Cincinnati, incorporated as a municipality, creating a fragment of black power in the Queen City area.[99] Robbins, south of Chicago; Brooklyn, Illinois; and Kinloch, Missouri, in the Saint Louis metropolitan area, were other examples of black municipalities along the fringe. Composed of modest frame structures, these communities bore no resemblance to Scarsdale or Shorewood. But like their more affluent counterparts, these black suburban municipalities enhanced the opportunity for a fragment of American society to determine its own governmental destiny; they offered an alternative to the white-dominated regimes of other suburban municipalities and of the big city. This was evident in an incident involving Robbins. When some black businessmen were denied service at a restaurant in a white suburb because of their race, they went to nearby Robbins and swore out a warrant for the restaurant manager's arrest for violating Illinois's civil rights law. An African American deputy served the warrant and brought the manager to Robbins, where he was incarcerated until he could raise the bail.[100] White suburban authorities and police officers in the white-dominated central city could not be counted on to enforce the law so vigorously. Robbins, however, was a community where African Americans could secure their legal rights. Just as white ethnics could find refuge in Hamtramck and Cicero from the moral codes imposed on them by teetotalers, blacks could go to Robbins to seek imposition of the civil right laws too often ignored by white authorities.

America's suburbs were, then, a diverse lot, but Scarsdale, Hamtramck, and Robbins all shared a degree of political autonomy that boded ill for a unified metropolitan life. Suburban municipalities added the force of law to the social, cultural, and ethnic rifts dividing metropolitan America. They still paled in comparison with the central city, and the big-city downtown remained a dominant focus affecting the lives of all disparate suburbanites. If, however, the suburbs continued to proliferate and the gravitational pull of the central city diminished, the prognosis for metropolitan unity was poor.

The Future

In 1945 urban observers were more focused on the future than perhaps at any time in American history. They realized there were serious urban problems that they would have to confront at war's end. The nation's major cities were showing signs of age, and to the humiliation of local boosters Boston, Philadelphia, Cleveland, and Saint Louis had all declined in population between 1930 and 1940. During the 1930s and first half of the 1940s, economic depression and the war effort had slowed new construction and prevented needed repairs. The result was physical decay and acres of new slums. Moreover, in the two decades before the war, the automobile had loosened the bonds tying the metropolis together and weakened the central business district. Observers knew that once rationing of gasoline and tires ended and manufacturers resumed production of automobiles, Americans would eschew public transit and move into the driver's seat in increasing numbers.

Among the foremost concerns generated by the automobile was decentralization. During the first half of the 1940s, urban experts repeatedly commented on the automobile-induced outward migration of population and business and warned of the dire consequences. In 1940 the distinguished planner Harland Bartholomew announced that "the whole financial structure of cities, as well as the investments of countless individuals and business firms, is in jeopardy because of what is called 'decentralization.'" The following year, a major Cincinnati real-estate broker identified as the nation's chief urban problem "the undue acceleration of population flight away from city centers causing rot and decay at their cores."[101] At the beginning of the decade, the Urban Land Institute, the research arm of the National Association of Real Estate Boards, issued a report, *Decentralization: What Is It Doing to Our Cities?* that explained the numerous "adverse results of decentralization." In 1941 the American Institute of Appraisers added lectures on "the disintegration and decentralization of urban communities" to its summer courses. The same year, a transportation consultant summed up the issue troubling many: "The basic question is whether we can retain the city as a central market place, and at the same time decentralize residences to the extent that everyone lives out in the suburbs or country."[102]

The natural consequence of decentralization seemed to be blight, and during the first half of the 1940s many bewailed the pernicious spread of physical decay in the cities and the resulting drop in property values (figure 1.7). Often blight was described as a disease or a spreading cancer. In November 1944 a *Saturday Evening Post* article, "Can the Cities Come Back?" described urban blight as "the consequence of an anemia which

FIGURE 1.7 Commercial blight in downtown Pittsburgh, 1940s. (Library and Archives Division, Historical Society of Western Pennsylvania, Pittsburgh)

follows the steady loss of a city's residents. Residents are to the city as blood corpuscles to the human body." Moreover, the *Post* claimed that the "disease shows signs of being progressive," and its spread "has seriously affected the cost of doing business in the cities, has reduced income, and naturally all this has had a depressing effect on central business-area property values."[103] In 1943 the nation's leading real-estate economist, Homer Hoyt, likewise claimed: "Like a cancer, blight spread[s] through all the tissues of the urban body and the urban organism [is] unable to cure itself except by a major surgical operation." A year later, a federal official expressed the view of many urban observers when he asserted that "urban blight and slums, next to the war, constitute the greatest threat which confronts the American people."[104]

Given the dire diagnoses of Hoyt and others, vigorous action seemed necessary. In *The City Is the People*, published in 1945, the planner-architect Henry Churchill claimed that "our cities, great and small, [were] falling apart, disintegrating" and examined how his fellow Americans could rebuild their metropolises.[105] Recognizing the adverse effect of decentralization and blight on municipal finances, in 1944 New York City's controller wrote that "the need of rebuilding our cities presents one of the greatest challenges to post-war America."[106] The following year, he discussed his search for an instrument by which cities "can rebuild not a small area here or there but the many huge areas of obsolescence which threaten them with strangulation."[107]

Because of the war in Europe and Asia, little material progress could be made during the first half of the 1940s in the battle against blight and decentralization. During the war years planners did, however, compile wish lists of public works for the postwar era. By 1945 New York City's proposed postwar program included projects costing an estimated $1.190 billion. In a publication surveying the proposals, city hall publicists boasted: "New York of Tomorrow . . . is to be a *new kind of city*—more beautiful, healthful and convenient; a more comfortable place in which to live, work and play."[108] To build support for its initiative, the city prepared a public exhibition of the proposals. According to one national magazine, "The exhibition at first appears to be a dream of Utopia," but "actually, it represents New York City as it can be in a very few years."[109] The planning commissions of Chicago and Detroit were likewise preparing lists of projects to improve the postwar city, as were Cincinnati's Joint Improvement Program Committee and Minneapolis's Postwar Progress Committee.[110] The Dallas city council hired Harland Bartholomew to draft a master plan for postwar development.[111] Meanwhile, San Francisco's Citizens' Postwar Planning Committee concluded that the city had "become careless and allowed itself to 'run down at the heels,'" but the committee urged San Francisco to "correct its deficiencies and take advantage of the opportunities now knocking at its door."[112]

Private groups were also mobilizing for the attack on blight and decentralization. In June 1943 concerned Philadelphians founded the Citizens' Council on City Planning, and two months later it sponsored a conference "on the subject of problems facing Philadelphia now and in the post-war period." Echoing the concern of urban citizens throughout the United States, in 1944 a council publication noted that "plans for rehabilitation of blighted and declining areas are imperative" and expressed consternation at "the spread of blight, the loss in real estate values, the tendency toward decline in population, and the migration of the higher income families to the suburbs."[113] To the west, Pittsburgh's leading business figures organized the Allegheny Conference on Post War Community Planning, and their counterparts in Ohio were forming the Planning Association for the Redevelopment of Cincinnati, dedicated to supporting "every movement of a broad nature that is for the improvement of living and business conditions in the Cincinnati area."[114]

Groups such as these lent their support to campaigns to secure the money and legislation necessary for postwar progress. In 1944 voters in Baltimore, Cincinnati, and Saint Louis approved bond issues totaling almost $100 million that were intended to fund postwar improvements.[115] In 1941 the New York state legislature approved the Urban Redevelopment Act, permitting local governments in that state to grant tax exemptions and the use of the power of eminent domain to private corporations that sought to clear and rebuild slum areas. The same year, Michigan and Illinois enacted similar measures, and by 1945 eleven additional states had adopted redevelopment acts.[116] The California Community Redevelopment Act of 1945, for example, authorized each California community to create a redevelopment agency to battle blight. By a two-thirds majority, the local legislative body could designate an area as needing redevelopment, and the agency would then formulate a plan for rebuilding it.[117] In California and elsewhere, the idea was to clear blocks of blighted areas, "the huge areas of obsolescence" so abhorrent to New York's controller, and redevelop them as modern, decent neighborhoods with up-to-date housing and other facilities. At the close of World War II, then, virtually nothing had been built, but the plans and legislation had been formulated. Once wartime restrictions on construction were lifted, it seemed as if the new battle on blight would begin. The cities were poised for the assault.

Of special concern to vigilant business leaders and embattled city officials was the purported threat to the central business district. The downtown area was the site of millions of dollars of real-estate investment and the generator of a disproportionate share of tax revenues. In any war on blight and decentralization, downtown had to be an impregnable citadel, a fortified zone whose defenses could not be breached. Although downtown seemed eminently vulnerable during the depression-ridden 1930s, the war years had brought new prosperity to the central business district. Office building vacancy rates dropped from about 18 percent in the late 1930s to an all-time low of less than 4 percent in 1945. In Hartford, Atlanta, and Dallas there was actually no available space. Department store sales soared from less than $4 billion in 1939 to more than $7 billion in 1945, and hotel occupancy rates likewise climbed from 66 percent in 1938 to an all-time high of 90 percent in 1944.[118] Despite these encouraging figures, downtown boosters were fearful that the doldrums of the 1930s would reappear and that the central business district would become less central to metropolitan life. Times were good, but in the minds of many the prognosis for the future was not so rosy.

Throughout the war years, city leaders could not escape the haunting fears of decentralization. "In recent years business men in the larger cities have become increasingly aware that the central business districts have not been progressing," wrote a prominent member of the Philadelphia Real Estate Board in 1942.[119] "On the contrary," he observed, "retrogression is very much in evidence." The same year, an expert on Detroit real estate agreed, concluding glumly that "people who constitute the best market for the central business district are moving farther and farther away from it."[120] At times, the fears bordered on paranoia, as in 1943, when a Milwaukee publication warned: "Strong forces are at work within the city to emasculate . . . the downtown business section." Because of "sectionalism" the central focus of Milwaukee life was losing its strength as the city became "a series of villages each fighting the other at every turn."[121]

Mayors, city council members, and municipal controllers were more concerned about assessment values than vacancy rates, and the figures in the assessment books lent tangible support to the fears for the future. Between 1931 and 1945, the taxable worth of Baltimore's core dropped 34 percent; from 1935 to 1944, the assessed value of Boston's central business district fell 24 percent; and between 1936 and 1945, the figure for downtown Detroit declined 15 percent. Even the economic resurgence of the early 1940s did not boost the dismal figures. From 1939 to 1947, the assessed worth of downtown Chicago slipped 13 percent, whereas the valuation of the city as a whole fell only 3 percent, and the taxable value of the suburban region of Cook County was up 6 percent.[122] Similarly, downtown Seattle's share of the city's assessed valuation declined from 24 percent in 1940 to 22 percent in 1945.[123] All this data added up to one fact for city controllers: unless something was done, the mother lode of taxes at the golden core of the metropolis would no longer be able to pay the municipality's bills.

Confronting their fears for the future, downtown business figures did take some action to buoy the fortunes of the core. In 1941 leaders in Baltimore's central business district organized the Downtown Committee, intended to "work for the downtown business section in precisely the same way the neighborhood improvement associations do [for] residential areas." The same year, downtown interests in Atlanta formed the Atlanta Central Improvement Association "to swing back the trend of decentralization and build up the heart of Atlanta's business district."[124] To draw more shoppers to the central business district, on 17 June 1944 the Downtown Association of Milwaukee sponsored a "Downtown Day." "Shop where you can supply all your needs!" the association's advertisements told Milwaukeeans. "Highlight the day by dining in downtown restaurants," the ads advised Wisconsin consumers. "Plan, too, to attend a downtown movie or stage show." Repeating its message, in 1945 the Milwaukee association plastered billboards and streetcars with the slogan "Downtown Has Everything" and blared it over the radio.[125]

The future of downtown depended on more than slogans and promotions. Among the proposals for future improvements was the construction of freeways to funnel workers and customers into the central business district. In 1941 a leader of Baltimore's Downtown Committee expressed a common view when he claimed that "the principal objective" of foes of decentralization was "to get persons in and out of the downtown area as quickly and easily as possible."[126] During the streetcar era, downtown had achieved its commercial supremacy because no area was so accessible, and it would supposedly retain its dominance during the auto age if the finest metropolitan highways converged on it. In 1940 Boston's Conference on Traffic presented a six-year, $20 million program for expressways, which, according to a local newspaper, would "take long-distance traffic off the Hub's narrow streets and . . . make the downtown section quickly accessible to the suburbs." These superhighways would be "a major step toward halting the decline in activity and the shrinkage of property values in the downtown area."[127] In 1944 a California highway engineer agreed when he claimed that expressways were a vital means "to remedy, or possibly to halt, the decentralization [of business] and the deterioration of [downtown] property values."[128] New York City planning commissioner Cleveland Rodgers added his support to this position, claiming that "Manhattan's greatest traffic need is for express ways which will bring automobiles of all kinds, including interstate buses, directly to the center of Midtown, with adequate terminal and parking facilities."[129]

Others seconded the need for parking facilities. Cities could not simply dump thousands of automobiles in the central business district without considering where to park them. Throughout the nation, postwar planning included parking surveys and proposals about where to store automobiles once the war ended. Generally planners favored building more garages near the major department stores to cater to short-term parkers who were devoting a few hours to shopping. All-day parkers who worked downtown needed to be relegated to lots or garages on the periphery of the central business district; shuttle buses could carry them on the last leg of their journey to their offices. All downtown leaders recognized the significance of the parking problem. In 1945 a parking study of the Los Angeles central business district sponsored by the Downtown Business Men's Association concluded: "No complete and permanent solution of the parking problem under post-war conditions can be offered except one which will involve the setting aside exclusively and permanently for parking, sufficient land properly located which will provide outdoor or indoor parking of approximately 45,000 car spaces within the Downtown Los Angeles Area."[130] The following year, a publication of the Urban Land Institute forthrightly announced: "The recent meetings of the Central Business District Council of the Urban Land Institute made it crystal clear that until the automobile parking problem is solved, no relief from the troubles that plague our central business districts can be expected." Parking was deemed "the most important single problem facing the central business districts of large cities today," and a solution to this problem was "essential to the preservation of an adequate central business section."[131]

Across the nation, urban leaders were, then, planning to set aside acres of downtown for tens of thousands of parking spaces to handle the automobiles funneled into the central business district by great expressways. They were dreaming of clearing miles of slums and creating new neighborhoods. Decentralization and blight were the twin enemies in the coming postwar battle for the cities, but urban leaders were mobilizing, and most believed they would prove victorious and at least halt the forces that seemingly threatened the city. They did not have a passive vision of the future. Instead, they were preparing for action.

Within the United States, however, there were some traitors to the cause of the city, rebels who sympathized with decentralization and viewed the city as not worth saving. Most notably among these few iconoclasts was America's greatest and most outspoken architect, Frank Lloyd Wright. Once when asked about renewing Pittsburgh, Wright observed, "It'd be cheaper to abandon it!"[132] Moreover, he believed that it would be not only cheaper but better to discard the old steel city. In his opinion, America's cities were great failures unworthy of a democratic nation and would best be abandoned. He expressed his views in *When Democracy Builds*, published in 1945.

This book was Wright's diatribe against centralization and his paean to decentralization. What central-city leaders deemed as a threat he viewed as a blessing, for centralization of business and population in urban hubs was a hideous relic of a benighted past. "Centralization, the social force that made the king an appropriate necessity," Wright announced, "is now the economic force that has overbuilt the pseudo-monarchic towns and cities of today." He expressed contempt for all the symbols of monarchical, undemocratic urban centralization. According to Wright, "The Skyscraper is a milestone and the gravestone of Capitalist Centralization!" "The great railway stations as the gateways of the old city" resulted from "the bad form of Centralization." The automobile and electrification, however, had liberated human beings from the necessity of living close together and had opened the way to the democratic life of decentralization. In 1945 Wright told his readers: "Yes, fond human dreams are about to be realized: the door of the urban cage is opening!" The great architect claimed, "Decentralization is salvation if we desire the free life of a genuine Democracy." At the close of World War II, "the true course for Democracy is now Decentralization."[133]

Wright called the ideal decentralized metropolis of the future Broadacres City. In fact, it was not so much a city as the negation of the whole idea of city. In Wright's utopian settlement, there would be at least one acre of land for each individual, and homes would be spread out across the countryside and linked by superhighways. Maximized mobility was central to Wright's new world. "The stems for the flowering of the new City," Wright wrote, "will be the great topographical road systems for ubiquitous mobility." He dreamed of "spacious landscaped highways," with no "main hard road" having fewer than three lanes and no super-highway fewer than six. The gasoline service stations that dotted the highways in 1945 would "survive and expand into various important distributing centers for merchandise of all sorts," providing many of the goods "that Marshall Field, Sears Roebuck, or Wanamaker now . . . distribute to the congested crowds senselessly swarming in from the country." Moreover, these wayside markets would enjoy "generous parking facilities beyond realization at present."[134] In Wright's mind, the future metropolis was sprawling, edgeless, and without a single focus. At regular intervals along the superhighways, retailing centers would develop, and the congested downtown of the past would disappear. Whereas others planned to strengthen the focus of the city and to reinforce centralization, Wright dreamed of a centerless city spread across the nation's broad acres, its disparate homes, offices, and offices linked by highways. He hoped to kill the traditional city, not to revitalize it.

In 1945, however, Wright's vision was an iconoclastic utopia alien to the thinking of hard-headed, practical policy makers. Although racial and class fissures as well as political boundaries divided the metropolitan population, metropolitan Americans still shared a readily definable urban space with clear edges and an identifiable center. And in 1945 the powers that be sought to preserve that city. Wright presented what seemed a far-fetched alternative lifestyle; it was not a lifestyle that business leaders, planners, or city officials were prepared to embrace.

2 Reinforcing the Status Quo

In 1956 architect-planner Victor Gruen presented his well-publicized and much lauded plan for rebuilding the central business district of Fort Worth. It was the culmination of twenty years of thought by American urban leaders and planners about how to thwart commercial decentralization and reinforce the existing single-focus city. In the plan, centripetal expressways carried traffic to a highway that looped around downtown Fort Worth. At each exit of the loop ample parking garages accommodated incoming drivers who then could walk the remaining few blocks to work or shopping in the compact, pedestrian business district. Although praised as innovative, Gruen's plan reflected the postwar desire to preserve the existing metropolis rather than radically change it. Accepting the orthodox wisdom of urban observers, Gruen posited that "just as the human body is dependent upon the heart for its life-giving beat so is the modern city dependent upon its heart—the central business district—for its very life."[1] Imagining the rebuilt Fort Worth of 1970, Gruen wrote of the office worker speeding conveniently to work in a downtown office tower, the department store executive enjoying vigorous downtown sales, and the housewife shopping downtown, lunching at a new tearoom, and taking in a movie before riding home with her husband. Fort Worth's future downtown was, then, the idealized downtown of the past, a hub of white-collar office workers, prosperous department store moguls, and consuming middle-class housewives. The downtown of the future was a white, middle-class domain; only well-dressed white people inhabited the drawings accompanying Gruen's text. Dark faces were absent from his vision of the future.

For Gruen and many others in the postwar years, the utopian city was nothing but a reinforced, cleansed version of the past. Policy makers and planners were not dreaming of a centerless Broadacres or a racially heterogeneous city. Instead, the desired metropolis of the future had a dominant downtown, an invisible black populace, and a female population dedicated primarily to consumption rather than production. Conservation, not revolution, was the goal of urban leaders in the late 1940s and first half of the 1950s who sought to perpetuate the existing single-focused metropolis. Moreover, the majority of Americans remained dedicated to the segregated black–white lifestyle, especially in the area of housing. Between 1945 and the mid-1950s, discourses on commercial revitalization dominated much of the rhetoric about cities. During the same years, maintenance of the color line, especially the line between black and white neighborhoods, produced sporadic violence, bitter attacks, and policies dedicated to keeping African Americans literally in their place. This decade witnessed an acceleration in suburbanization. But in the years immediately following World War II, massive housing subdivisions were the most notable manifestations of suburban development, perpetuating the earlier pattern of residential and industrial dispersion. The vast housing tracts renewed the suburban trend so evident in the 1920s.

Despite the designs of Gruen and others to maintain rather than revolutionize the existing metropolitan lifestyle, there was change. Efforts to recentralize and bolster the commercial core did not halt the gradual shift of retailing to the suburbs. There was incremental racial change, with some opportunities opening for urban blacks; racial boundaries were not necessarily insuperable. Moreover, the suburban migration offered portents of a new way of life. Yet the vision of Victor Gruen was not that of Frank Lloyd Wright. The metropolitan revolution would not transform America overnight. Inherited expectations held a firm grip on the American mind, and the nation would only slowly yield to the wave of centrifugal and racial change.

Bolstering the Center

During the late 1940s and the first half of the 1950s, earlier concerns about decentralization became more acute, but a growing corps of business and political leaders as well as planners seemed confident that the urban core would hold and emerge as a revitalized focus of metropolitan life. Committees and commissions mobilized the business community, mayors and highway engineers presented plans for expressways and parking garages, and planners unveiled schemes for core projects that would ensure that downtown remained the one real hub of the metropolis. Of special concern was the middle class, which was moving farther from the urban core but whose dollars and job skills were essential to downtown's continued supremacy. The decade following World War II was a period of trepidation about the future of the central business district but also an era of high hopes and big dreams. Certainly very few policy makers had given up on downtown or accepted the notion of an alternative to the single-focused metropolitan lifestyle that had developed during the previous century.

For anxious urban leaders, Pittsburgh was the uplifting symbol of urban redemption from blight and decay. At the close of World War II, few cities had such a benighted reputation as the soot- and smoke-ridden capital of America's steel industry. In 1946 a national magazine commented on "the multiple scuttles of soot one must devour per annum as a part of the price of living in Pittsburgh," where conditions were "hellish, tormenting, disease-abetting and spirit-wilting."[2] Reportedly, wives of would-be junior executives opposed transferring to the Steel City because of the community's dirt and gloom, and there were rumors that corporate headquarters were considering leaving the city. Quite simply, Pittsburgh was a prime example of what was wrong with America's urban hubs.

During the decade following World War II, the city's business leaders, working through the Allegheny Conference on Community Development, joined with the city's dynamic mayor to give Pittsburgh a face-lift. Tough antismoke ordinances forced businesses, households, and railroads to rely less on sooty bituminous coal and cleared the skies over the city. By 1950, a local leader could claim that "visibility [was] up by almost 70 percent, laundry and painting bills [had] gone down, buildings [had] been cleaned, and the whole aspect of the community [was] more cheerful and bright."[3] Additionally, the Allegheny Conference and its allies in city hall combined to clear the blight-ridden Point area, the gateway to downtown Pittsburgh. At the juncture of the Allegheny, Monongahela, and Ohio rivers, the Point was a shabby mix of railroad yards and aging warehouses; it seemed to sum up the image of Pittsburgh as an over-the-hill industrial city. During the late 1940s and first half of the 1950s, however, the state and city acting cooperatively leveled the fifty-nine-acre tract and transformed thirty-six acres into a state park on the site of the historic pre-Revolutionary forts Duquesne and Pitt. The remaining twenty-three acres became Gateway Center, where three gleaming stainless-steel office towers opened to tenants in 1952 and 1953 and during the following five years were joined by a new Hilton hotel, a state office building, and the telephone company headquarters (figure 2.1).

Meanwhile, in 1952 the forty-one-story Mellon–U.S. Steel Building opened in the heart of downtown Pittsburgh, as did a twenty-two-story hotel and the city's first modern downtown apartment house. The following year, the thirty-one-story Alcoa Building, the nation's first aluminum skyscraper, was dedicated, and in 1955 the completion of Mellon Square Park

FIGURE 2.1 Construction and demolition in Gateway Center, Pittsburgh, ca. 1951. (Library and Archives Division, Historical Society of Western Pennsylvania, Pittsburgh)

FIGURE 2.2 Mellon Square with the Alcoa Building in the left background, Pittsburgh, 1956. (Library and Archives Division, Historical Society of Western Pennsylvania, Pittsburgh)

rounded out a decade of achievement for downtown Pittsburgh (figure 2.2). Lauded by an Allegheny Conference publication as "a crowning achievement in Pittsburgh's Renaissance," Mellon Square was a nine-acre park in the center of the business district resting on top of a six-level, thousand-car underground parking garage. "The Park is an array of colorful fountains, fountain pools, cascades, terrazzo walks, and inviting granite benches," the conference boasted. "There are thousands of trees, plants, shrubs and flowers of many different varieties planted within its borders."[4] With thousands of flowers, cascading clear water, and shining aluminum and stainless-steel towers, the new core of Pittsburgh was the very antithesis of the image of the grimy old hub. It was visual proof that American cities could reverse themselves in a single decade.

Pittsburgh's leaders, however, did more than clear slums and erect skyscrapers. They also sought to adapt downtown to the automobile age. The chief highway project was the Penn-Lincoln Parkway, designed to provide expressway access to the central business district. Construction also began on the double-deck Fort Pitt Bridge leading into downtown, and work on the 3,600-foot Fort Pitt Tunnel was scheduled to commence in late 1956. This tunnel would burrow under Mount Washington and funnel traffic from the southern suburbs to the central business district. In addition, the number of off-street parking spaces in downtown Pittsburgh increased by 40 percent between 1946 and 1956. In the latter year, the Allegheny Conference claimed that almost one-fourth of the central business district had been rebuilt since the end of the war, a figure indicative of Pittsburgh's resurgence.[5] With new skyscrapers, expressways, and parking garages Pittsburgh's leaders had reinforced the urban core, ensuring that at least momentarily it would remain a suitable and convenient destination for middle-class workers and consumers.

The national media spread the Pittsburgh story to urban dwellers throughout the nation, giving hope to those seeking to preserve the traditional metropolis. In 1949 *Newsweek* reported that Pittsburgh was "no longer the smoky city or the tired milltown, but an industrial metropolis with a new bounce, with clear skies above it and a brand-new spirit below."[6] The same year, *Architectural Forum* called Pittsburgh "the biggest real estate and building story in the U.S. today."[7] In 1952 the *Washington Post* presented the Steel City as a model of revitalization that could teach some lessons to the nation's capital. The *Post* told its readers that "the spirit of Pittsburgh's rebirth, and it is hardly less than that, could be duplicated here."[8] At the close of the 1950s, a travel magazine summed up the urban Cinderella story when it labeled Pittsburgh "the city that quick-changed from unbelievable ugliness to shining beauty in less than half a generation."[9]

Responding to the much publicized success of Pittsburgh, business leaders in other cities organized their own versions of the Allegheny Conference. In 1948 the Greater Philadelphia Movement became the voice for Philadelphia's business elite and, together with the broader-based Citizens' Council on City Planning, pushed for the city's revival. In the early 1950s, Saint Louis's twenty-five most powerful business figures formed Civic Progress, Inc., to jump-start the Missouri metropolis, and in 1954 one hundred of the largest corporations in Cleveland established the Cleveland Development Foundation "to advance urban development through joint leadership of Cleveland business."[10] The following year, the chief executives of the one hundred largest firms in the Baltimore area founded the Greater Baltimore Committee, whose statement of purpose announced: "Our watchword should be *action now.* . . . We want sound planning, but we want action to implement the plans, and we want it now, not at some future time when we may not be around to see it."[11]

Leading metropolitan newspapers also called for immediate action and publicized projects that could reverse decentralization. In 1950 the *St. Louis Post-Dispatch* published a series of articles titled "Progress or Decay? St. Louis Must Choose." The initial installment in the series warned that if Saint Louis remained "content to jog along without aggressive action—there lurk[ed] decay, squalor, the threat of steady decline" and the promise that it "would take a back seat among American cities."[12] Although the *Post-Dispatch* series discussed a long list of necessary improvements, it made clear that recentralization and reinforcement of the urban core were essential to the future of the metropolis. "Without a vigorous Downtown, St. Louis loses its chief economic reasons for existence," the newspaper contended; "without a vigorous St. Louis, the whole metropolitan district falters and fails—economically, culturally, physically."[13] Two years later, the *Washington Post* copied the *Post-Dispatch* format in an eighteen-article series with the unoriginal title "Progress or Decay? Washington Must Choose!" The *Post* asked its readers: "Shall downtown Washington . . . continue its drift into blight, its business importance decreasing, its traf-fic arteries ever hardening, its slums daily growing? Or shall Washington make that massive frontal attack necessary to stop deterioration [and] to make downtown Washington a better, finer, more attractive place to live, work and shop?" Clearly the *Post* was on the side of progress rather than decay and was using its pages to mobilize local forces for the essential massive attack. Ending the series on an upbeat note, the newspaper con-cluded that "the story of the response of America's biggest cities to the cri-sis of downtown blight today is a heartening one for those who believe that democracy is a living thing in our vast urban areas."[14] In other words, the signs of redemption abounded; if willing to take action, Washington residents could share in the wave bringing new life to central business districts. Like the Greater Baltimore Committee, however, the *Washington Post* believed in action now. Washington had to choose progress and begin at once to reinforce its faltering core.

In one city after another, then, the message was similar. Pittsburgh had acted and achieved marked change; now the other cities had to do like-wise. The single-focus metropolis could survive, and swarms of middle-class Americans and their dollars could still be attracted to the core. If ma-jor cities chose progress, the middle-class housewife, white-collar office worker, and department store executive of the future would continue to find the downtown the most exciting and lucrative locale in the metropolis, the unrivaled center of metropolitan life.

Those who dreamed of revitalization shared a vision of what needed to be done. Like Pittsburgh, cities had to plan and build expressways and massive parking facilities that would draw workers and shoppers to the central business district. In the automobile age, as in the streetcar era, downtown had to remain the most accessible location in the metropolitan area. Long before the federal government elected to finance the massive 41,000-mile interstate highway program in the Federal-Aid Highway Act of 1956, cities across the nation were acting to create up-to-date highway systems. In the early 1940s, Los Angeles had already completed the Arroyo Seco and Cahuenga parkways, two links in its proposed freeway system, and by 1957 it could boast of 223 miles of limited-access highways.[15] In 1946 Detroit's city council authorized acquisition of rights-of-way for the Edsel Ford and John C. Lodge radial freeways (figure 2.3); by 1953, $105 million had been spent or committed for the expressways. As of 1953, the Detroit Municipal Parking Authority, created in 1948, was help-

FIGURE 2.3 Construction of the John C. Lodge Expressway in Detroit, 1950. (Walter P. Reuther Library, Wayne State University)

ing the central city further adapt to the automobile by maintaining four city-owned parking lots. Detroit's mayor predicted that "highways would lure residents of neighboring areas to shop [in Detroit]" and would "retard the decentralization of business into suburban areas which pay no Detroit taxes."[16] The leaders of Kansas City, Missouri, agreed with this sentiment; that city's master plan of 1947 proposed a system of expressways radiating from a loop highway encircling the central business district with parking lots conveniently adjoining the loop. The same year, Kansas City voters approved a $12 million highway proposal.[17] Meanwhile, in 1947 Philadelphia's city council ordered the drafting of plans for the Schuylkill Expressway, which would bring auto-borne employees and consumers from the northwestern fringe of the metropolitan area to the central business district. Six years later, construction began on this downtown feeder. During the early 1950s, Boston had begun work on the Central Artery, intended to accelerate the flow of traffic coming into the aging New England metropolis, and Bostonians were arguing over plans for the construction of a parking garage under the Boston Common.[18]

The central city, however, needed more than expressways and parking garages. It needed a revival in downtown construction and the creation of attractive new buildings where middle-class Americans could work, shop, and live. Although most cities could not match Pittsburgh's Gateway Center, there were encouraging signs of massive private investment in other central business districts. In 1947 promoter Arthur Rubloff unveiled his plans for a $200 million project to redevelop Chicago's upper Michigan Avenue as a magnificent mile of "office buildings, smart shops, hotels, and apartment buildings" that would enable the avenue to fulfill its "destiny and become one of the world's most beautiful streets." Saks Fifth Avenue and Bonwit-Teller were planning to move onto the street, which during the postwar era would achieve its destiny and realize Rubloff's dreams.[19] In 1952 the Pennsylvania Railroad began demolition of its grim downtown Philadelphia viaduct in preparation for the construction of the $123 million Penn Center, a gleaming new complex of two office towers, shops, and a twenty-two-story hotel.[20] In 1957 *U.S. News & World Report* recorded that since 1946, Dallas's "skyline has been revolutionized. Twenty-five big office buildings have risen downtown, four more are under construction."[21] In 1954 the forty-story Republic National Bank Building was completed, and in 1955 construction began on the equally tall Southland Center. Between 1954 and 1959, office space in downtown Dallas was increasing at the rate of 1 million square feet a year.[22] Meanwhile,

New York developer William Zeckendorf was transforming Denver, where in the mid-1950s he built the twenty-two-story Mile High Center office building as well as one of the nation's largest department stores, complete with underground parking for 1,200 automobiles.[23]

Nowhere was there such an outpouring of private investment as in Zeckendorf's hometown. During the decade after the war, 856 new office buildings rose in Manhattan, and in the mid-1950s New York was adding new office space at the pace of about 2 million square feet a year. In 1952 the sleek, glass-skinned Lever Building opened on Park Avenue, and other glass-and-steel towers would appear along the once residential thoroughfare during the following few years. In 1953 *Time* proclaimed: "Manhattan, written off long ago by city planners . . . because of its jammed-in skyscrapers and canyon-like streets, has defied and amazed its critics with a phenomenal postwar building boom."[24] By 1957, the chair of New York's planning commission optimistically observed: "There are indications that not only is the flow from the city to the suburbs slowing, but that the reverse flow is picking up." He claimed that "enough of a change is taking place to make it quite clear that we are moving into a new and significant situation."[25]

Although fearful of losses to suburban retailers, downtown department store moguls also expressed a faith in the future of the central business district and were spending millions of dollars that reinforced the centripetal pull of the urban hub. In the late 1940s and early 1950s, the Jordan Marsh department store erected a new building in downtown Boston, Halle's in Cleveland expanded its central emporium, Neiman-Marcus doubled the space of its downtown Dallas store, and Frederick and Nelson of Seattle spent $9 million to double its downtown selling space. Moreover, *Business Week* reported that Gimbel's in New York City was spending $5 million on its downtown facility and Chicago's Marshall Field Company was investing $19 million in renovations and improvements.[26] A survey conducted in Columbus, Ohio, Houston, and Seattle in the early 1950s found that consumers still preferred downtown to suburban shopping centers. In sixteen of the twenty-three "shopping satisfaction factors," downtown was the preferred destination, ranking especially high on the factors of "variety of styles and sizes" and "variety and range of prices and quality."[27] As downtown retailers constantly reminded their customers, the central business district had more of everything. To find what one wanted in clothing or furniture at a reasonable price, one still went downtown. "People still like to shop downtown," commented a

Philadelphia department store executive in 1954. "If we give them attractive stores with good stocks, they will continue to shop downtown."[28]

The millions invested by private entrepreneurs in department stores and office towers seemed to prove that there was still a good deal of life in the urban core. To reinforce the private assault on decentralization, however, some downtown leaders favored federal aid to redevelop the inner city. The result was Title I of the Housing Act of 1949, which authorized the federal government to pay for two-thirds of the net cost of purchasing and clearing blighted property for the purpose of redevelopment. Localities were to provide the other third. The funding was restricted to blighted properties that were predominantly residential or would be redeveloped predominantly for residences. In other words, Congress seemed to intend that the program would encourage slum clearance and provide new housing in the urban core. Although the land could be used for low-income public housing, proponents of inner-city revitalization envisioned new apartment complexes for middle-class urbanites. These complexes would supposedly anchor the middle class in the central city and ensure that their tax and retailing dollars did not end up in suburban coffers. The goal was, then, to preserve the established focus of the metropolis. With federal help, the traditional center would supposedly remain central to metropolitan life.

During the early 1950s, Title I was of limited significance compared with such privately financed projects as Penn Center, the massive private investment in Manhattan's office buildings, or the private and state–local government partnership responsible for the redevelopment of downtown Pittsburgh. From 1950 through 1956, the cost of construction begun under federal redevelopment amounted to a total of only $247 million.[29] By comparison, in 1955 alone urban governments sold $310 million in highway construction bonds, and between 1945 and 1957 almost $4 billion was invested in residential and office building construction in New York City.[30]

Although the federal government was a late recruit to the battle against decentralization, it did generate some projects in the early 1950s and certainly heightened the expectations for a reinforced and revitalized urban core. During the first years of the Title I program, New York City and its construction czar, Robert Moses, received the lion's share of the federal funds. A domineering, aggressive figure with a passion for reconstructing New York City, Moses quickly took advantage of the federal funds and erected apartment complexes primarily to house those who had too much money to qualify for public housing but too little cash to rent an apartment on the affluent Upper East Side of Manhattan. By the close of 1959, Moses's Committee on Slum Clearance had completed 7,800 Title I dwelling units, providing shelter for thousands of middle-income New Yorkers who otherwise might have migrated to the suburbs, beyond the reach of the city's tax collector and far removed from its retailers.[31]

Elsewhere, federally financed schemes proceeded more slowly but offered hope to those who sought to retain a middle-class presence in the inner city. In Detroit, the Lafayette Park complex of apartments and townhouses was intended to draw a more affluent population to the blighted core. As of the mid-1950s, there was still debate whether the project should include public housing for displaced black residents or be exclusively middle to upper income. An Urban Land Institute panel meeting in Detroit in 1955 recommended the latter, urging that the renewal effort "be directed towards a step-up in accommodations, not downwards to the bottom of the income group. Detroit has a great mass of good workers able to pay economic prices," the panel commented. "These are the great, solid heart of your city's life. Orient your program accordingly."[32] Other cities followed this same advice when developing federal renewal sites. Chicago's Lake Meadows project on the near South Side was designed for middle-class tenants, as was Saint Louis's downtown Plaza Square apartment complex. In Los Angeles, planners were proposing the clearance of the old wooden houses in the Bunker Hill district, adjacent to downtown, for the construction of high-rise apartments and the relocation of its low-income residents to public housing in largely Hispanic Chavez Ravine, a low-density shantytown. Land close to the urban core was supposedly too important to the economic interests of the city to remain in the hands of the poor. They had to be removed so that the core could survive as the great generator of tax dollars and prosperity. To the north, San Francisco authorities were proceeding slowly on a scheme to clear the Western Addition, an area with a large black and Japanese American population.[33] As yet, there were more proposals than actual blueprints and certainly more blueprints than construction, but Title I seemed to open the door of the federal treasury to those who sought to recentralize the American metropolis. And by the mid-1950s, many urban leaders were trying to make their way through that door.

Not only were central-city leaders using private and federal funds to reinforce downtown's dominant position, but they were mobilizing to protect major educational institutions threatened by blight and the poor African Americans that whites associated with blight. For example, in New York City's Morningside Heights district, Columbia University's leaders feared the encroachment of nearby Harlem and the resulting social and ethnic change that might repel both prospective students and faculty. Who, after all, would want to attend or work at a university in a slum? By 1950, about 10 percent of the neighborhood's population was black, and another 10 percent were recent immigrants from Puerto Rico. Landlords were converting formerly middle-class apartments into single-room-occupancy hotels that attracted low-income blacks and Puerto Ricans, including prostitutes and drug addicts. In 1947 in response to the perceived threat to their neighborhood, Columbia and other nearby institutions joined to form Morningside Heights, Inc., to curb the advance of Harlem and stabilize the social and ethnic composition of the community. In its war on blight, Columbia quite simply sought to make Morningside Heights safe for white, middle-class life. Among the first projects backed by Morningside Heights, Inc., was Morningside Gardens, a Title I middle-income apartment complex that was ethnically mixed but solidly middle class.[34]

Meanwhile, the University of Chicago was embarking on an even more ambitious program dedicated to saving its neighborhood for the middle class. Located in the Hyde Park district on Chicago's South Side adjacent to Bronzeville, the university was in the path of the expanding African American community; by the late 1940s, an invasion of poor blacks seemed imminent. Responding to this threat, in 1952 the university established the South East Chicago Commission, which drafted a plan for spot clearance of the area's most blighted structures and rehabilitation or conservation of the remaining buildings. The idea was to eliminate dilapidated housing with rents affordable to low-income blacks and upgrade or preserve the remaining dwelling units for middle-class occupants. In 1955 demolition began, and the following year the commission secured approval for $26 million in federal urban renewal funds. The neighborhood was not to be lily-white; middle-class blacks were not excluded. But Hyde Park was to remain a bastion against lower-class invaders. One comedian joked: "This is Hyde Park, whites and blacks shoulder to shoulder against the lower classes."[35]

In Chicago and New York City as well as Philadelphia and Pittsburgh, urban leaders were, then, attempting to hold the line against blight and the social transformation that accompanied the advance of this dread malady. Downtown had to remain a magnet for middle-class dollars, and Columbia and the University of Chicago had to remain appealing to affluent white students and faculty. Millions of dollars were being spent to ensure that the central city and its central business district remained the dominant heart of the metropolis. And so far the centrifugal forces of the automobile age had not destroyed the significance of the urban center in American life. In 1954 two urban geographers confidently observed that downtown "is so familiar to the average citizen that he is likely to take it for granted."[36] Whether the urban core would remain so familiar to the average American ten or twenty years in the future was a question that dominated the thinking of central-city leaders.

Holding the Color Line

Equally troubling to many urban Americans was the question of whether the color line would hold and white neighborhoods remain white. The migration of southern blacks to northern and western cities continued unabated during the decade following World War II as the possibility of better jobs and higher incomes attracted an unrelenting wave of African Americans. The result was a marked darkening of the complexion of America's central cities. In New York City, the black proportion of the population rose from 6.1 percent in 1940 to 14 percent in 1960; in Newark, it soared from 10.6 to 34.1 percent; in Philadelphia, the increase was from 13 to 26.4 percent; in Detroit, the African American share went from 9.2 to 28.9 percent; and in Chicago, it rose from 8.2 to 22.9 percent. In the late 1950s, Washington, D.C., became the first major American city with a black majority; the trajectory in other cities pointed to African American majorities within the next two decades. On the West Coast, black predominance seemed less imminent, but the African American share of the populations of San Francisco and Oakland skyrocketed tenfold between 1940 and 1960, from 1.4 to 14.3 percent.

In the minds of most white urban dwellers, all these figures added up to bad news. They viewed the black migration as an invasion threatening their previously homogeneous neighborhoods and the property values of their homes. Moreover, such sentiments were not confined to the southern or border states but were also prevalent in the far northern reaches of the United States, where relatively few blacks had yet penetrated (figure 2.4). In 1946 a poll found that 60 percent of Minnesotans surveyed believed that blacks should not "be allowed to move into any residential neighborhood where there is a vacancy," and 63 percent responded "no"

FIGURE 2.4 Antidiscrimination billboard sponsored by the Governor's Inter-Racial Commission in Minnesota, 1948. (*Minneapolis Star Journal Tribune*, Minnesota Historical Society)

to the question: "If you were selling your home and could get more from a Negro buyer, would you sell?"[37] In 1951 a poll of Detroit residents found that 56 percent of the whites surveyed favored residential segregation. An African American journalist summed up the postwar attitude when he observed, "The white population . . . has come to believe that it has a vested, exclusive, and permanent 'right' to certain districts."[38]

During most of the 1940s, racial restrictive covenants appeared to be the best defense against the perceived racial invasion. But in 1948, the United States Supreme Court, in *Shelley v. Kraemer*, held such covenants to be unenforceable. If courts enforced the racial restrictions, they would deprive blacks of equal protection of the laws, in violation of the Fourteenth Amendment to the Constitution. Thus white homeowners could no longer rely on the courts to evict black "invaders" from restricted properties. A serious breach had developed in the neighborhood defenses of the black–white city.

In the wake of *Shelley v. Kraemer*, however, the forces of segregated neighborhoods did not lay down their arms and abjectly capitulate. Instead resistance continued. Most realtors remained reluctant to sell or rent homes in white neighborhoods to blacks. Until 1950 the code of ethics of the National Association of Real Estate Boards specified that "a realtor should never be instrumental in introducing into a neighborhood . . . members of any race or nationality . . . whose presence will clearly be detrimental to property values in the neighborhood."[39] That year, the association modified this racist code, but most "reputable" realtors still deemed introducing blacks into white neighborhoods to be unethical and undesirable. "Ethical" operators steered blacks to black neighborhoods and whites to white areas.

The federal government likewise did not threaten the forces of residential segregation. The Federal Housing Administration (FHA) insured residential mortgages, guaranteeing to reimburse lenders should mortgagees default on their payments. Viewing racially mixed areas as bad investments, the FHA encouraged the adoption of racial restrictive covenants throughout the 1940s and would not insure mortgages on properties in neighborhoods where both blacks and whites lived. At the close of 1949, the FHA adopted a new policy of refusing to guarantee mortgages on homes subject to racial restrictive covenants finalized after February 15, 1950, but the federal agency continued to prefer white suburban subdivisions to mixed-race areas in the central cities. As of 1952, less than 2 percent of the 3 million dwellings with FHA mortgage insurance were available to blacks.[40]

Racial labeling in real-estate advertisements reinforced the discriminatory practices of realtors and lenders. During the late 1940s and early 1950s, the real-estate advertisements in many metropolitan newspapers identified whether the available house or apartment was for a "colored" occupant.[41] Blacks were expected to respond to only the advertisements marked "colored." Other residences in the listings were off-limits.

Neighborhood improvement associations also remained vigilant in the battle to protect white areas. On the South Side of Chicago, the Fernwood-Bellevue Civic Association, the Calumet Civic Association, and the South Deering Improvement Association fought the movement of black tenants into previously all-white public-housing projects. In 1948 a coalition of homeowners' associations in Detroit urged its members to "get busy on the phone" and tell real-estate brokers who sold houses to African Americans what they thought about the brokers' willingness to accommodate race invaders. Following the *Shelley v. Kraemer* decision, Detroit's Palmyra Home Owners' Association suggested new covenants that referred vaguely to "undesirable peoples" rather than specifically mentioning race.[42] In 1952 the A. P. Hill Civic Club of Memphis posted signs in the neighborhood reading "not for sale to Negroes" after some inquiries from blacks about purchasing homes in the area. Moreover, the club convinced city authorities to require developers to erect a steel fence to separate existing black and white residential zones in the North Memphis district.[43] Houston's Riverside Home Owners Protective Association organized following the purchase of a home in the neighborhood by an African American. The buyer was subjected to threatening telephone calls, and the *Houston Chronicle* reported that "several hundred white neighbors gathered in front of the house and a spokesman suggested 'If you leave this neighborhood you will live longer and be happier.' "[44]

Meanwhile, twenty organizations in Los Angeles banded together to bring legal action intended to ensure that restrictive covenants would continue to pose some threat. In *Barrows v. Jackson* Mr. and Mrs. Edgar W. Barrows brought suit for damages against their neighbor Leola Jackson, who had signed a restrictive covenant in 1944 and then in 1950 sold her property to blacks. Because of the *Shelley* ruling, the Barrows could not oust the black purchasers from their new home, but through their suit for damages they sought to coerce Jackson and other whites to adhere to their covenants. Not only did such Los Angeles homeowners' groups as the Vermont Square Neighbors, Harvard Neighbors Association, and Lafayette Square Improvement Association support the Barrows, but on appeal to the United States Supreme Court in 1953 they were joined by an improvement association in San Francisco, another in Kansas City, twenty-four associations in Washington, D.C., and sixteen in Saint Louis.[45] Despite this showing by white homeowners' groups across the nation, the Supreme Court ruled in favor of Jackson, handing the improvement associations yet another judicial defeat.

In Atlanta, the city's leaders sought to avoid lawsuits and neighborhood clashes by defining acceptable zones of expansion for the growing black population. In 1947 black developers and community leaders specified six areas reserved for new housing for African Americans, and white city officials privately agreed to the plan. To further avoid conflict, in 1952 Atlanta mayor William Hartsfield appointed the biracial West Side Mutual Development Committee to oversee peaceful expansion of the black population and to determine racial dividing lines. In effect, the committee was charged with partitioning the city's west side into white and black zones. Moreover, through the construction of new roads the city sought to create more effective racial boundaries. In 1954 Hartsfield urged immediate action on an access road to serve as a racial frontier. "As you probably know," the mayor told his construction chief, "the bi-racial committee is trying to assure residents of Center Hill and Grove Park that the proposed access road will be a boundary which will protect them as Negro citizens move farther out." The director of the planning commission reiterated this sentiment when he observed: "If the line can be stabilized, a potentially explosive situation will have been prevented, and both racial and political attitudes will be saved strain."[46] Thus to avoid strain and maintain stability, Atlanta's leaders believed that the residential color line had to be preserved. The result, however, was confinement for Atlanta's blacks. Although African Americans had negotiated the right to additional territory during the postwar decade, by 1959 they constituted 35.7 percent of the city's population but occupied only 16.4 percent of the land.[47]

Dedication to existing racial boundaries also thwarted the designs of public-housing officials seeking to build projects in outlying white areas. Low-rent public projects meant an influx of poor tenants, many of them black, and white homeowners were adamantly opposed to this threat to their property values and social status. In 1949 one of the major issues in Detroit's mayoral election was the prospect of outlying public-housing projects. Conservative Albert Cobo swept to victory, and the new mayor lived up to the expectations of many white homeowners when he announced: "I WILL NOT APPROVE Federal Housing Projects in the outlying single homes areas." According to Cobo, "When people move and invest in a single-family area, they are entitled to consideration and protection."[48] When in 1952 Cleveland housing officials proposed a project in the white Lee-Seville area, the neighborhood rose in revolt. "The community is divided, supposedly on the question of whether there should be more public housing or not," commented the city's public-housing director, "but the actual question is whether or not public housing should be built where both Negroes and whites could live together as American citizens should."[49] Cleveland's city council sided with opponents to the Lee-Seville scheme and resolved that in the future it would review for approval or rejection each public-housing proposal. In the mid-1950s, Chicago's city council took similar action to curb housing authority discretion and subjected proposed public-housing projects to the veto of the council member for the area affected.[50] This spelled doom for projects in outlying white areas. When in 1956 the Philadelphia housing authority unveiled plans for twenty-one public-housing sites, including some in white neighborhoods, the uproar was predictable. Again, most of the proposed projects were never built.[51] Throughout the nation, public housing was increasingly concentrated in inner-city, black neighborhoods. Massive, high-rise projects housing thousands of African Americans would become the new ghetto.

Sometimes defenders of the color line moved beyond appeals to city councils, lawsuits, and harassing telephone calls and resorted to violence. During the postwar decade, there were no full-scale race riots comparable to the Detroit outburst of 1943, but violence arising from fears of racial invasion was an ugly fact of urban life. This was especially true in Chicago, where working-class Catholics of southern and eastern European ancestry felt threatened by racial change. With most of their assets in their homes and limited housing options because of their modest incomes, they felt especially vulnerable. "I was born and raised on the near North Side," testified a South Side white woman on the verge of tears. "My father had to sell his home at a big loss when the Negroes moved into the neighborhood. Now are we going to have the same thing happen here?"[52] Blacks needed additional housing, and whites could ill afford the perceived threat to their property values. The combination was volatile.

One violent incident after another disrupted Chicago's South Side. In December 1946, a mob estimated at between 1,500 and 3,000 persons attacked police and vandalized property at Airport Homes, a veterans' housing project that was admitting black tenants. In August 1947, African Americans moved into the Fernwood Park public-housing project, igniting mob action by whites in the neighborhood. For three successive nights, crowds of whites gathered in the area around the project, stoned passing cars, including police cars, and attacked streetcars and buses carrying blacks. On the third night, 1,000 policemen were deployed to protect the Fernwood project and suppress a "howling screaming mob" of 1,500 to 2,000 whites.[53] In July 1949, the target of violence was a two-family home purchased by a black man in the white Park Manor neighborhood. In the aftermath of the incident, a city official summed up the damage: "All of the front windows with the exception of a few basement windows had been broken, and the brick front of the house was scarred and pitted by numerous bricks thrown against it." "We barricaded the doors with furniture and put a mattress behind it," recounted the wife of the black owner. "We crawled around on our hands and knees when the missiles started coming in through the windows. . . . Then they started to throw gasoline-soaked rags stuck in pop battles." The same year, the Englewood neighborhood exploded when rumors spread that a house was being "sold to niggers."[54]

The violence did not abate in the 1950s. In 1953 whites responded violently when the first blacks moved into the Trumbull Park public-housing project. At the height of the disturbance, a mob of two thousand whites gathered, and the now all-too-common stoning of windows, cars, and buses ensued as well as the throwing of lighted torches into the apartment of the hated race invaders. When additional blacks moved into the project, several women, according to the city's human relations commission, "literally hurled themselves, first at a truck loaded with the newcomers' furniture, and later at a new car driven by the head of one Negro family." One feisty "gray-haired woman of about 65 fell prostrate in front of the car. . . . When the halted car began to inch ahead, the woman clung to its front bumper."[55] The neighborhood newspaper fueled the anger of the Trumbull Park protesters when it editorialized: "The Negro can turn his neighborhood into a slum overnight. . . . Most of them live like savages. . . . Why don't they stay where they belong?"[56] Chicago's endemic racial violence persisted through the mid-1950s. The Chicago Urban League reported a total of 164 incidents of racial violence in 1956 and 1957, most of them in the transitional areas where African Americans were expanding into formerly all-white neighborhoods.[57]

The most highly publicized racial housing incident of the early 1950s was across the city limits in the adjacent municipality of Cicero. In July 1951, Illinois's governor had to declare martial law and dispatch the National Guard when a black man attempted to move into an apartment in the white ethnic community. From Tuesday to early Friday morning, whites attacked the offending apartment building with stones and burning torches. They ripped out walls and radiators, threw furniture out of windows, and tore trees up by their roots.[58] In what proved an effective display of racial hatred, Cicero whites made clear that their town was off-limits to blacks and would remain so.

The Chicago area, however, could not claim a monopoly on racial violence. Elsewhere, attempted breaches of the color line ignited harsh defensive action. Between the autumn of 1945 and early 1950, Detroit's Lower West Side suffered eighteen racial incidents. Neighborhood residents set fire to a house recently purchased by a black man, forced two African Americans from apartments in the area, ripped the porch from a black-owned home, and smashed thirty-five windows in two houses.[59] In 1949 and 1950, a rash of dynamitings targeted the homes of African

Americans who challenged the residential segregation prevailing in Birmingham, Alabama. Over a seventeen-month period in 1950 and 1951, thirteen dynamitings struck black homes in Dallas.[60] In 1951 white segregationists resorted to a series of dynamitings in order to dislodge blacks from a new housing project, Carver Village, in northwest Miami. The wife of Miami's mayor received telephone calls threatening that "if we didn't get the Negroes out of Carver Village within a month they would bomb it to pieces."[61] Then in 1952 a number of bombings rocked the houses of African Americans in a lower-middle-class neighborhood of Kansas City, Missouri.[62] Across the nation, whites were expressing a similar message (figure 2.5). They did not intend to yield their neighborhoods without resistance.

Yet gradually African Americans gained new territory, and the boundaries of the black ghetto in one city after another moved outward. Dynamitings and diatribes could not contain the black population, and racial boundaries were changing. Blacks moved farther south in Chicago and won new territory on the west side. The Bedford-Stuyvesant ghetto in Brooklyn absorbed new blocks, Cleveland's east side African American community spread further eastward, and Atlanta's blacks extended their west side domain. What did not change, however, were attitudes about racially mixed neighborhoods. Block by block, districts shifted from all-

FIGURE 2.5 Threatening note found at the site of a home bombing in Los Angeles, 1952. (*Herald Examiner* Collection, Los Angeles Public Library)

white to all-black as white residents yielded territory but did not shed their aversion for a racially heterogeneous lifestyle. In 1955 America's cities were, then, as segregated residentially as in 1945. The racial geography of urban America had changed somewhat, but the color line between blacks and whites remained strong. The black–white city of 1945 was very much alive in 1955.

While the residential walls between black and white remained strong, there was only modest improvement in job opportunities for African Americans. In most cities, blacks remained barred from positions in which they would have to interact with white consumers. Fearful of offending customers, many employers confined blacks to out-of-sight janitorial, stock-handling, and maintenance duties. Thus investigators working for the National Association for the Advancement of Colored People reported that in Washington, D.C., "occupations such as laundry truck drivers, ticket sellers in bus and railroad stations, desk clerks in hotels, and distributors of bakery and milk products" were as off-limits to African Americans in 1957 as in 1946. Those employees who delivered laundry, milk, and baked goods to Washington housewives and sold tickets and lodging to travelers in depots and hostelries had to be white. Moreover, other than the city's one black-owned bank, no financial institution in Washington employed an African American teller.[63] In 1951 an investigation of a major San Francisco bank found that there was only one black woman among the five hundred employees. The San Francisco investigators also found that blacks were notably absent from the serving staff of a popular restaurant chain but were employed as dishwashers, "cleanup men," and kitchen helpers.[64] As late as 1959, there were only eighty-six blacks among the twelve hundred employees of Detroit's major clothing stores for men, and no African American held a managerial or sales position.[65]

In the postwar decade, blacks continued to find unskilled and semi-skilled factory jobs, but skilled and managerial positions were difficult to obtain in the nation's manufacturing sector. As of 1954, the automobile industry could claim only forty-three African Americans in managerial jobs. Whereas some companies were willing to hire blacks, others excluded them and specified their preference for whites in job listings with employment services. For example, in June 1948, 65 percent of the job orders placed with the Michigan State Employment Service included racial preferences. The same year, an investigation of employment practices in Michigan found that "discrimination in hiring is on the increase. . . . Despite a serious labor shortage in Detroit, employers refused to employ qualified non-white workers."[66]

The job situation was not totally static. In 1948 Atlanta hired its first black policemen, although they were assigned to only African American neighborhoods and could not arrest whites.[67] By 1950, four department stores in Saint Paul, Minnesota, had broken precedent and employed eight black saleswomen. "It is becoming possible," the director of the local Urban League noted optimistically, "to match Negroes to jobs best suited for them." By 1952, an African American was on the research staff of the leading newspaper in nearby Minneapolis.[68] Because firefighters had to share living quarters while on duty, racial integration of fire departments proceeded slowly. But in 1955 San Francisco hired its first black firefighter.[69] With racial barriers largely intact, however, black hirings were often token and provided few opportunities for the mass of African American job seekers.

The postwar decade also witnessed some desegregation of public facilities. In 1949 Saint Louis opened its public swimming pools to African Americans. At Fairgrounds Park, however, a gang of young whites attacked black swimmers as a crowd of an estimated two thousand whites heckled African Americans who sought to use the pool. After a two-year court battle, in 1954 Kansas City, Missouri, opened the formerly white-only Swope Park swimming pool to African Americans. Mitigating this integration victory was the reluctance of whites to patronize the desegregated pool, with attendance falling to one-third its normal level during the first summer of integration.[70] In Washington, D.C., blacks were gradually admitted to white facilities. In 1949 the Roman Catholic Church instructed Washington's parochial schools to desegregate. Two years later, the lunchroom of the Hecht Company department store opened to blacks. Within a few months, other department stores and drugstores in the downtown shopping area followed suit and admitted African Americans to their lunch counters and restaurants. In the early 1950s, the National Theatre, Washington's only venue for Broadway productions, opened its doors to black patrons. Then in 1952 the District Medical Association agreed to admit African American members, and gradually private hospitals granted staff privileges to a few black physicians.[71]

In 1954 the United States Supreme Court, in *Brown v. Board of Education*, held that the segregation of blacks and whites in the public schools was unconstitutional. Since dual school systems were the norm in border and southern states, the *Brown* ruling seemed to promise dramatic change in cities below the Mason-Dixon Line. Yet in the mid-1950s, only communities in the border states took steps to dismantle their systems of separate black and white schools. In the cities of the Deep South, such as Atlanta, construction of separate schools for blacks and whites continued, and not until the early 1960s did the Georgia metropolis make even a token effort to desegregate its schools.[72] Just as *Shelley v. Kraemer* did not destroy the racial barriers in housing, *Brown v. Board of Education* did not suddenly end racial separation in schooling.

In the black–white cities of the mid-1950s, racial customs thus prevailed over judicial doctrine; life did not conform to the law. The color line held, and the lives of blacks and whites too often did not intersect amicably. They shared a city with a still dominant single hub, but they did not share the neighborhoods or necessarily the facilities within that city. The Supreme Court made high-minded pronouncements, but the way of life in the black–white city responded slowly to demands for change.

The Suburban Migration

While racial boundaries were holding and central-city boosters were attempting to preserve the magnetic pull of the urban core, a vast outward migration was under way along the metropolitan fringe. In sprawling cities such as Los Angeles, where the expansive San Fernando Valley remained largely undeveloped at the close of World War II, many of the migrants were moving into new houses within the central-city limits. But in other cities, especially in the Northeast and Midwest, where there was little vacant land in the core municipality, the migrants were pouring beyond the municipal limits and adding to the metropolitan population outside the reach of big-city mayors and council members. In 1940 only 32 percent of Americans in metropolitan districts lived outside the central city; by 1950, this was up to 41.5 percent, and ten years later the figure was 48.5 percent. In the single decade of the 1950s, this suburban population soared 56.3 percent as compared with a central-city increase of only 17.4 percent.

Virtually everyone during the postwar decade seemed to want a house in suburbia, a fact not ignored by Hollywood. In the 1946 Academy Award–winning film *The Best Years of Our Lives*, a returning GI reveals that his dream while overseas was "to have my own home. Just a nice little house with my wife and me out in the country, in the suburbs anyway."[73] In the 1947 Christmas classic *Miracle on 34th Street*, the little girl in the story wants Santa to bring her a home in the suburbs with a backyard swing. The following year, *Mr. Blandings Builds His Dream House* told of an advertising executive who seeks to fulfill his dream of a new home outside the city. The ex-GI, the young child, and the Madison Avenue executive all yearn for a suburban house, a place with grass, trees, breathing space, a swing, and the natural advantages unavailable in the city.

Housing construction figures reflected this yearning as millions of Americans moved into new single-family dwellings (figure 2.6). In 1947 the number of new housing starts rose above 1.2 million, double the figure for 1940, and remained above that mark throughout the rest of the 1940s and 1950s. It peaked at 1,952,000 in 1950, more than double the prewar record set in 1925. With low-interest, long-term mortgages insured by the FHA and Veterans Administration, millions of World War II veterans could now escape the central city and afford a house in suburbia. In 1945 a *Saturday Evening Post* survey found that only 14 percent of the

FIGURE 2.6 Housing tract under construction to meet the postwar housing shortage in southern California. (*Herald Examiner* Collection, Los Angeles Public Library)

respondents wanted a "used" house or an apartment.[74] An overwhelming majority of Americans dreamed of a new house, and at a rapid pace builders were realizing that dream for many eager buyers.

This housing boom and the burst of new suburban customers were perhaps the greatest phenomenon of the postwar decade. In 1953 *Fortune* breathlessly informed its readers in the business community of "the lush new suburban market" that was "made to order for the comprehending marketer."[75] A year later, the sales manager for Sears Roebuck seconded *Fortune*'s enthusiasm when he told an advertising convention: "This movement to the suburbs means more automobiles, more mileage per car and more multiple-car families. . . . I will leave it to your imagination to think what it means in terms of automotive home workshops, sporting goods, lawnmowers, garden tools, casual clothing." He concluded: "Man, oh man, think what this means in the sale of goods!"[76] In 1955 *U.S. News & World Report* summed up the suburban boom of recent years when it wrote of "the rush to the suburbs." "No matter where you look, you find suburbs mushrooming," reported the magazine.[77] The order of the age was suburban growth that, in turn, spawned new markets and exciting opportunities for profit.

Although many Americans viewed the suburban migration of the decade following World War II as an unprecedented phenomenon transforming the nation, in fact it was a continuation of the fast-paced suburbanization of the 1920s, which had been interrupted by the economic depression of the 1930s and World War II. During the 1920s, a suburban rush had also fueled a building boom, and millions of suburban-bound Americans had purchased new automobiles and radios from happy retailers. In the late 1940s and early 1950s, as in the 1920s, the most significant construction projects along the metropolitan fringe were housing subdivisions. Suburbia in 1950, as in 1930, was primarily a residential refuge. In other words, the suburban boom of the postwar decade was as much a continuation of the past as a departure. The rush to the suburbs was accelerating, with more new homes produced and more lawnmowers sold than ever before. But the outward migration to new homes did not mark a sudden rejection of the concept of the single-focused metropolis or a desire to shed the pattern of metropolitan existence prevailing before 1945. The suburban migration was not a revolution; it instead accelerated the existing pattern of evolution.

The greatest symbol of this quickening migration was Levittown, the massive 17,447-house community erected by Levitt and Sons on Long Island between 1947 and 1951. William Levitt, the mastermind of the project, was proclaimed the Henry Ford of housing because of his skill at mass-producing dwelling units. Describing how "each crew did its special job, then hurried on to the next site," *Time* reported that "new houses rose faster than Jack ever built them; a new one was finished every 15 minutes."[78] This fast-paced routine produced a four-room house on a sixty- by hundred-foot lot. During the first two years of construction, the houses were look-alike Cape Cod–style cottages, but in 1949 Levitt introduced his ranch-style model. Both the Cape Cod and ranch-style houses consisted of a living room, a kitchen (with a Bendix automatic washing machine), two bedrooms, and a bath downstairs and an unfinished second-floor attic that could later be converted into two additional bedrooms (figure 2.7). The houses sold for $6,990 at first; later Levitt and Sons raised the price to $7,990. But even at the latter price veterans could buy a home with no down payment and carrying charges of only $58 a month.[79] "No longer must young married couples plan to start living in an apartment, saving for the distant day when they can buy a house," *Time* told its readers.

FIGURE 2.7   Owners have remodeled the attics of their homes in Levittown, New York, adding needed bedrooms, 1950s. (Library of Congress)

"Now they can do it more easily than they can buy a $2,000 car on the in-stallment plan."[80]

Thousands of New Yorkers recognized this fact and flocked to the Levitt and Sons sales office. A postwar housing shortage had forced many young families to move in with their parents or in-laws or crowd into cramped, run-down apartments. For these poorly housed Americans, Levitt's suburbia represented a release from urban misery. In 1949 Levitt and Sons informed prospective purchasers that the first 350 in line on Monday, 7 March, would be able to buy one of the latest batch of Levittown houses. At 11:00 Friday night, the first applicant for a house showed up to form a line that had grown to almost fifty home-hungry buyers by Satur-day morning; by Sunday morning, nearly three hundred were camping out in sleeping bags and on lawn chairs awaiting the Monday sale. The *New York Times* reported that one waiting veteran heard the news that his wife had just given birth to twins at a local hospital. "Unperturbed, he re-ceived the congratulations of his companions and kept right on standing in line."[81] On 15 August 1949 Levitt and Sons sold 650 houses in only five hours, the seemingly insatiable yearning for suburbia enriching the Levitts at the rate of $1,000 per house.[82]

Spurred by the success of his Long Island development, William Levitt launched two additional giant housing projects during the following de-cade. In 1951 he opened the sales office for Levittown, Pennsylvania, twenty-two miles northeast of Philadelphia, and over the next five years built 17,311 houses for 67,000 residents. In what one observer called a "struggle against monotony," at the Pennsylvania project the same floor plan was "enclosed by four different types of exteriors, painted in seven varieties of color so that your shape of Levittown house occurs in the same color only once every twenty-eight times."[83] Then in 1955 Levitt an-nounced his purchase of almost all the land in Willingboro Township, New Jersey, where he would build a third Levittown. Although the lots and houses were slightly larger, the new Levittowns offered much the same product as their older Long Island counterpart. In each of the Levittowns young families would be able to buy affordable homes along the metro-politan fringe and become suburbanites.

The new communities were religiously diverse, welcoming Catholics, Protestants, and Jews whose ancestors had come from all corners of Eu-rope. Moreover, both white- and blue-collar families moved into the devel-opments, creating an occupational mix. Yet in some ways the residents of the Levittowns were very similar to one another. They were overwhelmingly young, married couples with small children or the prospect of off-spring in the near future. In 1951, 46 percent of the population of Levit-town, New York, were between the ages of twenty-five and thirty-six, and 41 percent were under ten years old.[84] A remarkable 30 percent were un-der the age of five. Pregnancy was so common that it was called "the Levit-town Look."[85] According to *Time*, "In front of almost every house along Levittown's 100 miles of winding streets sits a tricycle or a baby carriage. In Levittown, all activity stops from 12 to 2 in the afternoon; that is nap time." There were virtually no teenagers or senior citizens. "Everyone is so young that sometimes it's hard to remember how to get along with older people," observed one Levittowner.[86] In addition, 95 percent of the adults were married; single, divorced, or widowed individuals were rare. Fifty-four percent of employed Long Island Levittowners worked in New York City, the majority of these earning their living in Manhattan. And 53 percent of the Levittowners of 1951 had moved from New York City to the suburban development, with only 18 percent coming from suburban Nas-sau County, the site of Levittown, and 17 percent coming from out of state.[87] Levitt's Long Island development was, then, a community of sub-urban pioneers, newcomers from the big city who were beginning their families on the metropolitan frontier. The husband most often still com-muted to work in the city, and the wife stayed at home with small children or awaited the imminent prospect of birth.

Although some of the migrants to Levittown found it difficult to adjust to the new community and its little, look-alike houses, the prevailing sen-timent was favorable. One veteran who had shared a one-room apartment with his wife and a relative before moving to Levittown commented: "That was so awful I'd rather not talk about it. Getting into this house was like being emancipated."[88] The wife of another former GI wrote to a local newspaper: "Too bad there aren't more men like Levitt & Sons. . . . I hope they make a whopper of a profit."[89] With considerable hyperbole but some truth, Levitt himself observed: "In Levittown 99% of the people pray for us."[90] For some residents, the Levittown cottages were the first step on the path to upward mobility and were readily superseded by more expensive homes as soon as their bank accounts permitted. But a large number expressed their fondness for the community and faith in its fu-ture by remaining there and investing in their mass-produced houses. A 1956 survey found that of the 1,800 families who had migrated to Levit-town in 1947, 500 still resided there.[91] Alterations and home improve-ments were major industries in the community, and in 1957 a commenta-

tor reported that "it is hard in Levittown today to find a house with an un-
altered exterior—and rare to find two in a row with the same alterations."
Moreover, the value of Levittown houses, "increased by a demand that
cannot be met," had "been raised by these improvements," so that by 1957
altered houses were selling for as much as $21,000.[92] Demonstrating the
satisfaction of most homeowners, a 1957 survey found that 94 percent of
Levittowners would recommend the Long Island community to their
friends.[93]

Levittown, however, was not a harmonious utopia without conflict and
problems. Given the large number of children in the community, the
schools were predictably the chief focus of controversy. Between 1947 and
1957, the enrollment in School District Five, the largest of the four districts in Levittown, soared from 47 pupils attending a three-room school-
house to 16,300 students in fourteen buildings costing almost $23 mil-
lion.[94] In 1953 one commentator reported that "three years ago in
Levittown the schools had 3,000 children—and they were being taught in
Quonset huts. . . . This year they have roughly 9,000 children—and are
managing to absorb them only by holding split sessions." He concluded:
"No school system can indefinitely survive the impact of these gigantic
waves of children."[95] To finance this expansion, the property tax rate rose
from 73 cents per $100 of assessed valuation for the school year
1947/1948 to $6.06 per $100 for 1957/1958, the second highest rate of
the sixty-two districts in Nassau County. "Many residents who left New
York City because of high taxes, and because they wished to live and raise
their families in a suburban atmosphere," observed one Long Island publication in 1955, "are beginning to wonder if they have merely leapt from
the frying pan into the fire."[96]

Not only were the high taxes unexpected, but Levittowners had to adapt
to a new sense of authority over their schools. In the giant, heavily bu-
reaucratized, and highly centralized school system of New York City,
where the board of education was not elected but appointed by the mayor,
professional administrators ruled the educational process, and parents
had little voice or clout. But in Levittown, mothers and fathers enthusias-
tically filled the ranks of the Parent-Teacher Associations and attended
school board meetings, especially the annual budget meetings. In 1954
and 1955, a civil war erupted when the schools included in their classroom
exercises the playing of a recording of "The Lonesome Train," a cantata
that described the return of Lincoln's body to Illinois for burial. Claiming

that it was written by "known Communists," one group of parents wanted the cantata banned, whereas another faction defended it.[97] A PTA president who opposed the ban remembered that she "organized meetings and marches. The meetings were held on Friday nights and went on till early the next morning."[98] In May 1957, the fire department broke up a controversial school board meeting, claiming that the disorderly gathering was a fire hazard. When the meeting reconvened three days later at 7:30 in the evening, three thousand Levittowners crowded into the building, and not until 6:15 the next morning did the gathering adjourn after approval of a new school budget.[99] Underlying the school clashes were religious divisions. Jewish Levittowners generally supported a liberal curriculum and hefty spending; Catholic parents more often opposed what they perceived as radical influences and extravagant budgets.[100]

One group that the Levittowners of the late 1940s and early 1950s did not have to cope with was blacks. William Levitt restricted sale of houses to Caucasians, claiming that the prospect of racially integrated neighborhoods would deter buyers. "We can solve a housing problem, or we can try to solve a racial problem," Levitt contended. "But we cannot combine the two."[101] In 1949 a black veteran, James Mayweathers, waited in line from 7:00 A.M. Saturday to 7:30 A.M. Sunday to apply for the purchase of a Levitt house. On Sunday morning, Levitt informed him that blacks were not permitted to buy the new dwellings. The NAACP, the local of the United Automobile Workers Union, and the American Jewish Congress were among the groups to protest Levitt's discriminatory policy, but the developer remained dedicated to a whites-only policy.[102]

In 1957 the race issue exploded in Levittown, Pennsylvania, when the African American Myers family moved into a house at the corner of Deepgreen and Daffodil lanes. On the night of 13 August, two hundred people gathered outside the house; a barrage of stones ensued, smashing the living-room picture window. Later that week, the county sheriff declared the situation out of control as crowds formed before the house each night, and he asked for help from a state police detachment. The following week, state troopers wielding riot clubs broke up a group of four hundred people who had gathered to protest the sale of the house to the Myers family, and the Levittown Betterment Committee formed with the purpose of preserving the racial purity of the community. In September, the protests continued as automobiles filled with demonstrators drove by the Myers home late at night blowing their horns and playing the car radios as loudly as possible. Foes of integration gathered in an adjacent house flying the Confederate flag, sang "Old Black Joe," and played recordings of "Old Man River."[103]

Although most suburban subdivisions were off-limits to black purchasers, a few developers catered to African Americans. Thomas Romana's Ronek Park on Long Island offered one thousand small Levitt-type homes to buyers "regardless of race, creed or color," a cue to any alert home seeker that the development was in fact intended for blacks.[104] Suburbia, then, was not to deviate from the color line that prevailed in the central city. On the metropolitan fringe, as in the core city, there were to be white neighborhoods and black neighborhoods, but integrated living was rare.

The Levittowns attracted unequaled media and scholarly attention during the postwar years, but they were not the only mammoth housing developments arising along the metropolitan fringe. South of Chicago, American Community Builders (ACB), headed by former Federal Public Housing Authority commissioner Philip Klutznick, built Park Forest, a town of 31,000 residents. Like Levittown, it catered to the young families of veterans, although ACB first built rental garden apartments and then added thousands of single-family houses priced from $12,500 to $14,000. Klutznick was more idealistic than the pragmatic Levitt and sought not only to make money, but to fashion a model community. "We aren't interested in houses alone," Klutznick claimed. "We are trying to create a better life for people. In our view, we will have failed if all we do is produce houses."[105] With this in mind, he encouraged the first residents to incorporate Park Forest as a municipality so that they could participate democratically in the development of the community and not remain subject to the paternalistic rule of the developer. Klutznick dreamed of "a people's village, not a developer's fiefdom." This did not necessarily benefit him. "As the resident president of ACB," he later noted, "I was the natural object of protest movements."[106]

Not only were the Park Forest houses more expensive than those in Levittown, but the residents had a higher educational status and tended to be upwardly mobile white-collar workers. A 1950 survey found that the average adult male in Park Forest had more than four years of college education, and one observer reported that "the first wave of colonists was heavy with academic and professional people—the place, it appeared, had an extraordinary affinity for Ph.D.s"[107] But like Levittown, it also had an extraordinary affinity for children. In 1950 half the residents were under fourteen years old, and the high birth rate earned Park Forest the nick-name "Fertile Acres."[108] One early resident reminisced about the swarms of children he encountered on his first night in the community: "It seemed that they were all outside that night—60 noisy, running, scream-ing children swirling around us—it was incredible."[109]

The West Coast counterpart to Park Forest and the Levittowns was Lakewood, located south of Los Angeles. In 1950 three partners bought 3,375 acres of southern California farmland and launched the giant hous-ing development. By February 1952, an Associated Press story reported that "almost 8,000 homes have been completed by assembly-line meth-ods," and "beans and sugarbeets have been replaced by broad boulevards and quiet side streets, green lawns and frame homes." The developer of-fered seven basic floor plans, and the two- and three-bedroom houses sold for from $9,195 to $12,000. A veteran could acquire a two-bedroom model for a down payment of only $195. As an added attraction, each house came with an electric garbage-disposal unit, and the community boasted of being a "garbage-free city."[110] In 1954 Lakewood incorporated as a municipality, adopting the motto "Lakewood—Tomorrow's City To-day."[111] Three years later, it had an estimated 85,000 residents, most of them young couples with an abundance of children. Lakewood, like Park Forest and the Levittowns, definitely appeared to be tomorrow's city, a community of the young who were investing in the latest ranch-style houses and garbage disposals.

Because of their size, their rapid growth, and their large numbers of young people, seemingly representing the nation's future, the Levittowns, Park Forest, and Lakewood became well-known examples of the suburban trend; both in the 1950s and in later decades, they were viewed as stereo-typical postwar suburbs. Yet not all suburban migrants of the late 1940s and early 1950s were Levittowners seeking moderately priced, four-room, mass-produced houses. In fact, smaller developments in every price range were springing up along the metropolitan fringe throughout the nation. At the same time Levitt was selling his diminutive ranch models for $7,990, for $15,950 Pine Ridge Homes was offering its three-bedroom ("one paneled in knotty pine") and two-bath ranch houses in Long Island's "fine residential village of Flower Hill . . . only 19 miles from midtown New York."[112] On Long Island's south shore, Sam Harris was marketing the "Merrick Ranger," a three-bedroom, two-bath ranch house costing $16,990 and located in his "magnificent Merrick Oaks de-velopment," with its "thousands of towering, stately oak, beech and pine trees . . . framed by winding roads, paved sidewalks and curbs."[113] In an eight-hour period in 1949, developer Sam Berger sold 155 houses of the $13,500 to $16,000 price range in Great Neck, Long Island.[114] In 1947 the *New York Times* reported "a noticeable tendency in recent weeks toward the erection of residences definitely in the 'luxury' class." For example, two developers were subdividing a north shore Long Island estate into lots of an acre or more for sixty-six homes starting at $30,000, and in Englewood, New Jersey, the developer of South Hills Estates claimed to be responding to "an acute demand for $40,000 to $50,000 homes."[115]

Exclusive Scarsdale did not escape the wave of suburban newcomers, its population increasing over 36 percent in the 1950s. Yet Scarsdale was not Levittown and did not intend to be. In the fall of 1949, residents of the exclusive suburb became aware that a developer was preparing to build a subdivision of forty-six ranch houses with the same basic plan in their community. The village building inspectors temporarily halted the project by revoking the building permits, but many Scarsdale residents sought a permanent end to the threat from what one local leader called "the hit-and-run builders of look-alike houses." Consequently, in April 1950 the village board adopted an ordinance "to regulate similarity of appearance in any neighborhood." By forbidding repetition in the length and height of roofs, the placements of windows, doors, and porches, and the widths of houses in a single neighborhood, the board outlawed the look-alike models associated with large-scale builders such as Levitt.[116] By law, Scarsdale was in effect restricted to expensive, custom-built homes.

During the decade after World War II, suburbia was, then, no more uniform than in the prewar years. There were Levittowners who escaped from New York City, and Scarsdalers who sought to keep out Levittowners. Housewives were hosting Tupperware parties in Levittown and literary teas in Scarsdale; Levittown husbands were heading for the bowling alley, whereas their Scarsdale counterparts found refuge in the country club. Facile stereotypes about a homogeneous suburbia could not shed an accurate light on the outward migration of Americans. The metropolitan fringe was a diverse landscape, not a monotonous sprawl of unvarying housing tracts.

One can, however, make certain generalizations about the effect of postwar suburban migration on American life. As more Americans purchased homes in affordable suburban developments such as Levittown, home ownership became an increasingly significant factor in the American way of life. In 1940, 43.6 percent of American homes were owner occupied; by 1950, the figure was up to 55 percent, and in 1960 it was 61.9 percent. Whereas the number of owner-occupied housing units more than doubled from 15.2 million to 32.8 million during these two decades, the number of renter-occupied units remained virtually unchanged. In other words, the United States went from a renter majority to an owner majority. The result was an increasing concern for property values and the economic stability of neighborhoods. For the majority of homeowners, their houses represented their largest investment. It was their nest egg, a commodity that hopefully would appreciate in value so that the family could cash it in and buy an even better house in the future. Whereas renters had no vested interest in their dwellings or neighborhoods, home-owners most definitely did. As such, they were dedicated to excluding any-thing that endangered their investment, whether it be the African Ameri-can Myers family in Levittown, Pennsylvania, or the look-alike houses in Scarsdale. A greater proportion of Americans had a financial interest in the future development of their metropolis. They could not afford to allow their portion of the metropolitan turf to depreciate.

As Americans moved outward, farther from the public transit lines of the central city, they also became more auto dependent. Between 1945 and 1955, the number of automobiles registered in the United States more than doubled, from 25.8 million to 52.1 million, whereas the nation's pop-ulation increased only about 17 percent. In 1945 there was an automobile for every 5.5 Americans; ten years later, there was one for every 3.2. For new suburbanites, the automobile was a necessity, and the number of two-car families was growing. In the increasingly suburban world, failure to adapt to the automobile spelled obsolescence. A survey conducted in Columbus, Ohio, Houston, and Seattle in the early 1950s found that shop-pers still preferred the central-city downtown because of its "larger selec-tion of goods," but in each city the chief complaint about the core was "dif-ficult parking."[117] As auto-oriented suburbia grew, parking was becoming a prime concern that could not be ignored. Suburbanization meant in-creased auto dependence, which in turn meant the necessity of ample parking and abundant highways.

Yet another characteristic of the new suburban world of the postwar decade was its focus on children. Whereas in 1939 the American birth rate was only 18.8 per 1,000 people, by 1946 it was up to 24.1, and it re-mained between 24 and 27 through the end of the 1950s. Not since the early 1920s had the birth rate been so high, and a disproportionate share of the offspring were found in suburbia. In Levittown, Park Forest, Lakewood, and other suburbs across the nation, everyone noted the swarms of children. The crowded city—with its noise, crime, polluted air, and lack of open space—was deemed an undesirable atmosphere for young-sters; good parents were expected to move their children to suburbia. In the immensely popular 1950s television situation comedy *I Love Lucy*, the Ricardos leave their Manhattan apartment for a suburban home in Connecticut because their child needs the fresh air and elbow room of suburbia. For millions of American viewers, this seemed a natural move. New York City was no place to raise children; suburbia was the realm of the happy family.

Moreover, the focus on children meant a preoccupation with school-ing. School politics were serious business in the postwar suburbs, and parents were vigilant in their concern for the education of their offspring. Not only did Levittowners clash over supposed Communist-inspired school material, but Scarsdale residents battled over the purported Red in-fluence in their school system.[118] In lower-middle-class Levittown as well as elite Scarsdale, the Cold War was fought in the schools.

The family-oriented lifestyle of suburbia also was less formal than the big-city way of life. Harried by swarms of small children, young house-wives opted to dress more casually and were less likely to dress up when they went shopping. According to one observer of the suburban scene, slacks and shorts were "standard wear for both men and women at all times, including trips to the shopping center. Visiting grandparents in-variably are shocked and whisper: 'Why, nobody dresses around here!' "[119] Many suburbanites welcomed the release from the formality of down-town. An early 1950s shopping survey in Houston and Seattle found that one of the most frequently cited advantages of suburban shopping was that one did "not have to dress up."[120] The hat and gloves required of any decent woman in the metropolitan downtown were not necessary in sub-urbia. Nor did men feel compelled to wear a coat and tie, as they might in the central business district. Similarly, leisure activities were less formal. Backyard barbecues and television watching in one's own living room were casual alternatives to dressing up and eating out at a restaurant or going to a theater. One could experience the pleasures of a variety show or comedy while lounging on the couch wearing shorts. And one did not have to hire a babysitter.

Yet another consequence of the suburban migration was an increas-ing political fragmentation of metropolitan America. More suburbanites meant more suburban governments, and new municipalities and special districts sprouted up across the country in the late 1940s and 1950s. Between 1940 and 1960, the number of municipalities in suburban Saint Louis County, Missouri, soared from forty-one to ninety-eight, with an extraordinary forty-two municipalities created from 1945 through 1950. In southern California, Lakewood incorporated in 1954, opting to contract for most of its services from Los Angeles County while evading annexation to nearby Long Beach and retaining local community control over zoning and land-use planning. This option proved so attractive that twenty additional communities incorporated in Los Angeles County from 1956 through 1959.[121] Elsewhere, the increase was not always so dramatic, but even where there were few new municipalities, suburban migrants became residents of existing outlying units beyond the pale of big-city government and its concerns. For Levittowners, the politics of School District Five and its soaring tax rate became a more immediate concern than who was the mayor of New York City. In fact, suburbanites did not escape the problems of local government when they moved to the metropolitan fringe. Instead, they found new problems that reinforced the reality that they did not live in the central city but in an independent unit of government with its own dilemmas. In 1953 *Business Week* reported that "the swarming newcomers have found fresh air and homes—but they have created a very sticky problem in municipal finance."[122] Throughout the nation, the mass of suburban schoolchildren and the need for sewers, streets, and firefighters were imposing a heavy tax burden on the migrants. Yet this increasing body of metropolitan Americans no longer looked to a city hall in Manhattan or the Loop for an answer to these local government problems. Their local officials were a short drive away in their own suburban community. That was where their taxes went, and consequently that was their new civic focus.

The suburban migration was, then, producing changes in the metropolitan lifestyle. The central-city downtown remained, however tenuously, the center of metropolitan life, and the racially divided black–white city remained intact. But there was a changing lifestyle along the fringe, one that focused on homeownership, children, and automobiles. It was a more informal way of life and one independent of the politics and government of the central city. The postwar suburbanite was increasingly preoccupied with property values and highways rather than rents and streetcars. Coats and ties and hats and gloves were yielding to more casual attire, and the issue of schools attracted more attention than battles over subway fares.

Not everyone found the changing lifestyle appealing. Instead, the postwar era spawned a long list of rabid diatribes, journalistic commentaries, and supposedly scholarly analyses criticizing the suburban migration and life in the new housing developments along the metropolitan fringe. The most extreme of the critics was John Keats, whose 1956 novel *The Crack in the Picture Window* depicted life in the Levittowns and Lakewoods as a national disaster. He warned that "whole square miles of identical boxes are spreading like gangrene throughout New England, across the Denver prairie, around Los Angeles, Chicago, Washington, New York, Miami—everywhere." These developments were "conceived in error, nurtured by greed, corroding everything they touch." Moreover, they destroyed "established cities and trade patterns, pose dangerous problems for the areas they invade, and actually drive mad myriads of housewives shut up in them." The main characters of his novel were a benighted suburban couple named John and Mary Drone, whose very name reinforced Keats's belief that the postwar developments were "breeding swarms of neuter drones" who were "prey to drift and abyssal boredom" and who could not "be said to have lives of their own."[123]

No one matched the bitter verbiage of Keats, but many commentators of the late 1940s and 1950s joined in the antisuburban chorus. Although they presented themselves as informed social observers, their writings were in fact long on value judgments and short on supporting data. For these observers, suburbia was a homogeneous landscape of narrow-minded conformity where women and children were held in a stultifying captivity and life was a busy but shallow round of kaffeeklatsches and PTA meetings. In William Whyte's *The Organization Man*, published in 1956, suburbia was the natural home of a rising class of company men and their families who sacrificed their individuality to get ahead in the corporation. University of Chicago scholar David Riesman wrote of the suburban style of life, with its "ensuing loss of certain kinds of diversity, complexity, and texture," its "homogenizing modes of thought and feeling," and its "aimlessness, a pervasive low-keyed unpleasure." According to Riesman, "The suburb is like a fraternity house at a small college, in which like-mindedness reverberates upon itself as the potentially various selves within each of us do not get evoked or recognized."[124] In 1954 longtime social commentator Frederick Lewis Allen raised a common theme when he described the suburb "during the day [as] only half a community, an unnatural manless matriarchy" where the wife struggles "to rid herself of the frustrating feeling that the place where things are really going on is somewhere else."[125] The same year, an expert on child rearing wrote: "The children growing up in New Suburbia run the danger of becoming 'homogenized' . . . —the pressure to conform is intense, and stultifying." She further argued: "In this atmosphere children are likely to picture the good life in terms of uniform, standardized patterns; and that tends to block invention and experiment."[126] In 1955 an Episcopalian cleric wrote of "The Church in Suburban Captivity," the bride of Christ having been delivered into the hands of suburbanites whose gospel of advancement and individual success had corrupted her. In perhaps the most apocalyptic indictment of suburbia, he concluded: "Suburban domination may well be God's word of judgment upon us as his church. For our trespasses and complacency we have been delivered to Babylon."[127]

A land of absent husbands, frustrated wives, conforming parents, and dull, unimaginative children, suburbia in the minds of these commentators was a plague upon the nation. Its look-alike little houses and devotion to washing machines and television sets seemed to mark a nadir in American civilization. One of its few defenders among the high-minded writing class was the Pulitzer Prize–winning poet Phyllis McGinley. A wife and mother of two children who lived in an upper-middle-class New York suburb, she proclaimed in 1949 in an article in *Harper's Magazine*: "For the best eleven years of my life I have lived in Suburbia, and I like it." Noting that she had "yet to read a book in which the suburban life was pictured as the good life or the commuter as a sympathetic figure," she sang the praises of life on the metropolitan fringe. "How free we are!" she wrote of the suburban existence. "Free of the city's noise, of its ubiquitous doormen, of the soot on the windowsill and the radio in the next apartment."[128]

Millions of Americans seemed to agree with McGinley. Despite the diatribes against life on the fringe, the outward flow of people continued, and polls showed that the overwhelming majority of migrants were happy in their new homes. Moreover, there was no proof that a greater proportion of women went mad in Levittown than in Brooklyn or that Levittown children were unimaginative drones compared with their Brooklyn cousins. Nor did critics of suburbia ever seem to consider the monotony of giant city apartment buildings, where every unit had the same floor plan and one could identify one's own apartment only by noting the number on the door or memorizing how many doors it was from the end of the hall. City dwellers as well as suburbanites lived in repetitive little boxes. Suburbanites also were not the only Americans with a predilection for social homogeneity. As irate whites in Chicago and Detroit demonstrated, city dwellers were just as dedicated to keeping people of a different skin color out of the neighborhoods as suburbanites were. In Chicago, Riesman's Hyde Park neighborhood, although finally admitting affluent blacks, was spending millions of dollars to preserve its economic class homogeneity as the University of Chicago fought valiantly to exclude lower-class invaders from its share of the metropolitan turf. And the critics of suburbia were not immune from the intellectual conformity that supposedly blighted the suburban fringe. In their accounts of the suburbs, they parroted the same lines and repeated the same criticisms. Bound by stultifying cultural conventions, they were unable to comprehend the thinking of a housewife thrilled by a Bendix automatic washing machine. They suffered their own brand of cultural captivity.

In fact, the antisuburban tracts revealed less about life in suburbia than they did about the growing cultural chasm in metropolitan America. Metropolitan Americans did not share a view of the good life, and Levittowners and their ilk were incomprehensible to their critics, just as their critics proved beyond the understanding of Levittowners. The lifestyle aspirations of metropolitan Americans were increasingly divergent. For some, a suburban home was the great American dream; for others, it was the nation's nightmare. Moreover, the gap would not close. "To condemn Suburbia," Phyllis McGinley noted, was "a literary cliché," and it would remain so.[129] In future decades millions of Americans would invest their savings in single-family, detached homes and find happiness along the metropolitan fringe. Yet accompanying this outward migration was a continual barrage of assaults on the developers' rape of nature, the unthinking materialism of suburban consumer culture, and the conformity and homogeneity of suburbia. In America, life and letters were not congruent.

As yet, the increasingly divided metropolis still focused on a single hub, and the Detroit or Saint Louis metropolitan areas could accurately be regarded as consisting of the central city and its dependent outskirts. But as more Americans pursued their dreams in suburbia, the possibility of an independent new world beyond the central-city municipal limits seemed increasingly real. Already many of the new migrants were finding jobs outside the city. In 1956 a survey of Long Island Levittowners found that 66.2 percent of the families' principal wage earners had had jobs in New York City when they first moved to Levittown, and only 27 percent had worked in surrounding suburban Nassau County. Yet by 1956 the proportion working in New York City had dropped to 51.8 percent, with

43.8 percent employed in suburban Long Island.[130] Typical was the story of Al Utt. About the same time he moved to his Levittown ranch house in 1949, Utt gave up his job in Manhattan and secured employment in an aircraft plant near the giant housing development.[131] If an increasing number of Americans followed the path of Al Utt, they would spend their entire lives in suburbia, working, sleeping, shopping, and playing in the territory beyond the central city. Levittowners and their fellow suburbanites would then be no more tied to New York City than were residents of Albany. They would share the same state with Brooklynites or Manhattan dwellers but not the same city. The migration of Al Utt was, then, a movement away from the traditional notion of the metropolis and toward a posturban era, an age when Americans would inhabit vast, sprawling expanses of dense population without a unifying culture, government, or economy. By 1955, this metropolitan revolution had not yet occurred, but Utt and others like him were in the vanguard of change, pioneering the new world of the future.

3 | Coming Apart

In the late 1950s and early 1960s, the signs of a metropolitan revolution were undeniable. Not only did suburban housing tracts continue to proliferate, but mammoth shopping centers and malls joined them along the metropolitan fringe. New factories lined suburban highways, providing blue-collar jobs, and a number of new office and corporate campuses testified to the outward migration of white-collar jobs and executive decision makers. Along outlying thoroughfares, new chains of auto-oriented restaurants and motels meant that more people were eating and resting in the fringe areas rather than flocking downtown for food and hotel accommodations. Moreover, suburban lifestyle communities for older Americans were signs of a new fissure in the metropolitan map. Metropolitan culture was dividing along age lines, and seniors were escaping from the swarms of suburban children who were fast becoming rock-and-roll–loving adolescents. Meanwhile, a growing number of Americans were critical of schemes to bolster the traditional focus of metropolitan life, the downtown. Grand schemes for central-city revival seemed less desirable as the bulldozers began to clear tracts of urban land, displacing thousands of residents and businesses. Plans for inner-city superhighways likewise were losing their luster as urban dwellers came to realize the amount of destruction necessary to accommodate the automobile in cities designed for streetcars.

The metropolis appeared to be coming apart. Retailers were headed outward at an accelerating pace, and office workers were beginning to follow in their path. Senior citizens were withdrawing into enclaves of their own, and there was no consensus about plans to restore the traditional core. A growing number of Americans were living, working, and shopping in suburbia and had nothing to do with the central cities. A declining proportion of metropolitan residents were heading downtown for their paychecks or the latest in fashion; fewer were subject to central-city government and sending their children to central-city schools. The metropolitan center was weakening whereas centrifugal forces were mounting. Decentralization rather than recentralization was triumphing. The result was an increasingly dispersed metropolis with fewer bonds uniting its citizens.

The Emergence of Commercial Suburbia

Nothing testified to the loosening grip of a common metropolitan hub as forcefully as the emergence of suburban competitors to downtown retailing. Throughout the postwar period, suburbia had been capturing a growing share of retailing dollars, but the change was especially marked in the late 1950s and early 1960s. Between 1958 and 1963, retail sales in current dollars plummeted 23.5 percent in the central business district of Buffalo but rose 10.2 percent in the metropolitan area as a whole, dropped 18.6 percent in downtown Baltimore but increased 17.9 percent in that metropolitan area, and fell 17.7 percent in the Saint Louis central business district but climbed 17.4 percent in the metropolitan region.[1] This pattern was repeated across the country. Downtown retail sales were falling because suburban retailers were attracting the customers who had formerly headed to the urban core.

This spelled doom for some downtown stores. In 1956 Lewis and Conger, after serving customers in Manhattan for 122 years, moved its store to suburban Manhasset, and the following year Namm-Loeser Company closed its outlet in downtown Brooklyn but retained two modern Long Island branch stores.[2] After 104 years in retailing, in 1957 the R. H. White department store closed its massive emporium in downtown Boston, and in Pittsburgh two major downtown department stores, Frank and Seder

and Rosenbaums, went out of business.[3] In 1958 the floor space of Pittsburgh's downtown department stores exceeded the combined total for all
other department stores in the metropolitan area by 844,000 square feet.
By the close of 1963, the situation was reversed, with the combined area of
suburban department stores surpassing that of downtown outlets by
171,000 square feet.[4] Surveys of Christmas season shoppers told the same
story. During the holiday season of 1954, only 10 percent of all shopping
trips in Pittsburgh's Allegheny County were to suburban shopping centers; 41 percent were to the central-city downtown. In the Christmas season of 1960, however, 38 percent of all shopping trips were to suburban
centers, and the downtown's share was down to 35 percent.[5] For holiday
shoppers in western Pennsylvania, suburbia had surpassed downtown as
a magnet for retailing dollars.

The retailing picture in Cleveland was representative of that in the nation as a whole. During the 1950s and early 1960s, the city's major department stores found it necessary to establish new suburban branches as
their downtown stores struggled to produce profits. In 1951 the Bailey
Company opened a suburban store in Euclid and nine years later followed
with a branch in Mayfield Heights. In 1957 the May Company began to
open suburban branches, and the following year William Taylor's established a store in Southgate Shopping Center in Maple Heights. Throughout the 1950s, the Higbee Company refused to open suburban branches,
but it finally capitulated in 1961 with a store at Westgate Shopping Center
and two years later with another suburban shopping-center outlet. The
harsh consequences of decentralization became readily apparent when in
December 1961 William Taylor's downtown store went out of business, followed soon after in 1962 by the announced closing of Bailey's downtown
emporium.[6] The *Cleveland Plain Dealer* summed up the retailing realities
of the age when it reported that Bailey's was closing "because of a decline in
downtown business and the population growth in the suburbs."[7]

The great landmarks of this decentralization of retailing were the massive shopping centers arising along the suburban fringe. There were
some suburban shopping centers before the mid-1950s, but most of them
were small strip centers with a few stores lined up beside a supermarket
and pharmacy. In most metropolitan areas there was no suburban center
that posed a serious threat to the supremacy of the giant downtown emporiums in the marketing of apparel and accessories. In the mid- and late
1950s, however, a surge in the construction of ever larger and more elaborate suburban malls anchored by major department stores revolutionized

American retailing. For example, in 1954 Northland Shopping Center opened in Southfield, north of Detroit. Designed by architect Victor Gruen and financed by Detroit's largest department store, J. L. Hudson Company, Northland set a new standard for American malls. With one hundred stores along wide pedestrian malls and a Hudson's outlet, Northland offered a quantity and quality of merchandise traditionally found only in the central business district. Moreover, with ten thousand parking spaces and a suburban location, it was considerably more convenient than downtown for thousands of relatively affluent residents in Detroit's northern suburbs. A well-publicized success, Northland grossed $78 million in sales in its first full year, twice the anticipated level.[8] On the West Coast in San Mateo, south of San Francisco, Hillsdale Shopping Center also opened in 1954. With seventy-two stores and a branch of Macy's, it likewise spared suburbanites the necessity of a trip downtown.

Malls were rising in smaller metropolitan areas as well. In 1955 Dixie Manor center, located in the Louisville suburb of Shively, offered "acres and acres" of free parking. The *Louisville Courier-Journal* claimed that the facility, designed with a New Orleans motif, would "serve as a new downtown" for that area of Louisville's suburbs, and, comparing it with the prime downtown retailing area, the newspaper noted that it "had more store frontage . . . than on one side of Fourth St. from Market to Broadway."[9]

In 1956, however, the suburban shopping mecca truly took center stage as new malls of unprecedented size opened across the country. A leading expert on urban real estate estimated that more retail space in regional shopping malls opened in the two months of September and October 1956 than in the entire period from 1948 to September 1956.[10] Within a three-month period in 1956, three giant malls in Long Island's Nassau County welcomed their first customers. The Gertz department store anchored Mid-Island Mall in Hicksville, Gimbels was the leading retailer in Green Acres Mall in Valley Stream, and the largest of the three, Roosevelt Field, boasted of a Macy's outlet as well as eleven thousand parking spaces. The same year, hordes of shoppers descended on the new Seven Corners Shopping Center in suburban Virginia outside Washington, D.C. According to *Time* magazine, Seven Corners compressed "the equivalent of four city blocks of stores into a split-level building within one block of the shopper's car."[11] Another product of the 1956 shopping-center boom was Houston's Gulfgate, which claimed to be the biggest mall in the South.

FIGURE 3.1 Aerial view of Southdale Center, Edina, Minnesota. (Minnesota Historical Society)

The most influential and innovative of the 1956 malls was Southdale in Edina, outside Minneapolis. Unlike its open-air predecessors, Southdale was enclosed, the first climate-controlled suburban shopping center in the nation (figure 3.1). Designed by the ubiquitous Victor Gruen and built by Dayton's, Minneapolis's largest department store, Southdale included seventy-five stores arranged on two levels. At the core of the mall was a three-story garden court, air-conditioned in the summer and heated in the winter, with fountains, tropical plants, eighty canaries in a twenty-one-foot cage, and a sidewalk café (figure 3.2). A notable success, Southdale recorded sales that exceeded expectations, and during its first five years only four of the center's stores went out of business.[12] In early 1957 *Fortune* magazine reported: "The strikingly handsome and colorful center is constantly crowded, and the builders' estimate of 20,000 customers a day already has been surpassed." In fact, *Fortune* claimed that "on a recent Sunday, when the stores were closed, some 75,000 people drove to South-dale just to stroll around the court and window-shop on the upper terraces."[13]

FIGURE 3.2 Interior court of Southdale Center. (Norton & Peel, Minnesota Historical Society)

The good news from Minnesota and elsewhere inspired a continuing stream of new malls throughout the nation. Paramus, New Jersey, just west of New York City, became the ultimate mall town, with two regional centers opening in 1957. Macy's built Garden State Plaza, and Allied Stores was responsible for Bergen Mall. Together they had 128 stores and parking for more than sixteen thousand cars. Garden State Plaza alone had six shoe stores and seventeen apparel shops, offering a range of selection to satisfy the most careful shoppers.[14] Meanwhile, in 1958 Marshall Field's opened Old Orchard Shopping Center in Skokie, north of Chicago, and the same year developer James Rouse completed the nation's second enclosed center, Harundale Mall, outside Baltimore. He followed this in 1961 with the enclosed Cherry Hill Mall in southern New Jersey, east of Philadelphia. A year earlier, Rouse had summarized what these new developments meant for America when he observed: "It has been widely recognized that in the development of major regional shopping centers, we are really building new, well planned central business districts."[15] The proliferating malls were not just convenient supplements to the dominant downtown retailers. They were new downtowns that were displacing the old central business districts as the focus of metropolitan shopping. Shoppers were heading downtown less often and instead going to the mall.

At the mall, these shoppers found a retailing environment that differed from that of downtown. Whereas the central business district had traditionally attracted a diverse range of people from throughout the metropolitan area, the mall targeted a certain segment of consumers living within its sector of the metropolis. The shopping centers of Paramus aimed to serve the middle-class, white residents of Bergen County, New Jersey; Roosevelt Field catered to the same element in Long Island's Nassau and Suffolk counties; and Southdale was intended for middle-class customers from the western suburbs of Minneapolis. Whereas J. L. Hudson's downtown department store had a bargain basement for the budget-conscious shopper and the high-style Woodward Shops for well-heeled, fashion-conscious women, the branch store at Northland had neither. It was a one-class emporium aimed at the great middle range of American society that was moving to suburbia. Mall owners generally did not expect or desire that many inner-city poor or African Americans would stroll through their garden courts or linger in their sidewalk cafés. Nor did the malls' enthusiastic customers expect to mix with many persons of a different social class. Compared with downtown, the malls offered a socially homogeneous environment where suburbanites could shop among people like themselves without confronting the sidewalk panhandlers or "undesirable" characters that could be found in the urban core.

At the mall one could, then, escape the harsh realities of a heterogeneous metropolis evident in the central business district. This was especially appealing to middle-class whites as the central city became increasingly black and poor. Baltimore's Planning Council recognized the problem facing central-city retailers when it observed: "Greater numbers of low-income, Negro shoppers in Central Business District stores, coming at the same time as middle and upper income white shoppers are given alternatives in . . . segregated suburban centers, has had unfortunate implications [for downtown merchants]."[16] Because of their outlying locations and the absence or poor quality of public transportation serving them, the great, new shopping centers were for those Americans who could afford automobiles and homes in the suburbs. If one sought to shop out of reach of those who could not afford those advantages, one could go to the mall.

Not only was the mall socially homogeneous, but its environment was carefully controlled. Shopping-center developers sought to escape the haphazard development of the central business district and create an optimal world of retailing. They endeavored to attract the proper mix of tenants, and any business that would not draw customers or contribute to the overall well-being of the mall was not welcome. With its clean, modern, attractive appearance, the shopping center was intended to be an appealing refuge for consuming housewives and their families. Describing his plan for Roosevelt Field, architect I. M. Pei wrote of the "trees, flowers, music, fountains, gay awnings, and bold use of graphic art" that combined "to make the retail atmosphere."[17] *Fortune* magazine dubbed Victor Gruen "an architect of environments," because his shopping malls were stage settings for consumption, designed to make spending money more pleasurable.[18] Contrasting sharply with the random helter-skelter of traditional downtowns, the well-managed mall left nothing to chance. To guarantee "blightproof" environs for Gruen's pleasure dome of retailing the developers purchased almost five hundred acres of land surrounding Southdale.[19]

Promotional events added to the festive atmosphere. Fashion shows, concerts, art exhibits, and boat and automobile shows all attracted potential customers and proved lucrative to retailers. Mall developer James Rouse emphasized: "The integrated plan, the convenience, the easy, casual, relaxed atmosphere of the shopping center constitute a special opportunity for effective promotion." According to Rouse, "[The promotional events] may or may not have any direct and immediate effect on shopping traffic at the time of the particular event, but the cumulative effect of bringing people to the center at these times is to establish close identification by the public with the center, and thus serve ultimately to increase traffic and business."[20] In other words, attendance at a promotional event would strengthen the attachment of the potential customer to the mall. If consumers got into the habit of attending flower shows at the mall, they would be more likely to develop the habit of shopping there.

The socially homogeneous, controlled environment of the mall attracted a mix of customers different from that of the downtown department store's regulars. The downtown emporium was the domain of women, its services were aimed at female customers, and its tearooms were gathering places for "ladies." Typically, the middle-class housewife traveled alone on public transit to the central business district and spent the day in the department stores before returning home. But the shopping center was more family oriented, and developers soon discovered that men and children were more likely to go to the mall than to the downtown store. A Cincinnati study found that 85 percent of downtown customers shopped alone, whereas shopping-center patrons more often shopped with family members; only 43 percent did so by themselves. Similarly, a survey in Bergen County, New Jersey, in the late 1950s revealed that children and men were more often included in shopping trips after the Paramus shopping centers opened.[21] Because husbands were at work during the weekdays, shopping centers were busiest on evenings and weekends.

Reflecting this new reality, the promotions and facilities at the new malls targeted not simply women but the whole family. Among the activities at James Rouse's Baltimore shopping center were an outdoor automobile show, a "foreign car gymkhana," and an Armed Forces Week Show with weapons exhibits, all of which were expected to have more appeal for men than women. For children, there was a "county fair" with rides.[22] In order to attract people, many centers included auditoriums and meeting rooms that again drew more than the traditional female shopper. On three typical days, Northland Shopping Center's facilities hosted the all-male Rotary Club, a Boy Scout troop, a meeting of salesmen of the American Hardware Mutual Insurance Company, and the United States Coast Guard.[23] Mall managers realized that suburban housewives brought their children with them when shopping and were prepared for this influx of youngsters. The general manager of J. L. Hudson's Northland and Eastland shopping centers, outside Detroit, explained one of the most important functions of the mall police: "People in shopping centers seem to have the habit of losing their children. The police department helps find them." Moreover, "the police prevent youngsters from riding bikes on the malls or on the sidewalks to safeguard an environment which must be safe for shoppers and small children."[24] To cater to these children, Southdale included a play area in the basement where, according to *Fortune*, "there are small cars to drive, a zoo with live animals, a carrousel, and a bright maze where children stay happily distracted while their parents shop."[25] Although mall managers still expected women to be the principal shoppers and sought diligently to capture their dollars, the new shopping centers deviated from the old gender-bound Marshall Field's slogan of "Give the Lady What She Wants." The mall sought to give the whole family what it wanted.

A trip to the mall was not only a family experience but an automotive voyage. Unlike downtown department stores that had clustered at the hub of public transit, the new shopping centers were for drivers of automobiles. Recognizing that lack of parking was the chief complaint about downtown shopping, developers prominently advertised the thousands of free parking spaces available at the outlying malls. In 1956 *Business Week* reported: "Generally, it is now felt, the ratio of parking space to shopping space should be three or four to one."[26] Moreover, to accommodate women, who were perceived as less competent drivers, Virginia's Seven Corners Shopping Center provided nine-foot-wide parking spaces instead of the conventional eight-foot spaces.[27] Everything was done to aid the automobile borne. At Northland, the mall police force patrolled the parking lot to prevent theft, aided motorists with stalled cars, and furnished free gasoline to shoppers who ran out of fuel.[28] The nation, especially the suburban fringe, had eschewed public transit for the automobile, and shopping-center developers were well aware of the fact. The result was the standard shopping-center plan: an island of retailing surrounded by a sea of parking. The acres of asphalt were visual proof to any passerby that the mall possessed a vital ingredient to mid-twentieth-century American happiness that was lacking in the increasingly obsolete downtown.

A new shopping world was thus developing along the fringe. It was socially segregated, environmentally controlled, and designed for the automobile-borne family. Moreover, it attracted the customers. In 1958 a survey of shoppers in the Paramus area found that before the new shopping centers opened, 26 percent had gone to New York City to buy women's apparel and 35 percent had shopped in the county seat of Hackensack. After the opening of Garden State Plaza and Bergen Mall, 80 percent purchased their women's wear at these centers, whereas only 12 percent shopped in New York City and an equal percentage in Hackensack. "There is no longer much reason for women to make the trip to New York, or to put up with the inadequate parking and congested streets of the New Jersey cities," *Fortune* concluded.[29] On the West Coast, the decentralization of retailing was also proceeding at a rapid rate. In 1957 a woman who had moved from Omaha to the Los Angeles suburb of Lakewood confessed: "I've never been downtown. I'll probably never go."[30] Nor was there any reason for her to go. One observer noted of Los Angeles: "Although there is a neighborhood called downtown, there is no center: there is no area in which people by common consent congregate in their lighter moments."[31]

This was increasingly true of cities across the nation. In fact some of the mall designers and developers conceived of their creations as new community centers providing a focus for the emerging suburban world. "By affording opportunities for social life and recreation in a protected pedestrian environment, by incorporating civic and educational facilities, shopping centers can fill an existing void," Victor Gruen asserted. "They can provide the needed place and opportunity for participation in modern community life that the ancient Greek Agora, the Medieval Market Place and our own Town Squares provided in the past."[32] James Rouse similarly viewed the malls not simply as outlying centers for consumption but as new downtowns. For Rouse, the shopping mall represented a shift in the focus and center of metropolitan life. "The well-planned, well-managed shopping center is more than simply a new plan for retail expansion," he claimed. "It represents a massive reorganization of the urban community."[33]

Another symptom of the massive reorganization under way was the growth of office employment in the suburbs. In the late 1950s and early 1960s, low-rise office buildings and landscaped office parks were appearing along the metropolitan fringe throughout the United States. From 1959 to 1965 the number of office jobs in Long Island's Nassau County soared 41 percent, as compared with a 20 percent rise in manufacturing employment. In Southfield, Michigan, the home of Northland Shopping Center, corporate offices were also providing jobs for suburbanites. In 1955 Bendix Corporation built its general offices and research center in the Detroit suburb, and later in the 1950s Standard Oil and Reynolds Aluminum constructed low-rise regional headquarters. Eaton Yale and Town Corporation followed suit in the early 1960s, shifting its offices to Southfield, and in 1963 the first building in the Northland Towers complex, next to Northland Shopping Center, welcomed its initial white-collar tenants (figure 3.3). West of Chicago, in suburban Oak Brook, American Can Company opened offices in 1958, and two years later the community's developers laid out a 154-acre office park that lured an increasing number of new white-collar employers over the next decade. As early as 1952, the upscale Saint Louis suburb of Clayton attracted the corporate headquarters of the Brown Shoe Company, and in 1962 a thirteen-story office building opened, followed a year later by a sixteen-story office tower. In 1966 the *St. Louis Post-Dispatch* observed that the suburb's burgeoning skyline "no longer blended into the county's amorphous urban sprawl, but now appeared more like a little Tulsa or perhaps an Omaha, than just another incorporated outskirt of St. Louis."[34]

FIGURE 3.3   Office buildings at Northland Shopping Center, Southfield, Michigan, 1965. (Walter P. Reuther Library, Wayne State University)

On the West Coast, Stanford University was nurturing the suburban-ization of business. In 1951 its Stanford Industrial Park opened in Palo Alto, south of San Francisco. Intended as a site for light-manufactur-ing concerns, over the next two decades it proved especially attractive to research facilities and corporate offices employing white-collar workers. A major landmark in the park's development was the construction of Hewlett-Packard's corporate headquarters in 1957. By the early 1960s, the electronics firm employed three thousand people in four sleek, modern buildings set in a landscaped campus.[35] Such research campuses became the heart of the emerging Silicon Valley, which in the last decades of the century would emerge as the great hope of American business. By the early 1960s, then, the business vanguard was in suburbia. Palo Alto, not the "renaissance" city of Pittsburgh, was the nursery for America's corpo-rate future.

Indicative of the shifting base of American business was the develop-ment of campuslike corporate estates along the metropolitan fringe. Lead-ing the migration to suburban estates was General Foods. In 1954 it aban-doned its Manhattan offices for a new headquarters twenty miles to the north on a forty-six-acre tract in suburban White Plains. In this pastoral setting, corporate employees could escape the city and enjoy working as well as living in sylvan suburbia. The committee that searched for a new headquarters site described Manhattan as plagued by the "discomforts caused by dirt, dust, noise, and the ever increasing problem of traffic congestion." In contrast, at the opening of the new estate headquarters, the president of General Foods told his employees: "We shall . . . find ourselves working in a parklike setting and a more peaceful atmosphere with reduced nerve strain on everyone." The new headquarters offered employees "a chance to stroll on tree-lined paths at noon" as well as free parking in ample lots.[36]

In 1956/1957 Connecticut General Life Insurance followed the example of General Foods, abandoning its headquarters in downtown Hartford for a new command center on 280 acres in outlying Bloomfield. Like General Foods, Connecticut General relished the breathing space of the metropolitan fringe. "What acreage does," the company's president commented, "is to permit future expansion with a minimum of building difficulties and to provide employee facilities, especially parking, on a basis which is normally not possible in a more central location." Within a year of the opening of the new headquarters, the company already had to double the size of the parking lots to meet employee needs. "We accepted that most people wanted to drive to work," explained the company president.[37] Most of the site, however, remained meadow and woodland, providing both the natural beauty and the adaptation to the automobile that downtown Hartford could not offer.

The distinguished architectural firm of Skidmore, Owings, and Merrill designed the Connecticut General headquarters, earning acclaim for its gleaming, low-rise, glass-and-steel structure. During the following decades, the firm was to repeat its success in corporate estates elsewhere in the nation. For example, in 1957/1958 it designed the new General Mills headquarters on an estate in Golden Valley, Minnesota, just outside Minneapolis (figure 3.4). Again, it provided a long, low, sleek building set in handsomely landscaped grounds worthy of one of the nation's great corporations. And, again, it was well adapted to an increasingly auto-borne, suburban-based white-collar population.

As General Foods, Connecticut General, and General Mills left the city, however, they distanced themselves from less affluent urban Americans and the growing population of blacks who could not afford automobiles or would find it difficult, if not impossible, to purchase homes in suburbia. If the future of the American economy was on the fringe at the Hewlett-

FIGURE 3.4
Headquarters of General Mills in Golden Valley, outside Minneapolis. (Minnesota Historical Society)

Packard headquarters or other suburban research centers, the inner-city dweller faced the danger of being left behind. Cities that had traditionally provided economic opportunities for poor newcomers were losing their preeminence to more remote suburbs. Both the pedestrian concourses of the booming shopping malls and the tree-lined paths of the corporate estates and research campuses were far removed from the sidewalks of the inner city.

Not only were some of the nation's largest corporations finding new homes along the fringe, but suburbia was giving birth to some of the business giants of the next generation. Perhaps most notably, the restaurant industry was adapting to the suburban lifestyle and, in the process, igniting a fast-food revolution. Drive-in restaurants adapted to the automobile culture of the mid-twentieth century had flourished in southern California before World War II and become commonplace throughout the nation by the late 1940s and early 1950s. These restaurants, however, depended on carhops to take orders and serve the food. The fast-food empires were to eliminate the carhops and make it respectable for families to serve themselves and eat off paper wrappers and from paper bags rather than from china with silverware.

The greatest name in fast food was McDonald's. This chain, specializing in hamburgers and french fries, was to develop into one of the largest corporations in the world by exploiting the burgeoning suburban market. In 1939 two brothers, Richard and Maurice McDonald, opened a small drive-in in San Bernardino, California. In the late 1940s, they transformed their outlet into a walk-up, self-service operation with assembly-line production of a limited menu of hamburgers, fries, and beverages. Their business flourished, and in 1954 it attracted the attention of Ray Kroc, an Illinois salesman of milk-shake mixers. Kroc recognized the potential of the business and purchased from the McDonald brothers the right to franchise outlets throughout the country. Kroc opened his initial outlet in suburban Des Plaines, Illinois, in 1955, and in 1960 the two-hundredth McDonald's welcomed its first hungry customers. In 1961 Kroc bought out the McDonald brothers, and by 1965 there were 738 stores.[38] Until the early 1970s, McDonald's was almost exclusively a suburban operation, bypassing the once preeminent central cities to reap the lush profits available along the metropolitan fringe. Indicative of its suburban orientation, McDonald's established its corporate headquarters in the Chicago suburb of Oak Brook.

McDonald's triumphed because it fit well into the new suburban lifestyle. It was for people in automobiles; the early units had no dining rooms but ample parking space. One was expected to eat in the car, a practice suited to auto-borne people in a hurry. Although McDonald's prided itself on its low prices (the hamburger originally cost 15 cents and the fries, 10), Kroc definitely did not want his restaurants to be perceived as working-class greasy spoons or raucous teen hangouts. They were to serve the middle-class suburban family. With an obsessive devotion to cleanliness, Kroc sought to ensure that his stores were as immaculate as the kitchen of the most conscientious suburban housewife. Moreover, he banned pay telephones, jukeboxes, and vending machines from his restaurants. He believed that they encouraged loitering by teens and other undesirables and "would downgrade the family image we wanted to create for McDonald's."[39] McDonald's was not to be a cheap diner inhabited by lingering construction workers or unruly teenagers where a suburban housewife would feel uncomfortable about bringing her children. Instead, it was to provide inexpensive food in a safe environment for suburbanites who had something better to do than wait for a gum-chewing carhop to deliver a burger and fries.

Like Levittown, then, McDonald's was intended to offer the suburban lifestyle but at a cheap price. And like the shopping malls, it appealed to the family-oriented, auto-borne world of the metropolitan fringe. In 1955 the opening-day advertisement for the Des Plaines McDonald's proclaimed "bring the whole family" and "plenty of free parking."[40] Accommodating the family and plenty of parking: those were the keys to making money in the new suburban world.

McDonald's was not the only fast-food chain exploiting the new suburban market. In 1953 the first self-service Burger King drive-in opened in Jacksonville, Florida; five years later, the Burger Chef chain was founded, offering the "world's greatest hamburger" for only 15 cents; and Hardee's hamburger chain dates from 1960.[41] In the 1950s, Colonel Harland Sanders began marketing his chicken recipe; he had sold two hundred Kentucky Fried Chicken franchises by 1960.[42] Thus by the mid-1960s, the fast-food revolution had swept the metropolitan fringe, and millions of suburbanites were helping themselves to burgers and chicken in brightly lit and often garish fast-food emporiums lining the highways.

While Ray Kroc and his competitors were profiting from hungry suburbanites, other entrepreneurs were exploiting the outlying market for lodging. As more Americans traveled by automobile, the old downtown hotels designed to serve rail passengers seemed increasingly out of date and accounted for a diminishing share of the lodging business. From 1948 to 1964, the hotel share of hotel/motel revenues in the United States dropped from 92 to 64 percent. During the same period, the number of hotel rooms in the nation fell from 1,550,000 to 1,450,000; the number of rooms in motor hotels and motels rose from 304,000 to 1,020,000.[43] Yet during the first decade after World War II, finding a decent room in an outlying motel remained a daunting task. Most motels were small-time operations owned and managed by a husband and wife who provided a bed and bath but nothing comparable to the accommodations at the finest hotels. In the late 1950s and the 1960s, however, motel chains appeared that ensured a reliable standard of quality and introduced the automobile traveler to a new level of luxury.

The trend-setting chain was Holiday Inn. The founder of Holiday Inn and the Ray Kroc of the lodging industry was Kemmons Wilson of Memphis, Tennessee. A successful real-estate developer, Wilson recognized the shortcomings of roadside lodging on a trip with his wife and five children from Memphis to Washington, D.C. "It didn't take us long to find out that most motels had cramped, uncomfortable rooms—and that they charged extra for children," he later recounted. "Few had adequate restaurants and fewer still were air-conditioned. In short, it was a miserable trip." From this experience, he concluded that the motel industry was the "greatest untouched business in the country," and in 1952 he opened the first Holiday Inn along a major Memphis highway.[44] Unlike the miserable motels he had experienced en route to Washington, it had air-conditioning, a swimming pool, and a restaurant, and the father of five instituted a policy that there would be no extra charge for children sharing a room with their parents. During the chain's first years, Wilson attracted few franchisees, and not until the close of 1955 did he earn a profit. But the number of inns soared in the late 1950s from 26 with 2,107 rooms in 1956 to 162 with 15,249 rooms in 1960. By 1965, there were 587 Holiday Inns nationwide that offered nearly 70,000 rooms to highway travelers.[45] As did McDonald's, Holiday Inns prospered by exploiting the relatively untapped market along the metropolitan fringe. Not until 1963 did Holiday Inn open its first downtown facility.

Holiday Inn, like McDonald's, mass-produced a product adapted to America's increasingly suburban lifestyle. It supplied rooms and facilities of standardized quality aimed at the auto-borne, middle-class family. Just as McDonald's fries were reliably the same whether one bought them in Levittown or Lakewood, Holiday Inn provided a highly predictable product to the traveler on the fringes of Minneapolis and the outskirts of New Orleans. Moreover, with its policy of no extra charge for children and the lure of its swimming pool, Holiday Inn was just as family-friendly as Kroc's chain or Rouse's shopping malls. And, of course, a common denominator of the mall, McDonald's, and the Holiday Inn was ample parking. In the age of the ubiquitous motor vehicle, the option of being able to park one's car conveniently in front of the motel-room door was highly desirable. Whereas downtown seemed increasingly dingy, with more poor people and African Americans populating the sidewalks, McDonald's, the mall, and the Holiday Inn promised cleanliness and a safe, comfortable environment for middle-class whites. Consequently, these new manifestations of suburban commerce profited as the urban core declined.

Ray Kroc, James Rouse, and Kemmons Wilson thus proved that homebuilders such as William Levitt were not the only ones who could find their fortune in suburbia. The metropolitan fringe was a potential commercial giant that could give birth to the world's largest restaurant chain, rival downtown retailing, and revolutionize the lodging industry. By the mid-1960s, suburbia was no longer an outlying residential area unable to offer anything more than small convenience centers with a supermarket and drugstore, makeshift roadside hot-dog stands, and mom-and-pop tourist courts. It was the site of giant malls with scores of shops anchored by major department stores, corporate restaurant chains that generated billions in revenues, and motels and motor hotels that rivaled or surpassed the quality of downtown hostelries. In addition, office parks and corporate estates were accommodating thousands of white-collar workers who had formerly commuted to the urban hub. Commerce had emerged along the fringe, and the once dominant metropolitan downtown was no longer unrivaled as a center of enterprise. Reversing the traditional pattern of downtown as the chief business generator of the metropolis, both the McDonald's and Holiday Inn empires began on the outskirts and later moved toward the old core.

Moreover, as retailing, offices, and hostelries moved to the suburbs, so did employment. Outlying areas had been attracting industrial plants since well before World War II, but the outward flow of manufacturing also accelerated in the 1950s and 1960s. The net result was thousands of new blue-collar as well as white-collar jobs, yet another sign of suburbia's emergence in the business world. In 1957 the *New York Times* reported that "before the war commuters exceeded those locally employed by better than 3 to 2" in Long Island's suburban Nassau and Suffolk counties but noted that these figures had since reversed: "Local employment now provides jobs for 335,000 persons while 175,000 persons are commuters." A 1958 survey revealed that 64,300 persons actually commuted from New York City to work on suburban Long Island.[46] In 1960 nearly 60 percent of employed Levittowners worked in Nassau County, whereas only 36 percent held jobs in New York City.[47] On both the East and West coasts, the stereotype of the suburban commuter was increasingly out of date. According to the 1960 census, 73 percent of the employed residents in Orange County, California, south of Los Angeles, and 68 percent of the workforce of Suffolk County, New York, held jobs in their home counties.[48] The economic life of metropolitan America was no longer so focused on the single central hub. By 1965, the process of economic decentralization and the revolution in metropolitan life were well advanced.

Golden Years Ghettos

Not only were young families with children migrating to suburbia, but by the 1960s senior citizens were headed for the fringe and seeking to stake out a section of the metropolitan turf for their own exclusive use. As life expectancy increased during the twentieth century, the number of elderly rose. In 1900 those sixty-five or over constituted 4 percent of the American population; fifty years later, this was up to 8.1 percent; and in 1980 it was 11.3 percent.[49] Moreover, senior citizens were growing more independent and less willing to spend their later years in their children's spare bedrooms. The establishment of Social Security in 1935 had introduced a federal old-age pension, and in the prosperous postwar years senior citizens benefited increasingly from private pension plans and generous savings. Given their prosperity and relative good health, some of the elderly by the 1960s could afford to opt out of the traditional metropolis, with its age heterogeneity, and settle in tailor-made age-homogenous utopias on the outskirts. Their search for a world apart was just one more manifestation of the decline of the earlier single-focus metropolis, which had accommodated, however uneasily, all types of humanity. In a pattern repeated throughout the second half of the twentieth century, Americans were carving out lifestyle niches and segregating themselves from others who did not fit into their desired ways of life.

The pioneer retirement community was Sun City, Arizona (figure 3.5). Located thirteen miles northwest of downtown Phoenix in the Sonoran Desert, Sun City was the creation of builder Del Webb. Recognizing the attraction of the emerging Sun Belt to retirees, Webb decided to transform his desert tract into a community where at least one person in each household had to be fifty years of age or older and where there could be no children under twenty. At its opening on New Year's Day 1960, Sun City consisted of a golf course, small shopping area, recreation center, and motel as well as a group of model homes from which prospective buyers could select the style of their choice. And buyers flocked to the site, producing two-mile-long traffic jams on the highway from Phoenix. During the first weekend, Webb sold 272 houses, and for the entire year of 1960 he recorded sales of 1,472 houses and 262 apartments.[50] By the close of 1963, Sun City contained 7,500 residents and 3,600 houses and apartments.[51] The first houses were modest, concrete-block structures, with a two-bedroom model selling for $8,750 and a three-bedroom, two-bath house for

FIGURE 3.5   Aerial view of Sun City, Arizona, under construction, 1965. (Arizona State Library, Archives and Public Records, Archives Division, Phoenix, no. 97–0400)

$11,600.[52] There were only five basic models, although fifteen different exterior designs ensured some variety in the rows of houses along the palm-lined streets. Basically, however, Sun City, Arizona, was Levittown for the elderly, a mass-produced housing project from which the young couples and ubiquitous children of the Long Island community would be excluded.

Sun City's success spawned other retirement communities. In 1960 Webb also founded the less profitable Sun City Center, south of Tampa, and in the late 1970s he launched Sun City West, adjacent to his original Arizona community.[53] Meanwhile, Ross W. Cortese was building Leisure World retirement communities in Seal Beach, Laguna Hills, and Walnut Creek, California, before expanding to new sites in Maryland and New Jersey. Opening in June 1962, the Seal Beach community recorded sales of 6,500 units over a three-year period; at the Laguna Hills Leisure World, Cortese reportedly sold $50 million worth of homes in nine months; the Walnut Creek community outside San Francisco grossed $30 million in home sales in less than a year.[54]

Together, the Sun Cities and Leisure Worlds offered senior citizens a new lifestyle that defied traditional stereotypes about aging. Rather than viewing old age as a sedentary time for slumber and inactivity, these communities sold an active retirement. They were not simply housing developments; instead, they professed to be communities where senior citizens could eschew the rocking chair and enjoy to the fullest their retirement years. Webb claimed to be selling "a Way of Life."[55] In 1961 *Time* magazine reported on the "frenetic activity" at Sun City, Arizona, where golfers played the community course, "lawn bowlers practiced body English on the bowling green[,] the shuffleboard courts were jammed, and so was the community center swimming pool." At "some 40 different clubs, Sun City residents busily kept their hand in at every thing from chess to stone cutting. And—for those who had energy left—there was square dancing in the evening." According to *Time*, "jokers claim that the real reason for the ban [on children] is that children could not keep up with the pace of the city's residents."[56] A Sun City brochure from 1960 promised "active living for America's senior citizens" with "activities unlimited" and "fairways at your doorstep." Webb's development company preached to prospective buyers: "Wake up and live in Sun City for an active new way of life."[57]

Not only were the new retirement communities supposed to spare the elderly the frustrating boredom and inactivity of the metropolitan world beyond their gates, but they promised a homogeneous, classless environment where there was no need to keep up with the Joneses. *Time* found that "Sun City residents have shown strong egalitarian feelings and a desire to forget the past; they think of themselves as pioneers in a new, more or less classless community."[58] The Webb Company contended: "You cannot *buy* your way into Sun City society." Instead, the newcomer would develop friendships that *"cost you nothing."*[59] The similarity of the houses seemed to promote this classless attitude. "We all live in the same kind of house," observed the president of the Sun City Civic Association, "and we like it that way."[60] In fact, Sun City and the Leisure Worlds were uniformly white, middle-class communities. Like so many suburban enclaves, they were not classless but one-class towns. Class distinctions seemed to disappear because blacks and the poor were absent from the streets of Sun City.

The communities were appropriately labeled as cities or worlds because they were self-contained, restricted environments independent of the remainder of the metropolis. By 1980, Sun City had 45,000 residents, eleven golf courses, shopping centers distributed throughout the community, and a five-story hospital. A white brick wall enclosed the community; one observer noted: "Although the wall could not keep anyone out, it reiterated the autonomy of the inhabitants within." Established in 1963, the Homeowners Association enforced a growing list of deed restrictions, including ones that prohibited the hanging of laundry in public view and the housing of anyone under eighteen years old for more than ninety days. Sun City was an orderly community separate from the haphazard, slipshod metropolitan development so commonplace in America. In 1967 one commentator observed that it was designed to have "no rough edges, empty lots, junk at back doors, unpaved streets," no signs of "neglect or shoddiness." As the generation gap widened in the 1960s and early 1970s, the retirement community also provided what its inhabitants perceived as a refuge of civilized life in an increasingly barbaric world of long-haired, unkempt youth. One Sun City resident commented in the early 1970s: "We're examples of the vanishing American. . . . Most of the people you see here are of the generation where, look, you washed behind your ears and scrubbed your nails before you came to the dinner table."[61]

Perhaps the most extreme manifestation of Sun City's escape from the world of youth was its secession from the local school district. In a series of referenda, the elderly residents had repeatedly defeated bond issues for support of the area's Peoria School District, much to the disgust of parents in that district. Finally, in 1974, Sun Citians succeeded in winning voter approval for withdrawal from the school district, thus relieving themselves of all local school taxes. Clearly, Sun City residents felt they should not be saddled with the expense of supporting the education of children who lived in nearby subdivisions. They had moved to Sun City to live in a youth-free environment, and thus they deemed the education of children in the metropolitan area as none of their concern. In the 1990s, the residents of Sun City West attempted to secede from the Dysart School District, but district residents outside the retirement community were able to defeat the proposal. In California, Leisure World residents were not so antagonistic to funding public education and supported their local schools.[62] But at least in Arizona, many of the senior citizens opted out of paying for the world of youth.

Just as the growing number of automobiles was facilitating the transformation of the single-focus metropolis into a diffuse region of decentralized commerce and residence, Social Security, pensions, and longer life expectancy were permitting some of the nation's elderly to escape from the world of youth to walled golfing paradises. The shopping malls of James Rouse and Victor Gruen were carefully programmed business districts free from the haphazard development, dirt, and relative social heterogeneity of downtown. The corporate campuses of General Foods and General Mills were likewise controlled environments with carefully planned landscapes removed from the older corporate centers of downtown Manhattan and Minneapolis. Similarly, the creations of Del Webb and Ross Cortese were immaculate planned environments exempt not only from panhandlers, blacks, and debris, but also from long-haired hippies and screaming children. They provided an environment tailored to the active elderly, one that was as safe, reliable, and standardized as a Mc-Donalds or Holiday Inn. Enhanced mobility, prosperity, and improved health among the elderly were enabling older Americans to discard the traditional metropolis, where they had been forced to share space, environments, and governments with all types. By the mid-1960s, they increasingly enjoyed the option of escaping the vagaries of youth and fitting into a carefully conceived world of their own.

Rebelling Against Renewal

Further undermining the single-centered metropolis was a growing revolt against centripetal highway and renewal projects. During the twenty years following World War II, city leaders sought to reinforce the core through schemes to rebuild the gray areas around downtown, to upgrade central-city neighborhoods and lure back the middle class, and to funnel automobiles into the central business district and ring it with parking garages. In the early 1950s, planners' renderings of proposed projects stirred hope and enthusiasm, but when the bulldozers arrived in the late 1950s and early 1960s urban Americans became aware of the harsh costs of recentering the city. Highway construction and renewal would entail the displacement of thousands of residents and businesses, and many of the displaced were bitter about bearing an undue burden in the crusade to save the central city and its all-important core business district. For many Americans, renewal was not worth the sacrifice.

In cities across the nation, neighborhoods slated for destruction or radical change rose in revolt. Philadelphia's shabby, sparsely populated Eastwick district appeared to be a prime location for a massive redevelopment scheme aimed at retaining residents and industry in the central city. But the existing Eastwick residents felt otherwise, and in 1957 at a public hearing a crowd of 1,500 of them, in the words of one newspaper, "hooted, shouted and screamed its protest amid tears, accusations and charges of collusion." Dolores Rubillo, a leader of the Eastwick forces, called "this urban-renewal program as used in Philadelphia a socialistic move against the many for the capitalistic gain of the few. We revolt against it."[63] During the early 1960s, Chicago's Florence Scala led the fight against the destruction of the Harrison-Halsted community, slated to be replaced by a University of Illinois campus at the western gateway to downtown. In 1961 residents of the largely Italian and Mexican neighborhood marched on city hall and mounted a sit-in at Mayor Richard Daley's office. Scala explained to reporters, "Mayor Daley and others think it is easy to run roughshod over us, [but] we aren't going to take this lying down."[64]

In the Irish Catholic working-class Boston area of Charlestown, the Self-Help Organization–Charlestown (SHOC) adopted a "fanatically" antirenewal stance, hiring sound trucks to ply the streets and exhort residents to "Save Our Homes." In January 1963, a thousand SHOC members attended a public hearing where one renewal official described their behavior as "tumultuous." At a public hearing two years later, an angry resident expressed the feelings of many when he shouted: "I don't have to do it. It's my home and that's what I'm fighting for. You can stick the money up your ass."[65] In Boston's Allston-Brighton area, opposition was also bitter. In 1962 neighborhood Catholics attacked Monsignor Francis Lally, a member of the city's urban renewal board, screaming, "Shove it, Lally! You are a disgrace! Take the collar off! You're a pious hypocrite!" "To Hell with Urban Renewal" read signs throughout the neighborhood. When redevelopment appraisers arrived to value properties slated for destruction, local residents bearing brooms, sticks, spades, and shovels chased them away.[66]

In San Francisco, a revolt against centripetal highway construction spread throughout the city. During the early 1950s, many local business and political leaders deemed a program of freeway construction as essential if San Francisco and its downtown were to remain the heart of the Bay Area. The proposed routes of the expressways, however, angered the city's residents. In December 1955, a public hearing on freeway development attracted more than two thousand members of the West Portal Home Owners' Association, and four months later sixteen hundred attended a similar meeting with state highway officials. Expressing the concerns of many residents, one unhappy San Franciscan asked, "Why wreck our homes for

FIGURE 3.6 View of the historic Ferry Building in San Francisco, blocked by the Embarcadero Freeway. (San Francisco History Center, San Francisco Public Library)

traffic coming from outside the city."[67] Opposition intensified as San Franciscans realized that the construction of the elevated Embarcadero Freeway was about to obliterate their view of the historic Ferry Building (figure 3.6). This landmark had survived the city's famous fire and earthquake, but now it was hidden behind a concrete roadway, cut off from the core of the city. In January 1959, San Francisco's governing Board of Supervisors responded to complaints by voting to oppose the state's plans for freeway development in the city. Explaining their action, the supervisors contended that expressway construction involved "the demolition of homes, the destruction of residential areas, the forced uprooting and relocation of individuals, families, and business enterprises."[68] State highway engineers persisted in their plans for a freeway through a section of the city's historic Golden Gate Park. In 1965 a local radio newsman attacked this continuing devotion to destructive highway development when he warned that San Francisco would fall to "a ghastly combination of concrete monsters, side-by-side with immense parking garages, all of which will be overladen with the poisonous smog which is already choking the life out of us now."[69]

Meanwhile, a rising chorus of critics attacked the burden that centripetal highway and redevelopment schemes imposed on blacks. Highway planners routed Interstate 95 through Miami's Overtown district, thereby destroying the heart of the black community. In 1960 an African American citizens' committee in Birmingham, Alabama, protested that proposed freeways "would almost completely wipe out two old Negro communities [in] eastern Birmingham with their 13 churches and three schools." Some African Americans in Montgomery, Alabama, believed that state highway planners specifically targeted the homes and churches of the city's black civil rights activists. At a hearing in 1961, the black head of a property owners committee complained that the route "was racially motivated to uproot a neighborhood of Negro leaders."[70] But displacement was not restricted to the South. Minnesota highway planners routed Interstate 94 through Saint Paul's small African American community, uprooting one-seventh of the city's blacks. As one observer noted, "Very few blacks lived in Minnesota, but the road builders found them." With only some exaggeration, one public official reminisced about the condemnation process: "We went through the black section between Minneapolis and St. Paul about four blocks wide and we took out the home of every black man in the city."[71]

During the same years, urban renewal displaced many of the remaining blacks who did not live in the proposed paths of the new interstates. As early as 1949, an African American newspaper attacked nascent plans for redeveloping Washington, D.C., claiming that white proponents of renewal had "decided that the pauperized underdogs of color are too close to the nation's seat of government." To remedy this concentration of poor blacks, advocates of redevelopment sought to reverse the outward flow of the middle class through the lure of "attractive houses and lavish apartments close to government jobs." In 1957 the *Washington Post* dismissed such criticism when it argued: "No doubt many residents of the area will be loath to lose their homes despite the prevailing slum conditions. They should realize, however, that the net effect of this great redevelopment effort will be to make Washington a much more pleasant place in which to live and work."[72] In other words, poor blacks should willingly accede to the bulldozers and sacrifice their homes for what white planners and journalists deemed the greater glory of the city. In Tampa white business leaders would have heartily seconded these sentiments, for they were likewise proposing the destruction of black slums located too near downtown. Protesting the exclusion of blacks from Tampa's urban renewal decision making, a Florida civil rights leader observed that "the practice here has been to plan for rather than with local minority groups."[73]

Blacks in Oakland, California, felt that they too were being planned for and that schemes for recentering the metropolis took precedence over their interests. Between 1948 and 1962, downtown Oakland's share of retailing sales in the East Bay area dropped from 18 to 9 percent, and its portion of department store business plummeted from 40 to 20 percent. One possible means for reversing these figures was to redevelop West Oakland, the center of black population in the city. Oakland's renewal plan emphasized that "urban renewal in West Oakland . . . should reinforce the vitality of the downtown area, creating new job opportunities and a new tax base." Some West Oakland blacks, however, opposed clearance plans, organizing the United Tax Payers and Voters Union in 1960 in an unsuccessful effort to halt the demolition of their homes and businesses. Exacerbating the situation was the construction in the late 1950s of the Nimitz Freeway, which slashed a path of destruction through the black neighborhood.[74] In Washington, D.C., Florida, California, and elsewhere throughout the nation, blacks could not ignore the fact that white plans for salvation of the central city entailed the removal of African Americans. The planners' vision of a "pleasant place in which to live and work" was middle class and overwhelmingly white.

In a number of cities of the trans-Mississippi West, federally financed urban renewal proved so unacceptable that it never was implemented. Although business leaders in Omaha's chamber of commerce were eager to apply federal dollars to that city's graying core, the local electorate and city council were adamantly opposed to the program and repeatedly defeated renewal proposals. Consequently, there were no federal urban renewal projects in the Nebraska metropolis.[75] Because of its refusal to adopt zoning ordinances, Houston was automatically ineligible for federal urban renewal money. Moreover, Houston residents did not seem to care; one official observed that "urban renewal was not even in our lexicon."[76] Strong ideological scruples motivated opponents of federal urban renewal in Fort Worth, where the Citizens Committee for Protection of Property Rights led the crusade against government condemnation of blighted properties. In a 1966 referendum, Fort Worth conservatives decisively consigned urban renewal to oblivion when voters rejected it by a 4 to 1 margin.[77]

Nearby Dallas was equally offended by the prospect of federal assistance and never signed on to the program. In 1965 Salt Lake City voters rejected federal money by a 6 to 1 margin after a campaign that, according to one urban scholar, "described urban renewal as a violation of the divinely given right of property ownership."[78] In 1964 Denver residents defeated an urban renewal proposal, following the lead of a city council member who deemed public condemnation of land for resale to private interests as "immoral."[79] Two years later, Denver's electorate changed its mind and approved the scheme. Yet in Colorado as well as Utah, Texas, and Nebraska, many urban dwellers rebelled at a "socialistic" program of federal spending to aid private interests in the urban core. Ideology, racial self-preservation, and a simple devotion to one's home and neighborhood were arrayed against the bulldozers of recentralization.

Many of the reports about completed renewal projects aided opponents of redevelopment. In contrast to inspiring architectural drawings and the high-flown rhetoric of ground-breaking ceremonies, the reality of renewal often seemed bleak—if not downright cruel. Perhaps the most notorious renewal project was the West End of Boston, a much publicized monument to the shortcomings of federal redevelopment. In the early 1950s, the West End was a run-down tenement district with a predominantly Italian American population. Although located on the edge of Boston's central business district, it contributed few retailing dollars to the city's beleaguered downtown merchants and little to the municipal treasury. Convinced that the site could contribute more to the central city's economy, redevelopment authorities decided to clear the tract and evict its 7,500 residents, replacing their homes with luxury apartment buildings inhabited by affluent shoppers and taxpayers. In 1958/1959 wrecking crews leveled the area and scattered its denizens throughout the Boston area. As a consequence of their displacement, 86 percent of the former residents were forced to pay more for housing, the median monthly rent rising from $41 before relocation to $71 afterward.[80] Moreover, many of the former residents suffered psychologically from their forced removal. According to one study of those relocated, at least 46 percent of the women and 38 percent of the men suffered a "fairly severe grief reaction or worse." When asked about how they felt about their eviction, West End residents responded: "I felt as though I had lost everything," "I felt like my heart was taken out of me," "I felt like taking the gaspipe."[81]

What replaced the West End did not seem to justify the razing of homes and the devastation of a close-knit neighborhood. In 1963 a leading architectural critic described the site of the neighborhood as a "48-acre wasteland. On its edge have risen only two of architect Victor Gruen's forbidding luxury apartments, and a handful of drab townhouses looking for occupants."[82]

Unfortunately, the West End was not an isolated instance of the heartlessness of urban renewal. By early 1963, federal urban renewal projects had already evicted approximately 609,000 people, and federal authorities anticipated displacing over 3 million more by 1972.[83] Renewal agencies were expected to aid in relocating the uprooted, but relocation took a low priority among officials eager to replace the poor with middle-class shoppers and taxpayers. Between 1949 and 1964, only 0.5 percent of all federal renewal money was expended on relocation of individuals and families.[84] Former West End residents were not the only ones who suffered socially from the penurious relocation program. A 1966 study of those displaced by the Southwest urban renewal project in Washington, D.C., found that in the five years since relocation one-quarter of the evicted had not made one new friend among their neighbors. The study concluded that "New Southwest may yet develop into the 'Good City,' but its birth has been at a cost. It has risen over the ashes of what was a community of well-established, though poor, inhabitants."[85]

Like the West Enders, relocatees throughout the country were, moreover, shouldering an undue share of the financial burden in the battle to recenter the city. A 1960 study of those relocated from San Francisco's Western Addition found that their median monthly rent had been $39 before displacement and was $58 afterward; 83 percent paid higher rents as a result of relocation. Three years later, a study of Minneapolis found that 44 percent of the displaced had paid under $20 a month in rent before relocation, whereas only 3 percent did so in their new homes. The new homes also were not necessarily markedly superior to the old. A survey of relocated families in forty-one cities in the late 1950s found that approximately 60 percent moved into substandard dwellings.[86] Many relocatees found better homes, and the survey results were not all negative. Yet the notion that renewal produced grief, higher rents, and substandard housing for a substantial number of the poor could only add to growing doubts about the urban renewal crusade.

Small businesses likewise bore an undue burden in the fight to preserve a single central focus to the metropolis. By the close of 1961, federal urban renewal projects had already evicted 21,439 businesses, and authorities were predicting the dislocation of 300,000 firms by 1970.[87] A study of businesses displaced by highway or urban renewal projects in Providence, Rhode Island, from 1954 through 1959 found that about 40 percent of the firms in renewal areas and 30 percent in the paths of highways closed permanently as a result of displacement. Small groceries, restaurants, and bars serving a neighborhood clientele were least likely to survive. According to the Providence study, the owners of these endangered businesses "tended to know most of their customers who came disproportionately from a particular ethnic or racial group," and "because of this closer and apparently more recurrent relationship with their customers . . . these establishments were much more sensitive to the disruptive effects of the move."[88] In other words, it was the mom-and-pop stores owned by and serving immigrants rather than the chain retailer or large-scale department store that bore the heaviest burden of the centripetal highway and renewal schemes. "The loss was more than just a building—my work is gone forever too," lamented one displaced Providence business owner. "All of my customers have moved away. . . . [It] shook my confidence in my city and country—I never thought they would do such a thing."[89] The soon-to-be displaced owner of a small pastry shop on the West Side of Manhattan was equally outraged: "I've been in this location for over nine years. My wife and I worked like horses 12 to 14 hours a day to make something of this place. Now they come and kick us out."[90]

Adding to the indignation was the realization that much of the cleared land would remain vacant for years (figure 3.7). Although Congress created the federal urban redevelopment program in the Housing Act of 1949, by March 31, 1961, only twenty-five projects nationwide had been completed. In his 1964 study of renewal, Martin Anderson estimated that the average duration of a project from the beginning of planning to the completion of construction was twelve years, and a growing number of urban residents were convinced that their local projects would drag on for far more than a dozen years.[91] The clearing of Mill Creek Valley in Saint Louis left a sprawling wasteland known locally as "Hiroshima Flats." According to the *New York Times*, "Frustrated St. Louisans had to become accustomed to seeing a vast weed patch in the heart of their city." In 1964 the *Times* architectural critic, Ada Louise Huxtable, described Mill Creek Valley as "dotted by desultory building," with "a few apartments and town house groups of bravely cheerful design which seem to be whistling in the wilderness, and some spotty commercial and industrial enterprises."[92] Cleared between 1958 and 1961, Buffalo's 161-acre Ellicott renewal tract remained largely empty in 1964; a chamber of commerce staff member

FIGURE 3.7 Vacant urban renewal site in the center of Detroit, 1950s. (Walter P. Reuther Library, Wayne State University)

commented that this "29-block scar on the face of the city . . . could lead naïve lightplane pilots to assume the city was constructing a landing strip for them next to its busiest retail area."[93]

By the early 1960s, private investors in renewal projects were also expressing doubts about the government-subsidized effort to reinforce the urban core. During the second decade after World War II, New Haven, Connecticut, was a much admired showcase of urban renewal with plans for redevelopment that were the envy of public officials and downtown leaders throughout the nation. Yet in 1962, the primary private developer of New Haven's renewal project, Roger Stevens, admitted, "I'll never go into another one of these things."[94] Stevens explained: "I've had all the disadvantages of a political deal and none of the advantages, while I've had all the disadvantages of a private deal and none of the advantages."[95] By 1960, the Southwest project in Washington, D.C., was deemed a "short-run financial catastrophe" for its developers, and its principal investor remarked: "I never dreamed how long it would take with government red tape, and how much time it would require to get acceptance of a new community in a former slum area."[96] Meanwhile, middle-class high-rise apartment complexes on urban renewal sites in Detroit and Saint Louis did not spur a mass return of white consumers from the suburbs or mark the triumph of a Manhattan lifestyle in the Midwest. Lack of demand for new apartments, excessive red tape, delays owing to political meddling, and the cumbersome review process mandated by federal officials all meant that an urban renewal project was a risky investment at best. One could make more money with less hassle by building shopping malls in suburbia.

The most notable foe of the renewal and highway strategy of reinforcing the city center was Jane Jacobs. During the early 1960s through both word and deed, she assaulted prevailing notions about urban revitalization and presented an alternative vision. An editor of *Architectural Forum*, she was also a wife and mother living in the West Village area of Manhattan, and like other female foes of renewal, such as Dolores Rubillo and Florence Scala, Jacobs considered home and neighborhood rather than downtown skyscrapers and superhighways as the foundations of her city. Her principal concern was not the central business district tax base or department store business; rather, she sought to discover the formula for safe streets and healthy neighborhoods, desirable environments for herself, her children, and other residents and families of the central cities. Whereas downtown businessmen, many of whom lived in the suburbs, viewed success in terms of commercial construction figures and retail sales data, she found the secret to the vital city in the sidewalk life of the neighborhood. Ultimately, she did not seek to discover a plan for maintaining the urban core as the one dominant hub of the metropolitan area. Instead, she offered advice on how to make the city livable. If the city provided a rich, exciting environment for living, one by-product would be the return of middle-class money that the renewers so desperately sought.

Jacobs first captured the attention of her fellow New Yorkers when she led a crusade to save her own neighborhood from the renewal bulldozers. In February 1961, New York's mayor, Robert Wagner, proposed that the West Village be designated a blighted area targeted for urban renewal. Confronting this threat, Jacobs assumed leadership of the Committee to Save the West Village. "The aim of the committee is to kill this project entirely," she explained, "because if it goes through it can mean only the destruction of the community." A neighborhood coffeehouse owner fearful of displacement agreed with Jacobs: "It takes years to establish yourself and pay off your cost, and it is all wiped out if you are forced out by redevelopment."[97] The renewal authorities, however, were adamant about pursuing the project. The head of the city's redevelopment board asserted: "I am not exaggerating when I say that all of us here are firm in our fear that, if opposition is allowed to stop this . . . , the entire urban renewal program in the City of New York is in danger."[98] The *New York Times* agreed when it editorialized that "the city cannot surrender to the loudest voice and abandon all prospect of reversing the blight of the neighborhood slipping downhill."[99]

Jacobs and her West Villagers, however, would not back down. When in an open meeting the City Planning Commission voted to designate West Village as blighted, Jacobs and her villagers "leaped from their seats and rushed forward." According to the *Times*, "The commission chairman . . . sought vainly to restore order by pounding his gavel. Then he called on the police to remove the unruly from the room"; the officers "escorted several from the room and carried one man out feet first."[100] "We are not violent," Jacobs explained the next day. "We were only vocal. We were terribly alarmed at what is happening in our neighborhood and our city."[101] By the end of October 1961, Jacobs's forces proved victorious. Confronted with a tough reelection challenge, Mayor Wagner made a strategic retreat, sided with Jacobs, and arranged the withdrawal of the West Village renewal proposal.

The following year, Jacobs helped mobilize the antihighway forces when she served as chair of the Stop the Lower Manhattan Expressway Committee. Designed to link the Holland Tunnel on Manhattan's West Side with the Manhattan and Williamsburg bridges across the East River, the expressway would have cut a giant swath through Lower Manhattan, forcing almost two thousand families from their homes and displacing over eight hundred businesses. Jacobs attacked the expressway as a "monstrous and useless folly" and dismissed her opponents' contentions as "piffle."[102] Eventually, Jacobs again triumphed; the expressway was never built.

While Jacobs was embroiled in the West Village clash, her highly influential book *The Death and Life of Great American Cities* appeared, explaining the urban vision underlying her protests. Rejecting renewal dogma, she wrote: "There is a wistful myth that if only we had enough money to spend . . . we could wipe out all our slums in ten years, reverse decay in the great, dull gray belts that were yesterday's and day-before-yesterday's suburbs, anchor the wandering middle class and its wandering tax money, and perhaps even solve the traffic problem." Yet according to Ja-

cobs, the renewal-highway strategy had produced "middle-income housing projects which are truly marvels of dullness and regimentation, sealed
against any buoyancy or vitality of city life. Luxury housing projects that
mitigate their inanity, or try to, with a vapid vulgarity. . . . Expressways that
eviscerate great cities." Jacobs could only conclude: "This is not the rebuilding of cities. This is the sacking of cities."[103]

She contrasted the lifeless dregs of renewal with the vitality surviving
in a traditional inner-city neighborhood such as the North End of Boston.
Like the West End before its demolition, the North End was a predominantly Italian, working-class district of narrow streets and aged tenements. Here Jacobs found the life of the city. "Mingled all among the
buildings for living were an incredible number of splendid food stores, as
well as such enterprises as upholstery making, metal working, carpentry,
food processing," Jacobs wrote of the North End. "The streets are alive
with children playing, people shopping, people strolling, people talking,"
and "the general street atmosphere of buoyancy, friendliness and good
health was . . . infectious." Others had dismissed the North End as a slum,
but Jacobs deemed the lively neighborhood "as the healthiest place in the
city."[104]

For Jacobs, the mixture of commercial and residential, the aged buildings, and the density of population that she found in the North End were
the essence of a vital city. By comparison, modern high-rises surrounded
by open plazas and zoned exclusively for residential or commercial were
sterile, dead spaces that, if permitted to proliferate, would kill the city. According to Jacobs's gospel, bulldozing was not the way to salvation; preservation instead would lead to the heavenly city. Her rhapsodic descriptions
of urban street life and gritty city neighborhoods appealed to many readers no longer enamored with the renewal-highway strategy, which had
prevailed since the 1940s. For those frustrated with recent redevelopment
efforts, she was the prophet of a new appreciation of the traditional city.

Yet Jacobs did not actually speak to the concerns of downtown interests
dedicated to reinforcing the central focus of the metropolis. She explained
how to preserve what the city already possessed, but she did not realisti-
cally propose how to reestablish the dominance of the core in an age
seemingly out of step with traditional urban existence. She was a devotee
of sidewalks in an era when more Americans were buying more automobiles, and a lover of densely populated neighborhoods of apartments and
mom-and-pop stores in an age when the suburban migration to detached,
single-family homes and sprawling chain stores was proceeding with full

force. Jacobs was attracted to the "intricate sidewalk ballet" of her own West Village street at a time when most Americans were attracted by the promise of ample parking.[105] Jacobs's rhetoric had some appeal, but department store executives and beleaguered central-city mayors knew all too well that millions of American taxpayers and consumers preferred enclosed suburban malls to aging city streets and driving to walking. They had little faith that Jacobs's urban neighborhoods represented the vanguard of a centripetal revolution.

In fact, Jacobs did not offer a blueprint for a recentered city but a vision of a metropolis whose vitality derived from the vitality of its parts rather than the dynamism of its dominant core. What she liked about the North End and the West Village was that they were villages, intimate neighborhoods where the urban villagers knew one another and kept the sidewalks safe by paying attention to what was happening on their streets. She glorified the subdivisions of the metropolis because they offered a good way of life; she did not boost downtown in order to inflate the sales figures at Macy's. And Jacobs was not willing to destroy neighborhoods for the sake of funneling traffic to the core. For her, the interests of the West Village took priority over those of Wall Street, and a lively city was preeminently a metropolis of vital neighborhoods, not one with a vibrant heart and insipid limbs.

In coming decades, admirers of Jacobs's vision would settle and invest in urban neighborhoods, yet she and her followers did not reverse the prevailing centrifugal trend. McDonald's and Holiday Inns continued to proliferate along the metropolitan fringe, and corporate headquarters were joining them in suburbia. The centripetal expressways and renewal projects raised more wrath than municipal tax dollars or downtown sales figures. Despite the ambitious efforts of central-city promoters, metropolitan America was coming apart. Many Americans were finding bliss in Southdale Center; others like Jane Jacobs were discovering the good life in the West Village. But the impetus for drawing the whole together through a radical expressway and renewal strategy was waning.

4　The Debacle

"Riots, skyrocketing crime, tax problems that multiply raise this question: Can the big cities of this country ever stage a comeback?" In 1967 *U.S. News & World Report* posed this query, and its tentative conclusion was not optimistic. "The crisis of the big cities, coming to a head in recent years, continues without let up," the magazine observed. "And no real solution appears in the immediate future."[1] Many agreed with this assessment. In 1968 the mayor of Saint Louis admitted, "We just can't make it anymore," and his counterpart in New Orleans likewise noted, "The cities are going down the pipe."[2] Such rhetoric was commonplace in the late 1960s and 1970s. Urban America was definitely on the skids, and its plunge to oblivion seemed irreversible. This was the age of urban crisis when journalists and social scientists busily analyzed the ailing remnants of the city and periodically issued dire prognostications. The upbeat reports of renewal and revitalization so common in the 1950s seemed hopelessly naive by the 1970s, and according to all reports the American city was in shambles.

In fact, the worst fears of 1945 were being realized. Racial violence flared, and the Detroit riot of 1967 exceeded that of 1943 in casualties and damage estimates. All the human rights commissions and interracial committees had not been able to bridge the racial fissure dividing the black–white city. Moreover, the efforts of big-city mayors and downtown boosters had not been able to maintain the single-focused metropolis. By the 1970s, central cities were no longer central to the lives of many metropolitan Americans, and the sense that all metropolitan-area residents were part of one common city with common social, cultural, economic, and political interests was diminishing. A 1978 *New York Times* poll of 3,500 suburbanites in the New York City area found that 54 percent did not "feel part of the general New York City area," only 24 percent thought that events in the city had a "lot of impact" on their lives, and 25 percent said that they never went into the city. The *Times* concluded that these residents "no longer feel themselves subordinate to New York," and the suburbs had "surprisingly limited ties to the metropolitan core." Declaring victory for the dreaded forces of decentralization, the *Times* observed: "Suburban residents have established their own institutions and go about their lives in an increasingly separate world. They see their future even further from the city, rather than closer to it."[3]

Thus the disintegration of the city was readily apparent; the metropolitan community was clearly dissolving. In the late 1960s and 1970s, some optimistic entrepreneurs attempted to create new communities that would restore some semblance of social and cultural unity among metropolitan Americans. But these efforts foundered. Just as central-city leaders of the 1940s had feared, the divisions in the black–white city had worsened, and a new decentralized way of life had triumphed.

Central-City Decline

Indicative of the triumph of decentralization was the decline in the population of older central cities. During the 1960s, the outward flow of residents accelerated, with the population of Saint Louis dropping 17 percent, that of Cleveland and Pittsburgh falling 14 percent, and Cincinnati, Minneapolis, and Detroit each losing 10 percent of its population. These unfortunate northern hubs were becoming known collectively as the Rust Belt, a swath of decaying metropolitan space stretching from New England through the Midwest that was losing people and business to the surging Sun Belt areas of Florida, Texas, Arizona, and California. Benefiting from the advent of air-conditioning, such warm Sun Belt cities as Houston, Dallas, and Phoenix attracted thousands of newcomers, in sharp contrast to their northern counterparts. They boomed as the Rust

Belt busted. But nationally, the prevailing trend benefited small suburban municipalities, not the traditional central-city behemoths. And in the Sun Belt as well as the Rust Belt, central cities had to cope with the increasingly debilitating problems of crime, racial conflict, and clashes over such public services as policing and schools. Throughout the United States, the suburbs seemed ever more appealing, and in 1970, for the first time in American history, the nation's suburbanites outnumbered central-city dwellers. Whereas 46 percent of American metropolitan residents lived in central cities, down from 59 percent in 1950, 54 percent lived beyond the central-city boundaries in suburbia. By the 1970s, the United States was a suburban nation, with the majority of its metropolitan residents beyond the reach of central-city tax collectors and schools.

The decline in urban population continued during the early and mid-1970s. Between 1970 and 1977, the nation's central-city population dropped 4.6 percent, whereas the number of suburban residents rose 12 percent. As in the 1950s and 1960s, the outward migrants were disproportionately middle class, the very people necessary to pay the city's tax bills and fill its retail coffers. In 1970 the per family income in the nation's central cities amounted to only 85 percent of the per family figure for the suburbs; by 1977, this had fallen to 82 percent. Female-headed households, with no husband present, were increasing sharply in the central cities, up 27.5 percent between 1970 and 1977, but the number of traditional husband–wife families declined 7.6 percent. Since female-headed households were disproportionately poor, this again did not bode well for central-city controllers or retailers. Likewise, between 1970 and 1977, the disproportionately poor black population of the central cities rose 4.2 percent, as compared with a drop of 8.1 percent in the number of white residents.[4] Increasingly, the central city was a preserve for poor blacks and single mothers struggling to survive. It was the focus of life for the poor but was becoming alien territory to the affluent.

During the late 1960s and the 1970s, as during the earlier postwar years, the centrifugal flow of affluence was evident in the declining retail fortunes of the central cities. Business was discouraging in the late 1950s and early 1960s; now it was disastrous. Between 1967 and 1977, central business district retail sales, adjusted for inflation, fell 48 percent in Baltimore, 44 percent in Cleveland and Saint Louis, 38 percent in Boston, and 36 percent in Minneapolis. In 1967 the downtown flagship outlets still accounted for 46 percent of department store business, with outlying branches contributing 54 percent; in 1976 the figure for downtown department stores was down to 22 percent, with branch sales accounting for 78 percent.[5]

The plight of retailers along Baltimore's traditional shopping thoroughfare, Howard Street, was representative of the situation in many downtowns. Baltimore's downtown department store sales fell from $93 million in 1972 to $68 million in 1975. Responding to this drop, in 1976 Hutzler Brothers department store eliminated 20 percent of its Howard Street space, explaining that "for some time" the sales at a branch in suburban Towson had outpaced those at the downtown flagship. Hutzler's president lamented: "Downtown business is far from good, far from easy. . . . I don't know who is really doing a job [of bringing back sales]." The neighboring Hochschild Kohn department store likewise closed its sixth floor, thus eliminating 17 percent of its downtown sales space. Then, in January 1977, Hochschild Kohn announced that it would close its downtown store the following July.[6] In February, the president of the Stewart and Company department store added to the gloom when he warned that unless the city embarked on a massive downtown revitalization project "in the very near future, we cannot guarantee our continued presence in the center city." Meanwhile, downtown department store sales for the first half of 1977 were 15 percent lower than those for the same period of 1976.[7] In 1970 a marketing report on the suburbanization of retail trade summed up the new reality in America: "By the end of this decade the suburbs will be central and the central cities peripheral."[8] The success of Hutzler's Towson branch and the ongoing decline of Howard Street were visible proof of this transformation.

Downtown theaters and entertainment venues were even harder hit than department stores. Suburban mall theaters were supplanting the lavish downtown movie palaces that had dominated first-run film business in 1945. With ample parking and safe locations in the white, middle-class suburbs, the mall movie houses enabled metropolitan Americans to enjoy the latest Hollywood fare without the hassle of central-city traffic and beyond the threat of inner-city muggers and weirdos. Enhancing downtown's reputation as off-limits after dark was the fact that its remaining theaters increasingly specialized in pornography and violent films aimed at young black audiences. Moreover, a growing number of vacant downtown storefronts were attracting porn shops and sexually explicit peepshows. The once classy hubs of American entertainment were thus becoming the focus of a sleazy porn trade that offended and threatened many middle-class Americans.

In one city after another, a nationwide decline in censorship opened the floodgates for this wave of pornography. Boston's Combat Zone was the preeminent porn strip in New England and Minneapolis's Hennepin Avenue offered the latest in X-rated offerings. In Chicago, there was an outcry against the pornographic assault on the downtown Loop. "Just look at some of the creeps prowling the streets in daylight, attracted by hard-core porno films, X-rated garbage, and violence-oriented black exploitation movies," observed one journalist. "These scummy joints draw the kind of negative people who make honest folks uneasy, if not downright petrified."[9] The *Chicago Tribune*'s architecture critic remarked: "The feeling among some that these places are filled with perverts ready to commit mass rape cannot be laughed away." The theaters, however, were "only part of this change. Shabby little cut-rate shops and lunch counters, pornographic peep shows, and stores offering books catering to every sexual interest are also in the downtown mix."[10]

Yet even Chicago did not have enough theater-going "perverts" or "negative people" to keep all its downtown theaters in business. Between 1971 and 1977, six of the sixteen downtown movie houses closed, with a total loss of 8,697 seats, or 36 percent of the 1971 capacity. One of the shuttered theaters was the Oriental, where before its closing a Chicago film critic claimed to have found "foot-high trash from God knows when filling every row" of its infrequently used mezzanine. He also wrote of another "rodent palace downtown" where he engaged in a heated debate with a rival critic over whether a mouse or a rat had crossed the aisle during a film showing.[11]

Nowhere was the outcry against the blight of the entertainment district more pronounced than in New York City. For decades the focus of legitimate theater in the United States, famed Times Square was well on its way to becoming a porn zone by the early 1970s. In 1972 the *New York Times* editorialized: "Few things make a New Yorker feel worse than watching American and foreign tourists here walk past the Times Square porno-peepshows and dirty bookstores. The impulse is to shout, 'This is the underlife, not the real city.'"[12] A Broadway producer complained of "the swiftness of the area's relentless descent into squalor" and claimed that it threatened the future of American theater. Sixty-two prominent Broadway performers signed an appeal to the mayor, and there were even mutterings about a general theater strike to protest the city's unwillingness or inability to cleanse Times Square of its offensive porn shops and sexually explicit offerings.[13] By 1978, the city was formulating plans for revitalizing the theater district, but the area's growing population of winos added another blemish to its reputation. The owner of a hotel complained: "We've lost all our tourist and school-group business because people are scared of the drunks hanging around here." Another disgruntled business owner griped: "One of those drunks had the nerve to unfold a camp chair out front and start sunning himself."[14] No matter whether the offense took the form of porn shops or winos, the message was the same: New York's premier entertainment district was no longer as appealing to a middle-class clientele as it had been in 1945.

Meanwhile, the central city was losing its preeminence as the focus of metropolitan employment. The outward migration of manufacturing accelerated, eliminating working-class job opportunities. Since the end of World War II, growing reliance on trucking had encouraged manufactures to relocate to suburban sites adjacent to superhighways where they could build sprawling single-story plants better suited to assembly-line production than the existing multistory factories in the inner city. In the 1960s and 1970s, however, the pace of abandonment quickened, leaving a gloomy assortment of empty mills, especially in the older cities of the Northeast and Midwest. Between 1947 and 1967, New York City lost 175,000 manufacturing jobs, but from 1967 to 1977 manufacturing employment dropped an additional 286,000. From 1950 to 1967, the number of manufacturing jobs in Boston fell 21 percent; between 1967 and 1977, the loss was 36 percent. Philadelphia lost 40 percent of its manufacturing employment between 1967 and 1977, and the rate of decline in New York City, Chicago, Baltimore, Pittsburgh, and Buffalo was between 30 and 36 percent.[15] Shuttered factories were increasingly familiar sights in America's urban hubs, testifying to the industrial decline of the central city.

An increase in office employment compensated to some degree for the outflow of factory jobs. In fact, the thriving central-city office sector offered the best evidence that downtown was not headed for oblivion. Responding to the demand for downtown office space, developers erected scores of skyscrapers that literally overshadowed the high-rises of the past. In the early 1970s, New York City's 110-story, two-tower World Trade Center rose more than 100 feet higher than the city's previous record holder, the Empire State Building. During the late 1960s and early 1970s, Chicagoans constructed three new towers over 1,000 feet in height, the tallest being the Sears Tower, completed in 1974. Rising 1,450 feet and accommodating a daily population of 16,500, the Sears Tower was the tallest

office building in the world and visible evidence that the downtown Loop remained a vital hub of business. In Minneapolis, the IDS Center, completed in 1973, rose 57 stories and surpassed the city's once preeminent Foshay Tower by 300 feet. In 1972 San Francisco's 853-foot Transamerica Pyramid opened to tenants and soon became a signature landmark of the city (figure 4.1). Since 1927, Los Angeles's city hall, rising 454 feet, had been the tallest building in the southern California metropolis. But in 1968, the Union Bank Building surpassed it, and in the early 1970s the twin towers of the Atlantic Richfield and Bank of America buildings topped off at almost 700 feet. Finally, in 1973 and 1974, the United California Bank Building rose 62 stories above the city, soaring almost double the height of the once preeminent city hall. Long regarded as a moribund relic in a city known for pioneering decentralization, downtown Los Angeles seemed to be reestablishing itself as a place of commercial importance and as the office hub of southern California.

Yet the soaring skyscrapers told only part of the story. In fact, many office jobs were leaving the central city as corporations followed the earlier lead of General Foods and General Mills and established headquarters in the suburbs. From 1967 to 1974, the number of Fortune 500 headquarters in New York City dropped from 139 to 98, testifying to corporate America's rejection of the nation's largest metropolis.[16] Leading the exodus were Pepsico, American Can, and Bohn Business Machines, which announced their impending departures during a single week in February 1967. Pepsico was planning a corporate campus on the former grounds of the Blind Brook Polo Club in suburban Westchester County, and American Can was seeking to relocate on 228 acres in the upscale community of Greenwich, Connecticut. The same week, American Metal Climax and Union Camp admitted that they were considering leaving their Manhattan headquarters for the suburbs. Moreover, a leading location consultant claimed that fourteen additional corporations, with a total of 11,500 headquarters employees, were pondering a move from Manhattan to the metropolitan fringe. Meanwhile, Flinkote was already preparing to move from the city to a 35-acre tract in Westchester, and Corn Products, Inc., was planning to transfer to Englewood Cliffs, New Jersey, in the fall of 1967.[17]

Underlying this ominous flight from the nation's chief hub were numerous complaints about the problems of doing business in the city. High taxes, the misery of commuting, crime, and the need for more office space all played a role. "They all add up to the same thing," the location consultant concluded; "New York is not a happy place to be." Perhaps most disturbing was the consultant's claim that "complaints regarding clerical workers in New York City are universal."[18] Pepsico cited that as its chief reason for moving, and the *New York Times* noted the corporations' desire to tap "the employment potential of young housewives who are eager for office jobs close to home." Corporate America needed middle-class women with clerical skills or the ability to learn such skills, and those women had moved to suburbia. Thus the *Times* lamented the "lessened white-collar reserve within the five boroughs" owing to "the long-term exodus of high- and middle-income families to suburban communities."[19] Just as the middle class was abandoning downtown movie theaters and department stores, it was no longer as accessible to downtown corporate offices. Confronted by the alternative of hiring inner-city workers who struggled to fill out application forms or educated, middle-class suburbanites, the nation's largest corporations were opting for the latter.

Decaying central-city neighborhoods reinforced the dismal image of the urban core. By the late 1960s and 1970s a wave of abandonment swept inner-city neighborhoods as even the poorest Americans shunned them. Landlords no longer made repairs, collected rents, or paid taxes, and vandals stripped structures of plumbing fixtures, piping, hardware, and any other relic that could bring in a few dollars. Once solid structures that had earned lucrative rents were cast aside as worthless. The value of many inner-city blocks had dropped to nothing.

This phenomenon was especially evident in the older central cities of the Northeast and Midwest. In 1975 there were an estimated 62,000 abandoned dwelling units in Detroit and 33,000 in Philadelphia (figure 4.2). During the 1970s, wreckers demolished 15 percent of the housing in Saint Louis, with a loss of 4,000 units each year between 1970 and 1976.[20] In the most derelict neighborhoods of Saint Louis, approximately 16 percent of the buildings were abandoned.[21] From 1966 to 1974, the city

FIGURE 4.2
Sign of the times: the shell of a house in central Detroit, 1974. (Walter P. Reuther Library, Wayne State University)

of Cleveland appropriated over $4 million for the demolition of cast-off structures as an average of three dwelling units were abandoned each day.[22] Chicago's Woodlawn district was labeled "the zone of destruction." In the 1960s, its population dropped 36 percent, from 81,000 to 52,000, and by 1973 the city was bulldozing 500 housing units in the Woodlawn area each year, with a backlog of units slated for destruction mounting to 1,500.[23] But Woodlawn was not the only Chicago district being reduced to rubble. In the two-month period between September and November 1970, 2.6 percent of the dwelling units in the North Lawndale district were abandoned.[24] The number of dwelling units in Chicago's East Garfield Park area plummeted from 20,353 in 1960 to 10,933 in 1980.[25] Engulfed by the plague of abandonment and destruction half of East Garfield Park disappeared over the twenty-year period.

As was so often the case in the late 1960s and 1970s, the most dire news was from New York City. From 1965 to 1968, 5 percent of the city's housing stock, approximately 100,000 units, was abandoned. By 1975, the estimated number of abandoned dwelling units in the city had risen to 199,000.[26] The most notable concentration of vacant and burned-out structures was in the South Bronx. During the 1970s, commentators frequently described the devastated district as reminiscent of Berlin or Dresden after World War II or London after the Blitz. Yet in the case of the South Bronx, foreign enemies did not wreak the devastation; instead, it came from within. Seeking to collect insurance, landlords paid arsonists to torch their buildings. Realizing that burned-out households rose to the top of the eligibility list for public housing, some disgruntled tenants were also happy to set fire to their apartments. In 1975 two local youths, ten and fifteen years old, admitted responsibility for forty or fifty blazes, having taken on the job of torching the structures for fees of $3 and up.[27] Arson seemed to be the district's biggest business, and by 1974 the number of fires in the Bronx was triple what it had been in 1960, before the onset of devastation. During the 1978 World Series, every baseball fan in America became aware of the borough's plight when television cameras covering the game in Yankee Stadium shifted from the diamond and panned the blazing panorama of the nearby South Bronx. "The Bronx is burning," announced sports commentator Howard Cosell.[28] "It isn't pretty to watch whole communities self-destruct in the heart of the cities of the world's richest country," observed an article on the abandonment phenomenon.[29] Yet by the 1970s, millions of Americans were watching the ugly spectacle of self-destruction in the nation's largest city.

Although less dramatic than the burning of the Bronx, the statistics on central-city welfare recipients seemed to tell the same story of urban debacle. Despite overall prosperity and a low unemployment rate, the number of Americans on welfare rose 107 percent from December 1960 to February 1969, with the greatest increase occurring from 1965 to 1969. The sharpest rise in the dependent population was in the nation's five largest metropolitan areas, with an increase of 300 percent in New York City and 293 percent in Los Angeles County.[30] Long deemed the capital of capitalism, New York City was winning an unenviable reputation as "a welfare dumping ground." In 1960 almost ten times as many New Yorkers were employed as on welfare; by 1970 the ratio of employed to welfare recipients had declined to nearly five to one.[31] Just as Times Square no longer appeared so glamorous or Fifth Avenue department stores so bustling, the city's residents no longer seemed exemplars of the upward mobility resulting from private enterprise. Instead, the nation's largest city and other American urban centers were developing into hubs of despair and dependence.

Soaring central-city crime rates further testified to a deteriorating way of life. Between 1962 and 1972, the nation's murder rate doubled. In the early 1970s, southern cities proved especially lethal, with Atlanta winning the title of murder capital of America and New Orleans ranking a close second. In 1974 a mathematician at the Massachusetts Institute of Technology computed that a person born in a major American city and remaining there was more likely to be murdered than a World War II GI was to die in combat.[32] A radio ad in Washington, D.C., warned: "Most of us worry about heart attacks, automobile accidents, or cancer. But if you're a district resident between the ages of 15 to 44, you're more likely to die by the bullet. . . . So don't feel quite so secure if you've quit smoking and started wearing your seat belts."[33]

The nation's robbery rate also soared, more than doubling in the short period from 1966 to 1970. In New York City, renowned as America's mugging capital, the robbery rate far exceeded that of any other city. Describing how she adapted to the reign of robbery, one New Yorker explained that she never carried a wallet, relying instead on "a small change purse with some bus tokens, a credit card and a few dollars in case I meet a mugger."[34] Although many Americans deemed life in New York particularly hazardous, in cities throughout the nation urban dwellers were coping with an enhanced level of crime and disorder. In January 1973, the Gallup Poll reported that "one person in three living in big center-city areas" had been robbed, burgled, mugged, or suffered from vandalism during the previous year.[35]

Underlying much of the increase in crime and insecurity was a startling rise in narcotic drug use. During the 1950s, New York City's medical examiner reported an average of around a hundred narcotic-related deaths each year. By the close of the 1960s this figure had risen to over 1,200. Between 1963 and 1970, the estimated number of heroin users in Boston and Atlanta soared tenfold. Young males were especially vulnerable. In Washington, D.C., over 13 percent of males born in 1953 became heroin addicts, and in some parts of the nation's capital the figure rose to about 25 percent.[36]

Mounting fear of crime and violence further alienated middle-class Americans from the central cities. Racial prejudice underlay some of the fears, as whites felt threatened by the growing number of central-city blacks. Yet African Americans themselves were not exempt from the prevailing anxiety about an increasingly violent city. Explaining why whites avoided Chicago's downtown at night, a city official noted that an overwhelming majority of Loop filmgoers were black. "The white is intimidated by seeing a group of 24 black teen-agers coming toward him on a sidewalk." But then he added: "The black older guy is also intimidated just by seeing 24 teen-agers." In fact, in 1975 a *Chicago Tribune* survey found that only 26 percent of white respondents and 42 percent of black respondents would go to the Loop at night.[37] In other words, a majority of both races would not venture into the city's center after dark. Moreover, in another *Tribune* survey conducted at the same time crime ranked as the chief community concern among both black and white Chicagoans, and African Americans were more likely to have taken protective measures such as installing special locks or alarms.[38]

Mayoral candidates responded to mounting fears by campaigning as crime fighters. In both Philadelphia and Minneapolis, voters elected white former police officers who projected a tough-guy image to the mayor's office. In 1973 Tom Bradley, a black veteran of twenty-one years on the police force, won the mayor's race in Los Angeles after a campaign in which he spoke proudly of his law-enforcement background. The same year, African American Maynard Jackson successfully vied for Atlanta's highest position, promising to crack down on criminals and "bust the pusher." A black opponent for the Atlanta mayor's office warned voters: "If nothing is done, Atlanta will be just another big city, a southern version of New York, a city where muggers and robbers control the streets and where downtown is a no-man's land, where the central city is a battle-ground where the average man dares not trod."³⁹

In Atlanta, New York, Chicago, and Los Angeles, crime seemed to be destroying once great cities and forcing changes in the urban way of life. Fewer people were willing to go downtown after dark, and a stroll along the sidewalks of New York was a journey of fear rather than pleasure. Central Park was a place to be mugged, and Atlanta was a prime site for murder. "There is no keen and precise estimate of the extent to which fear of crime changes people's behavior," observed one student of the subject. "But it's enormous: they take taxis instead of walking; they barricade their houses; they construct medieval fortresses; they close up their cities tight after dark."⁴⁰ Victimized by thugs and thieves, America's central cities were becoming prisons of fear.

Culminating the downward spiral of the central cities was the fiscal crisis of the second half of the 1970s. Municipal governments in the older hubs moved perilously close to bankruptcy and became the financial basket cases of the nation. Unsafe, decaying, and abandoned, America's urban hubs ran out of money and faced the ultimate humiliation of fiscal debacle.

New York City's brush with bankruptcy dramatically demonstrated the weakness of central-city finances. For years, the city had borrowed to pay operating expenses and resorted to bookkeeping gimmicks to disguise its deteriorating financial condition. But by 1975, it had come to the end of its rope. The banks would no longer lend the city money; the nation's largest municipality was broke. The state of New York intervened and assumed charge of the city's finances, leading economist Milton Friedman to observe in December 1975: "New York City is now being run by the caretakers appointed by the state of New York. At the moment New York doesn't have any self-government."⁴¹ One of those charged with reordering the desperate finances of the city warned: "The pain is just beginning. New York will now have to undergo the most brutal kind of financial and fiscal exercise that any community in the country will ever have to face."⁴² By the close of 1975, New York City was, then, a ward of the state, and the new guardians of the incompetent city were dedicated to forcing it into shape.

Some observers, however, felt that New York City would never recover. "New York is not quite dead, but death is clearly inevitable," commented economist Robert Zevin. New York had lost "those things which define a city's vitality: the culture and ferment, material pleasures and comforts, exploration and invention, growth of old activities and creation of new ones which serve as positive attractions for immigrants and produce a flow of ideas and products for export."[43] Former city official Roger Starr proposed the planned shrinkage of New York, urging the abandonment of hopeless neighborhoods and the concentration of resources on areas capable of surviving. Attempting to salvage something from the city's debacle, Starr concluded: "Essentially, planned shrinkage is a recognition that the golden door to full participation in American life and the American economy is no longer to be found in New York."[44] Americans as a whole did not seem too eager to salvage the nation's largest city. Reflecting the mood of the electorate, President Gerald Ford rejected federal aid to the faltering city. The New York *Daily News* headline read "Ford to City: Drop Dead." Early in 1976, an article in the *New York Review of Books* perceptively observed: "As New York once carelessly discarded its own marginal neighborhoods, so America may have decided that New York itself can now be junked."[45]

Few cities had the luxury of gloating over New York's misfortune, for other hubs were also struggling to meet their expenses. In the fiscal year 1975/1976, Philadelphia recorded a $73 million deficit, and the projected budget gap for 1976/1977 was $100 million.[46] In 1974 Buffalo's finance commissioner seemed about ready to sacrifice his city's self-government when he remarked, "Perhaps we should just take the charter and the keys, send them to Albany, and say 'Okay, you solve it. We can't do any more.'"[47] The next year, local banks rescued Buffalo at the last minute, thus staving off a default on the city's short-term debt. The state of Michigan helped Detroit avoid bankruptcy in the second half of the 1970s. In 1978, however, Cleveland defaulted on its short-term notes, reinforcing that city's image as a deteriorating remnant of America's industrial past. Perhaps reassured by discovering a community in worse financial shape than New York City, the *New York Times* published an article headlined "Cleveland Caught in Long Decline" and pronounced soberly that "Ohio's largest city is chronically ill."[48]

By the second half of the 1970s, this chronic illness seemed of epidemic proportions. Just three decades before, New York City had been the hope of the world, the symbol of America's triumphant way of life. By 1975, however, some of its neighborhoods were being compared with the bombed-out Berlin of 1945, and commentators declared it no longer a place of opportunity. The New York City of 1975 evoked images of muggers, not Macy's, and of bankruptcy, not wealth. In one metropolitan area after another, the core was rotting; the centripetal way of life of 1945 had yielded to central-city debacle by 1975.

Race and Rebellion

Underlying much of the alienation of the white middle class from the central city were persistent racial animosities. Throughout the nation, the central cities were becoming increasingly black and as such were deemed off-limits to many whites. Between 1960 and 1980, the African American share of New York City's population rose from 14 to 25 percent, from 23 to 40 percent in Chicago, and from 29 to 46 percent in Saint Louis. By 1970 Washington, D.C.; Atlanta; Newark, New Jersey; and Gary, Indiana, were all majority African American. By 1980 Baltimore, Birmingham, Detroit, New Orleans, and Richmond, Virginia, had been added to the list of black-majority cities. In fact, by the latter date, Atlanta, Detroit, and Washington were over 60 percent black. Moreover, whites fully expected that it was only a matter of time before other hubs became predominantly African American. In 1966 *U.S. News & World Report* predicted that by the year 2000 Saint Louis, Philadelphia, New York City, and Chicago would be at least 50 percent black, and African Americans would constitute 66 percent of the population of Cleveland. The Bay cities of San Francisco and Oakland, Cincinnati, and Kansas City, Missouri, were expected to be at least 40 percent black. "If present trends continue," the magazine reported ominously to its white, middle-class readers, "Negroes will outnumber whites in 8 out of the 10 biggest cities in the U.S.—or come close to it—by the year 2000, a date that is now just 34 years away." Emphasizing the significance of these figures, *U.S. News* made clear that "this could mean Negro governments in New York, Chicago, Philadelphia, Detroit, Cleveland, St. Louis, Baltimore, and Newark." The magazine concluded: "Unless something occurs to check the current trends, some of the most important cities of this country are going to wind up under Negro control."[49] Both the census figures and the mass media were presenting whites with much the same message. In the near future, the nation's urban hubs were going to pass from their hands and become black metropolises. The central cities would no longer be central to white metropolitan life.

As the black presence in the central cities grew, it did not result in a marked increase in stable, racially integrated neighborhoods. Instead, as blacks moved into neighborhoods, whites moved out, so areas went from all white to all black in a relatively few years. Whites did not share residential space with African Americans and did not frequent areas deemed black. Thus there were carefully defined black districts that few whites penetrated. In Boston, the African American district was Roxbury; in Cleveland, the East Side was black, and the West Side was white; in Saint Louis, the North Side was black, and the South Side was white; in Los Angeles, the South Central area was the African American preserve.

Nowhere was the continuing black–white division more dramatically evident than in the massive public-housing projects. These central-city projects were becoming highly visible reservations for poor blacks; segregated zones of welfare, unwed mothers, and violent gang activity, they represented everything middle-class whites abhorred and feared. In the 1940s and 1950s, poor white families as well as blacks sought residency in public housing. But in the 1960s and 1970s, the projects became increasingly black and associated in white minds with a culture of poverty that was peculiarly African American. By the early 1970s, 70 percent of all public-housing households were nonwhite; public housing for the elderly still attracted a number of white tenants, but projects for families were overwhelmingly black. In Atlanta and Chicago, 95 percent of the non-elderly households were African American.[50] In Saint Louis, the Clinton Peabody Terrace project went from 6.1 percent black in 1957 to 96.1 percent black in 1974; the Cochran Gardens Apartments went from 16 to 98.8 percent African American over the same period; the increase in the Joseph M. Darst Apartments was from 18.9 to 98.9 percent.[51] Basically by 1974, family projects in Saint Louis were for African Americans.

Blacks as well as whites were very conscious that the African American population was being warehoused in government-sponsored reservations where they would be out of the way of more affluent Americans. In Chicago, blacks were isolated in rows of monolithic high-rises extending south from the Loop and separated from the rest of the city by the multilane Dan Ryan Expressway. In 1965 the *Chicago Daily News* ran a series of articles on the Robert R. Taylor Homes, described as a "$70 Million Ghetto" and "the world's biggest and most jam-packed public housing development." According to the *News*, the project was "virtually [an] all-Negro city within a city" that its own tenants labeled as "a 'death trap,' a concentration camp, and even, with sardonic self-derision, 'the Congo Hilton.' Here live 28,000 people, all of them poor, grappling with violence and vandalism, fear and suspicion, teen-age terror and adult chaos, rage, resentment, official regimenting."[52] The tenant-occupied towers of

FIGURE 4.3   Public housing at Hunter's Point, San Francisco. (San Francisco History Center, San Francisco Public Library)

Robert Taylor Homes were the very opposite of the oft-proclaimed American dream: ownership of a single-family, detached house on a plot of grass with shade trees. Whites were realizing this dream, but poor blacks were relegated to its antithesis.

On the West Coast, the most notable black public-housing reservation was Hunter's Point in San Francisco (figure 4.3). On an isolated peninsula in San Francisco Bay, this project was, according to the local housing authority, 95 percent black and 5 percent "Caucasian" and "Samoan."[53] Except for some dealings with welfare and housing authority personnel, the black residents of Hunter's Point had little contact with whites, and few white San Franciscans had ever been to the project. Even whites on the city police force generally avoided Hunter's Point, abdicating responsibility for it to the racially integrated housing authority security force. Hunter's Point was beyond the pale of white society; it was a community apart from the city and out of sight of San Francisco's more affluent residents.

Some of the black population was seeping beyond the central-city boundaries and settling in "better" neighborhoods. By 1969, African

Americans owned one-fifth of the houses in the Lomond neighborhood of the affluent Cleveland suburb of Shaker Heights.[54] In 1970 almost 15 percent of Shaker Heights residents were African American; ten years later, the figure approached 25 percent. Meanwhile, nearby middle-class Cleveland Heights went from less than 1 percent black in 1960 to 25 percent black in 1980. In the Chicago area, the middle-class suburb of Oak Park had 132 African American residents in 1970; ten years later, 5,929 blacks lived in the community. In southern California, thousands of upwardly mobile blacks moved into the single-family tract houses along the tree-lined streets of suburban Compton, although in the 1970s they were joined by an increasing number of poorer refugees from the central city. The black migrants to suburbia, however, were the exception to the rule. Most African Americans remained confined in segregated neighborhoods of the central city, removed from a white population that was resigned to the abandonment of the urban core.

The well-publicized riots of the 1960s heightened white fears of central-city blacks and, if anything, widened the racial divide. Racial violence was nothing new to the nation's urban areas, but the chain reaction of disorder during the 1960s shocked Americans. Extensive television coverage brought the reality of rebellion to the living rooms of Americans in even the most remote corners of the nation. Residents of lily-white suburbs could not avoid what was occurring in the central cities. Each evening, the television networks broadcast racial violence into their homes.

In the summer of 1964, New York City ushered in the age of disorder, suffering the first of the riots. As did so many of the 1960s disturbances, it began with a police incident. Thomas Gilligan, a white police officer, shot and killed a fifteen-year-old African American boy who had rushed at Gilligan with a knife. Incensed by what they perceived as yet another example of white police brutality, blacks rioted in both Harlem and the Bedford-Stuyvesant area of Brooklyn, smashing windows, setting fires, and looting stores. One rioter was killed, 118 persons were injured, and 465 arrested.[55] During the remainder of the summer, lesser riots broke out in Rochester, New York, and Philadelphia.

Yet it was Los Angeles's Watts riot in the summer of 1965 that brought the purported urban crisis to the forefront of the nation's consciousness. Like the New York City disorder of the previous year, police action sparked the rebellion. On a sweltering evening in August, the California Highway Patrol pulled over twenty-one-year-old Marquette Frye for drunk driving. A crowd gathered around the stopped car, and Frye and his mother and brother began arguing with the police. An angry Mrs. Frye jumped on a police officer's back. The white patrolmen dragged into their squad car a young black woman in a loose smock who appeared to be pregnant; the authorities claimed that she had spit on an officer. As the police pulled away with the Fryes in custody, the irate mob responded with a barrage of rocks and bottles.

For six days, rioting spread through Los Angeles's Watts neighborhood and adjoining black districts. Middle-class black leaders sought to pacify the mob, but young African American rioters were not willing to follow the lead of their more affluent elders, who appeared to be allies of the hated whites. When a black state legislator who was attempting to halt the violence refused to join in the rock throwing, a young rioter responded: "Hell! You're with the Man."[56] Thirty-four people died in the uprising; 1,032 required treatment for injuries; and 3,952 were arrested. Rioters burned, damaged, or looted almost one thousand buildings with a total estimated property loss of $40 million (figure 4.4). One unemployed man explained why so many joined in the looting: "They wanted everything the

FIGURE 4.4   Building on fire during the riot in the Watts neighborhood, Los Angeles, August 1965. (*Herald Examiner* Collection, Los Angeles Public Library)

whites had, including color TV. They saw the stores were open. If you are hungry and don't have no money, you want anything and everything."[57]

Although nothing in the summer of 1966 matched the intensity or destruction of the Watts uprising, there was enough civil disorder in America's cities to keep white fears of racial rebellion very much alive. In July, Chicago suffered an outbreak of rock throwing, arson, and looting that resulted in three deaths and 533 arrests. The same month, rioting broke out in the Hough area of Cleveland, leaving four blacks dead.[58] In San Francisco, Hunter's Point erupted after a white police officer shot and killed a fleeing sixteen-year-old black boy who had refused to halt for questioning. Again, there was some looting, rock throwing, and minor arson. In calmer years, the Hunter's Point disturbance would not have been deemed a riot but simply an insignificant outburst of neighborhood unrest. By 1966, however, the news media was labeling every mob action by angry blacks as a riot, and to uneasy white San Franciscans it seemed that their city was on the verge of another Watts. As in other cities, prominent blacks attempted to calm the youthful rioters. But when a black member of San Francisco's governing Board of Supervisors spoke to the angry Hunter's Point demonstrators, he was greeted with rocks and jeers. "That cocksucker forget he's black," remarked one Hunter's Point resident, "but when we put them fuckers on the run, they sure let him know at City Hall right away."[59] Altogether there were forty-three reported race-related civil disorders and riots in 1966, but 1966 was relatively quiet compared to the violence of the following year.[60]

During the first nine months of 1967, there were a reported 164 disorders. In mid-June, Tampa and Cincinnati erupted; in late June, Buffalo was the scene of rioting. The following month, the race rebellion spread to Newark. Black rioters stole or damaged over $8 million of merchandise in the New Jersey city, and before order was finally restored, twenty-three people had been killed.[61]

In late July, Detroit suffered the most destructive and lethal riot of the 1960s. Again, a police incident ignited the black population. On a steamy summer night, Detroit police raided an illegal drinking establishment in a black neighborhood and arrested the eighty-two people patronizing the bar. A crowd gathered to witness the arrests and became angry because of the police officers' supposed brutal treatment of those arrested. According to one police officer, a black youth incited the crowd, shouting, "Black Power, don't let them take our people away; look what they are doing to our people.... Let's kill them whitey motherfuckers ... let's get the bricks and bottles going."[62] The bricks and bottles did get going as well as the now all-too-familiar looting and arson.

In Detroit, as elsewhere, African American leaders attempted to quiet the angry mob. When black congressman John Conyers tried to disperse the crowd, one bitter rioter shouted: "Why are you defending the cops and the establishment? You're just as bad as they are!" Later a discouraged Conyers complained: "You try to talk to those people and they'll knock you into the middle of next year."[63] For five days, the wave of violence continued. In Detroit, however, some whites joined with the blacks in the looting. Twelve percent of the adults arrested were white, as were two of the seventeen looters who were killed.[64] Seemingly, rebellion in Detroit was an integrated affair.

The extent of the violence shocked the nation. Forty-three people were killed in the Detroit riot, and 7,200 were arrested; there was an estimated $45 million in property damage. The fire department reported 682 fires resulting from the riot; the blazes demolished 412 buildings (figure 4.5).[65] In the black neighborhoods of Detroit, ruins of destroyed businesses testified to the implosion of the central city.

FIGURE 4.5   Aerial view of Detroit on fire during the riot of July 1967. (Walter P. Reuther Library, Wayne State University)

In the wake of the 1967 riots, President Lyndon Johnson appointed the National Advisory Commission on Civil Disorders to investigate the nature and causes of the urban uprising. Released in early 1968, the commission's report concluded: "Our nation is moving toward two societies, one black, one white—separate and unequal." It further argued that "within two decades, this division could be so deep that it would be almost impossible to unite: a white society principally located in suburbs, in smaller central cities, and in the peripheral parts of large central cities; and a Negro society largely concentrated within large central cities."[66] By bluntly exposing the nation's developing racial division, the commission sought to shock the white public into embracing a program of healing action. But the commission's conclusions were hardly surprising or shocking. Anyone with even a superficial knowledge of the black–white city would have realized that the United States was not moving toward two societies, separate and unequal; two societies, separate and unequal, had existed for centuries. Rather than describing a fearsome future, the commission was restating an American tradition. Moreover, there was already "a white society principally located in suburbs" and "a Negro society largely concentrated within large central cities." And the message conveyed to many white Americans by the riots was that this was how it should remain. White Americans should confine themselves to the safe suburbs and avoid the increasingly black central cities. Despite the commission's well-meaning call for change, many white Americans felt the answer to the "urban crisis" was to live, work, and play in the suburbs and abandon the central city to troublesome blacks.

In its emphasis on the black–white division and its narrow focus on race, however, the commission report downplayed some salient features of the urban unrest. The disturbances of the 1960s were not traditional race riots like the Detroit melee of 1943. In 1943 and in earlier riots, black and white mobs clashed, attacking anyone of a different skin color. In the 1960s riots, blacks attacked white police and white-owned businesses in African American neighborhoods, but they did not invade white neighborhoods or attack whites outside the black ghetto. Few of the casualties of the 1960s riots were white civilians; most of the whites injured were police officers or firefighters. Moreover, white mobs did not take to the streets and attack African Americans. The 1960s riots were rebellions against authority: against "the man," those with power who, like the white police, were pushing blacks around or, like white-owned neighborhood businesses, were unfairly exploiting them. And to some degree, the riots were a rebellion against even black authority figures. Repeatedly, rioters jeered white-collar black peacemakers; they were no better than "the man." A survey of rioters in Newark found that 50.5 percent believed that "Negroes who make a lot of money are just as bad as whites."[67] The riots in Los Angeles, Newark, and Detroit were not simply black–white clashes; they were attacks by powerless blacks on neighborhood businesses that exploited their patronage and on police who treated them like dogs. Many rioters deemed successful blacks who cooperated with the hated white authorities as little better than the whites.

No group had more reason to rebel than the young black males who constituted a disproportionate share of the rioters. Their youth, race, and gender made them the focus of police scrutiny; if there was trouble, they were assumed to be the troublemakers. Moreover, they suffered the highest rates of unemployment. White businesses were moving to suburbia to hire young white, middle-class women. They were not anchored in the central cities by a desire to employ African American males. For whites in business and law enforcement, the young black male did not conjure up an image of honesty, reliability, or obedience. The white power structure deemed young black males the enemy, and in the riots of the 1960s, young African American men rebelled against that structure.

It made little difference to middle-class whites, however, whether the riots of the 1960s were simply antiwhite or anti–middle class. Either way, they were the target. What was evident was that much of the central city was out of bounds to them. Newark and Detroit were no longer their cities. They belonged to rebellious blacks and thus were not desirable places to invest and live in or even to visit.

Reinforcing the perception of rebellion were government-sponsored community action programs. In 1964 President Johnson launched his War on Poverty, a federal initiative to level the social and economic playing field in America. One vital element of the federal scheme was the community action councils, which were to guide the assault on poverty in poor neighborhoods throughout the nation. There was to be "maximum feasible participation" by the poor on these neighborhood councils. In the minds of many Americans, the program was intended to empower the poor, specifically poor blacks, and enable them to seize control of their destinies from the prevailing white power structure. According to one contemporary observer, the federal bureaucrats in charge of the War on Poverty "operated on the assumption that the involvement of the poor in policy-making was necessary in order to redistribute power in the cities;

without power redistribution, they believed, there would be no great improvement in the lot of the Negro poor."[68]

The notion of a federally funded revolution understandably troubled many white central-city officials. In San Francisco, for example, Mayor John Shelley fought an unsuccessful battle with local black activists over control of the city's community action program. At the meeting of the United States Conference of Mayors in 1965, an embittered Shelley joined with Mayor Samuel Yorty of Los Angeles in introducing a resolution that accused the federal antipoverty agency of "fostering class struggle." Two years later, Shelley concluded: "Maximum feasible participation . . . are words that expanded the social revolution in San Francisco into a chain reaction of unrest and distrust that has left its mark on every major civic improvement project attempted here in recent years."[69] The white mayor of Newark agreed, charging the local community action agency with stirring dissent in the days before that city's riot. Community action employees had participated in the antipolice rally that preceded the riot, and community action equipment was used to produce leaflets calling for the protest demonstration.[70] At a time when white mayors were under siege and attempting to administer collapsing cities, they certainly did not welcome such federally sponsored assaults on their authority or the stability of their communities.

The community action program did empower a new corps of black leaders, most of them middle class, and provide jobs for favored followers of those leaders. But it created more conflict and controversy than economic uplift. Commenting on the Hunter's Point neighborhood of San Francisco, one student of the program concluded: "Maximum feasible participation of the poor meant that upwards of a hundred persons were able to secure some full- or part-time staff positions and several hundred more were involved in block meetings concerned with improving some of the worst abuses in public housing. Hopes were raised, but the extent of changes brought about in this ghetto were negligible." The editor of the local antipoverty newspaper summed up the situation: "The most outstanding thing is that everything is the same."[71] For whites, however, all the talk of black empowerment and social revolution simply reinforced the notion that the central city was off-limits. In their minds, black power meant the exclusion of whites.

A rising number of African American victories at the polls proved even more significant in the struggle for black empowerment and the advance of white alienation. As the black population increased in central cities, African Americans won more political offices, and in 1967 Cleveland and Gary became the first major American cities to elect black mayors. Three years later, Newark voters chose an African American as their city's chief executive, and in 1973 blacks won the mayor's office in Detroit, Atlanta, and Los Angeles. These victories did not signal a new era of racial tolerance in America's cities. Instead, urban voters split largely along racial lines, with blacks winning because they constituted a majority or near majority of the population. Race dominated the Cleveland campaign of 1967; the white opponent of victorious Carl Stokes complained: "Over in the Negro part of the city the ministers and newspaper editors and everybody else were saying, 'Vote color,' and over in the white community Stokes was saying, 'No, don't vote color—consider a person on his qualifications, not on account of his color.'"[72] Some whites were also recommending that the electorate vote color. "Vote Right—Vote White," read an anonymous leaflet distributed in some white neighborhoods before the election.[73] Gary's black candidate, Richard Hatcher, declared independence from the white-dominated Democratic organization, proclaiming, "Plantation politics is dead." Such rhetoric worried some of Gary's whites. One white resident said of his neighborhood before the election: "Every racist in the area . . . were out in the open, up and down the street."[74]

The election returns demonstrated the racial split. Hatcher won more than 96 percent of the black ballots but only 14 percent of the white vote; Stokes captured an estimated 95 percent of the African American vote yet only 19 percent of the white.[75] In Newark, the white police director said the mayoral battle of 1970 was a "black versus white situation," "a battle for survival." Raising visions of apocalyptic doom he told a white audience: "Whether we survive or cease to exist depends on what you do on [election day]."[76] This racial divide was evident in the election returns: Newark's black candidate won nearly unanimous backing from African Americans and no more than 20 percent of the white ballots.[77] In Detroit's 1973 contest, the African American Coleman Young secured 92 percent of black votes; his white opponent was the choice of 91 percent of white voters.[78] Meanwhile, in Atlanta the black victor received 95 percent support from African Americans and an estimated 17.5 percent of white votes.[79] Only in Los Angeles was a black candidate able to draw strong support from both black and white voters. Elsewhere race determined the people's choice.

Once they took office, black mayors were able to translate political power into new opportunities for their African American supporters. Between 1973 and 1978, the share of managerial positions in Detroit's city government held by blacks soared from 12 to 32 percent, and the black share of professional positions in Atlanta's municipal bureaucracy rose from 19 to 42 percent. Victory at the polls meant more African American department heads, municipal engineers, and city attorneys. Similarly, in Detroit and Atlanta, the percentage of the cities' business in the form of purchases and contracts going to minority-owned firms increased from 2 to 3 percent in 1973 to 33 percent in 1978.[80] Although the beleaguered older central cities were not the rich prizes they had once been, political power produced important gains for blacks long closed out of the inner circle at city hall.

Yet as blacks took power, whites felt increasingly insecure about their position in the central cities. Rhetoric about "a battle for survival" struck a chord with whites facing the possibility of displacement. Exemplifying the racial tensions arising from African American empowerment was the highly publicized clash over school government in New York City. During the late 1960s, New York's African Americans grew increasingly frustrated with the city's highly centralized education bureaucracy. Black children were not receiving adequate education, and responding to a growing chorus of complaints the city embarked on an experiment in neighborhood control. In 1967 three experimental districts were created where the schools would be governed by neighborhood boards. One of the districts comprised the predominantly black Ocean Hill–Brownsville area of Brooklyn.

The white-dominated teachers union, however, soon clashed with the black-dominated neighborhood board and the black administrator of the Ocean Hill–Brownsville district, resulting in a bitter barrage of attacks and counterattacks. White teachers received "hate literature" demanding that only black or Puerto Rican teachers be employed in Ocean Hill–Brownsville. Moreover, one manifesto proclaimed: "All 'whitey' textbooks must be burnt and replaced by decent educational material. 'Whitey' art and John Birch–type social studies must be replaced by African arts and crafts and African history." "The Black Community Must Unite Itself Around the Need to Run Our Own Schools and to Control Our Own Neighborhoods Without Whitey Being Anywhere on the Scene," announced one leaflet placed in teachers' mailboxes. "We Want to Make It Crystal Clear to You Outsiders and You Missionaries, the Natives Are on the Move!!! Look Out!!! Watch Out!!!! That Backfire You Hear Might Be

Your Number Has Come Up!!!!" The many Jewish teachers felt especially threatened when the literature warned: "Get Off Our Backs, or Your Relatives in the Middle East Will Find Themselves Giving Benefits to Raise Money to Help You Get Out from Under the Terrible Weight of an Enraged Black Community."[81]

The neighborhood board denied any responsibility for the hate literature and denounced anti-Semitism. But the well-publicized conflict in the nation's largest city was added proof of the racial chasm dividing the nation. A committee appointed by the mayor to investigate the Ocean Hill–Brownsville conflict found that "an appalling amount of racial prejudice—black and white—in New York City surfaced in and about the school controversy. Over and over again we found evidence of vicious anti-white attitudes on the part of some black people, and vicious anti-black attitudes on the part of some white people."[82] Given such racial vitriol, many middle-class whites had to conclude that the suburbs were the best place for them.

Clinching the case against the central city was the battle over busing. In 1954 the United States Supreme Court, in *Brown v. Board of Education*, held racial segregation in the public schools unconstitutional, and by the 1970s the courts were interpreting this to mean that school districts had to ensure that the student body of each school had a racial mix proportionate to the racial mix in the district as the whole. In one city after another, federal judges ordered busing of children to schools outside their neighborhoods in order to achieve racial balance. This might require the transportation of students to schools miles from their all-white or all-black neighborhoods.

Throughout the nation, school districts engaged in lengthy court battles to avoid busing. And polls showed that white parents were overwhelmingly opposed to the integration policy. Some whites transferred their children to private schools; others opted to move out of central-city school districts and thereby avoid busing orders. Parents complained bitterly about the possibility of their children being sent miles from home to distant neighborhoods. Proponents of school integration, however, contended that foes of busing were simply racists. "It's Not the Distance, 'It's the Niggers,'" the NAACP Defense Fund bluntly observed.[83] Whatever the motives for opposition, busing was a key factor in determining where whites chose to live. If they could avoid the transportation of their children to distant institutions, they would do so. The result was further abandonment of the central city. In the minds of most whites, busing further raised the penalty for living in the urban core.

The greatest battle over busing was fought in Boston. In 1965 the Massachusetts legislature adopted the Racial Imbalance Act, which defined any school that had more than 50 percent nonwhite students as racially imbalanced and ordered local districts to eliminate such concentrations of minority pupils. For the following nine years, Boston's school board refused to allow anything more than token action to correct imbalances. Its Irish Catholic members, led by Louise Day Hicks, stirred not only racial animosities but also class conflict. They emphasized that upper-middle-class lawmakers from the suburbs were imposing this scheme of social engineering on working-class Bostonians. Attacking the coauthor of the imbalance law, a resident of the upper-middle-class suburb of Brookline, Hicks argued: "The racial imbalance law does not affect Brookline, so he smugly tells the elected officials of Boston what they should do. I, for one, am tired of nonresidents telling the people of Boston what they should do." Shifting the blame for social ills to the more affluent whites outside the city, Hicks challenged suburban residents to "help the poor city correct the situation. Take the Negro families into your suburbs and build housing for them and let them go to school with your children."[84] Another school board member attacked an approach to government that mandated "that suburban patricians rule urban plebeians from 9 A.M. to 5 P.M. It seems to be an elitist concept which would rule the destinies of the great 'unwashed' (us) through inquisitions, innuendo and high-powered Madison Avenue scare techniques."[85]

In 1974 the clash entered a new phase when federal district court judge W. Arthur Garrity, a resident of the affluent suburb of Wellesley, found the Boston school authorities guilty of maintaining segregated schools and ordered busing to achieve racial balance. Opposition to Garrity's busing order was especially vehement in the working-class Irish neighborhood of South Boston. At the opening of the school year in September 1974, 90 percent of South Boston's white students participated in a school boycott, staying away from their classes. According to *Time* magazine, "a jeering, mostly teen-aged crowd of whites threw stones and bottles at two yellow buses that carried the 56 black students who showed up for opening day" at South Boston High School. After school that afternoon, "whites brandished lengths of rubber hose and clubs and again threw bottles at the buses." The next day, black students were confronted by "several dozen white mothers, who chanted, 'Southie won't go!' and by some 200 stone-throwing white youths."[86]

South Boston whites not only opposed the importation of African American students but were, if anything, more opposed to the transfer of their children to schools in black Roxbury, a district perceived as danger-ous and crime ridden. One white parent of a boy slated for busing ex-plained: "I worked nine years in Roxbury as a street cleaner, and I'll never let him go there."[87] Raising the specter of rapacious black sexuality, an-other white father observed: "The question is: Am I going to send my young daughter, who is budding into the flower of womanhood, into Rox-bury on a bus?"[88]

In the working-class Charlestown district of Boston, the opposition was virtually as intense. Charlestown whites had earlier fought the physi-cal engineering plots of urban renewal authorities to disrupt their enclave, and now they mobilized against the social engineers of busing. In fact, whites throughout the city opposed busing, and many of those who could afford to move to suburbia did so. Meanwhile, poor whites and poor blacks remained in the central city, embroiled in racial conflict.

In the early 1970s, some federal judges, however, attempted to foil flee-ing whites by mandating interdistrict busing between cities and suburbs. Most notably, in 1972 federal district court judge Stephen Roth ordered busing between the city of Detroit and fifty-three independent suburban school districts. Roth found Detroit school authorities guilty of actions that promoted racial segregation in the city's public schools, but he held that busing solely within the increasingly black city was not an adequate remedy. Shifting students between the black areas of Detroit and the re-maining white city neighborhoods would still result in schools that were largely black. To achieve truly integrated schools, there would have to be busing between the predominantly black city and the predominantly white suburbs. Under Roth's scheme, a total of 310,000 black and white children over a three-county area would be transported from their school districts to others in order to achieve racial composition in each classroom proportionate to the racial composition of the student population of the metropolitan area as a whole. The outcry against the decision was deafen-ing (figure 4.6). In effect, Roth was using the equal protection clause of the United States Constitution to eradicate the boundaries between the central city and the suburbs and discard not only the concept of the neigh-borhood school but the principle of local self-rule.

FIGURE 4.6
Antibusing demonstra-
tors in Michigan, early
1970s. (Walter P.
Reuther Library, Wayne
State University)

The suburban school districts appealed to the United States Supreme
Court, where attorneys for the NAACP defended Roth's ruling. Speaking
of the central city and suburbs, the NAACP general counsel argued: "They
are bound together by economic interests, recreation interests, social concerns and interests, governmental interests of various sorts, and a transportation network."[89] In other words, socially, economically, and culturally
the metropolitan area was a single entity. Consequently, busing advocates
believed that all its subdivisions should share in the legal remedy proposed
to achieve equal educational opportunity.

In 1974, in *Milliken v. Bradley*, the Supreme Court disagreed, overrul-
ing Roth's draconian scheme by a 5 to 4 vote. Speaking for the five-person
majority, Chief Justice Warren Burger contended: "No single tradition in
public education is more deeply rooted than local control over the opera-

tion of schools." Deferring to this tradition, the Court was not willing to uphold Roth's interdistrict scheme for racial mixing. Burger held that "without an interdistrict violation . . . , there is no constitutional wrong calling for an interdistrict remedy."[90] According to the majority, there was no evidence that the suburban districts had taken any unconstitutional actions to promote racial segregation in the Detroit schools, so Roth could not require them to be part of the remedy for correcting such segregation within the city of Detroit. The lower courts could order busing between black and white neighborhoods within the city of Detroit, but the suburbs could not be forced to be involved. Detroit's segregation problem was legally none of the suburbs' business. They were separate entities; they were not part of the central city's racial problems and thus need not be part of the mandated solution. Burger in effect excused white suburbanites from the hated remedy of busing. Central cities across the nation remained subject to busing orders, but for the most part busing between cities and suburbs was not necessary.

In this decision, the Supreme Court added the Constitution's imprimatur to the destruction of the single-focus, interconnected metropolis. Contrary to the argument of the NAACP counsel, the Detroit metropolitan area was not a single entity bound together socially, its peripheral parts legally responsible for its core. Instead, it was a disparate mass of population in which the outer, predominantly white parts had no responsibility for the predominantly black core. The tradition of local control had trumped the notion of metropolitan interdependence. The periphery could abandon the center and pursue its independent course. In the 1978 *Times* poll, New York suburbanites had not felt part of a single metropolitan area, and neither had they believed that what went on in the central city affected them. *Milliken v. Bradley* was the constitutional equivalent of these findings. What happened in bankrupt New York City or poor, black Detroit need not concern people living, working, and shopping in separate communities twenty-five or thirty miles from decaying central-city downtowns.

The Supreme Court confirmed the suspicions of working-class whites stranded in the central city of Boston. The burden of righting the wrongs of the past were on them, the poorest of the white population; working-class whites in Charlestown were saddled with the white man's busing burden, just as they had been targeted as the victims of the urban renewal crusade. They were the ones chosen to face the bulldozers as well as the buses. Judge Garrity and his neighbors in Wellesley need not be part of the wrenching remedies for America's urban ills. During the 1970s, the central city seemed not only a welfare dumping ground but a convenient dumping ground for America's guilt. Those with money, mainly whites but also some middle-class blacks, could escape. But the less affluent residents of South Boston and Roxbury would have to pay the price for the nation's social ills.

Creating a New Alternative

Confronted by the debacle in the central cities and the monotony of malls and tract houses in the suburbs, some Americans of the 1960s posited the need for a third alternative. They found inspiration for this new option in Europe. Since World War II, the governments of Great Britain and Scandinavia had invested in the creation of "new towns," carefully designed communities in outlying areas to house the growing number of metropolitan residents. Admired by American visitors, these new towns seemed an answer to America's metropolitan dilemma. Through the creation of entire new communities, Americans could supposedly correct the urban flaws resulting from the unplanned development of the past. Rather than segregating rich and poor, white and black, the new cities could embrace social and racial heterogeneity and provide housing and jobs for a diverse and hopefully harmonious population. Moreover, through enlightened planning, the new communities could halt mindless urban sprawl and offer something better than the prevailing pattern of unrelated housing subdivisions and garish commercial strips along traffic-jammed highways. They could also provide adequate open space and recreational facilities and preserve rather than bulldoze the natural beauty of the countryside. And they could foster imaginative modern architecture rather than create additional rows of the banal boxes with neocolonial trim so typical of suburbia. The dream was, then, to apply the ingenuity of planners and architects to the urban dilemma and produce something better than what existed. Urban America had seemingly failed; now was the time to start from scratch and build new cities.

One person who believed that new towns were a viable response to metropolitan ills was Robert E. Simon. In 1961 Simon purchased eleven square miles of undeveloped land in northern Virginia eighteen miles west of Washington, D.C., and began planning a community known as Reston. Its master plan, completed the following year, envisioned a city of

75,000 residents that would include detached single-family homes, town-houses, and apartment buildings as well as industry and retailing. Residents would enjoy a full range of cultural and recreational facilities. In other words, it was not a subdivision; it was intended to be an entire city.

Yet it was to be a carefully planned city quite unlike the aging, troubled metropolises of the eastern United States. Reston was to consist of seven villages, each with a village center featuring shops and recreational facilities. Walking paths were to link the villages, offering an alternative to excessive dependence on the automobile. Aesthetics were important to Simon. He sought to preserve the site's natural topography and woodlands and favored innovative, architect-designed housing. The first village constructed, Lake Anne, was a modernist version of the Italian fishing village of Portofino, complete with apartments and shops enclosing a waterfront piazza. Sailing, golf, horseback riding, swimming, and other forms of recreation were to play a significant role in the lifestyle of the new town. "The main idea," Simon explained, "is that in this age of leisure people should have a wide choice of things to do which are stimulating, pleasurable, exciting, fun."[91]

Reston, however, was not planned to be simply a leisure age retreat for white, upper-middle-class Washingtonians. It was intended to offer housing for low-income families as well as the more affluent. A 1968 editorial from the Reston newspaper expressed the multiclass, multirace vision of the community's pioneers: "Many of us came to Reston believing, at least hoping, that the town was the answer to the urban dilemma our nation faces—that the vast economic gap between the haves and have-nots could somehow be bridged."[92] An early African American resident of Reston summed up the sentiment succinctly: "New towns are the black man's hope."[93]

A similar philosophy underlay the development of Columbia, Maryland, a new town between Baltimore and Washington with a target population of about 100,000. By 1963, shopping-mall entrepreneur James Rouse had assembled fourteen thousand acres of land for this community, which was intended to serve as a model for private developments throughout the nation. "The surest way to make the American city what it ought to be," Rouse observed, "is to demonstrate that it is enormously profitable to do it a better way." Disgusted by the unplanned suburban sprawl that was laying waste to the American landscape, Rouse believed that heretofore the wrong way had prevailed. "Sprawl is ugly, oppressive, massively dull," he complained. "It squanders the resources of nature—

forests, streams, hillsides—and produces vast, monotonous armies of housing and graceless, tasteless clutter." He believed that the sprawl resulting from traditional subdivision development was "inhuman. The vast, formless spread of housing pierced by the unrelated spotting of schools, churches, stores, creates areas so huge and irrational that they are out of scale with people."[94]

Seeking to re-create the human scale that he knew as a boy growing up in a small town on the Eastern Shore of Maryland, Rouse conceived of his new city as a group of distinct villages, each with about twelve thousand residents and a village center consisting of stores, schools, and community facilities. The villages would be organized around an urban downtown, the common focus of this new city. Village life would supposedly nurture an intimacy and fellowship lacking in the sprawling, unplanned metropolis. "A broader range of friendships and relationships occurs in a village or small town than in a city," Rouse believed; "there is a greater sense of responsibility for one's neighbor and a greater sense of support of one's fellow-man." But Columbia was to have the advantages of a city as well as those of a small town. Rouse hoped to attract thirty thousand jobs to the community, thus offering residents a full range of employment opportunities. Moreover, one-fifth of Columbia's area would be devoted to open space, with woodland trails, golf courses, riding stables, lakes, tennis courts, and swimming pools providing unequaled recreational options.[95] Columbia was not to be a residential suburb dependent on a larger city for employment and recreation but a self-sufficient community where one could live, work, and play.

Like Reston, it was also intended to provide a home for all races and social classes. Rouse boasted that the new community would have housing for everybody from the company president to the janitor. Each village was intended to include upper-middle-class, single-family homes as well as subsidized rental apartments for those who could not afford market rates. "Like any real city of 100,000 Columbia will be economically diverse, polycultural, multi-faith and interracial," Rouse declared in 1967.[96] At a time when class and racial differences were ripping apart existing cities, both Columbia and Reston would provide an alternative; they would supposedly breach the social and cultural chasms in the nation and provide models for tolerant, harmonious living.

On the West Coast, the new town of Irvine, California, was also capturing the imagination of Americans who hoped to create a better way of metropolitan life. By the late 1950s, southern California's metropolitan frontier was fast approaching the 120,000-acre Irvine Ranch in Orange County. Rather than opt for piecemeal development of its vast property, the Irvine Company decided to create a planned new community of 100,000 residents on the ranch site. Approved by Orange County authorities in 1964, the master plan for the new town, like those of Reston and Columbia, provided for a city composed of a series of distinct villages. A particular style of architecture and landscaping would distinguish each village. One would be California ranch style, another Mission style, and still another would have a Cape Cod motif. And each would have a village shopping center. As in the eastern new towns, there would be ample recreational facilities for leisure-conscious residents. Planned to be a self-sufficient community Irvine was to be a hub of manufacturing, retailing, and office employment as well as the site of a new branch of the University of California. Less idealistic than Rouse and Simon, the Irvine Company originally was not committed to accommodating lower-income residents in subsidized housing.[97] Yet like its eastern counterparts, the new town of Irvine was a clear departure from the unplanned sprawl that had traditionally characterized American metropolitan development. It was a carefully designed city, not just one more housing subdivision.

As the first structures arose in the new towns during the mid-1960s, it was clear that the dreams of their developers were not identical. Simon was more interested in innovative modernist architecture than was Rouse or the Irvine Company; a vision of small-town fellowship particularly motivated Rouse; and the Irvine Company was more concerned with the ideal, and ultimately lucrative, development of its property than with bridging the nation's racial and class divisions. Yet together, the new towns seemed to promise a better metropolitan future. Through enlightened planning, Americans could perhaps create new cities that righted the wrongs so obvious in Los Angeles, Chicago, and New York.

Three towns alone, however, could not change America. To spread the gospel of Simon and Rouse throughout the nation, new-town advocates turned to the federal government, lobbying Congress for a program that would foster additional communities. The result was a series of measures, the most notable being Title VII of the Housing and Urban Development Act of 1970. This legislation authorized the federal government to guarantee bonds issued by developers to finance new towns that, like Reston and Columbia, were to offer housing for blacks as well as whites and lower-income Americans as well as the middle class. In other words, if the developers defaulted on their bonds, the federal government was obligated to assume the debt payments. The law further permitted the federal government to make direct loans and grants for planning and public facilities to new-town developers. Basically, Title VII was intended to aid private developers willing to take the risk of investing in large-scale, innovative schemes. The bond guarantee would encourage lenders to advance the money necessary for the construction of entire new cities, and the government loans and grants were similarly intended to ease the burden of initiating the ambitious projects.

The legislation stirred considerable interest among private developers, with the Department of Housing and Urban Development receiving almost one hundred applications and preapplications for Title VII assistance from 1970 through 1974. Thirteen projects actually received bond guarantees and embarked on the federally sponsored pursuit for new and better communities.[98] One of the projects, for example, was Jonathan, twenty-five miles southwest of Minneapolis. The dream of a wealthy Minnesota businessman and environmentalist, Jonathan was planned to be a city of fifty thousand residents. Its developers sought to preserve the site's meadows, wooded ravines, and wetlands while also promising "exciting innovations in housing designs and systems." The community experimented with modular "stack units," and one newspaper account described Jonathan as "dotted with striking, unusual houses" (figure 4.7).[99] With both subsidized and market-rate housing, the Minnesota new town attracted what a local pastor called "an amalgamation of a great assortment of people—conservatives, militants, escape artists, chronic transients. It's the closest thing to a cross-section, representative community that I've found, a microcosm of a major city." He claimed, "We range from Ph.D.'s to ex-cons."[100]

Other federally aided new towns also seemed to offer exciting alternatives to the status quo. Shenandoah, thirty-five miles southwest of Atlanta, was designed to be a solar-powered community housing seventy thousand residents. Among its first structures were a community center heated and cooled by solar power and a solar-energy model home.[101] Thirty miles north of Houston, Woodlands was a Title VII new town with a projected population of 150,000 and a special sensitivity to the natural environment. Its development plan promised that "procedures and techniques for land planning, land development, and construction will be established

FIGURE 4.7 Modernistic housing design in Jonathan, Minnesota, 1975. (Steve Plattner, Minnesota Historical Society)

to preserve and enhance the natural surroundings and create a healthful, ecologically sound, aesthetically pleasing community."[102] The Texas new town developed an innovative natural drainage system, winning plaudits from environmentalists. One leading ecologist said of Woodlands: "Builders found that they could love money and trees at the same time."[103]

Initial enthusiasm for the federal new-towns program, however, quickly changed to despair. By the close of 1974, the federal new towns were in serious financial trouble, and in January 1975 the Department of Housing and Urban Development announced that it would not process any further applications for new-town development. Instead, it would devote its resources to salvaging the existing projects. In 1976 the federal government decided to purchase seven of the thirteen faltering new towns and terminated two of the seven as no longer feasible.[104] One of those terminated was Newfields, outside Dayton. Developers had projected that by 1975 there would be 919 housing units in the Ohio new town; in November of that year, only 65 units were actually standing and a mere 25 occupied.[105] A 1976 government report on the new communities said of Newfields that "a market for a new town does not exist" in the Dayton area and noted that the federal government planned to turn the failed town into a residential development of no more than five hundred acres. Similarly, the core area of the defunct new town of Ganada, east of Rochester, New York, was to be developed as "a conventional subdivision."[106]

The data from one community after another was dismal. By late 1976, two and a half years after development began, Shenandoah was far from its goal of 70,000 residents, having a total population of only 7. At the close of 1982, it had risen to 750.[107] Four years after groundbreaking, Maumelle, outside Little Rock, Arkansas, consisted of sixty-five dwelling units, forty-two of which were occupied.[108] In late 1974, Jonathan defaulted on a $468,000 interest payment on its bonds, forcing the federal government to intervene and come up with the sum. At the beginning of 1975, the Minnesota new town was up for sale.[109] No longer were there optimistic projections of a city of 50,000. In late 1976, the Department of Housing and Urban Development was predicting that Jonathan's population "could increase to 5,000 in 5 years and to 15,000 in 20 years." It failed to reach these figures; six years later, at the end of 1982, it had an estimated 3,125 residents.[110]

Even the highly vaunted new towns of Reston and Columbia were not proving to be ideal investments. As early as 1967, Gulf Oil Company, Reston's chief financial backer, took control of the community away from Robert Simon because of fears that the new-town project was approaching bankruptcy. Although the Virginia community's financial prospects improved during the late 1960s and early 1970s, in 1975 the *Washington Post* reported that Reston was "still losing money daily."[111] In January 1975, James Rouse was forced to negotiate emergency refinancing of Columbia owing to what he described as "the precipitous collapse of the real estate industry." Columbia land sales plummeted from an average of $24 million a year in 1971 through 1973 to only $6.5 million in 1974.[112] Compelled to cut expenses, Rouse also laid off approximately half his employees. Through the 1970s, Reston and Columbia continued to grow in population, but not at the rate originally projected.

Unfavorable economic conditions were partially responsible for the crisis in new-town development. During the years 1973 to 1975, a combination of economic recession, record-high interest rates, and double-digit inflation meant that few Americans were in the market for houses and that the price of borrowing and building was soaring. In other words, developers' expenses were rising at the same time their revenues were diminishing. Yet in its analysis of the troubled Title VII program, the De-

partment of Housing and Urban Development contended that the economy was not wholly to blame for the new-town fiasco. "While adverse economic conditions exacerbated the program's difficulties," the department
noted, "these difficulties would have occurred in any event" owing to de-
fects in Title VII itself and to the administration of the new community
initiative. Because of the federal bond guarantee mechanism, developers
incurred excessive initial debt; moreover, they "did not receive Federal
grants of the types and amounts necessary to offset" this burden.[113] In addition, the Department of Housing and Urban Development did not have
adequate staffing or the necessary expertise to implement a successful
program. Repeated complaints by developers about administrative delays
and red tape seemed to support the latter conclusion. Overall, the federal
government, and state and local governments as well, needed to commit
itself more fully to promoting the innovative developments if Americans
were actually to enjoy the benefits of new-town living. America could not
create model cities on the cheap.

Yet there was another problem that new-town advocates were reluctant
to confront. Perhaps Americans were not all too eager to embrace life in a
new town. Slow sales not only reflected the shortcomings of the federal
government and the developers but also testified to a lack of interest
among home buyers. Commenting on Jonathan's unimpressive growth, a
former marketing director noted that architectural innovation had little
sales appeal in a metropolitan area where "95 per cent of the people want
traditional housing."[114] A University of North Carolina study of resident
attitudes in new towns concluded that "people may have moved to
Jonathan in spite of its housing, since it was not viewed by many residents
as a key aspect of the community's appeal" and postulated that "the character of housing" in the new town might have accounted "for the very slow
sales pace."[115] Similarly, the idea of economic and racial diversity did not
appeal to many perspective residents. Concluding that Shenandoah "suffered from a marketing problem," a study found that "county officials and
residents . . . perceive[d] it to be a 'low-income project,' since almost one-
half of its units constitute some form of assisted housing." In 1979 a
marketing report on Park Forest South, a federal new town outside
Chicago, found that the community had a poor reputation among white,
middle-class home seekers in part because of "the involvement of the
federal government" and "a growing minority presence among the project's residents."[116] The Irvine Company had originally not included low-

income housing in its plans, and later attempts to accommodate the less affluent were not appreciated by many of the new town's residents. In 1974 the mayor of Irvine explained her constituents' aversion to low- and moderate-income housing: "The quality of life in our community began as a concern for the environment, for saving the eucalyptus trees. Now it means exclusion of blacks and chicanos."[117]

In other words, the dreams of Robert Simon and James Rouse did not necessarily coincide with those of the average home buyer. Planners and professors might inveigh against sprawl, strip malls, and the ubiquitous golden arches of McDonalds, but sales figures demonstrated that a big yard, a big parking lot, and a Big Mac appealed to millions of Americans. Conventional subdivisions proved quite satisfactory to most Americans; consequently, there was no particular reason for them to flock to new towns. Moreover, many middle-class whites were adverse to risking their investment in a new home by settling in a community that included low-income blacks and public housing. Economic and racial integration might be a socially desirable goal, but when a family was making the largest investment of its life, safety seemed more important than social reform. Similarly, an investment in a solid neocolonial manse with conventional heating and cooling seemed much wiser than sinking one's money into stack modules or solar-energy experiments. Idealistic multimillionaire developers and the federal government might be able to afford philanthropic reforms and daring experiments; the average home owner could not. Woodlands, the one Title VII community ultimately deemed a success, turned itself around not through ecological experiments or social class mixing but by attracting the Houston Open golf tournament to its freshly sodded links.[118] In the America of the 1970s, golf could win more home buyers than could good deeds.

By 1975, then, the old central cities appeared to be going down the drain, and the idealistic option of creating new cities was being jettisoned. The traditional single-focus metropolis with its powerful downtown hub had largely disappeared, yet Americans did not seem too eager to accept the carefully planned communities of James Rouse or Robert Simon as a substitute. Instead, an amorphous suburbia was prevailing. This sprawling, unfocused mass, exempted by the Supreme Court from responsibility for the nation's racial ills, was becoming the American norm.

5   The New Metropolitan World

Each week, the opening credits of the 1970s *Mary Tyler Moore Show* depicted young, single, attractive Mary Richards driving into Minneapolis to apartment life in a converted Victorian house and a downtown, white-collar career. Mary ended her journey in the very heart of downtown Minneapolis, where she exultantly tossed up her hat as the accompanying theme song promised that she was going "to make it after all." In the mid-1950s, the married mother Lucy Ricardo had left her Manhattan brownstone for a home in suburban Connecticut; now in the 1970s, Mary Richards was coming back to the city to find fulfillment. Television was not life, but the return of situation comedy to the city as represented by Mary's triumphant arrival reflected an underlying cultural shift in metropolitan life during the 1970s and 1980s. Just when America's central cities seemed irretrievably doomed, there were signs of new life in their moribund bodies. Like Mary Richards many young, single, white-collar Americans were moving into old houses in the central cities and finding that the core promised opportunities not available in the suburbs. Moreover, with them came the dollars of consumers and developers. The central city was not dead; it might just make it after all.

During the late 1970s and the 1980s, urban observers were eager to proclaim the supposed resurrection of the central cities. In 1977 *U.S.*

News & World Report published an account headed "Why More and More People Are Coming Back to Cities."[1] The following year, *Saturday Review* fueled the upbeat mood with its article "America Falls in Love with Its Cities—Again," which told of a "monumental renaissance that has given new life to cities like Cincinnati, Minneapolis, Detroit, Hartford, Atlanta, Birmingham, and a dozen other cities."[2] Meanwhile, *Harper's* printed "The Urban Crisis Leaves Town."[3] In January 1979, *Newsweek* cautiously titled its announcement of the urban renaissance "A City Revival?" but the opening lines of the article expressed less doubt about the rebirth. "There is a new hope abroad in the cities," the news magazine reported, "a sense that the older cities of the Northeast and Midwest are staging a Big Comeback from the urban crisis of the 1960s."[4] By the mid-1980s, a planning journal was characterizing Saint Louis as "Comeback City," a former deputy mayor was telling readers of the *New York Times Magazine* "The Good News About New York City," and the leading scholarly journal in urban studies was publishing a symposium titled "Whatever Happened to the Urban Crisis?"[5] Journalists, planners, public officials, and scholars all seemed to believe that America's cities had turned the corner. They were no longer headed for oblivion but seemingly on the course to new life.

This shift in direction, however, did not mark the beginning of a new era of metropolitan recentralization. During the late 1970s and the 1980s, Americans did not fashion new bonds between the core and the fringe and re-create the interconnected, single-focus metropolis that existed at the close of World War II. Instead, central cities pursued a different path to profitability. They sought to carve a distinctive market niche that would distinguish them from suburban competitors. The central city would not advance by asserting itself as the hub of all metropolitan life, the focus of all retailing, entertainment, business, and government. It would sell itself as offering an "urban" way of life different from the prevailing suburban norm, a lifestyle that would appeal to young, childless professionals, tourists, and convention goers. Attempts to reestablish past supremacy seemed increasingly futile, but efforts to offer a distinctive way of life attractive to a certain market segment of Americans could reap profits. Thus the older central cities could prove their viability by selling a product not to be found in suburbia. They were no longer the mecca for most Americans, but urban boosters hoped a sizable number might join Mary Richards in her pilgrimage to the core.

Meanwhile, the metropolitan fringe headed off on its own. The long-standing trend toward decentralization continued, if not accelerated, as a growing number of Americans spent their entire lives outside the urban hub, sleeping, working, and playing in the spreading, amorphous mass of development that bore little resemblance to the traditional city and was a world apart from the core. Impressive new commercial centers appeared, stirring excitement among commentators, who labeled them "edge cities." These collections of office buildings, malls, and hotels were deemed the centers of the future. Yet in mobile suburbia, there was no real center. Auto-borne Americans could and did head in every direction and no longer needed to focus on any one center or hub, whether urban or suburban.

By the close of the 1980s, metropolitan America was a sprawling mass offering a lifestyle smorgasbord. In the central city were charming recreations of an imagined past; in edge cities were glittering malls and glistening high-rises, portents of an imagined future. Metropolitan areas offered a variety of lifestyle entrées to suit the tastes and predilections of a broad range of Americans. Some were following Mary Richards, taking the centripetal journey to the historic hub; more were trying to make it along the fringe. By the late 1980s, metropolitan America offered it all.

Back to the City

Underlying the new optimism about the urban core was a much publicized back-to-the-city movement. After decades of outward migration to suburbia, the white middle class seemed to be headed back to the old neighborhoods, where they were investing in real estate and renovating aging structures that until recently appeared destined for abandonment. This return of the white middle class became know as gentrification; the gentry were reclaiming down-at-the-heels neighborhoods and making them upscale. Especially prevalent among the gentrifiers were young, upwardly mobile professionals, the so-called Yuppies. Young, confident, childless whites found the crime and inferior schooling of the central cities less threatening than did families with children to protect and educate. Moreover, they were not dependent on a suburban McDonalds to satisfy their screaming youngsters' demands for Happy Meals. Suburbia had always been deemed a good place to raise children, a safe, wholesome environment with ample play space and quality schools. Suburbia also offered blue-chip homes, safe investments for those seeking to build up the equity that might be necessary to put offspring through college or later secure a place in a retirement community. For those who were young, venturesome, and childless, however, these suburban advantages were less appealing. Many of them were ready to take the chance on inner-city neighborhoods where they could join other Yuppies and escape the child-oriented, fast-food, mall life of the fringe. If they worked in the central-city downtown, inner-city residence offered an added attraction. It meant a shorter commute and fewer hours trapped in an automobile inching through rush-hour traffic.

By the late 1970s and 1980s, this Yuppie market segment of American society was growing at an unequaled pace. The huge population of baby boomers who as children had been so ubiquitous in Levittown, Park Forest, and Lakewood was coming of age and in the market for an exciting new lifestyle. From 1975 to 1982, the number of young adults in the twenty-five to forty-four age category increased by more than 13 million, constituting 73 percent of the nation's population growth during those years. By comparison, the number of Americans under twenty-four years old grew by only 2 million.[6] Children were no longer ever present, and birth rates had declined; the rate for whites in 1982 was only 14.9 per 1,000 population, as compared with 23.8 per 1,000 in 1955, during the baby boom. Consequently, family size was contracting. Between 1970 and 1982, the number of households with only one or two persons increased almost threefold and accounted for 55 percent of the nation's households by the early 1980s.[7] In other words, the number of Americans who needed a multibedroom house in suburbia with yard space for a swing set and access to good education was not increasing as rapidly as was the population of young, childless individuals who were more likely to know the location of singles bars than schools.

Another factor encouraging gentrification was the increase in white-collar jobs in the central cities. Manufacturing employment continued to plummet as blue-collar jobs moved to the suburbs, to smaller communities in the South, or out of the country or simply yielded to automation. Between 1977 and 1987, New York City lost 232,000 manufacturing jobs. Yet New York's overall private-sector employment rose 342,000, with the finance and business services category making up 70 percent of the increase. Employment doubled in the securities industry as Wall Street boomed while the city's factories closed.[8] In Boston between 1976 and 1985, the number of jobs in professional services rose 62 percent; in business services, 55 percent; and in the finance/insurance/real-estate sector, 32 percent. During the same period, manufacturing employment in New

England's hub city was down 21 percent.[9] The number of young white-collar men and women employed in the central city was rising markedly, and the old blue-collar base was disappearing. The Yuppies were on the rise; the working class was in decline.

The rising white-collar class and the developers serving them also benefited from federal tax incentives that spurred the rehabilitation of old inner-city structures. The tax acts of both 1976 and 1981 allowed handsome tax credits for rehabilitating historic buildings. For many Americans seeking to escape the heavy burden of federal income taxes, this was a welcome invitation to invest in the aging core and upgrade structures for the expanding Yuppie population.

Although the impact of urban rehabilitation efforts was not uniform throughout the nation, a number of cities experienced reinvestment in old neighborhoods. One of the hot spots for gentrification was Washington, D.C., with its large population of white-collar government employees and its army of professionals in law firms dealing with federal agencies. In the city's Adams Morgan district, young, relatively affluent whites took up residence; consequently, all three of the area's census tracts showed a "whitening" of the population between 1970 and 1980. The average sales price for single-family houses in Adams Morgan soared from $34,512 in 1973 to $123,362 in 1979; the area's rate of increase was 70 percent greater than the rate of increase for home prices in Washington as a whole. "They're asking ridiculous prices," observed a longtime resident as early as 1975. "You have a vacant house and they grab it like wildfire."[10] Other Washington neighborhoods were also feeling the impact of gentrification. "Four years ago, the only places in Washington where white people were willing to buy older homes and renovate were Georgetown and Capitol Hill," commented a local contractor in 1977. "Now, it seems to be happening all over."[11] Expressing the euphoria of real-estate interests, in 1979 one Washington realtor noted with some exaggeration: "There is no longer any area in the city where you can drive for five blocks and see continuous slums."[12]

To the north, in Philadelphia, Queen Village was an emerging favorite of Yuppie rehabilitators. Located just to the south of the central business district, the formerly working-class neighborhood of aging row houses was suddenly becoming upscale. In the two census tracts wholly within Queen Village, the proportion of the population that was black fell from 45 to 21 percent between 1970 and 1980; the share of adult residents with college degrees soared from 4 to 41 percent; and the number having professional or managerial occupations rose from 11 to 44 percent.[13] In 1979 a resident of Queen Village described the transformation: "This used to be an old-fashioned neighborhood; now it's a playground for professionals."[14] By 1980, Queen Village could boast of forty-three restaurants and bars catering to well-heeled Yuppies, twenty-two of these having opened in the short period between 1977 and 1979.[15]

The mecca for back-to-the-city Yuppies in Chicago was the Lincoln Park/Lake View East district. "Everywhere in the Lincoln Park/Lake View East area is evidence of a growing interest in rehabbing and revitalizing diverse housing stock that ranges from ornate, picturesque Victorian stone and frame houses to two-, three- and six-flats, to brownstones and graystones," reported the *Chicago Tribune* in 1984. One of the commercial streets was "booming with shops catering to young professionals," and "areas that once suffered from urban blight, poverty and gang troubles now see a lack of parking as a big headache." Lincoln Park/Lake View East was the type of area where one could patronize gift shops with names like Pass The Salt & Pepper and enjoy the fare at Mama Desta Red Sea, Chicago's first Ethiopian restaurant.[16] By 1980, the median value of owner-occupied houses in Lincoln Park had risen to $123,700, as compared with the citywide median of $47,200.[17] Typical of the residential offerings in the area was a complex of rental units "with hardwood floors, fireplaces, modern kitchens and exposed brick walls" that, according to a spokesperson for the owner, was on an "attractive tree-lined street near trendy boutiques and theaters." Recognizing the targeted market for her property, she concluded, "It's a vibrant area for young professionals."[18]

Across the country in one city after another, older neighborhoods were becoming trendy and attracting Yuppie dollars. Old Louisville was the principal example of gentrification and rehabilitation in Kentucky's largest city. In 1970 all four of the district's census tracts had median family incomes well below the citywide median; by 1980, the median family incomes in three of the four tracts had risen well above the citywide figure.[19] In Saint Louis, the elegant nineteenth-century Lafayette Square neighborhood won acclaim for its successful rehabilitation. "The Lafayette Square of the 1980s barely resembles the run-down neighborhood of the 1960s, in which shabby Victorian houses overlooked a block-sized park full of overgrown vegetation and rusting, rotting furniture and fences," reported one observer. "Today, virtually every house has been restored to its former stately appearance while a few continue to be wrapped in scaffolding."[20] Meanwhile, in Seattle the Capitol Hill and Madrona neighborhoods were attracting the attention of gentrifiers. A 1978 study found that more than three-quarters of the newcomers to Madrona were professionals, whereas less than one-third of those moving out of the neighborhood had professional occupations. Complaints of "white reinvasion" and white block-busting were heard in areas of Madrona that in earlier years had become predominantly black.[21]

Often the gentrifying neighborhoods did not shift directly from working-class black or white to upper-middle-class professional. In many cases, a bohemian phase of settlement by hippies and artists preceded the transformation to a Yuppie haven. For those escaping the alternative of life in suburbia, a counterculture reputation was not necessarily repulsive and frequently proved attractive. Such neighborhoods did not represent the family-oriented norm of the suburbs; instead, they seemed to promise an offbeat flavor enticing to many young, childless professionals. Moreover, artistic creation lent a touch of class to an area, no matter how poor the resident artists. At the beginning of its gentrification cycle, Seattle's Capitol Hill district had, in the words of one observer, "developed a widely held image as a lower-class 'Bohemian' neighborhood where all types of behavior were observed and for the most part tolerated."[22] During the early 1970s, anti–Vietnam War activists had pioneered the resettlement of Adams Morgan in Washington, D.C.; the leading student of that neighborhood described its progressive gentrification as a shift from "counter culture" to "quiche culture."[23] Lincoln Park's Wells Street had once been the center of Chicago hippiedom. "Barefoot, long-haired young people gathered there, crowding into its coffeehouses and folk music cafes," reported the *Chicago Tribune*.[24] In addition, the North Side area was the home of the city's experimental theater companies, and its Old Town Art Fair earned Lincoln Park a reputation as a creative environment.

The most notable example of artist-induced revitalization was the transformation of SoHo in Lower Manhattan. A district of aging manufacturing lofts, in the 1960s SoHo began to attract an increasing number of artists who sought large work spaces and cheap rents. In 1968 SoHo's first commercial art gallery opened for business, and during the 1970s the area became the center for artistic creation in New York. Moreover, it had growing appeal for those who sought to share in the district's bohemian, although increasingly upscale, lifestyle. In 1974 *Art News* published an article titled "SoHo: Brave New Bohemia," and *New York Magazine* declared SoHo "the most exciting place to live in the city." A number of manufacturing concerns remained in the neighborhood, but by 1977 there had been some residential conversion in 55 percent of all SoHo loft buildings. Transforming large manufacturing spaces into apartments became all the rage, even among people who had never held an artist's paintbrush. In 1977 *Apartment Life* magazine asked its readers, "Loft Living: Can You Make It on the Urban Frontier?"[25] If one wanted to secure a place in the fashionable vanguard of urban life, be a trendsetter rather than a follower, loft conversion was the course to pursue. Loft seekers soon pioneered conversions in the nearby Manhattan neighborhoods of Tribeca and NoHo, and throughout the country the transformation of old warehouses and factories into upscale apartments attracted the dollars of urban rehabilitators. By 1980, SoHo had clearly arrived and was a model for other aspiring neighborhoods. That year, an article in *Art News* characterized it as "still funky but oh so chic SoHo," a district transformed "from a dark Dickensian industrial area to one of chic restaurants and boutiques."[26]

As SoHo gained artistic renown, it attracted a growing number of tourists. Published in 1978, a 274-page guidebook to the district opened with the breathless statement: "You are now about to enter SoHo, one of the most exciting 'new' neighborhoods in New York City." Included in its pages was a directory of sixty-five SoHo boutiques and shops, eighty-five art galleries, and twenty-five restaurants.[27] Some high-minded critics rebelled at the invasion of tourists into this sanctum of art. In 1978 one such disenchanted observer wrote an essay titled "SoHo: Disneyland of the Aesthete?" in which he claimed that the district offered "too much in the way of 'fun boutiques,' 'interesting restaurants,' and 'unusual nightspots" to raise any questions about value in art."[28]

America's West Coast provided the best example of the shift from hippie domain to gentrified enclave. In the late 1960s, San Francisco's Haight-Ashbury district was the capital of the hippie world, its "Summer of Love" in 1967 attracting tens of thousands of young people seeking a psychedelic high. Although still a counterculture icon, the area deteriorated into a heroin ghetto by the early 1970s. During the 1970s, however, its avant-garde reputation, together with its supply of affordable housing convenient to downtown, attracted a new population of venturesome young white professionals. By 1978, the *Wall Street Journal* was able to report that the former hippie magnet was turning "into a bastion of the middle class." In 1970 the average price of houses in Haight-Ashbury was $33,000, 8 percent above the citywide median; ten years later, it was more than $150,000, 44 percent over San Francisco's median. In 1970 the district was 33 percent black; in 1980 blacks constituted only 20 percent of

Haight-Ashbury's population. One resident reminisced: "When I bought my house in Upper Ashbury from a black family in 1970, there was a hippie commune living in the other unit of the building. . . . There were a lot of families with kids around then, and a lot of blacks." But by 1980, he claimed there were "hardly any" blacks or children left. "My street has been bought mainly by young white professionals."[29]

Such marked changes did not appeal to everyone, and during the late 1970s and the 1980s many felt threatened by the white Yuppie invaders. The newcomers ushered in a wave of redevelopment that seemed destined to erase the indigenous lifestyles of the counterculture devotees or the working-class residents who had formerly claimed the neighborhood as their own. In 1978 a McDonald's opened on the main street of Haight-Ashbury, and in 1986 a Gap clothing store joined it, marking the triumph of the mainstream middle class over those who had rejected the homogeneous, conformist culture of chain stores.[30] Similarly, Yuppie bars supplanted working-class taverns in neighborhoods that had traditionally provided comfortable refuges for blue-collar families. Moreover, rising real-estate values meant increased rents and soaring property tax assessments that counterculture habitués and working-class residents could not afford. Gentrification seemed to spell displacement for many incumbent residents of rehabilitated neighborhoods. And fear of displacement stirred protests.

The complaints were heard in cities across the nation. In Philadelphia, a former Queen Village resident expressed the impending threat from well-heeled newcomers: "We are at their mercy. . . . They have the money. I just hope that they don't do us in." A black clergyman commented on the displacement of his Queen Village parishioners: "The process looks to me inexorable. Money follows money—and it's just eating the neighborhoods alive!"[31] In Seattle's Capitol Hill district, opponents of gentrification took action, throwing balloons filled with red paint against the white walls of a chic neighborhood restaurant. In a letter to the restaurant's owners, they expressed their antagonism to gentrifiers: "Good morning, Fat Cats. The paint on your establishment is a protest against your rich white intrusion into this poor, multi-racial community of Capitol Hill."[32]

Throughout the 1980s and into the early 1990s, gentrification sparked sporadic battles between longtime residents and newcomers. In 1990, for example, blacks were fighting whites over the designation of the Church Hill neighborhood in Richmond, Virginia, as a historic district. Working-class black residents believed that historic status would raise property values and consequently property taxes and accelerate the pace of white gentrification in the community. They also recognized that it would impose the rehabilitators' aesthetic judgment on them. Exterior changes that did not conform to the rehabilitators' notion of "historic" would not be allowed. Aluminum siding and shiny metal screen doors would not be welcome; the white newcomers' taste for wood surfaces would prevail. "Leave us alone," complained one African American woman. "If you want restrictions for yourself, fine, but don't impose them on me." Another black resident claimed the historic-district designation would "rob us of our homes and our community." Speaking of a purported conspiracy by real-estate interests to displace black residents, he warned, "There is a plan, and it's long-term." An observer summed up the racial reality of the issue: "Most of the people who are adversely affected by the district are black, most of the people who are for it are white."[33]

Many of those threatened by displacement sought protection from policy makers. For example, in 1985 Jersey City voters threatened by an increasing population of well-heeled professionals ousted the incumbent progentrification mayor and elected in his stead a candidate dedicated to "balanced development" and protection for low- and moderate-rent tenants.[34] The following year, the leader of the antigentrification effort in Baltimore's Upper Fells Point neighborhood testified before a congressional committee, appealing for protection from displacement. A lifelong resident of the mostly Polish and Ukrainian working-class area, she complained that rising tax assessments would prevent blue-collar offspring from remaining in the neighborhood. "I went and hollered about my assessment," she explained, and the assessor "told me right to my face: My child can't live in that house after I'm gone." She told the *Baltimore Sun*: "I'll be damned if somebody is going to throw me out of here with high taxes."[35] Meanwhile, in 1988 Chicago manufacturers secured passage of a planned manufacturing-district ordinance that would keep most nonindustrial commercial development as well as residences out of designated factory zones and thereby halt the displacement of industry by loft-hungry developers seeking to create a Midwest version of SoHo. In the words of one planning journal article, this was a means for "protecting industry from Yuppies and other invaders."[36]

Perhaps the most publicized and bitterest conflict over gentrification occurred in New York City's East Village. An aging tenement district, this Lower Manhattan neighborhood experienced a wave of abandonment in the 1970s as landlords no longer found the buildings worth maintaining.

In the late 1970s, however, counterculture artists began moving into the remaining low-rent structures, and during the first half of the 1980s the East Village emerged as the hub of New York's radical art scene. By 1984, there were over seventy commercial galleries in a fourteen-block area. Formerly denounced for defacing the city's walls and subways, graffiti became an art form in the East Village, as did assemblages made of junk and spare parts rescued from vacant lots. The East Village was the latest manifestation of Manhattan bohemia; one art critic described it as "a neighborhood that encourages one to be the person he is with greater ease than other parts of the city." With art came middle-class whites and the developers eager to accommodate them. In 1985 a Citibank executive expressed the prevailing business sentiment regarding the East Village: "This can't be a slum forever. . . . I know what young professionals are thinking. This could be another SoHo."[37]

These, however, were fighting words. Faced with possible displacement, many of the remaining low-income residents, squatters in the abandoned tenements, and neighborhood radicals in general rallied against the Yuppie invasion. "Die Yuppie Scum" appeared on buildings and sidewalks in the neighborhood. In 1982 protesters marched from the East Village to City Hall Park, where a crowd of more than two thousand demonstrated against the city's support for gentrification and burned the mayor in effigy.[38]

Tension persisted throughout the 1980s and peaked in August 1988, when the police attempted to enforce a curfew and evict homeless squatters and other "undesirables" from Tompkins Square Park in the heart of the East Village. They met resistance from what one author has described as "alarmed and outraged punks, post-hippies, [and] housing activists" who carried banners reading "Gentrification Is Class War" and chanted, "It's our fucking park, you don't live here!" Forty-four people were injured in the fray, casualties of a cultural clash that was evident, although less boisterous, in many American cities.[39]

Despite the shouts and complaints, gentrification proceeded, especially in cities with strong downtown office sectors staffed by well-paid young employees eager to avoid the commute to suburbia. It was especially significant in Boston, New York City, and San Francisco; it was hardly evident in the decaying industrial cities of Detroit and Cleveland. And in freshly minted cities like Phoenix and Las Vegas, there were few old structures to lure rehabilitators. A glance at population and income statistics would reveal that gentrification did not radically shift the overall course of American urban development. In most of the older central cities of the Northeast and Midwest, as well in the southern cities of Richmond, Norfolk, Atlanta, Birmingham, and New Orleans, the population continued to decline. Moreover, the percentage of city dwellers living in poverty continued to rise. Gentrification transformed select neighborhoods; it did not produce a citywide return of the middle class. Where it existed, however, gentrification marked a noteworthy stage in metropolitan development. Central cities were profiting from their age, the one characteristic that the suburbs could not match. The aged hubs might have been relics from the past, but smart developers realized that they could market such relics.

Moreover, rehabilitators could target a growing clientele that cared little about the quality of schools or a child-friendly environment but preferred an avant-garde edginess and ready access to the increasing number of downtown white-collar jobs. Brokerage firms, corporate law offices, and advertising and accounting giants were the growth industries, and their employees were edging aside the working-class Poles and Ukrainians of Upper Fells Point, the "post-hippies" and squatters of the East Village, and the artists who could no longer afford a loft once gentrification had transformed a neighborhood. Tight-knit working-class neighborhoods were endangered as central-city factories shut down and the population of Yuppies increased. No longer the preeminent focus of metropolitan endeavor, older central cities could successfully cultivate a market niche and draw some portion of America's affluent populace. But in the process, those who could not afford upscale rents or taxes might have to relinquish their claim on a share of the city.

The emphasis on historic rehabilitation and the bygone charm of urban living was also evident in some much publicized downtown commercial projects. In the 1960s, San Francisco's Ghirardelli Square demonstrated the potential for recycling old, discarded inner-city structures (figure 5.1). A collection of former factory buildings, it was transformed into a complex of seventy-five shops and restaurants attracting consumer dollars, especially those of tourists.[40] Not until the late 1970s, however, did a growing interest in historic rehabilitation combine with a new vision for revitalizing the central cities to spawn a number of marketplaces similar to the San Francisco model. Known as festival marketplaces, these projects eschewed the traditional suburban-mall model of dozens of chain stores anchored by two or three big department stores. Instead, like old-fashioned city markets, they accommodated small retail stalls as well as

FIGURE 5.1 Ghirardelli Square enlivened the nighttime scene in central San Francisco. (San Francisco History Center, San Francisco Public Library)

pushcarts. They sold a colorful array of wares in an atmosphere intended to make shopping not simply a mundane chore but a festive occasion. Contributing to the festival atmosphere were mimes, balloon sellers, strolling musicians, and jugglers, the very type of off-beat characters generally not found in the more staid environment of the suburban mall. The chief developer of festival marketplaces was James Rouse, the creator of the new town of Columbia, Maryland. "There's a yearning for life at the heart of the city—a yearning for active places with personality and human scale," Rouse contended.[41] And through his festival marketplaces, he sought to give Americans a new urban heart and infuse the core with an upbeat personality.

The most notable of the festival marketplaces, and the one every city wanted to replicate, was Boston's Faneuil Hall Marketplace. Although the marketplace was named for adjacent Faneuil Hall, a historic site of eighteenth-century Revolutionary agitation, its centerpiece was Quincy Market, a handsome Greek Revival structure completed in 1826 (figure 5.2). After 150 years of accommodating butchers and produce stalls, Quincy Market had become an obsolete relic seemingly inappropriate to

FIGURE 5.2   Quincy Market at Faneuil Hall Marketplace, Boston. (Library of Congress)

the slick new corporate center of Boston. In the early 1970s, however, Rouse teamed with architect Benjamin Thompson to bring life back to Quincy Market and some old-fashioned human scale back to downtown Boston. According to Thompson, the new marketplace "would be carefully laid out as a downtown bazaar, to gain the variety, color, balance and constant change that is missing from today's piecemeal development of inner cities." The emphasis would be "on provision of fresh foods, meats, seafood, baked goods and delicacies to serve area residents on a daily basis." Moreover, Thompson envisioned an "intense chaotic mix" of small retailers "with a colorful diversity of life and events competing on a day-to-day basis." The architect believed that the Boston marketplace had a "chance of regaining that genuine character of a city center" with "variety and abundance" and "the communal security of personal contact and mutual exchange." Thompson argued that people "hunger for the festive activity and action that markets add to the central city," and he sought to satisfy this hunger.[42]

When Faneuil Hall Marketplace opened in August 1976, Thompson and Rouse seemed to have succeeded beyond all expectation. An estimated 100,000 people turned out for the event, and in 1978 *Fortune* magazine reported that the marketplace "attracted a phenomenal 10 million visitors annually, about as many as visit Disneyland in California."[43] In the *New York Times Magazine*, one devotee of the marketplace described it as "lavish with heaped fruit, vegetables, meat, flowers and baskets, a sensuous still life reminiscent of Les Halles, Campo dei Fiori in Rome, and innumerable other traditional marketplaces throughout the world." More important, she noted that "people are back on the scene, in crowds that are, if anything, too enthusiastic."[44] In 1978 another commentator described Quincy Market as "a mass of throbbing humanity" that had "turned downtown Boston into *the* place to be."[45] By 1980, the architecture critic of the *Washington Post* was declaring Faneuil Hall Marketplace "a triumph and turning point in the life of great American cities." He reported that "millions from all over the Boston region are drawn to its more than 150 restaurants, food stalls and retail shops set in a festive atmosphere that is at once 'quaint' and modern and on both counts refreshingly genuine." It was "a continuous festival with all kinds of people enjoying their freedom from cellophane and Muzak, in which most of America's joy and nourishments are wrapped."[46]

The Thompson–Rouse team was to repeat its success with Harborplace in downtown Baltimore. The waterfront along Baltimore's Inner Harbor had been cleared years before, so there was no historic structure to transform into a marketplace. Instead, Thompson designed two waterside pavilions that resemble in form and scale wharf buildings but were intended to house 140 food stalls, specialty shops, and eateries. Police estimated that 400,000 people crowded into the market area on opening day in July 1980; during its first year, Harborplace welcomed 18 million visitors and boasted sales figures more than double the receipts of a typical regional mall.[47] On opening day, one local resident admitted that she formerly "was embarrassed to say I was from Baltimore. It was so zero here." But now she proclaimed: "Baltimore has become a place[;] it's a place people wouldn't ignore."[48] *Time* did not ignore it. "From early morning until well past midnight," the magazine reported, "natives and tourists by the thousands turn Baltimore's Inner Harbor into a continuous celebration: milling on the promenades, perching on the bulkheads, dangling feet in the drink, flirting on the benches, lounging in the outdoor cafes, ogling, jogging, strolling, munching, sipping, savoring the sounds and sweet airs."[49] The old waterfront of Baltimore was no longer a deserted reminder of the city's decline; it was a magnet for the strolling, lolling, shopping populace.

Following the triumph first in Boston and then in Baltimore, cities across the country were clamoring for help from the Rouse–Thompson team. As early as 1978, Thompson's wife and architectural associate remarked: "Every city in America must have called us and said, 'We have the place.'"[50] On taking office in 1978, Mayor Edward Koch of New York, bent on restoring his city's economic health, visited Faneuil Hall Marketplace and told Rouse, "I want one of those for New York."[51] Rouse and Thompson obliged, developing South Street Seaport along the East River in Lower Manhattan, the first stage of which opened in 1983. A mix of historic and newly constructed buildings, South Street Seaport was intended to capture the maritime spirit of old-time New York and proved a popular lunch-hour destination for nearby Wall Street workers as well as a magnet for tourists.[52] In 1983 Rouse also opened Waterside in Norfolk, Virginia, a festival marketplace that, according to one planner, "quickly ascended into the retailing stratosphere."[53] The Rouse interests then proceeded to develop Sixth Street Marketplace in Richmond, Virginia; Water Street Pavilion in Flint, Michigan; and Portside in Toledo, Ohio. In Saint Louis, the Rouse Company took on the redevelopment of the city's giant, late-nineteenth-century Union Station. Within the abandoned railroad depot, the company created a two-level mall for shopping and eating together with a beer garden, a one-acre lake, and a 550-room hotel.

The Rouse Company closed the 1980s by assuming management of Underground Atlanta, the Georgia capital's bid for a downtown festive spirit. An area of old commercial buildings beneath the city's railroad viaducts, Underground Atlanta had flourished for a time in the 1970s as a gas-lighted collection of bars and shops. A reputation for crime, however, had led to its closing in the early 1980s. Atlanta's mayor, Andrew Young, was dedicated to reopening the historic district, and many Atlantans felt action was necessary, especially after travel writer Arthur Frommer had described their city after dark as "a graveyard, a scene of death and desolation, a nullity as far as the life, culture and camaraderie present in numerous other cities." After an investment of $142 million and under the management of the Rouse Company, the reconstructed district of twenty-two clubs and restaurants and nearly one hundred shops reopened in 1989. Signs and brochures advertising the event read: "The Fun's Back in Town!" Recognizing the need "to create something attractive enough that will draw people from the suburbs to the city," a Rouse Company executive claimed to have "put together something so dazzling it separates itself from any other experience in Atlanta."[54]

Without the aid of Rouse and his company, other cities were proceeding with commercial rehabilitation of old buildings and districts, although not necessarily in the form of festival marketplaces. In Denver, the renovation of aging commercial structures in Larimer Square sparked a new appreciation of historic buildings that led to the rehabilitation of the lower downtown district, known as LoDo. LoDo was to become an area of trendy lofts for downtown living and popular bars and restaurants that attracted nighttime crowds to the city's core. Beginning in the mid-1960s, Seattle's late-nineteenth-century business center, Pioneer Square, underwent a transformation, shedding its past reputation as the preeminent skid row of the Northwest and becoming by the 1980s a tourist destination. The pride of Seattle's historic preservationists, however, was Pike Place, a waterfront public market built in the early twentieth century. A grimy assortment of ramshackle structures, Pike Place was saved from destruction in 1971 when Seattle's voters rejected a proposed urban renewal project for the market's site. During the 1970s, Pike Place was carefully rehabilitated, its original down-at-the-heels ambience being preserved. Unlike Faneuil Hall Marketplace or Harborplace, where James Rouse demanded standards of cleanliness that would satisfy any suburban-mall shopper, Pike Place was maintained as an "authentic" market where fish mongers sold king salmon from grubby stalls, scruffy farmers hawked their produce, and an array of handicrafts, both treasures and junk, were available to venturesome shoppers. In the words of one observer, it was "no sanitized Disneyworld" but had "jumble and chaos to spare." By the late 1980s, it was attracting 7 million visitors annually, more than double the number before its renovation.[55]

The back-to-the-city commercial initiative, however, was not universally successful. Some of the much vaunted festival marketplaces quickly proved financial failures. In 1988 the Rouse Company divested itself of Richmond's Sixth Street Marketplace, which was losing around $100,000 a month. Toledo's Portside and Flint's Water Street Pavilion also failed.[56] Despite Rouse's views to the contrary, there was not enough yearning for a return to the heart of Flint or to downtown Toledo to support the enterprises. By 1989, Norfolk's Waterside also was not earning a profit, and in the 1990s the city was forced to subsidize it, spending $11.6 million to keep the marketplace in business.[57] Even Faneuil Hall Marketplace and Pike Place disappointed some of their original backers. To the dismay of Benjamin Thompson, armies of tourists with an appetite for fast food engulfed the Boston marketplace. Ten years after the opening of the rehabilitated Quincy Market, Thompson observed: "The Marketplace was never planned as a tourist attraction." Instead he had envisioned it as a bazaar for local residents, "a place to gather day and night to enjoy colors, smells, and the simple pleasures of watching others."[58] But the tourists had come, and food merchants found that they could make more money selling their sausages and cheese to hungry lunchtime crowds than to shoppers doing their weekly marketing. Thompson's bazaar was becoming a food court rather than an emporium of sights and smells where locals would discover community. Gritty Pike Place likewise lured tourists who were not in the market for fresh produce or fish but would buy the many handicrafts and trinkets on sale. Thus craft vendors crowded out farmers. In the mid-1990s, a Seattle architecture critic lamented: "As tourism grows it dilutes the market's authenticity and interferes with the purposes for which it was founded."[59]

Yet for city officials and urban boosters, tourist money was just as welcome as local money. The marketplaces and renovated districts might not have been fulfilling the romantic visions of some critics, but the most successful projects were drawing cash into the urban core. And together with the new wave of gentrified neighborhoods, they represented a significant departure from past approaches to bolstering the central cities. The urban revitalization plans of the late 1940s and 1950s had sought to strengthen the centripetal pull of the one dominant hub by refashioning that hub in accord with all the latest developments in urban transportation, architecture, and planning. They had sought to buttress the core through high-speed expressway access to downtown; through the construction of ultramodern high-rises to house the middle class, which supposedly craved a Manhattan lifestyle; and through the building of sleek, new office towers that supplanted the grimy remnants of the Victorian era. Desiring to erase the dirty past, these urban renewal schemes had aimed at breakneck modernization. But this strategy had failed. The central city lost its unchallenged preeminence and became simply the oldest and largest municipality in an increasingly amorphous mass of metropolitan development, a place that most metropolitan residents avoided and many ignored. In the late 1970s and the 1980s, however, neighborhood rehabilitators and some urban developers like James Rouse turned instead to exploiting the very element that earlier boosters had attempted to mask: the urban past. The gentrifiers and Rouse presented a selective vision of this past that emphasized lively markets, colorful waterfronts, and charming neighborhoods; the steel, soot, hectic pace, and huddled masses of America's urban tradition were missing from their back-to-the-city vision. Yet this vision seemed to offer a viable alternative to the suburbs, where little of the built environment predated 1945. For at least some consumers, the reconstructed urban heritage of Rouse and the gentrifiers was an appealing commodity that was worth buying.

Moreover, it was an attractive commodity to millions of tourists and suburban visitors because it did not represent the metropolitan norm. The rehabilitated structures and districts of the central cities were something unusual, something that did not exist just down the suburban streets where most Americans lived. Although Thompson and others who were originally enamored with the marketplaces seemed to believe that butchers' stalls and produce stands had a "genuine," "real" quality, in the 1980s they were not genuine or real. They were exotic and unusual, something worthy of a visit by a tourist. Cellophane and fast food were the genuine commodities of the late twentieth century; mounds of fresh fish and farmers with homegrown produce were charming anomalies. Likewise, aluminum siding was the "natural" building material of the era; the wood clapboards so dear to rehabilitators were a throwback to an earlier age. The success of the marketplaces and the gentrified neighborhoods depended to a degree on how much they evoked not the genuine life of the 1980s but a carefully contrived image of the urban past. For most Americans of the 1980s, reality was in the suburbs; Thompson, Rouse, and the rehabilitators were fashioning an alternative for those seeking at least a momentary escape. They were marketing charm and festivity in a metropolitan world of parking lots and chain stores.

Their alternative had to be carefully contrived because that was the only way to get people with money back to the inner city. Americans did not actually have a centripetal yearning, an innate desire to return to a common meeting ground in the urban core where they could commune with their brothers and sisters from throughout the metropolitan area. They had to be drawn there by the hoopla and hokum of the festival marketplace. Downtown was no longer a place where one had to go; the journey to the core was not a necessity of life, as it had been in 1945. But if James Rouse could recruit enough jugglers and steel bands and if people could be convinced that a trip to a bar or restaurant in LoDo or Underground Atlanta was a fun alternative, then the urban core could remain in the running for metropolitan dollars and still assert itself as someplace special. Rouse and the gentrifiers were not reestablishing the central city as the unchallenged metropolitan focus. They were creating a market niche for the long-troubled cities that might prevent them from becoming small islands of office towers moribund after 5:00 P.M. and surrounded by seas of slums.

It was a market niche, however, that appealed to the white-collar settler or tourist rather than the indigenous blue-collar masses. Strolling mimes would lure few stevedores or truckers to the festive markets, and enraptured references to Les Halles and Campo dei Fiori were expressions of America's upper-middle-class culture. Moreover, the gentrified neighborhoods were, by definition, areas that attracted the gentry. Meanwhile, the remaining working-class residents in those neighborhoods watched their property taxes rise, taxes that went to pay for subsidized marketplaces and rehabilitation schemes. Throughout the half century after World War II, mayors and urban business leaders sought to draw middle-class money to the core. The back-to-the-city movement was just one more stage in that effort. Working-class city dwellers might benefit from the restaurant jobs created in revitalized neighborhoods, but back-to-the-city initiatives were aimed preeminently at accommodating the middle class and its money.

The Making of Gay Ghettos

One group that was establishing its own niche in the American metropolis of the 1970s and the 1980s was the gays. There had always been a homosexual population in America's cities, and certain bars and night spots had long been identified as gathering places for this contingent. Yet the gay presence was largely underground. Heterosexual Americans preferred not to think about gays, the police harassed them, and politicians would have nothing to do with them. In June 1969, however, a police raid on a New York City bar catering to gays, the Stonewall Inn, ignited a riot as the bar's customers and sympathetic bystanders responded to the harassment with a barrage of rocks and bottles. The Stonewall Riot marked the beginning of the gay liberation movement, dedicated to asserting the rights of homosexuals and relieving them of the need to remain underground. During the following two decades, openly homosexual communities developed in cities across the nation, and certain neighborhoods became renowned as gay ghettos. Just as senior citizens had discovered an enclave suited to their needs in Sun City, so homosexuals were to develop their own fragments of the metropolitan turf adapted to their predilections.

The most famous gay community to emerge was the Castro in San Francisco. It was a homeland for those seeking a refuge for an alternative lifestyle; one person called it "a gay Israel." In 1976 San Francisco police estimated that about eighty homosexual men were migrating to the city each week, and the Castro and its environs were the focus of their life. By 1980, approximately 12 to 15 percent of the city's population was homosexual.[60] Moreover, 50,000 to 100,000 gay tourists descended on the Castro each year to patronize the gay-friendly bars and bathhouses unavailable in less tolerant communities.[61] According to the local guide of homosexual-identified businesses and social gathering spots, there were only 66 such establishments in San Francisco in 1972 but by 1982 the number was up to 307.[62] Nine gay newspapers also served the Castro community. At the annual Gay Freedom Day Parade, the homosexual population was able to express itself in a way that would not have been appreciated in family-oriented suburbs, Sun Belt retirement communities, or blue-collar ethnic enclaves. In 1978 the Local Lesbian Association Kazoo Marching Band paraded with the Dykes on Bikes, the Gay Pagans, and a contingent of sadomasochists carrying a sign reading "Black and Blue Is Beautiful."[63]

Property values and business sales soared in the Castro as the homosexual population increased, and gay gentrification appeared to buoy the city's economy. The publisher of a leading gay periodical observed: "Our cities are in very bad trouble as the groups moving into them are generally without skills, education, or affluence. The gay immigrants have these things, and they have a real interest in the cities."[64] San Francisco's new role as a homosexual mecca thus seemed to ensure new economic life for the central city. The Yuppie migrants to the Castro's gay ghetto might well compensate economically for low-income blacks relegated to Hunter's Point.

San Francisco's homosexual population was also asserting its political power and influencing the course of urban government. The most notable gay political leader of the late 1970s was Harvey Milk, known as "the Mayor of Castro Street." In 1977 Milk was elected to San Francisco's governing Board of Supervisors, a victory that was acclaimed as one more landmark in the gay liberation movement. Milk's term, however, was cut short when the following year a disgruntled ex-supervisor and former police officer, Dan White, walked into city hall and murdered both Milk and Mayor George Moscone. Campaign literature distributed during White's race for supervisor expressed his animosity toward the city's gay invaders and other alternative lifestyles. "I am not going to be forced out of San Francisco by splinter groups of radicals, social deviates, and incorrigibles," it read. "You must realize there are thousands upon thousands of frustrated angry people such as yourselves waiting to unleash a fury that can and will eradicate the malignancies which blight our beautiful city."[65] By killing Milk, White seemed to be expressing the fury of these frustrated angry people.

White's murder trial in May 1979 resulted in a conviction for manslaughter and a maximum sentence of seven years, eight months' imprisonment. Angered by the jury's leniency, a mob gathered in the Castro and marched on city hall, where, five thousand strong, the protesters shouted, "Get Dan White. Lynch him."[66] They stormed the municipal building and shattered the structure's windows. They also battled police and set fire to squad cars. By midnight, the riot had subsided, but it was clear that San Francisco's gays were not about to yield to legal prejudice. They had migrated to the Castro to find liberation, and they were intent on defending their new status and alternative lifestyle.

The San Francisco homosexual community did not, then, retreat from political activism. Instead, there were other openly gay or lesbian political officials in San Francisco, and the Castro was a hub of political activism. In 1987 a gay San Francisco columnist asserted: "Politicians can be destroyed by the gay vote. As long as we keep our vote, they're going to kiss our ass for a long time." The respondents to a 1989 survey reiterated this sentiment. Seventy percent of San Francisco's homosexuals said they had "a lot" or "a moderate amount" of influence over local government decisions, whereas only 48 percent of the city's heterosexual respondents believed they had that degree of political efficacy.[67] Through boldly asserting their lifestyle in the Castro, gays and lesbians had emerged as a citywide power.

Elsewhere this was happening as well. The center of homosexual life in Chicago was the North Side lakefront area, with male gays attracted especially to Lake View East and lesbians more prevalent farther north in Uptown. In 1983 the cochair of the Police Relations Committee of the Illinois Gay and Lesbian Task Force observed that "in the last 10 years, Chicago has really changed. The bars used to be dangerous places. Public restrooms became ghettos for gay encounters." That was "all gone now," for "at least on the North Side, being gay is accepted as a way of life. Now there is a whole gay community with a variety of outlets from churches to health clinics to choirs." Given what the *Chicago Tribune* referred to as the "buying power of Chicago's free-flowing gay dollar," Windy City retailers were beginning to court homosexual customers. According to the *Tribune*, a North Side grocery piqued "the appetite of its gay clientele with suggestive photographs of fruits and vegetables that resemble male anatomy." The grocery's owners explained: "When the gays see those photos, they know they're welcome in our store. . . . It's our subtle but sure way of appealing to an important market."[68]

Chicago's annual Gay and Lesbian Pride Day parade celebrated the emergence of the homosexual community. In 1983 it included ninety-three floats and assorted vehicles, about 1,300 marchers, and a convertible carrying the city's former mayor, Jane Byrne, whose presence reflected the growing political clout of Chicago homosexuals.[69] Yet the gay–lesbian community was clearly a world apart from most Chicagoans, its lifestyle offensive or inexplicable to many residents of the metropolis. In 1985 a heterosexual columnist observed: "For the uninitiated, certain aspects of Chicago's gay pride parade can be quite a jolt." Noting that "this is a public celebration of sexual freedom and that's not an easy theme to put on a float," he reported that the most memorable parade displays "tend to look something like a bacchanalian orgy on wheels."[70]

In Seattle, Broadway, the main street of the Capitol Hill district, became the center of gay commerce and entertainment. In Capitol Hill, as in San Francisco and on Chicago's North Side, gays were prominent among the gentrifiers who were bringing money back to central cities and making old neighborhoods suddenly fashionable as well as profitable. "Broadway was having a tough time," reminisced the owner of the district's first gay bar. "They were thinking it was going to die and the neighborhood would become a ghetto of some kind." But his business boomed, as did others along the increasingly upscale street. Some less affluent homosexuals resented the degree of gentrification. "The rich white pricks are trying to move lesbians and other poor women and men out of Seattle," claimed one angry activist in 1978. "Take Monkey Shines on the corner of Broadway and John, which used to be the Congo Room, a restaurant where dykes worked and ate. Since it has become Monkeys, dykes don't work there, most can't afford to eat there." Yet Broadway would continue to attract both money and homosexuals, becoming the site of Seattle's annual gay–lesbian parade. According to one observer of gay Seattle, by the early 1990s "everyone from beer companies to floral shops to the police and fire departments had entries" in the parade, and "mayors and politicians . . . would be walking in them, just a few spots back from the bare-breasted dykes on motorbikes who always led."[71]

One homosexual community declared political independence from its heterosexual environs, becoming the first municipality with a gay-dominated government. In the early 1980s, West Hollywood, California, was an unincorporated island bordering Beverly Hills on the west and otherwise surrounded by the city of Los Angeles. More than one-third of the 36,000 residents were homosexuals, almost 90 percent were renters, and only 6 percent were under eighteen years of age. It was, then, a far cry from the stereotypical family-oriented, home-owning suburb, but in 1984 it chose to join the ranks of suburban municipalities, becoming the eighty-fourth city in Los Angeles County. Rebelling against existing rule by Los Angeles County authorities, the renter population, both homosexual and heterosexual, was especially dissatisfied with the weak protection afforded by the county's rent control ordinance. Moreover, that modest safeguard against rent inflation was due to expire the following year, leaving West Hollywood tenants vulnerable to escalating housing costs. Yet many West Hollywood residents also viewed incorporation as a welcome means to gay empowerment (figures 5.3 and 5.4). "West Hollywood is journey's end for a wave of refugees from sexual tyranny as practiced in most parts of middle America," observed the *Nation*, and incorporation would provide these gay refugees with an independent homeland, a center of gay power.[72]

On election day 1984, West Hollywood's voters not only approved incorporation by an overwhelming majority but also selected a five-person city council, three of whom were homosexuals. The first mayor was a thirty-one-year-old lesbian. Reporting on these unprecedented political

FIGURE 5.3 A group of men called the West Hollywood High Cheerleaders in the Gay Pride Parade, 1988. (Paul Chinn, *Herald Examiner* Collection, Los Angeles Public Library)

FIGURE 5.4 Opening day at the Gay and Lesbian Fair and Parade in West Hollywood, 1989. (Steve Grayson, *Herald Examiner* Collection, Los Angeles Public Library)

developments, *Newsweek* labeled West Hollywood "the new Gay City on the Hill," and the *New York Times* referred to it as a "Gay Camelot."[73] West Hollywood seemed to live up to these labels, its city council approving a series of unconventional measures that defied American tradition. To protect cross-dressers, the council adopted an ordinance that forbade a restaurant or bar to refuse service to a customer in attire not "customarily associated with his or her biological sex." It also approved a "domestic partners" ordinance, permitting a gay alternative to marriage.[74] And in an action that would have been deemed worthy of Ebenezer Scrooge in any other municipality, it voted that city hall should remain open on Christmas Day.[75]

West Hollywood, like the Castro, was, then, establishing itself as a hub of the gay lifestyle and using its municipal powers to reinforce this position. In the amorphous mass of metropolitan southern California, it was the gay ghetto, a lifestyle enclave in the increasingly fragmented, centerless population sprawl stretching from Mexico to Santa Barbara. In this vast metropolitan smorgasbord, it offered an option appealing to a segment of the American population that had broken free from the imposed sexual regime of the past. Metropolitan fragmentation opened the path to liberation for the gays of West Hollywood.

Life in the Edge City

While gentrification and gay migration were transforming some central-city neighborhoods, the metropolitan fringe was continuing to spin off from the central city and was pursuing its own course of development. By the late 1980s, the centripetal pull of the historic hub was simply a faint tug, drawing some outlying residents to periodic visits to central-city sports stadiums, museums, and concert halls and perhaps to an exploratory foray to see a heavily hyped festival marketplace. An increasing number of suburbanites were tourists in the central city, visitors sampling the attractions but with no ongoing stake in the life or business of the hub. A minority of suburbanites commuted to central-city jobs each day, but at the same time a growing number of central-city residents were headed in the opposite direction, traveling from their homes in the historic core to employment in the suburbs. The suburbs were no longer deserving of the name, for they were no longer subordinate to the central urb. They were a world of their own.

Enhancing the significance of the metropolitan fringe was the growth of the suburban office sector. Gradually over the previous half century, business had migrated to the suburbs. During the 1940s and 1950s, manufacturers built sprawling single-story plants with ample parking along outlying railroads and highways. In the late 1950s and the 1960s, suburban retailing surged forward as giant outlying malls secured a growing share of consumer dollars and eclipsed downtown department stores as the preeminent shopping meccas. In the late 1970s and the 1980s, suburbia surpassed the central city in the one remaining area of economic endeavor: the office sector. Office construction was booming in many central-city downtowns, and new skyscrapers were raising the spirits of urban boosters. But the pace of office construction was even greater in the suburbs. Scores of buildings to accommodate the rapidly multiplying army of white-collar workers were arising along every outlying freeway and clustering at busy interchanges.

Data on office space offered statistical proof of a phenomenon evident to even casual observers of the metropolitan scene. In 1981, 57 percent of America's office space was in traditional downtowns; by 1986, this was down to 43 percent, with 57 percent of office space located elsewhere in the nation's metropolitan areas.[76] In 1984 and 1985, only one-third of the office space under construction was in central business districts; two-thirds was in outlying areas.[77] New York City remained the nation's preeminent office center, but even there the central city was losing its edge. Between 1970 and 1988, New York City's share of its metropolitan area's office market dropped from 83 to 59 percent as Long Island, northern New Jersey, and the suburbs north of the city attracted a disproportionate percentage of white-collar business. In 1989, 52 percent of the six hundred largest publicly held companies based in the New York region had their headquarters in the suburbs; only a minority remained in the city.[78] Throughout the nation, data on office dispersion testified to the startling change in America's commercial geography. By the beginning of 1991, Boston's central business district accounted for only 28 percent of its metropolitan area's office space, the figure for downtown Miami and Kansas City was 37 percent, and in Denver it was 33 percent.[79]

A number of factors contributed to this office diaspora. The crime, high taxes, exorbitant office rents, congested thoroughfares, and limited parking of the inner city repelled many Americans, making the prospect of a suburban job more attractive. Tired of lengthy commutes, executives sought to relocate their offices closer to their suburban homes and avoid the problems and inconvenience of the city. There was also a gender factor influencing the move to suburbia. Studies consistently showed that women commuted shorter distances than men, and it was widely believed that suburban offices could more readily attract the labor of skilled, educated suburban women than could distant downtown establishments.[80] Women seemed to want to be closer to home, and suburban offices were nearer the residences of those women firms sought to hire. A leading student of burgeoning suburban commerce contended that "developers viewed it as a truism that office buildings had an indisputable advantage if they were located near the best-educated, most conscientious, most stable workers—underemployed females living in middle-class communities on the fringes of the old urban areas."[81] In the 1960s, corporations had moved out of New York to take advantage of this suburban asset, and the preference of suburban women for suburban jobs seemed to be of increasing significance to office location in the 1970s and 1980s as the number of women entering the workforce soared. Between 1957 and 1990, the share of married women in the age category twenty-seven to fifty-four who were employed outside the home rose from 33 to 68 percent.[82] And a large proportion of these women were finding jobs in suburbia, a relatively short commute from their homes.

During the 1980s, the growth in suburban office space and commercial development in general attracted increasing attention among journalists and scholars who attempted to understand this new world that defied traditional notions of a business core and residential fringe. Department stores, hotels, offices, everything that was once confined to downtown were now found along the fringe. The periphery was no longer peripheral to metropolitan existence, and the center was no longer central to the lives of metropolitan Americans. Urban America seemed to be turned inside out, and the new metropolitan map was disorienting to those accustomed to the traditional conception of the city. This transformation had gradually taken place over the past three decades. By the 1980s, however, it was evident to even the most obtuse observers, and commentators felt compelled to make some sense of it. One author after another endeavored to name the new metropolitan form. Outer city, suburban downtown, technoburb, and urban village were among the alternatives proposed for the prominent new commercial districts along the metropolitan fringe.[83] There was a new beast in the metropolitan menagerie, and observers struggled to name it.

The label that proved most popular was "edge city," a tag created by the leading observer of the new phenomenon, *Washington Post* journalist Joel Garreau. In his 1991 book on the subject, Garreau defined edge cities as suburban commercial hubs with at least 5 million square feet of leasable office space, "more than downtown Memphis," a minimum of 600,000 square feet of leasable retail area, and more daytime workers than nighttime residents. He identified 122 full-fledged edge cities across the country, from Massachusetts's Burlington Mall area in the East to Oregon's Beaverton-Tigard-Tualatin in the West. The edge city was, then, a nationwide phenomenon, and one that was transforming American life. "Americans are creating the biggest change in a hundred years in how we build cities," Garreau told his readers. "Every single American city that *is* growing, is growing . . . multiple urban cores." These were the "new hearths of our civilization . . . in which the majority of metropolitan Americans now work and around which we live."[84]

No matter whether they were called edge cities or something else, these new commercial agglomerations could no longer be ignored. They were everywhere, and they took various forms. A number were actually located in the business districts of older upscale suburbs. For example, downtown Bethesda, Maryland, along Wisconsin Avenue sprouted office towers, becoming a leading edge city in the Washington, D.C., area. In 1986 a planning journal described it as having "been transformed from a quiet suburb to a booming 'outer city' with 10-story hotels and 20-story office buildings."[85] Saint Louis's upper-income residential suburb of Clayton had attracted office employment and high-rise structures in the 1960s, and during the 1980s it continued to thrive as one of the leading downtowns in Missouri.[86] On the West Coast, the once-decaying downtown of genteel Pasadena emerged as a major edge city in the Los Angeles area. Between 1980 and 1986, twenty-eight mid- and high-rise office structures rose in the reborn suburb as it became a center for back-office insurance and banking operations that sought to tap the middle-class, suburban labor force of the booming San Gabriel Valley. Sixty thousand southern Californians commuted to work in the city of 128,500 residents; only about 25,000 Pasadenans commuted outward to employment elsewhere. One article on the edge-city phenomenon reported that "the character of downtown Pasadena has changed radically. . . . Entire blocks of handsome 1920s and 1930s two-story commercial buildings have been restored, and restaurants, espresso bars, and shops are now moving into ground-floor retail space that had gone begging for many years."[87]

To the north, an edge city was developing in downtown Bellevue, Washington, a posh community east of Seattle. A prime residential address, Bellevue was tagged "the BMW capital of America."[88] But it was also an emerging commercial center, boasting 9 million square feet of office space in 1988. Its office inventory already far exceeded that of downtown Tacoma, western Washington's second largest city.[89] By the beginning of 1991, there were plans for a thirty-five-story office tower designed by a leading New York architectural firm, and Bellevue boosters fully expected that employment in the suburban downtown would double during the next decade.[90] One of Bellevue's city-planning staff explained: "We've decided we're going to be an urban place" with a pedestrian-oriented downtown reminiscent of older communities.[91] No longer simply an upper-crust retreat from busy Seattle, Bellevue had become a business center in its own right and was designing its own urban core to rival that of the central city.

Many other edge cities did not arise in existing suburban business districts but sprouted from previously undeveloped fields around thriving suburban shopping malls. Perhaps the most cited example of an edge city, Tysons Corner, Virginia, outside Washington, D.C., developed around a giant super-regional mall. In the late 1980s, the *Washington Post* reported that this commercial hub, which as recently as the 1950s had consisted of only a crossroads general store, was "now bigger in terms of office space than all but 15 downtowns in the country and has more of a skyline than some." It was "easily the largest downtown in Virginia or Maryland" and was also "bigger than downtown Miami."[92] To the south, in the Atlanta metropolitan region, the Cumberland-Galleria edge city developed around Cumberland Mall, a shopping center that opened in 1973 with four major department store anchors and over 1 million square feet of retail space. By 1982, Cumberland Mall's annual retail sales were more than double the sales figure for downtown Atlanta. Located at the interchange of Interstates 285 and 75, the Cumberland node became a major office center in the 1980s; by 1989, it offered more commercial office space than Atlanta's central business district and provided employment for 75,000 Georgians.[93]

In the Midwest and West, shopping malls were also the nuclei of booming commercial zones that arose over the course of two decades. In the Chicago area, office structures sprang up around Oak Brook Mall, among them the corporate headquarters of McDonalds. Soaring thirty-one stories above the Illinois prairie, Oakbrook Terrace Tower was a monument to suburbia's commercial success. To the north, in Schaumburg, Illinois, giant Woodfield Mall generated retail sales more than equal to the combined totals of downtown Saint Louis, Kansas City, and Omaha and also spawned adjacent office development.[94] In southern California, Orange County's South Coast Plaza projected $715 million in sales in 1987, more than downtown San Francisco.[95] Among its offspring were not only office buildings and hotels but also an adjacent $73 million performing arts center. According to *New York Times* architecture critic Paul Goldberger, the opening of the performing arts center in 1986 represented "a kind of coming of age for far-flung American suburbs." Over the past generation, "suburban areas have been filling up with bigger and bigger buildings within which the activities for which people once went into the city are increasingly being conducted: working, shopping, even vacationing" (figure 5.5). All that was missing were "big-time performing arts centers and large art museums . . . —the only things that belied these new settlements' image of complete self-sufficiency." But now Orange County had "built itself as big a performing arts center as almost any city ha[d]."[96] The edge cities seemingly had everything: retail sales, corporate headquarters, and symphony orchestras.

Other outlying commercial areas were not nodes centering on a mall but instead strips of development stretching miles along suburban interstate highways. New Jersey's Princeton Corridor, along U.S. Route 1, was among the nation's most prominent linear cities. In 1986 one leading

FIGURE 5.5 Orange County edge-city landscape, with an expensive townhouse community in the foreground adjacent to a golf course and office towers in the background. (*Herald
Examiner* Collection, Los Angeles Public Library)

commentator on suburban development estimated that by the mid-1990s
the total office space along the corridor would surpass that of downtown
Milwaukee or downtown Newark.[97] Another observer viewed the corridor's transformation less positively, describing it as "one of the nation's
most dramatic examples of suburban development gone wild."[98] Northwest of Washington, D.C., the Interstate 270 corridor in Montgomery
County, Maryland, was another example of miles of office parks, hotels,
malls, and restaurants, offering all the cuisine, comforts, merchandise,
and employment traditionally found in the central-city downtown. Meanwhile, south of Minneapolis the seven miles of Interstate 494 stretching
from Bloomington to Edina and skirting the metropolitan airport constituted by the early 1980s the second largest employment hub in the Twin
Cities area and the Twin Cities' "nighttime capital" and center for business meetings. It boasted more hotel rooms than existed in the downtowns of Minneapolis and Saint Paul combined (figure 5.6).[99]

   Although the interstate highways were clearly vital to the life of most of
the new suburban business clusters and strips, a few edge cities devel-

FIGURE 5.6 High-rise hotel along the Interstate 494 corridor south of Minneapolis. (Steve Plattner, Minnesota Historical Society)

oped in part because of their location on transit lines. This was the case in Arlington County, Virginia, where the Washington area's rapid transit lines were magnets for development. The completion of Arlington's transit lines in 1979 escalated the pace of development at each of the five stations along the Rosslyn–Ballston corridor. New offices offered employment to an army of white-collar workers. In 1985 Rosslyn–Ballston had a daytime population of 51,600, compared with its resident population of 23,900. By the early 1990s, the end-of-the-line Ballston transit stop sported a twenty-six-story hotel–apartment tower and a twelve-story office building.[100]

Still other of the new suburban downtowns were creations of a single developer seeking to fashion a perfect commercial hub from scratch. Columbia, Maryland; Reston, Virginia; and Irvine, California, were among Garreau's edge cities. By 1986, Reston had surpassed downtown Richmond, Virginia, in office space, and in 1990 the first phase of its Town Center opened. Intended to resemble a traditional high-density, urban downtown, Reston's new hub included twin eleven-story office buildings, a 514-room Hyatt Regency Hotel, and a full complement of shops, restaurants, movie theaters, and apartments sited on a grid of streets typical of older central cities.[101] Meanwhile, Texas developer Ben Carpenter transformed his sprawling ranch near the Dallas–Fort Worth Airport into the new city of Las Colinas, complete with a high-rise urban center. With a flamboyance worthy of Texas, Carpenter constructed a canal reminiscent of those of Venice in the heart of his new city. Sidewalk cafés, arched bridges, and imported water taxis reinforced the romantic Venetian theme. Yet Las Colinas was not a place for dawdling over cappuccino or engaging in Mediterranean reveries. It was a center of business. By 1989, more than nine hundred companies had located in Las Colinas, and in the fall of that year the corporate giant Exxon announced its plans to abandon New York City and relocate its international headquarters in the Texas edge city.[102]

Although varied in nature, the outlying commercial districts shared a common characteristic. They were not new substitutes for the old downtowns of 1945, serving the same functions as the traditional centers but in different locales. They were not the focus for an entire metropolitan area, a common hub of significance to everyone in the metropolis. Instead, they were commercial clusters that had developed for various reasons at scattered sites throughout metropolitan areas. They offered jobs and shopping for some metropolitan residents but were alien territory to others who worked and shopped an hour's drive away in another sector of the metropolitan sprawl. Most of the edge cities were not cities in the traditional sense, communities that residents identified with as their hometown, places that they claimed to be from. No one was from Tysons Corner or rooted loyally for a Tysons Corner team. The edge cities were places where metropolitan Americans shopped or worked until a glitzier mall or a more fashionable office address lured them to a new location along the freeways. They were the consummation of the revolution that had transformed metropolitan America since 1945. Tysons Corner and its ilk were commercial zones within an amorphous, centerless population mass that no longer had any unified focus or clear boundaries. They were not cities but the most visible landmarks of the postcity era when traditional concepts of urban and suburban seemed increasingly obsolete.

Perhaps no place summed up this metropolitan revolution so well as Perimeter Center, an edge city north of Atlanta. Its very name was a contradiction of terms: the perimeter was, by definition, not the center. But in the new world of the 1980s, the fringe could with some justification claim to be the core. With more commercial office space than either downtown Atlanta or the Cumberland–Galleria area, Perimeter Center was the leading office node of Georgia. A thirty-one-story tower completed in 1988 and soon to be joined by an equally lofty twin testified to the perimeter's centrality to southern business life. Yet in 1986, an observer noted that the view from the top floor of a Perimeter Center high-rise was "mostly trees and lawns, not other office buildings."[103] Moreover, there were no sidewalks connecting the disparate structures; instead, one was expected to drive from building to building in this suburban space. The pedestrian life and unremitting concrete of the traditional urban core was missing. The new world was one of trees and towers, Hyatt Regency hotels just minutes from upscale housing subdivisions. It was a world with seeming opposites juxtaposed to form a markedly untraditional mix.

In 1987 historian Robert Fishman perceptively described the new metropolitan world that was no longer urban or suburban but "defined by the locations [Americans] can conveniently reach in their cars." According to Fishman, "The true center of this new city is not in some downtown business district but in each residential unit. From that central starting point, the members of the household create their own city from the multitude of destinations that are within suitable driving distance." In this new world, "one spouse might work at an industrial park two exits down the interstate; the other at an office complex five exits in the other direction; . . . the family shops at several different malls along several different highways; . . . all they need and consume, from the most complex medical services to fresh fruits and vegetables, can be found along the highways."[104] Freed from centripetal transit lines and enjoying the independence afforded by automobility, metropolitan Americans of the late 1980s had found that the traditional city was no longer necessary. Instead, they could fashion their own city from the smorgasbord of facilities and lifestyles offered in the sprawling populated mass surrounding them. They could partake of a gentrified lifestyle, taste the offerings of a festival marketplace, frequent an upscale shopping mall, or invest in a four-bedroom manse freshly minted in a field producing corn just two summers earlier. American metropolitan areas offered seemingly limitless options, and the tens of millions of Americans fortunate enough to have an automobile and a credit card could select from the manifold offerings and create a city to suit their tastes.

Many outlying residents, however, were not altogether pleased by some of the options appearing along the metropolitan fringe. High-rise office towers, scores of new retail outlets, and the construction of major hotels all seemed to threaten the traditionally suburban qualities that they valued. They had moved to suburbia to escape the commercial hubbub of big offices, big stores, and big hotels. They sought instead the sylvan and the charming, life in a quaint and quiet world. Confronted by the threat to traditional suburban advantages, many outlying residents rebelled against the new development. During the 1980s, slow-growth movements appeared in metropolitan areas across the nation, and antideveloper sentiment soared. The long-standing decentralization trend seemed to have gone too far; the undesirable qualities of the traditional center had migrated to the periphery, infecting the quality of life and endangering the preferred lifestyle of many outlying residents.

Especially aggravating was the mounting traffic problem on suburban highways. Throughout the nation, frustrated drivers complained about the congested thoroughfares and feared the approach of an apocalyptic gridlock trapping them all in their cars and dashing dreams of mobility. Contributing to the jams was the poor state of suburban public transit, which forced commuters to edge cities to rely almost wholly on private automobiles to get to work. In 1975, 41 percent of rush hour traffic on freeways in urbanized areas moved at a pace of less than thirty-five miles per hour; by 1985, after a decade of edge-city development, this figure was up to 56 percent.[105] One executive along the Princeton Corridor claimed that commuting on congested U.S. Route 1 could prove so tiresome that it "just stays with [employees] all day."[106] A sociologist at the University of California at Irvine predicted that by the twenty-first century, traffic in Orange County would become so harrowing that "the people in Irvine . . . will rarely decide to go to another village. They will stay in their own small areas."[107] Already there were dire tales of traffic jams. Characterized as "a metaphor for commuter gridlock" by a local newspaper, the Long Island Expressway was the scene of a fourteen-hour jam in August 1985 when a truck accident closed all six lanes. "There was no movement whatever," reported one Long Island motorist. "People were pulling to the side, fanning themselves and relieving themselves."[108] The president of a transportation-consulting firm predicted: "Traffic conditions will get worse, there's no doubt about it."[109] In 1987 a leading urban economist concluded: "Throughout the country, suburban traffic congestion has become the hot issue as a result of this development buildup."[110]

One area where it was a steaming issue was Fairfax County, Virginia, the site of Tysons Corner. Once an upper-middle-class retreat for commuters to Washington, D.C., Fairfax County by 1986 had more office space than the three largest cities in Virginia combined and was, according to the *Washington Post*, "widely considered to be the economic engine driving the state."[111] It also had some of the worst traffic jams in the state. To limit the breakneck growth and its adverse consequences, in December 1986 the county planning commission sent to the governing Board of Supervisors a zoning proposal that would cut by as much as 75 percent the permitted density of new office buildings. County developers and business groups vigorously opposed this curb on their enterprise. A newspaper ad paid for by the local chamber of commerce bore the headline: "Fairfax County's Proposed Solutions to Traffic LOWER YOUR STANDARD OF LIVING." The advertisement contended that "stopping business development in Fairfax County will not solve the county's transportation problems. All it will do is erode the county's tax base, increase the tax burden on homeowners, raise the county's unemployment rate and ultimately diminish the quality of life in the county."[112] At hearings on the proposal, a zoning lawyer agreed. "What the hell are we going to do?" he asked, "retreat 20 years back in time?"[113]

Proponents of the limit on commercial growth felt, however, that dire conditions required drastic action. A county supervisor stated forthrightly: "We've got a problem in Fairfax County. We have gridlock."[114] The county planning director explained that there was "a devastating imbalance between the land-use plan and transportation plan." Referring to the city long regarded as symbolic of developmental sprawl run amok and bumper-to-bumper traffic, a planning commission member complained: "It shouldn't always look like Los Angeles around here."[115] Fairfax residents seemed to concur with this view. A poll reported that more than two-thirds of those surveyed favored the growth limit, and an overwhelming majority believed that fast-paced commercial development was threatening the quality of life in the county.[116]

Fairfax County's Board of Supervisors rejected the planning commission proposal, granting developers a momentary reprieve. The election of November 1987, however, became a referendum on development, with slow-growth and pro-growth candidates vying for control of the Board of Supervisors. On election day, the slow-growth forces won a decisive victory, capturing a 7 to 2 majority on the county board. Moreover, the county's leading proponent of growth limits defeated the incumbent pro-growth chair of the Board of Supervisors by a 3 to 2 margin.[117] In the wake of the victory, the prospects for more Tysons Corners seemed dim, but some were skeptical that political victory could halt the onslaught of commerce and clear the clogged highways. "Everyone wants the traffic to go away," observed one doubter. "Well, it's not going to go away. We live in an urban environment."[118] "A lot of people have promised no growth," remarked another skeptic. "I want to see how well they walk on water."[119]

The battle in Fairfax was a microcosm of what was occurring along the fringe in metropolitan areas across the nation. The traditional middle-class suburban lifestyle was clashing with the edge-city onslaught. Suburban residents who had sought to escape from the city now felt that the city had caught up with them, dashing their hopes for a life immune from urban congestion. Feeling betrayed, they rebelled. Others, however, proclaimed development inevitable and desirable, acquiesced to the wave of urbanization, and believed that only a miracle could clear the highways and restore the sylvan tranquility of an earlier era.

The antidevelopment movement was not as pronounced in mid-America as on either of the coasts, but the clash between the traditional suburban ideal and the new edge-city realities was evident there as well. In 1988 the *Chicago Tribune* reported: "It's a cliché heard time and again in suburban zoning and annexation battles and cries for preservation of open space: 'We don't want to be another Schaumburg!'" The site of giant Woodfield Mall, nine major hotels, and 45,000 jobs, the community of 64,000 residents northwest of Chicago had an image of "a suburb that grew too fast, has too many people and too many cars, and is lacking in the quality of life that suburban living is supposed to offer." One open-space advocate remarked of Schaumburg: "I drove through once and got out as quickly as I could." Schaumburg's village manager responded defensively to criticisms of the congested local thoroughfares: "Sure, rush-hour traffic is a problem. It is a problem in the whole metropolitan area. We have it, but so does Hoffman Estates, Streamwood, Arlington Heights and all the others." In any case, he claimed the community was attempting to solve the problem of traffic "or at least make it bearable."[120]

When the Chicago White Sox proposed moving from their ballpark in the inner-city neighborhood of Bridgeport to a new facility in suburban Addison, the ensuing conflict cast an especially revealing spotlight on the metropolitan revolution troubling many Americans. Tom Zver, president of Addison's King Point Homeowners Association, led the fight to prevent construction of a new stadium adjacent to the Kings Point subdivision. Zver said that he had moved to suburbia to "roll up the sidewalks at 6 o'clock and settle in for a quiet night in front of the VCR. I've always loved the suburban life, the quiet." Speaking of the proposed stadium, Zver lamented: "Now I'm gonna look out at an 11-story monstrosity. It's gonna tear my heart out." But Zver and the Kings Pointers found allies

among Bridgeport residents who also deplored the potential loss of a sa-
cred part of their urban neighborhood. "God forgive me," confessed one
Bridgeporter, "but I look to the ballpark as a holy place. To me it's street
sound, it's background music." This defender of his urban heritage explained: "What it all comes down to, it's like seein' the house you grew up
in bein' torn down, or the old neighborhood dyin'." Zver summed up the
mutual interests of the suburban Addison residents and urban Bridge-
porters when he remarked, "The bottom line is we're fighting for the
same thing: tradition."[121] Zver cherished the suburban tradition of quiet
and tranquility; the Bridgeport residents worshipped the urban tradition
of ballparks, beer, and sports-loving throngs. In the age of edge cities and
decentralization, Addison appeared to be losing its suburban-ness and
Bridgeport its urban-ness. Eventually, Zver and his allies succeeded in
keeping the White Sox far away from the Kings Point subdivision. The
team rebuilt its ballpark in inner-city Bridgeport. Yet the episode was indicative of the change that had transformed metropolitan America, a
change that was unfathomable and deeply disturbing to many defenders
of the tradition of the hub and periphery.

Nowhere, however, was the rebellion against the onslaught of development and urban-ness more intense or widespread than in California. The
nation's most populous state, California seemed to be bursting with people, malls, offices, and all manner of sundry development. In 1989 a
statewide poll found that 65 percent of respondents wanted to discourage
population growth in their communities, and 84 percent believed that
traffic congestion on the freeways had gotten worse. A San Francisco urban studies professor concluded that "the basic message is one of doom."
The San Francisco Examiner likewise said of the poll findings: "The overwhelming conclusion was that most Californians believe that their quality
of life has deteriorated."[122]

The discontent was evident in the booming edge city of Walnut Creek
in Contra Costa County, east of San Francisco. From 1980 to 1986, office
space in the once quiet community doubled, and, according to one planning journal, "as the in-commuting increased, traffic at major intersec-
tions in Walnut Creek deteriorated to what traffic engineers call the 'E'
level of service—just short of gridlock." "This used to be a community
that had a sense of place," reported an economist studying the area. "Now
all of a sudden it's urban, and it never expected that to happen."[123] In 1985
voters reacted, first passing an initiative that reduced the city's height
limit to six stories and then adopting a second measure banning all com-

mercial construction until traffic flow improved. Moreover, they elected two slow-growth proponents to the city council. "It is an absolute milestone," proclaimed one of the victorious growth-control council members. "It just shows it can be done. . . . I think it'll go right through the country." The mayor of nearby Concord agreed that the slow-growth victory in Walnut Creek was a wake-up call to public officials. "This is an absolute signal to every middle-class suburban community in the Bay Area that if these issues are not resolved by the elected officials, the public will step in and do it," the mayor concluded after the 1985 election.[124]

Meanwhile, southern Californians were fighting similar battles. In 1986 in the affluent Orange County community of Newport Beach, an organization called Gridlock fought to quash an Irvine Company proposal to build three additional office towers in the Newport Center complex. Antidevelopment forces claimed that the new structures would generate forty thousand additional automobile trips each day and "further transform picturesque Newport Beach into a crowded urban center." Gridlock proved successful at the polls, thwarting the plans of the Irvine Company. In the wake of the victory, a controlled-growth city council member explained: "The fundamental message of Tuesday's election is that citizens want to slow down the pace of development and avoid overdevelopment."[125] In 1988 voters in the Orange County communities of San Clemente, Costa Mesa, and San Juan Capistrano also approved slow-growth initiatives, although a countywide growth-control measure suffered defeat at the polls after a $1.6 million campaign by developers (figure 5.7). The signs of dissatisfaction were widespread. A poll of Orange County residents in 1989 found that 51 percent wished they lived elsewhere.[126] A study of the southern California growth war concluded that there was "a single unifying theme—'we don't want to become another Los Angeles.'"[127] Los Angeles and other central cities were the antithesis of the suburban dream; they represented the hated environment of bigness and congestion that suburbanites sought to escape. Yet by the late 1980s, the specter of the big city was haunting the escapees in Fairfax County, Addison, and Orange County. Just as Tom Zver had nightmares about an eleven-story stadium arising in his backyard, Orange Countians feared that what had happened to Los Angeles was now happening to them.

By the close of the 1980s, then, the metropolitan revolution not only had destroyed the urban centrality of the once central cities but was endangering the suburban sense of being away from it all. In the new met-

FIGURE 5.7   New housing sprawling across the hills of Orange County, California, at the time of the slow-growth initiative, 1988. (Javier Mendoza, *Herald Examiner* Collection, Los Angeles Public Library)

ropolitan world, there was no longer any center or any edge. Thousands of office workers commuted in all directions, shoppers found fashion miles from the historic core, and farmers' fields sprouted corn one summer and glass-encased high-rises the next. The nation's metropolitan areas had been transformed, but millions of Americans were having trouble adjusting to the revolution. Gentrifying neighborhoods and gay ghettos offered lifestyle enclaves for a minority of metropolitan Americans. For the majority who lived in that vast expanse traditionally known as suburbia, their lifestyle seemed at risk.

6 | Beyond the Black–White City

"Our nation is moving toward two societies, one black, one white—separate and unequal," concluded the National Advisory Commission on Civil Disorders following the riots of 1967.[1] This statement summed up the prevailing vision of ethnicity in the United States during the first three decades after World War II. America was a black–white nation, a bifurcated entity divided between African Americans who, according to the commission, seemed destined to take over the central cities and whites who would create their alternative society in the suburbs. The cultural conception of race was two-toned, with a minority at one end of the color spectrum and a majority at the other. To bring together these extremes seemed imperative to the welfare of the American city. Solving the black–white racial dilemma was the great goal of American urban policy.

Other ethnic groups existed, although their presence was obscured by the prevailing black–white conceptualization of American society. In the late 1940s and the 1950s, Puerto Ricans flooded into New York City, adding a new Latin element to the metropolis. The millions of Americans who saw *West Side Story* on the stage or screen were aware of the Anglo–Puerto Rican clash in New York, yet in the 1960s this was a sideshow commanding far less attention than the center-stage black–white dilemma. Large numbers of Mexican Americans had long inhabited areas of the Southwest, and in a city such as San Antonio the most notable ethnic division was between Anglo and Hispanic. Moreover, there were well-known Chinatowns in San Francisco and New York City, testifying to the presence of an Asian minority. Exceptions to the prevailing black–white conception of American society, Asians, Mexicans, and Puerto Ricans were not deemed of sufficient significance to warrant a national advisory commission or extended hand-wringing over their impact on the future of the nation. For policy makers, scholars, journalists, and the American public in general, the race problem meant the antagonism between whites and blacks. Other groups were outside the dominant conceptual framework.

During the last three decades of the twentieth century, however, the ethnic composition of the nation changed markedly, giving rise to a new vision of ethnicity in metropolitan America. A massive influx of immigrants from Latin America and Asia compelled Americans to accept a more complex picture of the metropolitan population. These newcomers did not fit the old formula of a monolithic white majority versus a monolithic black minority. The two-toned society was yielding to a nation of various shades with large contingents of immigrants who did not necessarily identify with either of the two traditional players in the racial game. Some native-born Americans had trouble adjusting to the change. Whites had to recognize that the complexion of metropolitan America was growing darker. Perhaps more problematic was the struggle of blacks to accept that the complexion of the city from their standpoint was growing lighter. As Americans refashioned their cultural vision of urban ethnicity, there were new ethnic conflicts. The long-standing bifurcated concept of majority versus minority died hard, but by 2000 perceptive observers had to admit that the old black–white world of the early postwar years had passed. At the close of the century, many central cities were not growing more black, and many suburbs were not white preserves. Newcomers had created an ethnic pattern that defied the prognostications of earlier prophets.

The Newcomers

Underlying the ethnic changes in metropolitan America was a shift in immigration patterns. Owing to restrictive immigration laws, the economic depression of the 1930s, and World War II, the number of migrants to America during the period 1920 to 1960 was far below that of earlier decades. Whereas 14.7 percent of Americans were foreign-born in 1910, in 1970 the foreign-born share reached a new low of only 4.7 percent. Moreover, before the 1960s the overwhelming majority of newcomers were from Europe, federal legislation having severely limited the entry of Asians. For the 150 years from 1820 through 1969, 79.9 percent of the nation's immigrants were from Europe, only 2.7 percent from Asia, and 7.5 percent from Latin America and the West Indies.[2] During the first two decades of the postwar era, then, the number of newcomers was modest, and the share of native-born Americans was growing. In addition, the word "immigrant" conjured up images of white Europeans arriving from Poland, Germany, Ireland, or Italy. The tired, poor, huddled masses welcomed by the Statue of Liberty had come from that relatively small slice of the world between the Urals and the North Atlantic.

During the last three decades of the twentieth century, all this changed. The immigration rate soared, reaching a peak in 1990/1991. By 2000, 10.4 percent of the nation's population was foreign-born. Moreover, most of these newcomers bore little resemblance to those who had arrived at Ellis Island in the early twentieth century. Only 12.3 percent of the more than 16 million immigrants arriving from 1981 through 2000 were from Europe; 34.7 percent were Asians; 48.9 percent were from the Americas.[3]

A number of factors facilitated this flow of newcomers and influenced its composition. Most notably the passage of the Hart-Celler Act in 1965 eliminated the old system of quotas, whereby the federal government had preferred northern European immigrants over newcomers from southern and eastern Europe and permitted only a small number of new residents from Asia. Rather than allocating quotas on the basis of nationality, the Hart-Celler Act established family relationship and occupational skills as the principal criteria for admission to the United States. Henceforth, the federal government would give preference to those seeking to come to the United States to reunite with family members and to those with scarce or desirable skills that could enhance the American economy or quality of life. In other words, educated professional and technical workers were preferred over the unskilled, who might well struggle to find employment and depress American wage levels. Further enhancing the flow of immigrants was America's willingness to waive immigration restrictions for refugees from Communist regimes. As the world's leading foe of Communism, the United States felt compelled to open its doors to victims of left-wing governments, no matter their ethnicity. An additional factor facilitating the wave of immigration was the nation's porous borders, through which millions of illegal newcomers could pass. By 2000, there were an estimated 7 million unauthorized immigrants in the United States, almost 5 million of them having come from Mexico.[4] The federal government was unable to prevent the illegal passage of Mexicans across the nation's southern borders, and the consequence was a surge in the foreign-born population of the Southwest.

These factors resulted in an immigrant population that was highly diverse in social and educational background. Many well-educated Asians gained entry under the provisions of the Hart-Celler Act. Unlike the stereotypical immigrants of the past, they were middle class and college trained. Moreover, America's refugee policy opened the floodgates to displaced capitalists whose entrepreneurial skills and ambitions clashed with Communist dogma. Vehement anti-Communists, these newcomers posed no threat to the nation's prevailing ideology but instead reinforced the image of the United States as the world's chief bulwark of capitalism. The illegal immigrants were for the most part desperately poor, compelled by economic necessity to defy the law. Because of their precarious legal status, they could be readily exploited by American employers, paid less than minimum wage, and forced to work in conditions that no native-born American would tolerate. The new immigrants thus comprised college-educated professionals as well as the poor and unschooled, the ambitious capitalist entrepreneur as well as the exploited proletariat.

On arriving in America, these varied immigrants did not disperse evenly across the nation. Instead, a few areas attracted the bulk of newcomers. Unlike those of the nineteenth and early twentieth centuries, the immigrants of the late twentieth century were found disproportionately in the Sun Belt and were less common in the old manufacturing heartland. In 2000 the Miami–Fort Lauderdale metropolitan area was the most "foreign" region in the country; 40.2 percent of its population had been born outside the United States. The figure for Los Angeles–Riverside–Orange County was 30.9 percent, and for San Francisco–Oakland–San Jose, it was 27 percent. In contrast, the foreign-born constituted only 2.6 percent of the population in both the Pittsburgh and Cincinnati metropolitan areas. Of the older hubs of the Northeast and Midwest, only the New York City area, with 24.4 percent of its population born outside the United States, was among the principal destinations for the new immigrant population.[5]

Miami's preeminence as a magnet for newcomers was owing primarily to the massive influx of Cubans, who were in the vanguard of the new immigration. From the coming of power of Fidel Castro in 1959 through

1962, 215,000 Cubans fled their homeland and arrived in the United States. Known as the Golden Exiles, these initial migrants included a disproportionate share of Cuba's professional and managerial class and were on average far better educated than the Cuban population as a whole. Despite periodic crackdowns on migration by the Cuban government, an additional 578,500 arrived from 1963 through 1980.[6] Not all settled in South Florida. A notable Cuban settlement developed along the west bank of the Hudson River in West New York and Union City, New Jersey. But Miami became the capital of Cuba in exile and the most Cuban city in the United States. By 1990, the population of the city of Miami was 62.5 percent Hispanic, including many Nicaraguan refugees from the left-wing Sandinista regime. Yet the largest contingent of Miami's Hispanics was the Cubans, who constituted 38.9 percent of the city's population.

Visitors to Miami were struck by its Latin, and specifically Cuban, flavor. In 1980 an article in the *New York Times Magazine* reported on "the Latinization of Miami," informing readers that "more than half a million Cuban refugees have transformed a declining resort town into a bustling bicultural city."[7] In 1985 *Time* magazine described Miami's Calle Ocho district: "Open-air markets sell plantains, mangoes and boniatos (sweet potatoes); old men play excitedly at dominoes in the main park. Little but Spanish is heard on the streets and indeed in many offices and shops. A Hispanic in need of a haircut, a pair of eyeglasses or legal advice can visit a Spanish-speaking barber, optometrist or lawyer."[8] The writer Joan Didion claimed that "the entire tone of the city, the way people looked and talked and met one another, was Cuban. . . . There was even in the way women dressed in Miami a definable Havana look, a more distinct emphasis on the hips and décolletage, more black, more veiling, a generalized flirtatiousness of style not then current in American cities."[9] The widespread use of Spanish testified to the strong and persistent Cuban influence. In 1980 a survey of Cuban households in Miami found that 92 percent of the respondents spoke only Spanish at home, and 57 percent of Cubans relied primarily on Spanish at work. Moreover, 64 percent listened to Spanish-language radio, and less than 20 percent read English-language newspapers.[10] In 2000, forty years after Castro's triumph, 51.5 percent of the 3.6 million people five years old and over in the Miami–Fort Lauderdale metropolitan area spoke a language other than English at home, the overwhelming majority of these communicating in Spanish.[11]

As the Cuban population soared, the zone of Cuban settlement spread outward through much of Miami–Dade County. The center of Cuban Miami was Little Havana, an aging, inner-city area around Calle Ocho. But there was no Cuban ghetto. Instead, the newcomers moved west from Little Havana into the suburbs of West Miami and Sweetwater as well as northwest into Hialeah. By 1980, fifteen of the twenty-seven municipalities in Dade County were at least 15 percent Hispanic, and Latins constituted 81 percent of the population of Sweetwater, 74 percent of the inhabitants of Hialeah, and 62 percent of the residents of West Miami. The exclusive suburb of Coral Gables was not off-limits to the newcomers; 30 percent of its residents were Hispanic.[12]

The Cuban presence in Coral Gables and other upper-middle-class areas was visible proof of the relative economic success of the immigrants. Miami's Cubans were not an economically oppressed ethnic minority trapped on the lower rungs of the social ladder and barred from opportunities for success. Instead, they earned a reputation as ambitious entrepreneurs who buoyed rather than depressed the local economy. By the early 1980s, Dade County could claim more than 18,000 Cuban-owned businesses, including more than 60 car dealerships, around 500 supermarkets, and approximately 250 drugstores. In addition, there were sixteen Cuban American bank presidents.[13] In 1990, 42 percent of all businesses in Dade County were owned by Hispanics, three-quarters of them controlled by Cubans.[14] Attracted by Miami's bicultural, bilingual environment, banks and corporations seeking to do business with Latin America established branches in the South Florida city, leading the president of Ecuador to dub Miami "the capital of Latin America." Miami became the vital business link between Latin America and the United States, and commentators attributed this to the Cuban newcomers. In 1980 one observer noted: "It is an article of faith in Miami that without the impetus provided by the Cuban-exile community the city today would be just another Sun Belt spa well past its prime." The same year, the city's mayor, who was of Puerto Rican origin, confirmed this view: "Miami would not be what it is, or where it is, if it were not for the Cuban community." Although, he claimed, "most Hispanic communities" were "not very demanding and . . . happy with very little," the Cubans were "extremely competitive, . . . extremely aggressive. Not only do they want the best, they want it first."[15] Moreover, Cuban leaders were not modest about their contribution to the city's economy. "We Cuban people have made Miami," boasted one of Miami's Cuban executives. "Thanks to the freedoms here in America, we're combining our natural Cuban energies with American knowledge, American know-how, to create a new more passionate American."[16]

Cubans were not only establishing themselves in the private sector but also taking charge of local government. As early as 1973, a Cuban was elected to Miami's governing commission. Twelve years later, a Cuban was chosen mayor of Miami, and another was appointed city manager. By the late 1980s, the cities of West Miami, Sweetwater, Hialeah, and Hialeah Gardens also had Cuban-born mayors. And in the 1990s, a Cuban assumed the office of county executive. In 2000 a *Miami Herald* poll found that at least 80 percent of Miami's non-Hispanic whites and blacks as well as 63 percent of the Cubans believed that Cubans controlled the area's politics.[17] "Nowhere else in the country, and possibly in American history, have first-generation immigrants so quickly and thoroughly appropriated political power," concluded a scholarly analysis of Miami's political scene.[18]

Although dominant in South Florida, Cubans were far outnumbered nationally by the largest contingent of Hispanic immigrants: the Mexicans. According to the Immigration and Naturalization Service, they constituted 24 percent of the newcomers arriving from 1981 through 2000, and the 2000 census reported that the almost 8 million persons of Mexican birth resident in the United States accounted for 28 percent of the nation's foreign-born population.[19] Nowhere were Mexican Americans more numerous than in the Los Angeles area. In the mid-1990s, one scholar proclaimed that "Los Angeles has become the capital of Mexican America and the single largest Mexican concentration outside of Mexico City."[20] By 2000, more than 3 million people of Mexican birth or ancestry lived in Los Angeles County, constituting 32 percent of the county's population. They accounted for 15 percent of all Mexican Americans in the United States. Moreover, there was no sign that the latinization of Los Angeles was abating. Between 1990 and 2000, the Mexican population of the Los Angeles area rose 44 percent, as compared with a 13 percent rise in the overall number of inhabitants.[21]

The long-standing heart of Mexican American settlement was East Los Angeles. Most of the newcomers to this area were poor, coming to the United States to better their economic condition. And many were illegal immigrants. Consequently, the old East Los Angeles barrio spreading eastward from Boyle Heights reflected the poverty of Mexico rather than the affluence that moviegoers associated with southern California. According to one observer from early 1990s, "In the bars and restaurants of Boyle Heights, bedraggled youngsters go from table to table pleading with people to buy novelties like those found in the stalls of Tijuana. Outside

FIGURE 6.1
Some of the fifty undoc-
umented immigrants
found in a garage in
Compton, California,
1984. (Philip Kamrass,
Herald Examiner Collec-
tion, Los Angeles Public
Library)

on the sidewalks, their mothers, often with infants in their arms, stop
passers-by and beg for money." The lack of affordable housing forced
many of the newcomers to live in illegally converted garages, and the *Los
Angeles Times* reported on 200,000 "garage people" who lived with little or
no heat, plumbing, or windows (figure 6.1).[22]

Yet the rapidly rising Mexican population was not confined to East Los
Angeles. Instead, it spread through much of the region, moving into
housing once occupied by other ethnic groups. For example, South Central Los Angeles, the traditional hub of black life in southern California,
experienced a Latin invasion. By 1990, only 53 percent of South Central's
population was non-Hispanic black; 44 percent was Latino. The Watts
neighborhood, which had lent its name to the riot of 1965, was 43 percent
Hispanic.[23] Meanwhile, middle-class Mexican Americans moved eastward, settling throughout the San Gabriel Valley and finding homes in the
distant reaches of San Bernardino and Riverside counties. The suburbs

were not off-limits to the growing Mexican American population. At the beginning of the twenty-first century, one scholarly study said of this outward flow: "In the entire history of American suburbanization . . . there is no comparable instance of an ethnic or linguistic group moving to the suburbs in such overwhelming numbers and density."[24]

Mexicans were also the leading immigrant group in the Chicago area. Although the Hispanic presence was not nearly as pronounced as in southern California, the Land of Lincoln was acquiring a Latin flavor. By 2000, there were almost 800,000 Mexican Americans among the 5.4 million people in Chicago's Cook County. During the last decades of the twentieth century, the Lower West Side, stretching westward from the once Czech district of Pilsen, emerged as the center of the local Mexican community. Twenty-Sixth Street, the area's chief shopping strip, was dubbed "Avenida Mexico," and, according to one estimate, by the mid-1980s more than three-quarters of the businesses along the thoroughfare were owned by Mexican Americans. The annual Fiesta del Sol, held in August, and the Mexican Independence Day Parade in September as well as the opening of the Benito Juarez High School in 1977 were signs of the new Mexican American preeminence. The once Lithuanian Providence of God Roman Catholic Church became a Spanish-speaking parish. Nearby, the Polish St. Adalbert's Basilica adapted by adding a picture of Our Lady of Guadalupe, and the German Lutheran St. Matthew's Church sported the alternative name of Iglesia San Mateo, with Lutheran services in both English and Spanish.[25] As in Los Angeles, Mexican Americans were not confined to older inner-city neighborhoods but spread into nearby West Side suburbs. Once a predominantly central and eastern European working-class town, by 2000 Cicero was 68 percent Mexican. Farther out, in the pre–World War II suburban bungalow belt, Mexican Americans constituted 31 percent of Berwyn's population.

Increasing numbers translated into increasing political power for Mexican Americans. In 1981 Henry Cisneros won election as mayor of San Antonio, the first Mexican American mayor of a major city in the United States. Two years later, the Mexican American Federico Peña won the mayor's office in Denver. During the 1990s, both Cisneros and Peña served in President Bill Clinton's cabinet. In the Los Angeles area, the political triumphs were less dramatic, and Mexican Americans failed to acquire a proportionate share of public offices. Handicapping Mexican American office seekers was the relatively low proportion of Mexican immigrants who became citizens. In 2000 only 20 percent of American residents of Mexican birth were citizens and thus enjoyed voting rights. In contrast, 58 percent of American residents of Cuban birth were citizens.[26] Yet there were victories. In 1985 a Mexican American won a seat on the Los Angeles city council, and six years later another secured a place on the powerful county board of supervisors. Finally, in 2005, a Latino was chosen mayor of Los Angeles. In California, as in Florida, Hispanics were seizing the reins of power.

Although Mexicans were the largest Hispanic group in the United States, millions of other Latin Americans migrated northward during the last three decades of the twentieth century. The largest Hispanic immigrant group in the New York City area was the Dominicans. Almost 800,000 people born in the small Caribbean nation of the Dominican Republic or of Dominican ancestry lived in the New York City area by 2000, more than double New York's Mexican population. Washington Heights, at the northern end of Manhattan, became a Dominican enclave, although by the end of the century the Dominicans were succeeding the outward migrating Puerto Ricans in the nearby West Bronx. Between 1990 and 2000, the number of Puerto Ricans in New York City proper dropped 12 percent as this older, more established Hispanic group followed European Americans to the suburbs.[27] Yet Dominicans filled the apartments left behind, participating in one more stage of the city's seemingly endless history of ethnic succession. In 2000 the New York area was home to 247,500 Ecuadorians as well and almost an equal number of Colombians.[28] These South Americans were especially numerous in the ethnically diverse borough of Queens, where they shared space with Asians and native-born European Americans.

During the 1980s, civil wars in Central America spurred the migration of Salvadorans, Guatemalans, and Nicaraguans. The Nicaraguans added to Miami's Hispanic population, the Salvadorans constituted the largest portion of the Latino immigrants in Washington, D.C., but Los Angeles was the destination for the lion's share of Central Americans. By 2000, the Los Angeles area was home to approximately 800,000 Central Americans, with almost 400,000 Salvadorans alone. In fact, the Los Angeles metropolitan area housed almost 50 percent of all Central Americans in the United States and nearly 60 percent of the Salvadorans. Southern California's Central Americans were generally poor, with little schooling by United States standards, and a large share had entered the country illegally. They were disproportionately engaged in household services, and the stereotypical Salvadoran or Guatemalan immigrant woman was a servant or hotel maid. Although they were not clustered in any single ethnic ghetto, the largest concentration of Central Americans was in the Pico–Union/Westlake district, immediately to the west of downtown Los Angeles, and farther northwest in Hollywood.[29] These areas housed the standard assortment of restaurants, groceries, and other enterprises catering to ethnic needs, all testifying to the burgeoning diversity of life in southern California.

Although Latin America was contributing the largest share of the nation's new immigrants, the influx of Asians was almost as dramatic. By the beginning of the twenty-first century, there were 8.5 million persons of Asian birth residing in the United States. Like the Hispanics, they were not evenly distributed across the nation but instead heavily concentrated in California and the New York City area. In 2000 the Honolulu metropolitan area led the nation in percentage of population of Asian origin, but most Hawaiian Asians were not recent immigrants but long-standing residents. Of the metropolitan areas ranked second to nineteenth in percentage of Asian population, thirteen were in California, three were in northeastern New Jersey, one was New York City, and the other was the Seattle area. Yet there were lesser concentrations of Asian population in other parts of the country. For example, the traditionally Jewish Chicago suburb of Skokie was 21 percent Asian, stereotypical suburban Glendale Heights to the west in DuPage County was 20 percent Asian, and Asians constituted 14 percent of the population of the edge city and mall hub of Schaumburg.[30]

As these suburban addresses indicated, many of the Asians merged readily into American middle-class life and earned praise as a "model minority." Although some rejected this tag as just another example of stereotyping and as a convenient means for masking the unevenness of Asian achievement and the difficulties some newcomers faced, the model image survived and found some statistical support. Data for 1990 from the Los Angeles region recorded that among persons twenty-five years or older, 40 percent of the area's foreign-born Chinese, 54 percent of its foreign-born Filipinos, 55 percent of its Indian immigrants, and 38 percent of newcomers from Korea had a college degree or more, as compared with only 31 percent of the native-born whites and 16 percent of the native-born blacks. Of foreign-born Asians in the age category twenty-five through sixty-four, 39 percent had high-skill occupations, as compared with 44 percent for whites and 31 percent for blacks, but among native-born Asians in the Los Angeles region the share holding these elite jobs rose to 50 percent. In

1989 the median household income of Los Angeles's foreign-born Asians was $40,000, as compared with $43,000 for whites and $26,000 for blacks; for Asians born in the United States, it was $48,000.[31] These newcomers were not, then, the stereotypical downtrodden, deprived masses of American immigrant lore. On average, they were better educated than the American norm, and after one generation in the United States they surpassed by a considerable margin older settlers in household income. The relatively impressive statistics were in part owing to the preference given to the skilled and educated by the federal immigration law. Whereas millions of unschooled, unskilled, and impoverished Latin Americans entered the country illegally, relatively few Asians did so. It was easier to sneak across the Rio Grande than the Pacific Ocean, which gave Latin Americans a distinct advantage in evading American immigration law. Geography dictated that Asians conform to the federal government's immigration standards.

Perceived as hardworking, skilled, highly intelligent, law-abiding, and ambitious by the American majority and its media, Asians were the poster children for those proclaiming the merits of the new wave of immigration and the emerging diversity and inclusiveness of the nation. In its 1985 special issue on America's immigrants, *Time* magazine observed favorably of the newcomers: "So many of the Asians come from the middle class, or aspire to the middle class, and are driven by a stern Confucian ethic." Moreover, it quoted a demographer who characterized the Asians as "the most highly skilled of any immigrant group our country has ever had."[32] Reporting in 1991 on the migration of local Asians to suburbia, the *Chicago Tribune* expressed the prevailing media view: "The common American perception of Asians as educated, hard-working professionals has ultimately worked in their favor." When the *Tribune* wrote of the Asian stores along Argyle Street on Chicago's North Side, it expanded on this favorable image. "Wander down Argyle, right into Asia, where the food is fresh and the faces friendly," the newspaper told its readers. In the older black–white city of Chicago, minority faces were not perceived by the white majority as friendly. Here, however, was a new, and seemingly better, minority whose neighborhood was a welcoming, pleasurable destination. In the words of the *Tribune* Argyle was a "street of dreams."[33] Earlier minority streets had been the stuff of white nightmares.

The largest group of Asian immigrants was the Chinese. In 1960 there were 237,000 Chinese Americans; in 2000 there were 2.8 million. During the intervening four decades, more than 1.3 million newcomers legally entered the United States from China, Taiwan, and Hong Kong.[34] The ouster of the Taiwan-based Republic of China from the United Nations in 1971, the fall of Saigon in 1975, the gradual establishment of relations between the United States and Communist China during the 1970s, and British plans to relinquish Hong Kong to Communist China all seemed to threaten the interests of anti-Communist Asian capitalists and encouraged an influx of Chinese immigrants to the United States, the one eminently secure bastion of anti-Communist capitalism in the world. Many of the Chinese immigrants were not wealthy, but a good portion of the newcomers had money and skills that they sought to invest and utilize in America.

The influence of the new Chinese Americans was especially evident in the suburbs of the San Gabriel Valley, east of Los Angeles, and specifically in the city of Monterey Park. This suburb had developed largely during the first two decades following World War II when thousands of middle-class, single-family homes typical of American suburbia arose to house native-born white Anglos. The community did, however, attract a number of upwardly mobile Hispanics and a few Asians, mostly Japanese Americans. In 1960 it was 85 percent non-Hispanic white, 12 percent Hispanic, and 3 percent Asian. During the 1960s, the Hispanic share increased markedly and then leveled off after 1970. Yet the Asian proportion continued to soar, reaching 34 percent in 1980 and 58 percent in 1990.[35]

Most of the newcomers were Chinese, and by 2000 Chinese/Taiwanese constituted over 40 percent of Monterey Park's population. During the 1970s, Chinese American real-estate developer Frederic Hsieh promoted this immigration, advertising Monterey Park as the "Chinese Beverly Hills" in Chinese-language newspapers throughout Asia. Monterey Park was sold as the place to go for those who wanted a safe haven in North America. A brochure issued by a Taiwan-based immigrant consulting firm promised: "In Monterey Park, you can enjoy the American life quality and Taipei's convenience at the same time."[36] This advertising attracted immigrants with cash and ambitions. "The first stop would be the Mercedes dealer and the second stop would be the real estate broker," observed one Chinese American who served as a liaison to the newcomers. Speaking of these immigrants he claimed: "This group of businessmen—entrepreneurs—were bolder, more boisterous, more demanding and sometimes even cunning."[37]

The influx of Chinese residents spawned a multitude of new businesses catering to Asians. By 1989, six of the city's eight supermarkets were Chinese owned. In 1981 Diho, a branch of a Taiwan-based supermarket chain, opened; later the Hong Kong Supermarket welcomed its first customers on the site of a former skating rink. Indicative of the changing times, the American chain store Alpha Beta gave way to a supermarket with the name Ai Hoa, which was Chinese for "Loving the Chinese Homeland."[38] According to one student of the city, "In the new supermarkets, Chinese is the language of commerce, and the stores feature fifty-pound sacks of rice, large water tanks with live fish, and rows of imported canned goods that are generally unrecognizable to a non-Chinese shopper."[39] By the close of the century, Monterey Park was headquarters for three Chinese-language newspapers distributed internationally, could boast of numerous Chinese-owned mini-malls housing hundreds of shops, and had more than sixty Chinese restaurants. In 1977 Frederic Hsieh had told the local chamber of commerce, "You may not know it, but this [Monterey Park] will serve as the mecca for Chinese business."[40] Twenty years later, his prediction had proved remarkably accurate. Moreover, just as the Cubans were praised for rejuvenating Miami, the Chinese were widely credited with having brought new life to the commerce of Monterey Park and the surrounding San Gabriel Valley communities. "Business strips once moribund have been revitalized with an infusion of Asian (Chinese) enterprise and money," reported the *Los Angeles Times* in 1987. "Lots that were vacant only a few years ago now support an odd meld of suburban mini-malls and pulsing Far East marketplaces."[41]

By the 1990s, Monterey Park had won a reputation as America's first suburban Chinatown. Nicknamed "Little Taipei," Monterey Park was supposedly a diminutive version of Taiwan's capital transplanted to southern California. As such, it was a comfortable and appealing environment for Chinese newcomers. Just as West Hollywood was a community designed for gays and Beverly Hills for the wealthy, Monterey Park was a preserve for Chinese Americans. One Chinese woman explained why her compatriots congregated in Monterey Park: "Living here we feel just like home. There are so many Chinese people and Chinese stores, restaurants, banks, newspapers, radios, and TV, almost everything you need." "Want to know why I moved here?" responded another Chinese resident. "Let me tell you something: I usually have a morning walk along Monterey Park's streets. You know what? All I see are Chinese, there are no foreigners at all!"[42] In the typical amorphous American metropolitan mass of the 1990s, there was no longer a single, common focus of urban life, acknowledged by all residents. Instead, there was a multitude of fragments. And Monterey Park was the fragment for the Chinese. In fact, it was known as a center of business and residence throughout much of the Chinese world. "You're from Los Angeles?" a Taiwan resident asked a visiting Californian. "Isn't that near Monterey Park?"[43] For the Chinese, Los Angeles was a suburb of Monterey Park.

Monterey Park, however, was not actually the Chinese Beverly Hills. That title correctly went to nearby San Marino. One of the wealthiest communities in southern California, with a median household income of $117,000 in 1999, San Marino was a quiet retreat of palatial homes and lush plantings, a symbol of material success. In 2000 almost half its thirteen thousand residents were Asian, with Chinese/Taiwanese accounting for over 40 percent of the population. San Marino dramatically demonstrated that at the close of the twentieth century, foreign-born and minority did not necessarily equate with poverty. No one could deny that many Chinese could not even afford more humble Monterey Park. Less affluent and less educated than their West Coast counterparts, New York City's Chinese immigrants crowded into tenements in Manhattan's Chinatown or migrated to working-class and lower-middle-class neighborhoods in Brooklyn and Queens.[44] But the ethnic lifestyle of the San Gabriel Valley did challenge long-established stereotypes. At least in California, the old pattern of poor minorities confined to the central city and excluded from more affluent white suburbs no longer prevailed.

The Chinese were not the only Asians earning a reputation as entrepreneurs. From 1976 to 1990, the number of Korean immigrants averaged thirty thousand a year, the wave of newcomers peaking in 1987. As South Korea's economy improved in the 1990s and the relative standing of the United States as a land of opportunity diminished, the influx declined, averaging only seventeen thousand annually from 1991 through 2000.[45] But by the close of the century, Koreans had established a definite presence in the United States, winning a reputation as hardworking small-business owners. In 1986 an estimated 45 percent of Korean newcomers in Los Angeles and Orange counties were self-employed, the highest rate of self-employment for any minority or immigrant group (figure 6.2), and the figure for New York City's Korean immigrants was at least as high.[46] A large portion of those who were not self-employed were working in small Korean-owned businesses, preparing to strike out on enterprises of their own. Explaining this predilection for self-employment, one Korean-born lawyer observed: "One thing about Koreans is that they don't like to be dominated by anybody."[47]

On both the West and East coasts, Koreans carved out an economic niche for themselves. In New York City, they became known for their

FIGURE 6.2 Los Angeles congressman appealing to his increasingly diverse constituents in a parade through Korea Town, 1984. (Mike Sergieff, *Herald Examiner* Collection, Los Angeles Public Library)

small produce stores. By the late 1990s, there were approximately two thousand Korean-owned stores specializing in fresh fruits and vegetables in the city, constituting about 60 percent of New York's independent produce retailers. There were also about 1,500 Korean-owned dry cleaners in New York, and Koreans controlled 50 percent of the city's manicure salons. In southern California, Koreans owned thousands of small grocery and liquor stores and operated swap meets. These meets were gatherings of small dealers who sold a wide variety of merchandise for cut-rate prices. Not confined to ethnic enterprises, southern California's Koreans owned an estimated 550 American fast-food businesses by the mid-1990s.[48] Moreover, many of these newcomers embraced a work ethic that native-born Americans often professed but seldom practiced. "We should work harder than other Americans," remarked the Korean owner of a dry-cleaning chain in southern California. "Otherwise we cannot succeed."[49]

Although Korean immigrants operated businesses throughout Los Angeles and New York City, they became known specifically for their willingness to establish stores in poor black and Hispanic neighborhoods, tapping markets that non-Hispanic white entrepreneurs and major chain retailers avoided. At the beginning of 1992, Los Angeles's *Korean Times* estimated that 80 percent of the businesses in the city's principal African American area were owned by Koreans, including one thousand swap meet stores and six hundred outlets selling groceries, liquor, gasoline, and other merchandise.[50] Earlier in the twentieth century, Jewish immigrants had filled the retailing needs of poor minority neighborhoods ignored by more established native-born merchants. During the last two decades of the century, Koreans supplanted the Jewish retailers in the black ghettos of Los Angeles and New York City, seeking to make a profit where few others dared to operate.

Joining the Koreans in the struggle for success were hundreds of thousands of Filipinos who, among the Asian newcomers, were second in number only to the Chinese. Filipino immigrants were largely concentrated in California, and Daly City, immediately south of San Francisco, became the Filipino version of Monterey Park. By 2000, a majority of the city's 104,000 residents were Asian, and more than 30 percent of the total was Filipino. "Over the past two decades, Filipino immigrants have flocked to Daly City, transforming the bedroom community into a mini-metropolis with a distinctly Pacific flavor," reported one observer in 1996. "Filipino restaurants dot the city's shopping strips," he noted; "*bagoong, tinapa, daing, kamote,* and *kamoteng kahoy*—staple foods in rural Philippines—are readily available in dozens of Oriental stores." If Monterey Park was "Little Taipei," Daly City was "Little Manila," a hub of transplanted Filipino life in northern California. "When people talk of Daly City, they talk of Filipinos," commented a prominent local Filipino American. "I've seen Filipino movies in which a character would say: 'If I go to America, I'd go to Daly City.'" Suburban Daly City represented making it for many Filipinos who had spent their first years in America in the crowded central-city neighborhoods of San Francisco. "This city has been good to us," asserted a boosterish Filipino American realtor. "We can raise our children well, acquire property, and not be exposed to hostility and discrimination. We're free to pursue our American dream."[51]

Also pursuing that dream was a wave of newcomers from India. Whereas Filipinos preferred the West Coast, the largest concentration of Indians was in the New York City area, especially in the borough of Queens, where one could shop at the India Sari Palace, bank at a branch of the State Bank of India, worship at a Hindu temple or a Sikh *gurdwara,* and watch devotees accompany a Hindu deity's chariot through the streets during the festival of Ganesh Chaturthi. Generally well educated and members of India's upper or middle classes, the immigrants had high expectations for material success, and many realized their goals. By the close of the century, an increasing number were moving to the suburbs of Long Island and northern New Jersey, drawn by the opportunity of owning a home and sending their children to better schools than the central city afforded. Suburban Long Island movie theaters ran films from Bombay, and as many as fifteen thousand South Asians jammed the Coliseum in Long Island's Nassau County several times each year to see live performances by Bombay movie stars.[52] Although admitting that some Indian immigrants were limited to "mundane or even menial jobs," a student of the South Asian newcomers concluded that "overall this is an immigrant group whose education, hard work and ambition have boosted them to middle- or upper-middle-class status within U.S. society."[53]

The one Asian group that offered less statistical support for the notion of the model minority was the Southeast Asians from Indochina. Largely impoverished refugees fleeing the Communist takeover of the area in the 1970s, these newcomers on average had less education and less financial resources than the Indians, Filipinos, Koreans, or Chinese. The United States government attempted to distribute Indochinese refugees throughout the nation, but a disproportionate share settled in California, with the largest concentration in Orange County, south of Los Angeles (figure 6.3). A "Little Saigon" with numerous businesses catering to Vietnamese newcomers developed in the city of Westminster, and the proliferation of small Vietnamese-owned businesses contributed to the prevailing stereo-

FIGURE 6.3 Example of southern California's growing cultural diversity: Vietnamese ceremony, 1980s. (Dean Musgrove, *Herald Examiner* Collection, Los Angeles Public Library)

type of Asians as successful entrepreneurs. Although the Indochinese ranked behind their fellow Asian immigrants in terms of household income and college education, some believed that they were on the way to prosperity. In 1990 a study of southern California's Southeast Asians reported that "the number one concern of the refugees in Orange County is unemployment" but concluded that the immigrants "have already contributed to the booming Orange County economy by providing a labor force that is hard working, thrifty, competitive, and with strong family values. Employers surveyed about their experience of having Southeast Asians as employees are overwhelmingly positive."[54]

Vietnamese, Indians, Filipinos, Koreans, Chinese, Dominicans, Salvadorans, Mexicans, Cubans all joined blacks and non-Hispanic whites to form what New York City's mayor David Dinkins celebrated as a "gorgeous mosaic." Metropolitan America could no longer be viewed as simply black and white; it was rich in various hues with a mix of people from throughout the world. The result was a new amalgam quite different from that existing in America's urban centers in 1945. Nowhere was this gorgeous mosaic more evident than in the Elmhurst–Corona district of Queens in Dinkins's own city. In the late 1990s, an anthropologist reported: "On a heavily Latin American block of Roosevelt Avenue in Elmhurst, an Indian, a Chinese, and a Korean store coexisted with seven Colombian, Dominican, and Argentinean firms; and facing William Moore Park in Corona, one Jewish, one Korean, two Greek, and two Dominican stores were scattered among fourteen Italian businesses." Moreover, "at La Gran Victoria, a Dominican Chinese restaurant in Corona Plaza, a Chinese waiter speaking fluent Spanish served four young Latin Americans who ordered Chinese dishes, and nothing from the *comidas criollos* side of the menu." In addition, he recorded that the Chinese-owned Century 21 Sunshine Realty employed speakers of "Mandarin, Taiwanese, Cantonese, Hakka, Spanish, Italian, German, Polish, Korean, and 'Indian,'" and the Colombian-owned Woodside Realty Corporation could deal with customers in Spanish, Hebrew, Korean, and Mandarin as well as English.[55]

Such a babel of tongues confirmed New York City's long-standing reputation as a port of entry for America's immigrants. In the late twentieth century, however, Dinkins's gorgeous mosaic was not only found in the central city but in once homogeneous suburbs. A study published in 1989 found that the most ethnically diverse city in the United States was not New York or Chicago but the upper-middle-class Los Angeles suburb of Cerritos, a community especially notable for its wide range of Asian nationalities.[56] Nor did suburban communities grow any less diverse during the following decade. In 2003 *USA Today* carried a front-page story that proclaimed " 'New Brooklyns' Replace White Suburbs." "A whole class of traditional, white-bread suburb has turned into a new kind of city" reminiscent of Brooklyn in the past, incubators for hardworking immigrants on the path to middle-class life. According to the newspaper, Anaheim, California; Irving, Texas; and Pembroke Pines, Florida—all distant geographically from Ellis Island and in lifestyle from the old immigrant hub on Manhattan's Lower East Side—were the crucibles for the American future where the promise of the gorgeous mosaic was being realized.[57]

In the last decades of the twentieth century, then, the ethnic portrait of metropolitan America was changing markedly. The signs of change were everywhere. Our Lady of Guadalupe was receiving a place of honor in a Polish basilica, the Ai Hoa market was supplanting the Alpha Beta, South Central Los Angeles was turning from black to brown, and residents were speaking Chinese in San Marino and Spanish in Coral Gables. Immigrants from Taiwan dreamed not of the Statue of Liberty but of Monterey Park, and Daly City was the focus of Filipino aspirations. Americans had moved beyond the black–white city.

The Uneasy Transition

Not everyone, however, was happy about the changes occurring in metropolitan America. For some native-born Americans, both black and white, the new ethnic diversity was troubling and even threatening. As neighborhoods changed and foreign tongues and different complexions became commonplace in nearby shopping streets, some Americans felt that they were losing hold of their communities and becoming aliens in places where they had lived all their lives. Unfamiliar sights, sounds, smells, and manners offended their sensibilities. A number of the native-born also perceived the newcomers as economic competitors. Given the widespread perception that many of the immigrants were hardworking go-getters, employers might naturally prefer the newcomers to native-born job seekers (figure 6.4). Moreover, the sight of successful, well-heeled "foreigners" cruising the streets in Mercedeses could prove disturbing to native-born residents who had never been able to rise one rung on the economic ladder and feared slipping even lower. Altogether, the strangeness of the newcomers could prove unsettling, and their success

FIGURE 6.4   Anti–illegal immigration billboard in Los Angeles. (Michael Edwards, *Herald Examiner* Collection, Los Angeles Public Library)

raised doubts that the fulfillment of the American dream was reserved only for Americans.

Among non-Hispanic whites, anti-immigrant sentiment focused on the newcomers' refusal to give up their native languages. Miami was the scene of one of the earliest English-only battles. In 1973 the Dade County Commission decided to adopt a bilingual policy, publishing official documents in both English and Spanish, hiring Spanish-speaking personnel to serve Hispanics, and posting signs that offered information in both languages. In 1980, however, an Anglo group called Citizens of Dade United led a referendum campaign to eliminate bilingualism in the county. If adopted, the referendum measure would prohibit "the expenditure of county funds for the purpose of utilizing any language other than English, or promoting any culture other than that of the United States." Moreover, it required that "all county government meetings, hearings, and publications shall be in the English language only." One of the leaders of the referendum campaign, a multilingual Russian Jewish immigrant, explained that because of the prevalence of Spanish she "didn't feel like an American anymore" in Dade County.[58] "How come the Cubans get everything?" she asked, and she made it clear that she wanted Miami to return to "the way it used to be."[59]

Other non-Hispanics agreed. One English speaker complained: "Our people can't get jobs because they can't speak Spanish." Another laid it on the line: "Hey, buddy, if you want to speak Spanish, go back to Cuba." The Spanish-American League Against Discrimination led the fight against the proposal, and a spokesperson for the United Cuban-Americans of Dade County protested: "There are 200,000 Cubans here who can't speak English, but they pay taxes and they buy Coca-Cola."[60]

On election day, however, the antibilingual forces triumphed as the electorate split along ethnic lines. An estimated 71 percent of the non-Hispanic whites supported the measure, whereas 80 percent of Hispanics casting ballots voted against it.[61] Yet the victory was largely symbolic; it did not halt the widespread use of Spanish in the Miami area or return Dade County to the way it used to be. In 1986 a *Miami Herald* columnist observed: "A good many Americans have left Miami because they want to live someplace where everybody speaks one language: theirs."[62]

Language also became the crux of controversy between non-Hispanic whites and Asians in Monterey Park. In 1985 the National Municipal League and *USA Today* named Monterey Park an "All-American" city in recognition of its ethnic inclusiveness and its efforts to incorporate immigrants into the community. Yet beneath the facade of harmony were interethnic tensions that manifested themselves in complaints about the proliferation of business signs in Chinese. Critics of Chinese signage claimed that if storeowners failed to include an English translation on their signs, then firefighters and police would not know where to answer a call. Monterey Park's city attorney, however, claimed that "the police and fire know what is there, no matter what language you put on it" and argued that "it was just absolute nonsense to suppose that there was some public welfare reason for the fight that went on; it was political." Although the Chinese American mayor acceded to pressure and proposed an ordinance requiring an English translation on Chinese signs, some residents felt that this was not enough, presenting arguments that supported the city attorney's contention that public safety was not the principal concern. In a letter to the local newspaper, Frank Acuri expressed the anger of many residents when he said the proposed signage ordinance did not "address the real issues. The problem is that Asian businesses are crowding out American businesses in Monterey Park. . . . Stores that post signs that are 80 percent Chinese characters make us feel like strangers in our own land. . . . I will go a step further than the proposed law and say that all signs must be completely in English."[63]

Acting on his sentiments, Acuri and another resident, Barry Hatch, organized a petition campaign to make English the official language of Monterey Park. Acuri claimed to enjoy diversity, but he complained that "now all of a sudden, to have a group come to our city, which in this case is Chinese people, with enough money so they can buy our city, buy our economy and force their language and culture down out throats, this is what's disturbing to people in Monterey Park." Hatch concurred: "When we look up and see all these Chinese characters on signs—why, it feels foreign to us. It is one bold slap in the face, which says to us, 'Hey, you're not wanted.'"[64] Eventually, the city council passed a resolution that favored making English the official language of the United States. Reacting to the English-only sentiment, a group of Asians, Hispanics, and Anglos joined together in the Coalition for Harmony in Monterey Park and forced the council to rescind the measure.

Monterey Park was not the only community embroiled in battles over Chinese signs. By 1994, ten cities in the San Gabriel Valley had taken measures to require English on business signs.[65] The Chinese could and did continue to expand their commercial role in the valley, but sensitive city officials preferred that they not advertise their takeover too blatantly. They could profit but should avoid slapping those like Barry Hatch in the face.

Led by the Japanese American former United States senator from California S. I. Hayakawa, an organization called U.S. English promoted the English-only cause nationwide, seeking a federal constitutional amendment to make English the nation's single official language. Colorado governor Richard Lamm vigorously supported the effort, claiming: "We should be a rainbow but not a cacophony. We should welcome different people but not adopt different languages." No federal amendment was adopted, but Californians acted to make English the official language of their state. In 1986 they approved Proposition 63 by a 3 to 1 margin; it directed the legislature to "take all steps necessary to insure that the role of English as the common language of the state of California is preserved and enhanced" and prohibited any law that "diminishes or ignores the role of English."[66] The *New York Times* editorialized that the Proposition 63 campaign "smacked of a mean-spirited, nativist irritation over the influx of Mexicans and Asians."[67] Los Angeles mayor Tom Bradley warned that the proposition could "stir hatred and animosity. It could tear us apart as a people."[68] Eight years later, Californians adopted the equally divisive Proposition 187, which cut off state services to illegal immigrants. Aimed especially at the many illegal newcomers from Latin America, the proposition won support from two-thirds of the state's non-Hispanic whites, whereas Hispanics opposed it by a 3 to 1 margin.[69]

In California, Florida, and elsewhere, the non-Hispanic white reaction to the newcomers was not, then, altogether positive. English-only campaigns reflected anxiety about ethnic change and a perceived cultural threat deeper than just Chinese characters on business signs. Despite the laudatory talk about model minorities and their contributions to American society, the influx of hardworking Asians and enterprising Cubans was deemed by some as a threat to the comforting homogeneity of their white, English-speaking world. Yet when compared with earlier white opposition to the arrival of blacks in their neighborhoods, the response to the Asians and Hispanics was relatively mild. In the late 1940s and early 1950s, barrages of stones and bottles welcomed "race invaders" in the white areas of Chicago and Detroit. By comparison, a 1986 account of Chicago's Lower West Side reported that "by and large, the transition from an Eastern European neighborhood to a predominantly Hispanic one has been peaceful."[70] Whites required Chinese storeowners to include English translations on their business signs; whites did not burn down their stores or attack their homes. Violent mob action did not greet Cuban newcomers to Hialeah or Coral Gables or accompany the latinization of Anaheim or the Filipino migration to Daly City.

Moreover, white reaction to the newcomers did not replicate earlier attitudes of the black–white city. In Miami and southern California, many non-Hispanic whites were resentful not of the inferiority of the immigrant groups or of their depressing effect on property values. Instead they resented the pretensions or manifestations of superiority among some of the newcomers. Cubans were seen as getting it all; Chinese-only signs advertised to Anglos that their patronage was not desired; repeated complaints of too many Asians in Mercedeses expressed bitterness that the American dream was being realized by non-Americans while still proving elusive to the native-born. Everyone recognized, and some complained, that the Chinese inflated property values in the San Gabriel Valley, and Cubans were widely viewed as having boosted the fortunes of Miami. Poor Mexican and Central American immigrants might be criticized as relatively unschooled burdens on the native-born, middle-class taxpayers, but the newcomers of the late twentieth century were not seen uniformly as weighing down the nation's standard of living or draining the public treasury.

Many white Anglo complaints also focused on the self-imposed cultural segregation of the newcomers and their unwillingness to integrate into American society. A Westminster, California, city council member denied Vietnamese military veterans permission to parade, telling them: "It's my opinion that you're all Americans and you'd better be Americans. If you want to be South Vietnamese, go back to South Vietnam."[71] Vietnamese veterans should not march separately but join in the American parade; Chinese should advertise in English like good Americans; Cubans should speak English and give up their obsession with returning some day to a liberated Cuba. The white, native-born population believed that immigrants should speak English and become like "us." This was a different message from that prevailing in the black–white city of 1945. Blacks were expected to remain apart; in the minds of many whites, blacks did not have the innate capacity to become like "us."

Compared with the white, Anglo response, the African American reaction to the newcomers was often more troubled and sometimes violent. The poor Latin immigrants threatened to take low-skill jobs away from blacks, and the entrepreneurial Asians and Cubans often worked their way into the middle class by profiting from businesses in black neighborhoods. The newcomers too often seemed like both competitors and exploiters, getting ahead at the expense of the native-born minority that had long suffered white oppression. Moreover, the concept of model minorities, widely disseminated by the media, was a veiled insult to African Americans. It implied that some minorities familiar to white Americans were not model, and everyone knew which one minority was deemed less than model. When the model attributes—hard work, ambition, higher education, and strong family ties—were listed, they seemed to describe everything the stereotypical black welfare mother of white imagination was not. And when Koreans, Indians, and Cubans boasted of having worked their way to success despite their minority status and alien origins, it appeared to be an unspoken challenge to the long-standing black minority to energize itself and do likewise. There were new minorities on the block who were seemingly showing up the old minority, and the resulting black resentment was understandable.

Black-Cuban hostility was a major theme in the history of late-twentieth-century Miami. In the minds of many blacks, the influx of Cubans deprived African Americans of the opportunity to get better jobs or develop businesses because Anglo employers and bankers preferred hiring and lending to white Cubans rather than to black Americans. It was reported that in 1960, blacks owned 25 percent of the gas stations in Dade County and Cubans owned 12 percent. By 1979, the figure for blacks was 9 percent and for Cubans 48 percent.[72] Cuban businesses proliferated, seemingly depriving blacks of the opportunity for enterprise and upward mobility. "The only things blacks have in Miami are several hundred churches and funeral homes," complained one observer in the early 1980s. "After a generation of being Southern slaves, blacks now face a future as Latin slaves."[73] In the 1990s, a local black civil rights leader expressed his exasperation with the economic consequences of the takeover by Spanish-speaking Cubans: "There have been enough people brought to the country that have the jobs now, that the African American used to have and could have. But because No. 1, he doesn't speak Spanish, it's difficult to get the job. . . . It excludes me from work in my own community—in my own country."[74] A resident of Miami's black slums reiterated this sentiment: "They bring everybody to Miami. Nicaraguans, Cubans, Haitians. And we're still on the bottom. We can't even get to the first step to make it to the top."[75]

The animosity between blacks and Cubans was evident in the local media. In 1990 the African American *Miami Times* editorialized about the "Cuban Mafia" who controlled Miami, "bullying and threatening all those who do not toe the line."[76] A survey of the *Miami Times* editorials from the early 1960s to the early 1990s found that only 11 percent of the newspaper's references to Cubans were positive, 60 percent were negative, and the remainder neutral.[77] The African American newspaper did not always side against the newcomers. It opposed the 1980 English-only initiative as racist, although in 1988 it refused to denounce a proposed Florida constitutional amendment that would declare English the state's official language. A 1980 *Miami Herald* poll demonstrated that anti-Cuban feelings were stronger among blacks than among non-Hispanic whites. When asked whether the influx of Cubans before 1980 had a positive or negative effect on Miami, only 29 percent of the Anglos answered negatively, as compared with 45 percent of the black respondents.[78]

Local African Americans seemed especially exasperated that Cubans showed relatively little concern for race relations and few of the signs of racial guilt that blacks expected from white people in the post–civil rights era. "[Native whites] are racists by tradition and they at least know what they're doing is not quite right," commented one black Miamian. "Cubans don't even think there is anything wrong with it. That is the way they've always related, period."[79] In the 1980s, one observer of Miami concluded that "in South Florida, one almost has the feeling that the Cubans wonder what these black people are doing in this second Havana," and a 1990s study of Cuban–black relations reported that "the Spanish-language daily press is marked by a lack of interest toward blacks."[80] In 1993, after the black *Miami Times* criticized Cubans for their insensitivity toward African Americans, the newsletter of an organization of Hispanic county employees explained Cubans' refusal to bear the burden of racial guilt: "It may be okay with Anglos, since, historically, they are guilty of enslaving and degrading blacks for centuries; they owe blacks. But folks, we Hispanics owe blacks nothing." It asked: "What are we guilty of? Of hard work, not only as bankers and entrepreneurs, but also as humble laborers and peddlers? Keep it clear in your head that we have never coerced assistance from anyone, but would much rather roam the streets of Miami selling limes, onions, flowers, peanuts, etc. Some folks should try this, it is hard work, but not bad."[81] In other words, blacks should stop blaming innocent Cubans, get off the welfare rolls, and get to work. It was a message that did nothing to heal ethnic wounds in South Florida.

By 1993, these wounds were festering, owing to a number of well-publicized clashes between the newcomers and the old-time minority. In 1980 rioting swept through the black Miami neighborhood of Liberty City after the acquittal of white police officers charged with the fatal beating of a black man. Although the outbreak was not specifically aimed at Hispanics, the rioters did not discriminate between Anglos and Cubans. "During the riot, we hit everybody, Anglo, Cuban, it didn't matter," a black leader admitted.[82] Then, in 1982, a Cuban American police officer shot and killed an African American in the black ghetto of Overtown, touching off three days of rioting. And in 1989 a Hispanic officer shot and killed an African American motorcyclist, again resulting in three days of rioting by local blacks. Although the officer was actually Colombian, for blacks it was just one more example of Cuban oppression. "What I want to know is how come it's always the Cubans that's shooting the niggers," asked a local African American. A black former police officer admitted: "The Cubans will shoot a nigger faster'n a cracker will."[83]

Then, in 1990, the black South African leader and renowned foe of racial apartheid Nelson Mandela visited Miami and ignited a clash that widened the chasm between blacks and Cubans. Mandela had expressed support for Cuban Communist leader Fidel Castro and had personally thanked Castro for his support for the battle against apartheid. This incensed Miami's Cuban community, and five Cuban American mayors from Dade County, including the mayor of Miami, signed a statement condemning Mandela. The Miami City Commission also refused to adopt a resolution honoring the black foe of racial oppression. "We're really disappointed by these actions that serve not only to exacerbate deep wounds but to further entrench the racial polarization that has our city in its grip," observed the publisher of the black *Miami Times*. A black civil rights leader proclaimed: "We're tired of this racism, and we're not going to tolerate it anymore."[84] Local African American leaders called on national organizations to boycott Miami as a conference and convention site. Over the next two and a half years, the city lost an estimated $50 to $60 million in convention business owing to the boycott, the cost of the bitter rift between the Hispanic and African American communities.

In southern California, the rift was perhaps not so pronounced, but there was tension owing in part to competition between blacks and Latinos for low-skilled jobs. Moreover, it seemed that the newcomers had an advantage in the contest for employment. By the early 1990s, Los Angeles janitorial firms had largely replaced their unionized black workers with nonunion immigrants. A 1992 article in *Atlantic Monthly* commented on the "almost total absence of black gardeners, busboys, chambermaids, nannies, janitors, and construction workers in a city with a notoriously large pool of unemployed, unskilled black people." It claimed that "if Latinos were not around to do that work, nonblack employers would be forced to hire blacks—but they'd rather not. They trust Latinos. They fear or disdain blacks." The article concluded that "to Anglos, Latinos, even when they are foreign, seem native and safe, while blacks, who are native, seem foreign and dangerous."[85] Employing sophisticated statistical analysis, a scholarly study published in 1996 came to much the same conclusion, finding that "both Latino immigration and racism play significant roles in disadvantaging African Americans in terms of joblessness and earnings."[86]

Even more important than scholarly conclusions was the widespread perception among the black community that Hispanics were a threat. Indicative of this was the conflict over the much publicized 1992 campaign of African American Danny Bakewell to shut down Los Angeles construction projects that failed to employ blacks. In response to this crusade, Hispanic Xavier Hermosillo organized teams of undercover construction workers armed with video cameras who taped Bakewell's efforts to replace Hispanics with blacks.[87] Seemingly any employment for Latin newcomers was deemed a loss for African Americans, and Bakewell sought to stanch this flow of jobs to nonblacks.

Tied to the clash over jobs was discontent over the distribution of political power. Control of city hall meant public-sector jobs as well as public programs sensitive to the needs of the dominant ethnic group. This became the crux of controversy between African Americans and Hispanics in the black-dominated suburb of Compton. By the 1990s, a majority of the children in Compton's schools were Latino, but the blacks who controlled the school board were reluctant to spend money on bilingual education. "This is America," remarked one black school trustee. "Because a person does not speak English is not a reason to provide exceptional resources at public expense." Black youths fought Latino teenagers in the city's public schools, a videotape showed a black Compton police officer beating a Hispanic youth, and African American officials refused to share a sufficient portion of public-sector jobs with the lighter-skinned invaders from south of the border. One local Hispanic claimed: "A few years ago the white man was doing this to the black man and now black men are doing this to brown people." A black pastor agreed: "We are today the entrenched group trying to keep out intruders, just as whites were once the entrenched group and we were the intruders."[88]

Many black leaders were sensitive to Hispanic concerns in southern California and supposed manifestations of discrimination against the newcomers. The black president of the Los Angeles Urban League condemned Proposition 187, telling African American voters: "There are black people and other minority people who are at odds over jobs. But if you're black and you vote for 187, you're not just voting against Hispanics, but you're also voting for the kind of thing that has been used against blacks since time began."[89] The local chair of the NAACP also declared that he would vote against 187. But he recognized correctly that a large number of blacks would support the initiative. Given the "long-running tensions between the black and Latino communities," the NAACP leader argued, "many black people don't care that Proposition 187 is being financed by racist organizations. . . . If the initiative creates a McCarthyite police state, the attitude is, 'So be it.'"[90]

The sharpest conflict, however, arose between African Americans and Asians, specifically Koreans. The Asian newcomers became leading retailers in black neighborhoods, and tension between customers and merchants was manifest in cities across the country. A survey of newspapers in thirty-nine American cities found reports of forty black-led boycotts of Korean-owned stores in thirteen of the cities during the 1980s and first half of the 1990s. These included the boycott of a flea market in Miami, a minimart in Philadelphia, a beauty shop in Indianapolis, and a shopping center in Dallas. Moreover, there were reports of sixty-six violent incidents between African Americans and Koreans in sixteen cities, including thirty-two shootings. In twenty-six cases, an African American shot a Korean, and in the remaining six incidents a Korean was the shooter.[91] Often the boycotts and violence arose from a scuffle between a Korean shopkeeper and a black customer who was suspected of shoplifting. But African Americans also complained of poor merchandise, high prices, and generally rude treatment by Korean retailers. And many blacks regarded the Koreans as economic parasites draining the African American community of cash and contributing little in return.

In 1990, for example, a conflict between Korean merchants and black customers in Chicago's Roseland district raised many concerns commonly expressed in other cities as well. A flier distributed among African Americans bore the headline, "Lets Take Control of Our Community!" Referring to Korean storeowners, it asked: "Why don't they: Treat us with respect. Bank in our banks. Provide substantial employment. Donate to our community activities." Reiterating this, one black resident complained: "They take out money but they don't put anything back into the community." Another expressed the widespread resentment of suspicious Korean merchants who seemed to regard every black person as a likely shoplifter. "The worst thing is being watched like a hawk the whole time you're in the stores. I don't want to be followed around like I'm some thief."[92]

The most highly publicized boycotts of Korean businesses were in New York City, revealing the ugly tensions underlying Gotham's gorgeous mosaic. As early as 1981, New York's black newspaper, the *Amsterdam News*, wrote of the "anti-Korean hysteria" among Harlem's African American storekeepers, noting that "the situation is tense among both sides of the business community, and is seen in some circles as by far the most explosive issue to come out of the Black community since the Harlem riots of 1943." The next year, the Afrikan Nationalist Pioneer Movement initiated a "Buy Black" campaign aimed at ridding Harlem of Korean merchants.[93] The first boycott of a Korean store in Harlem began in October 1984 and lasted for more than three months. Demonstrators handed out fliers calling on blacks to "Boycott all Korean merchants."[94] The most notable boycott, however, was the campaign against the Red Apple and Church Fruits stores in Brooklyn in 1990/1991. Lasting for 505 days, it brought the black–Asian conflict to the attention of all New Yorkers and widened the division between militants on both sides. Although the protest arose from a tussle between Korean store employees and a black woman suspected of shoplifting, a boycott flier made it clear that there were larger issues at stake. "The question for Black folks to consider is this: 'Who is going to control the economic life of the Black community?'" the flier explained. "People understand that this struggle we are presently engaged in is a continuation of our historical struggle for self-determination."[95]

For Koreans, however, it was a struggle to maintain their right to do business in whatever neighborhood they desired. Around seven thousand Koreans, or approximately 15 percent of the Koreans in New York City, participated in a "peace rally" calling for an end to the boycott. Reminding Koreans of their own past oppression, speakers at the rally compared the boycott with the Japanese occupation of Korea during the first half of the twentieth century. The underlying message was that just as they had liberated themselves from the Japanese, they would overcome the black boycott leaders. Polls showed that only a minority of black New Yorkers supported the boycott, yet in the public's mind the clash was a clearly defined battle between Asians and blacks. A *New York Times* editorial headlined "These Boycotts Are Racist, and Wrong" summed up prevailing opinion among both white and Asian New Yorkers.[96]

In Los Angeles, there were fewer and less protracted boycotts, yet no one could ignore the signs of deep anger and bitterness between blacks and Asians. In March 1991, a Korean storekeeper in the South Central district shot and killed a fifteen-year-old black girl, Latasha Harlins, after a fight over a container of orange juice that Harlins was supposedly stealing. In November, a white judge sentenced the Korean woman to five years' probation and ordered her to pay a $500 fine and Harlins's funeral expenses. The light penalty for what many blacks regarded as simple murder outraged the African American community. One Korean American remarked: "That probation decision just drove a deep wedge right between the black and Korean communities. There was no middle ground; you were either for us or you were against us."[97]

Adding to the tense conditions was the release of the song "Black Korea" by Los Angeles rapper Ice Cube. Expressing rage at Asian store owners, Ice Cube rapped:

Don't follow me, up and down your market
Or your little chop suey ass'll be a target
of the nationwide boycott.

Then he went further, yelling:

> Pay respect to the black fist
> or we'll burn your store, right down to a crisp
> And then we'll see ya!
> Cause you can't turn the ghetto—into Black Korea.[98]

Having already suffered fire bombings and fatal attacks from black robbers, Korean merchants reacted strongly to Ice Cube's lyrics. "This is a life-and-death situation," commented the executive director of the Korean American Grocers' Association. "What if someone listened to the song and set fire to a store?"[99]

The following spring, a number of blacks did act out Ice Cube's lyrics and wreak havoc on Korean-owned businesses. In April 1992, a jury acquitted four white police officers who had been videotaped beating black motorist Rodney King. The Rodney King verdict, coming just months after the light sentence imposed in the Harlins case, ignited three days of violent rage. Surpassing in violence the Watts riot of 1965, the Los Angeles uprising of 1992 resulted in more than fifty deaths, over fourteen thousand arrests, and about $1 billion in property damage (figure 6.5). Both

FIGURE 6.5 Looting in Los Angeles during the riot of April 1992. (Gary Leonard, Security Pacific Collection, Los Angeles Public Library)

blacks and Latinos participated in the rioting, the number of Hispanics arrested actually exceeding the number of African Americans; but the black participants seemed to be more violent, whereas the Latinos were more often looters seeking free merchandise. The chief victims were Korean Americans. Although Koreans accounted for only 1.6 percent of Los Angeles County's population, they bore the lion's share of property loss. Korean stores suffered an estimated $359 million in damage. According to city government records, one-third of the businesses damaged within the city of Los Angeles were owned by Koreans, and about three-quarters of the stores on the State Insurance Commission's list of damaged properties were Korean-owned.[100] Most agreed that rioters specifically targeted the businesses of the hated Koreans. "There is no doubt that in the violence following the verdict Korean merchants were, in fact, targeted for destruction," commented a leader of the Southern Christian Leadership Conference. "There was a nasty anti-Asian, anti-Korean mood circulating throughout the streets of L.A. We can't deny it and we have to deal [with] that, straight up."[101]

There even were repercussions for Korean merchants in other cities. On the second day of the Los Angeles uprising, black rioters looted and burned two Korean-owned supermarkets in Las Vegas. That same evening, demonstrating African Americans in Manhattan smashed the windows of several Korean retailers, and most of New York's Korean merchants kept their stores closed during the Los Angeles rioting. In Atlanta, black college students attacked two Korean-owned stores, causing $300,000 in damage.[102]

Adding to the injury of Korean Americans was a campaign to prevent many of them from rebuilding their businesses in Los Angeles's South Central district. Many of the businesses destroyed were small combination grocery and liquor stores that some African American leaders believed contributed to the area's crime and moral decay. Consequently, they successfully intervened to halt the reestablishment of a number of the liquor retailers. The district's black city council representative stated: "An institutionalized form of oppression . . . the overconcentration of liquor outlets in my community drives down the quality of life."[103] Yet a Korean observer reported: "A lot of people in the Korean community felt liquor stores were just another code word for 'get Koreans out of our neighborhood.'"[104] Thus in the wake of the riot, the clash continued. Many blacks viewed Korean merchants as oppressors; many Koreans viewed blacks as exclusionary racists.

By the close of the twentieth century, then, the nation's newcomers seemed to add to the frustration of African Americans, who traditionally had been closed out of opportunities for advancement. In the 1960s and 1970s, a growing black presence in American cities offered blacks the prospect of parlaying their numbers into electoral victories. More black voters meant more black officeholders and, consequently, more public-sector jobs and public contracts. Yet during the last decade of the century, even the advantage of numerical supremacy was slipping away as cities across the nation were becoming less black. In Boston, Providence, Hartford, New York City, Newark, Washington, D.C., Atlanta, and Miami, the African American share of the population declined during the 1990s. The first major city to become majority black, Washington was growing lighter, its African American share falling from 66 to 60 percent. This same trend was evident in Chicago, Oklahoma City, Dallas, Fort Worth, San Antonio, Houston, Denver, and Phoenix. The drop was especially noteworthy on the immigrant-rich West Coast. Between 1990 and 2000, the black share of Los Angeles's population slipped from 14 to 11 percent; in San Francisco, the African American portion fell from 11 to 8 percent. In the much contested city of Compton, the drop was from 55 to 40 percent. During the 1980s, New York City, Chicago, and Los Angeles each elected African American mayors. During the 1990s, the executive office in each city returned to white hands. Given the changing demographic realities African American politicians had to form rainbow coalitions and join in America's gorgeous mosaic. Yet bitter conflicts with newcomers threatened to jar loose pieces of the mosaic, leaving a scattering of fragments of clashing colors. A New York landlord discussing prospective tenants seemed to sum up the worst possible scenario for African Americans in the multihued metropolis when he concluded: "Afghanistan is okay. Anything, but not black."[105]

In any case, the familiar pattern of the black–white city had largely disappeared by the close of the century. Latinos were looting Asian stores in a riot ignited by the acquittal of Anglo whites who beat up an African American. There was a sometimes confusing array of characters in the new metropolitan drama, and the story of conflict and competition was becoming more complex. Ethnic tensions persisted and in some areas became more acute. Yet the nature of the struggle between the ethnic fragments of metropolitan America was changing. The standard black–white scenario was obsolete.

After the Revolution

"What's Edison? Is that a city? I just never hear of it," responded New York's former mayor Edward Koch on learning in the summer of 2003 that the federal Office of Management and Budget had renamed the nation's largest concentration of population the New York–Newark–Edison metropolitan area. The name change was yet another sign of the revolution that had occurred since 1945. A New Jersey township of strip malls, subdivisions, and office parks was now officially deemed worthy to be joined with New York City as a metropolitan presence. Yet unlike the hubs of the past, it was a relatively invisible presence, unknown to a leading public official who had spent his entire life within fifty miles of the township. "For all too long, the major so-called suburbs or edge cities have been lost in the shadow of New York," Edison's mayor commented. "We're not lost anymore. We've wandered in from the wilderness."[1] But to Koch and many others, Edison was still lost, an obscure place they had to search for on a road map. By 2003, metropolitan America was no longer a world of easily identifiable places known locally and nationwide but an agglomeration of population and business with some historically famous old centers and many anonymous municipalities. The self-proclaimed "crossroads of New Jersey," Edison won its metropolitan distinction because it was at the intersection of expressways, and expressway interchanges had largely supplanted cities as metropolitan foci. Like other metropolitan residents, Koch had heard of the highways but not the place, for the place-names of cities and towns counted for much less in the post-urban world of the twenty-first century.

Trapped by past conceptions of the city and of metropolitan centers, the Office of Management and Budget felt compelled to insert the name Edison. But the linking of Edison and New York City as seeming equals simply highlighted the outmoded thinking of the federal agency. Edison and New York City were two different phenomena, apples and oranges, one the product of the pre-1945 age of cities and the other an example of the post-urban era of the late twentieth century. Metropolitan America was no longer organized around single dominant centers, as it had been in 1945; neither was it truly polycentered, with a few readily identifiable hubs. To identify metropolitan regions by the names of supposed centers was an anachronism, for metropolitan America was increasingly centerless. Yet it was not a featureless sprawl of indistinguishable elements or a uniform expanse of low-density settlement reminiscent of Frank Lloyd Wright's Broadacres. Instead, it was rich in diversity, a historical accretion of settlement patterns and lifestyles that reflected the felt needs of millions of Americans of the past and present. Metropolitan America included the remnants of traditional cities like Boston, New York, Pittsburgh, and San Francisco, as well as pre–World War II posh enclaves like Scarsdale, post–World War II residential behemoths such as Levittown, edge cities of the 1980s, and an array of malls, big-box stores, office complexes, and chain restaurants and hotels built at the close of the twentieth century.

Traveling through a metropolitan region, one did not pass from one hub to another but instead through layers or patches of settlement, each different and catering to different residents and workers and different lifestyles. Metropolitan America was edgeless and centerless; its place-names denoted governmental units like Edison Township rather than cohesive, clearly defined communities. It defied the traditional logic regarding cities, yet it suited the diverse lifestyles of the post-urban era. Freed from past strictures on sexual behavior, gays could congregate in some central-city neighborhoods, and childless professionals could likewise enjoy what they deemed a desirable urban lifestyle in the historic centers. Families still gravitated to the good schools of suburbia, and, subsidized by Social Security, retirees found happiness in walled communities of their own. There were Hispanic enclaves and suburban Chinatowns with signage incomprehensible to English speakers but welcoming to thousands of newcomers seeking to transplant Taipei to southern California.

Rather than a city with a readily mapped core and edge, metropolitan America was a mélange reflecting the social and cultural diversity of the nation. Liberated from reliance on a centripetal public transit system that funneled everyone and everything to a common core, auto-borne Americans of the late twentieth century escaped to separate spheres suited to their needs. Some headed for Edison; others, for Manhattan. A continuous zone of dense population stretched along the mid-Atlantic, the Florida peninsula, and the southern California coast. Yet there was no longer a coherent city, simply a mass of settlement accommodating a variety of lifestyles and people whose paths no longer intersected at a shared center.

The Edgeless City

In 2003 urban scholar Robert Lang issued a new communiqué from the nation's little-understood metropolitan expanse. Challenging Joel Garreau's decade-old prediction that edge cities were reestablishing dense, mixed-use, identifiable centers in the metropolitan mass, Lang claimed that instead the prevailing pattern was the edgeless city, "a form of sprawling office development that does not have the density or cohesiveness of edge cities" but accounted "for the bulk of the office space found outside downtowns." According to Lang, "Sprawl is back—or, more accurately, it never went away." "Isolated office buildings or small clusters of buildings" were spread over "vast swaths of metropolitan space," and as a prime example Lang offered Edison's central New Jersey, where "edgeless cities stretch over a thousand square miles of metropolitan area."[2] In other words, the multicentered metropolis was seemingly as passé as its single-centered ancestor. Metropolitan American was continuing its relentless advance across the countryside, eschewing concentration for sprawl.

Anyone driving the highways of New Jersey, Georgia, Florida, Illinois, Texas, or California would have strongly seconded Lang's findings. Commercial outlets spread in all directions and small office buildings with large parking lots proliferated at a faster pace than suburban high-rises served by multilevel garages. Strip centers skirting highways and giant discount stores convenient to motorists proved more attractive to time-conscious shoppers than many of the older malls that had dominated retailing for the past four decades. For the many customers who did not want to linger or stroll, a dense concentration of businesses had little appeal. If commerce was spread out along the highways, motorists could move as rapidly as possible along these asphalt conveyor belts, collecting goods and services as they passed. After all, one did not go to the dentist, grocery, or video store to experience some city planner's notion of diverse urbanity or to partake of some uplifting ambience. The idea was to get in, do one's business, and get out as quickly and conveniently as possible. Taking advantage of drive-through windows at drugstores, banks, and fast-food restaurants, customers might not even need to leave the comfort of their cars but instead could experience to the fullest the automobility of the edgeless city.

Meanwhile, housing subdivisions sprouted in barren fields, and the rate of residential sprawl seemed to accelerate. Once quiet suburbs emerged among the ranks of the nation's most populous cities, leading urban commentators to dub them boomburbs. By 2000, Virginia Beach could boast of 425,000 residents, up from 5,000 in 1950 and almost twice the population of Norfolk, the historic hub of tidewater Virginia. The Phoenix area included seven "suburban" cities with populations over 100,000, led by Mesa, with almost 400,000 inhabitants. Moreover, the growth of the Arizona boomburbs was not abating; in the mid-1990s, houses were reportedly consuming the Arizona desert at the rate of an acre per hour.[3] Both Virginia Beach and Mesa were already more populous than such traditional hubs as Minneapolis, Pittsburgh, Saint Louis, and Cincinnati. In California, there were twenty-five boomburbs with populations of more than 100,000, and the Denver metropolitan area was the site of three of these outlying giants, the largest being Aurora, with 276,000 people. Dallas was ringed by seven boomburbs that topped the 100,000 mark, headed by Arlington, whose population grew from 8,000 in 1950 to 333,000 in 2000. In these cities, growth was a way of life during the late twentieth century. Between 1986 and 1989, a breakneck annexation campaign more than doubled Aurora's area to 140 square miles. A Denver newspaper accused Aurora of being "bent on annexing Kansas and beyond."[4] "Arlington is a pro-growth town," observed a former planning official of the Texas city at the close of the 1980s. "Always has been, always will be."[5] Many observers felt that the physical evidence of unthinking, sprawling growth was all too obvious in many of the boomtowns. An early-twenty-first-century visitor to Aurora wrote of the Colorado giant: "It has no discernible downtown, no town center, just mile after mile of strip malls, small mom-and-pops, ethnic restaurants, and ranch-style housing developments."[6]

The boomburbs were not only large, and growing larger, but most were becoming more diverse, defying long-standing notions of ethnic and lifestyle homogeneity in suburbia. A University of Michigan study completed in 1999 judged Aurora "the most integrated city in the United States," and Aurora's school system claimed that sixty-eight languages were spoken in the city's households. In 2000, 20 percent of the population was Hispanic, and 12 percent was African American. The Aurora community services directory was printed in English, Spanish, Korean, Vietnamese, and Russian. "Everywhere you go, it's like you're in a different country, with all the cultures and people," observed an enthusiastic Aurora resident. "I feel sorry for people who live in all-black or all-white neighborhoods because they don't know what they're missing."[7]

Not only were there booming young cities welcoming people from around the world, but small towns and unincorporated areas in outlying counties were exploding with newcomers who had few or no ties to the region's historic hub city. By 2000, three suburban counties in the Atlanta area had over 500,000 residents, with Gwinnett County's population having soared from 32,000 in 1950 to 588,000 fifty years later. In 2004 Gwinnett County's school system was the largest in Georgia, with a more diverse student population than that of the predominantly black city of Atlanta. Twenty-three percent of the students were African American, 17 percent were Hispanic, and 10 percent were Asian American. Moreover, at the turn of the century, there seemed no prospect that Gwinnett's growth or that of surrounding counties would soon cease. In 1999 *Time* magazine ran a picture of new houses in Gwinnett County with the caption "Spread Alert" and questioned whether this was "part of the fastest widening human settlement ever."[8]

Many residents of the ever more populous political units of the edgeless city maintained a carefully controlled lifestyle and a sense of grassroots rule by resorting to the private governments of homeowner associations. Large, diverse counties or boomburbs could not provide government tailored to a single subdivision, but the associations could, thus preserving the local control traditionally valued in suburbia even while populations soared. In the crime-ridden, threatening metropolitan world of the late twentieth century, the proliferating homeowner associations also offered the sense of security associated with small towns and traditional residential suburbs. This was especially evident in the growing number of gated communities, walled subdivisions that were off-limits to nonresidents. Homeowner associations maintained the surrounding walls as well as the community's private streets and the recreation areas open only to subdivision residents and their guests. Many such communities hired guards to staff gatehouses or imposed a system of key cards or entry codes that ensured only authorized persons could enter the subdivision. Originally popular among Sun Belt retirees, gated communities attracted a growing portion of the population during the 1990s, especially in the boomburb regions of California, Arizona, Texas, and Florida. In 1994 approximately one-third of southern California's new communities were gated, and according to one estimate the nation's gated community population soared from 4 million in 1995 to 16 million in 1998. A study based on the 2001 American Housing Survey found that over 7 million American households were within walled communities.[9]

Various factors encouraged this retreat behind walls and the resort to private homeowner governments. Fear of outsiders and the crimes they might commit motivated some to seek a life behind gates and security guards. A South Florida developer observed: "People are a little neurotic. [Those] who have suffered from crime or know someone who has are sitting there all day like Chicken Little waiting for the sky to fall in." A resident of a southern California subdivision that installed gates in the 1990s explained: "Before it was gated I had to keep everything locked. There were transients coming through, walking up and down the street."[10] Yet prestige was an added advantage. "People like to live within walls because they give the illusion of security," remarked a Dallas security consultant. "And it has acquired a certain social connotation as well. It's become the thing to do, like having a doorman or a chauffeur."[11] Moreover, many residents believed that the walls and subdivision associations created a more neighborly community, a small-town feeling. "In any homeowner association I think you'd have more community spirit than just on a block," commented a California resident. "I guess the gates make it a family." And a Dallas developer asserted: "The number one issue as I see it is that people want a sense of community. I think that is more what the gate is about, more so than security." He believed that "the main thing is 'I want a small town atmosphere in my big city. I want to be part of a community where I can be friends with all these people who are similar to my background.'"[12]

In the seemingly limitless, centerless expanse of metropolitan America, walled subdivisions created identifiable, defined communities for their residents. For their residents, the walls provided needed edges in the edgeless city, boundaries that distinguished neighbors from intruders, the privileged from the poor, and the protected from the vulnerable. Implied in the concept of community was the notion that some belonged and some did not. In the amorphous sprawl of turn-of-the-century America, walled subdivisions made residents feel they were part of a community, fenced off from the dangerous and the undesirable. Many observers deplored the gated community phenomenon. A leading urban planner warned: "These walls and gates are leading to more segregation and more isolation, and the outcome is going to be tragic for all of us." But a resident of a gated community in the Dallas area boomburb of Irving thought otherwise: "It seems like a secure, established neighborhood where our kids can run around without having to worry about traffic." Claiming that in a city neighborhood "you never know what's going to happen," he concluded that "in a gated community you can control some of that."[13]

Another emerging element of the landscape of the edgeless city was the giant windowless retail outlet known as the big-box store. By the close of the twentieth century, fewer large, enclosed malls were being built, and some were standing derelict as shoppers turned from the mall's department store anchors and headed instead for the big-box emporiums of discounters that lined suburban highways. With low prices and huge inventories, these discount chains lured millions of bargain-hungry shoppers. In 2000 Wal-Mart, with 4,190 stores, was the world's largest retailer, reaping four times the revenues of the nation's second-largest chain and ten times the sales of Federated Department Stores, the owner of Macy's. Number three in the United States and four in the world was the home improvement giant Home Depot, and the upscale discounter Target ranked number six in the nation (figure 7.1).[14] Target was founded in 1962 as the discount outlet for Minneapolis's Dayton's Department Store. By the close of the century, Dayton's had purchased Detroit's premier department store, Hudson's, as well as Chicago's Marshall Field's. Yet in 2000, 83 percent of the company's pretax profits came from its discounter. Acknowledging the triumph of its big-box discount offspring over its aging department stores, the parent company changed its name from Dayton Hudson to Target.[15]

The triumph of big-box retailers was yet another stage in the shift of shopping from a centripetal pursuit to a centrifugal one. For the largest selection of merchandise at the best prices, the shopper of the early twenty-first century headed not toward the city center but outward from

the historic hub to suburban highways. At the beginning of the century, there was no Target store in Manhattan, but Manhattanites commuted outward to suburban outlets. "I'm beyond obsessed with Target," confessed one Manhattan business owner, who traveled to suburban New York or New Jersey each weekend to satisfy her obsession. Another well-heeled Manhattanite told of her discovery of Target in suburban Long Island: "I came out with two shopping carts full of stuff. They had to help me out the door. It's so cheap! It's amazing!"[16]

Wal-Mart best exemplified this reversal of the traditional pattern prevailing before 1945. Founded by Arkansas's Sam Walton, it first thrived by catering to underserved small-town customers and then expanded into suburbia. Finally, by the turn of the twenty-first century, it was entering the central cities. In 2003 it had outlets in seven of the top ten urban markets; the exceptions were Chicago, Detroit, and New York City. A retail analyst observed: "Urban areas are the last frontier for Wal-Mart other than international markets."[17] The same year, the giant discounter announced plans to open its first stores in the city of Chicago. Local labor unions responded with bitter attacks on the chain, which relied exclusively on nonunion labor. Yet many African Americans living near the proposed Wal-Mart sites favored the prospect of a big-box store in their neighborhood. A local pastor claimed that 99 percent of his congregants already shopped at suburban Wal-Marts, driving miles to satisfy their retailing needs. Expressing the opinion of many of her constituents, the city council representative for a black West Side neighborhood asserted: "If our money is good to spend in the suburbs, then it's good to spend here." "We need a Wal-Mart around here," remarked a West Side shopper. "I can't find any place in this neighborhood that sells decent clothes or furniture I can afford."[18]

Both well-heeled Manhattanites and poor Chicagoans were headed outward from the underserved central city to the great edgeless-city emporiums of the twenty-first century. In 1945 Macy's, in the heart of Manhattan, was the world's biggest retailer; in 2000 Bentonville, Arkansas, was the headquarters of the world's preeminent retailer. In 1945 shoppers traveled downtown to find the most merchandise and seek the best prices; in 2000 the treasure troves of shoppers were along New Jersey interstates and on Illinois acreage that had produced corn only a few years earlier. At the beginning of the twenty-first century, New York City and Chicago were the last frontiers of the world's largest retailer, the last places it chose to locate. The metropolitan revolution had turned the retailing world inside out.

Although millions of Americans were flocking to big-box stores, gated communities, and boomburbs, a cadre of highly vocal critics was keeping alive the tradition of antisuburban diatribes. "The United States has become a predominantly suburban nation, but not a very happy one," pronounced critic Philip Langdon in 1994. According to him, suburbs were "fostering an unhealthy way of life," and, echoing the screeds of the 1950s, he believed that suburbanization had produced "a bitter harvest of individual trauma, family distress, and civic decay."[19] Among the most vehement of the turn-of-the-century foes of suburban sprawl was James Howard Kunstler, who in a series of books leveled an unrelenting barrage of rhetoric on the edgeless city. It was "depressing, brutal, ugly, unhealthy, and spiritually degrading," a landscape of "jive-plastic commuter tract home wastelands, . . . Potemkin village shopping plazas with . . . vast parking lagoons," and "Orwellian office parks featuring buildings sheathed in the same reflective glass as the sunglasses worn by chain-gang guards." It was "destructive, wasteful, toxic," a blight on the nation and a plague on its people.[20] At the close of the century, *Time* magazine concluded with some exaggeration: "Everybody hates the drive time, the scuffed and dented banality, of overextended suburbs."[21]

Whereas many of the earlier diatribes of the 1950s, 1960s, and 1970s had focused on the suburbs' destructive impact on the central city, the attacks of the 1990s emphasized the edgeless city's toll on the natural environment. Influenced by the widespread embrace of environmentalism, critics in the late twentieth century claimed that suburban developers were at war with nature itself. The advance of suburban sprawl seemed to be accelerating, consuming the nation's fields and forests at an ever-increasing rate. In a 1999 article on suburban "hypergrowth," *Newsweek* reported that in the Denver area farmland was "falling to sprawl at a rate of 90,000 acres per year"; in Austin from 1982 to 1992, there was a "35 percent increase in open space lost to development"; and between 1990 and 1996, metropolitan Akron experienced a "37 percent decrease in population density and [a] land area increase of 65 percent."[22] According to an account of the sprawl problem published in 2000, America was "presently experiencing an unprecedented loss of 'open space'—productive crop and pasture lands, along with forest woodlands, fragile wetlands, and other natural wildlife habitats."[23]

Exacerbating the problem were the poisonous fumes and debilitating traffic snarls produced by the mounting number of automobiles transporting edgeless-city commuters. Kunstler described the Atlanta metropolitan area as "one big-ass parking lot under a toxic pall from Hartsfield [Airport] clear up to the brand-new completely absurd Mall of Georgia."[24] Everywhere the traffic seemed to be getting worse, polluting the air and damaging the lives of the auto dependent. The federal government found that between 1990 and 1995, the amount of time mothers spent behind the wheels of their cars rose by 11 percent. *U.S. News & World Report* concluded: "Moms spend more time driving than they spend dressing, bathing, and feeding a child." A California psychologist reported that about half the married couples he counseled suffered from commuter-related stress. "They come in having only a dim awareness that commuting is the problem," he noted. "Instead, they say we're quarreling too much, and the affection's gone, and so is the sex."[25]

Sexual intercourse, connubial affection, motherly devotion, atmospheric purity, flora and fauna, civic loyalty, and individual happiness all seemed to be victims of the relentless sprawl of the edgeless city. The indictment was as powerful in the 1990s as in the 1950s. Gwinnett County, however, was the new offender par excellence, replacing Levittown as public enemy number one. "They ran the environmental people out of here a long time ago," reported a Gwinnett County developer in 2000. "You've got no trees. You've got no streams. You've got no mountains. It's a developer's paradise."[26] But for Kunstler, Langdon, and a growing number of environment-conscious Americans, Gwinnett was hell.

A few foes of edgeless-city sprawl were willing to take violent action to curb development. Between January 2000 and August 2001, ecoterrorists set fire to more than a dozen new houses in New York, Indiana, Colorado, and Arizona.[27] On Long Island, they also spray-painted "Stop Urban Sprawl!" on a new home. "The Earth isn't dying, it's being killed," read a threatening communiqué from the pro-sabotage Earth Liberation Front, "and those who are killing it have names and addresses."[28]

More often, however, foes of sprawl resorted to the ballot box in repeated attempts to impose restrictions on development and preserve open spaces. In November 1998, 240 state and local measures to preserve or purchase open space were on the ballot in states across the nation, with voters approving 72 percent of them. Eight of the ten statewide measures to set aside open land won voter endorsement.[29] For example, New Jersey's electorate agreed to spend $1 billion over a ten-year period to preserve half the remaining undeveloped land in the state as open space. "Americans are finally realizing that once you lose land, you can't get it back," remarked New Jersey's governor.[30] Meanwhile, in 1997 Maryland adopted "Smart Growth" legislation that permitted state subsidies for new roads, sewers, and schools only in "priority funding areas," zones deemed suited for development. Developers seeking to plant new subdivisions in rural areas, thus perpetuating sprawl, could not count on state support for the infrastructure necessary to accommodate new homeowners. Similarly, in 1998 Tennessee approved legislation requiring municipalities and counties to draft comprehensive plans designating urban growth boundaries; state funding would be restricted to the development zones within these limits.[31]

Oregon, however, was the preeminent antisprawl state and a much-admired model for foes of the edgeless city. In the 1970s, it had adopted a policy of urban growth boundaries, designed especially to keep the Portland metropolitan area from sprawling southward into the rich farmland of the Willamette Valley. Basically, beyond these boundaries developers could not build. The consequence was denser development within the limits. Whereas in the late 1970s the average lot size in the Portland area was 13,000 square feet, by the late 1990s the figure was down to 6,700 square feet. In 1999 *Time* magazine reported: "Outside [the growth boundary], where open land is strictly protected, there's mostly just the uninterrupted flight of greenery we call nature. Unspoiled stretches of the Willamette River Valley start 15 miles from city hall."[32] James Kunstler also approved, lauding Portland as the exception to the dismal American rule. "Because people live there at a high density," he asserted, "the city can support a variety of eating places, bars, cafes, clubs. . . . The texture of life is mixed, complex, and dense, as a city ought to be." In his opinion, Oregonians were having "to find new ways of doing things: of making a living without destroying land, building real towns and city neighborhoods instead of tract housing pods and commercial strip smarm, [and] eliminating unnecessary car trips and commutes."[33]

The Portland experience was also welcome news to an emerging planning movement known as the New Urbanism. Led by architects Andres Duany and Elizabeth Plater-Zyberk, New Urbanism was the planning arm of the antisprawl crusade, dedicated to creating traditional-style neighborhoods with smaller lots, narrower streets, front porches, and corner groceries. Density and walkability were to replace the sprawl and automobile dependence of the edgeless city. Basically, New Urbanists sought to re-create the neighborhoods of the pre-1945 era before Levittown, Southdale Center, McDonalds, and the interstate highway system had corrupted American life. In their manifesto on New Urbanism, Duany and Plater-Zyberk urged their followers to remember the refrain: "No more housing subdivisions! No more shopping centers! No more office parks! No more highways! Neighborhoods or nothing!"[34]

A scattering of New Urbanist communities attracted considerable attention at the close of the twentieth century. The initial New Urbanist offering was Seaside, Florida, a small resort community designed by Duany and Plater-Zyberk in the 1980s. They followed this with Kentlands in suburban Maryland. The Disney Corporation signed on to the movement, constructing the New Urbanist community of Celebration adjacent to its Florida Disney World. In each of these communities, the planners eschewed the cul-de-sacs, expansive lawns, and front-facing garages of standard edgeless-city subdivisions, building instead houses with small yards and garages on back alleys within walking distance of stores and schools. Rejecting stark modernist architecture and opting instead for houses outwardly reminiscent of the eighteenth and nineteenth centuries, the designers of these communities created an environment that some found antiseptically cute. Kentlands and Celebration were carefully contrived refuges from the edgeless city that seemed about as real as Disney World's Main Street. Yet as the chorus of complaints about sprawl grew louder, the New Urbanist devotion to density and reduced reliance on the automobile attracted many adherents among planners and architects.

Some, however, questioned propaganda regarding sprawl and rebelled against the arrogance of planners and architects who claimed to know what was best for seemingly dim-witted Americans who for decades had preferred a big yard, a big car, and the ample private space afforded by suburbia rather than the density of the central city. Randal O'Toole denounced the planning tyranny of his home state of Oregon, claiming that all urban lifestyles from high density to low density were "valid lifestyle choices and they work for the people that live there." Yet, according to O'Toole, "if smart-growth planners had their way, almost everyone except a few rural workers and their families would be confined to high-density, mixed-use urban neighborhoods.... The arrogant notion that a small elite can and should make important lifestyle choices for everyone else is at the heart of the war on the suburbs."[35] An economist with the Reason Public Policy Institute seconded this notion when he observed: "You can't develop a public policy around stopping people from moving to the communities and homes they want to live in, at least not in the United States. Not yet."[36] In the pages of the *New Republic*, Greg Easterbrook made much the same point when he noted: "The reason Americans keep buying more housing, more SUVs, more swimming pools, and other space-consuming items is that they can afford those things.... If prosperity puts the four-bedroom house within reach for the typical person, it's hard to see why public policy should look askance at that."[37]

Not only did the antisprawl, smart-growth crusade smack of arrogant planning dictation, but it seemed motivated by the selfishness of those who already enjoyed open space and wanted to keep their less fortunate brothers and sisters out. Easterbrook noted that "if communities take the kind of steps that would really stop sprawl, they would confer a windfall on those already entrenched while damaging the prospect of those who long to attain the detached-home lifestyle."[38] Another observed: "Suburbanization by other people is what's unpopular; people love living in the suburbs, they just don't want anyone else out there with them."[39] Too often it seemed as if wealthy estate owners, gentlemen farmers, and those already established in rambling manses on two-acre lots were trying to keep house-hungry newcomers from wreaking "environmental" damage on their zones of privilege. Moreover, too often it appeared that urban growth boundaries would simply inflate the cost of land open to development, dooming middle-class purchasers and upwardly mobile immigrants from Mexico, China, and India to a life in an attached townhouse with a yard just large enough for a flower bed and walls that failed to keep out the sound of wailing babies and blaring radios from the unit next door.

In any case, the New Urbanists and their ilk seemed as yet not to represent the American norm. Despite all the rhetoric about banal subdivisions and the soulless highway culture, new home sales in edgeless-city developments were not abating and business at Wal-Mart and Target was booming. Gas-guzzling sports utility vehicles were big sellers for the auto industry, and the line at the drive-up window at McDonalds was not dwindling. Americans did not welcome the prospect of new houses blocking their scenic suburban views or additional cars on the highways slowing their journeys to the big-box store. Yet they themselves did not want to give up life in the edgeless city. If Americans wanted to live in a traditional neighborhood, they could have moved there. Plenty of homes were for sale in pre-1945 neighborhoods where one could stroll the sidewalks to public transit lines that would carry one downtown. Some were selecting this lifestyle option, but, the New Urbanists and sprawl busters to the contrary, more Americans seemed to prefer living in the edgeless city.

The Perpetual Renaissance

While the edgeless city sprawled outward with new Wal-Marts, subdivisions, and office parks, the older central cities survived and continued their seemingly perpetual search for renaissance. In fact, at the close of the century, the news from the historic urban core was unusually upbeat. The 2000 census showed that the population decline in the hub cities had slowed, leading a Brookings Institution study to write of an "urban turnaround."[40] In both Chicago and Minneapolis, the population increased 4 percent during the 1990s, the first rise in either city since the 1940s. During the 1950s and 1960s, Boston, Providence, and Worcester had been counted out as dying centers of a region whose heyday had long passed, but in the 1990s each of these cities posted population gains, demonstrating that they could not be dismissed as has-beens. Even the cities that continued to lose population did so at a reduced rate. In the 1970s, the number of residents in Cleveland had dropped 24 percent; in the 1990s, the decline was only 5 percent. Similarly, Detroit's population plummeted 20 percent in the 1970s but only 8 percent in the 1990s. Most of the decline in the 1990s seemed to be the result of smaller households rather than wholesale abandonment of structures such as plagued the older centers in the 1970s. In 2000 there was nothing to compare with the devastation of the South Bronx a quarter century earlier.

Some of the supposed turnaround might have been owing to improved census coverage in 2000, as compared with 1990. It was widely believed that the Census Bureau had failed to count many urban dwellers in 1990, thus shortchanging older hubs. In 2000, however, Census Bureau efforts seem to have improved, producing a more accurate count. Yet the influx of immigrants from Latin America, Asia, and Europe seeking inexpensive housing in the inner cities also appeared to explain some of the change. New York City's population rise of 9 percent clearly was owing to new-comers from abroad who were reinforcing the city's role as a multicul-tural mecca. Moreover, gentrification probably accounted for a share of the good news. The city had not lost its allure for at least some of the young and childless. Popular television programs such as *Seinfeld* and *Friends* broadcast an appealing picture of Manhattan apartment life that partially erased the adverse images of mugging, rioting, and decay inher-ited from the late 1960s and the 1970s. For millions of television viewers in the 1990s, the city was a place of laughs and romance where attractive young people struggled only with the tribulations of situation comedy and not with the traditional urban conflicts arising from ethnicity, poverty, crime, or class strife.

In addition, the older hubs retained their long-standing grip on the American psyche. Million of suburban Americans still referred to them-selves as being from New York, Philadelphia, Chicago, Atlanta, and San Francisco even though they had never lived within those cities and rarely set foot in them. Although they did not contribute to the tax base, census data, and retail sales figures of the central city, in some way it was still their city, part of their identity when they defined where they were from. They departed from and arrived at airports bearing the names of the his-toric hubs, watched television newscasters who reported what the local big-city mayor said and did, and read the metropolitan daily newspapers published in the old downtown. The historic hubs were not what they used to be, but they were not forgotten and could not be wholly ignored.

Despite the persistent significance of the core municipalities and the supposed urban turnaround, the role of the older centers in American life

remained insecure, and mayors and downtown business leaders continued to seek an elixir that would provide lasting revitalization. Downtown
was no longer the focus of retailing and no longer the hub of office employment. The so-called central cities had to remain the center of something if they were to continue to merit the label "central." Moreover, they
had to fashion a lucrative role for themselves if they were to generate
enough tax revenues to support public services and create enough jobs to
support their residents. Thus city leaders remained dedicated to making
their cities destinations, places where people would come and spend
money. The center had to have some magnetic attraction for those with
cash, and in the 1990s, as in earlier decades, the search for this attraction
preoccupied urban policy makers.

A favorite element in efforts to recenter metropolitan America was the
sports team. By the end of the century, little united the residents of a metropolitan area other than a common allegiance to the local professional
sports team. Affluent white residents in Oakland County, Michigan, did
not mix with poor black inhabitants immediately to the south in the city of
Detroit, nor did they have many links with blue-collar whites in adjacent
Macomb County. Oakland and Macomb countians did not frequent downtown Detroit; they no longer shopped or worked there. The various com-
ponents of the metropolitan population of southeastern Michigan feared,
resented, or ignored one another. But they were all fans of the Detroit
Tigers baseball team, the Detroit Lions football team, and the Detroit Pis-
tons basketball team. The one uniting bond that identified them as De-
troiters, even though most did not live in the city of Detroit, was a loyalty
to sports teams bearing the city's name. It was this uniting loyalty that
many urban leaders believed could refocus the edgeless city, diverting
some of its wealth and many of its people to sports events in the historic
hub. The common allegiance to the local team was one of the few good
cards that central cities had left in their hands, and in the 1990s urban
leaders sought to trump suburban successes by playing it.

One city after another embarked on expansive programs to build sports
facilities that would draw people and money to the aging core and boost
its fortunes and morale. With noteworthy consistency, scholarly studies
demonstrated that the millions of public dollars spent for downtown stadiums and arenas would not yield sufficient tangible benefits to warrant
the state, county, or city financial commitment. Central-city boosters
claimed, however, that the sports facilities were worth the public-sector investment. In 1996 a Saint Louis economic development director con-

tended: "There are intangible benefits . . . corporate recruiting, community attitude and reintroducing people to a city. . . . As people come downtown and get comfortable there, they are more likely to come down again, hang out and spend time."[41] In 1997 the Minnesota Twins financial adviser agreed when he told a legislative committee, "No one can tell me that it's not better to have three million people a year coming to downtown Minneapolis to watch baseball than having none."[42] Backers of a ballot proposal for a tax levy to finance a stadium in downtown Cleveland emphasized the positive economic impact on the city's core when they adopted the slogan, "More Than a Stadium."[43]

In Cleveland, Minneapolis, and Saint Louis, it was more than just a question of sports facilities; it was also one more attempt at recentering metropolitan America and reasserting the historic hub's once unquestioned claim to be central to at least one aspect of American life. Identifying the crux of the issue, one student of the impact of sports on cities asked: "In a city with a full set of urban challenges, is the new image created by these public investments worth the commitments if there is no direct economic impact? Is the myth or illusion of activity created by the glamour from sports and downtown crowds worth what the public sector spent?"[44] Most urban leaders answered with a definite yes.

This was evident across the country. For example, in Baltimore a state sports authority built Camden Yards ballpark for baseball's Orioles as yet another step in the city's long-term campaign to attract visitors. Chicago's mayor arranged a complex financing package to pay for the renovation of downtown Soldier Field, ensuring the continuing presence of the football Bears in the city's core.[45] In 1996 the public sector agreed to contribute 48 percent of the estimated $505 million necessary to build a new downtown ballpark for the Detroit Tigers and a football stadium for the Detroit Lions. The *Detroit Free Press* announced this deal with the euphoric headline "Detroit Comeback" and claimed that the city's investment would pay off because of new "development expected near the project and a new image for downtown."[46] Perhaps no city relied more heavily on sports to recenter the metropolitan population than long-troubled Cleveland. As part of a downtown revitalization scheme, city leaders arranged for the construction of a new baseball park, an adjacent professional basketball arena, and a nearby football stadium. By doing so, they ensured that the baseball team would remain in town, they lured the basketball team from its previous home in suburban Richfield, and they secured a new football franchise after losing their team to Baltimore a few years earlier.[47] Thus Cleveland firmly reinforced its big-league status, despite its long economic and population decline, and it attracted millions of sports fans to the downtown area. Although no longer as significant a retailing destination or as prominent a business center, downtown Cleveland was at least the unquestioned professional sports hub of northeastern Ohio.

Cleveland and its urban ilk were also resorting to other ploys to lure people back to the historic metropolitan center. During the 1990s, both the $92 million Rock and Roll Hall of Fame and the $55 million Great Lakes Science Center opened in downtown Cleveland to serve as magnets drawing additional visitors to the core.[48] In 1992 the New Jersey Sports and Exposition Authority opened the New Jersey State Aquarium in downtown Camden, a gritty community perennially on the list of the nation's most troubled cities.[49] Throughout America, ever-larger convention centers were constructed to draw out-of-town spenders to the city core, with some succeeding and others struggling to attract the bookings necessary to survive.[50] A new panacea was casino gambling. No city grew at a faster pace in the late twentieth century than Las Vegas, the world's gaming capital. Given its success, some urban leaders turned to gambling as an untapped attraction that would make their cities destinations for millions of Americans. In the 1990s, casinos opened in both East Saint Louis and Gary, cities that vied with Camden for the distinction of worst in the nation.[51] Although they did not spur a revolution in the economies of the two cities, the casinos did provide much needed revenues for municipal treasuries and enable local officials to finance public services. "From an economic development perspective, it has been a boon for us," reported Gary's economic development director, though he admitted that "Gary was in pretty dire straits when they came in." According to the director of Gary's chamber of commerce, the casinos at least gave the city "something else to be seen as besides another buckle in the Rust Belt."[52]

Another revitalization initiative of the 1990s aimed at attracting housing to the downtown area. By boosting the residential population of the central business district, cities would supposedly ensure twenty-four-hour vitality in the core and secure new customers for the remaining downtown businesses. There were reports of new downtown residents not only in Manhattan or such traditional bastions of gentrification as Boston, Philadelphia, Chicago, or San Francisco. The centripetal movement seemed to be occurring in a broad variety of cities across the country. By December 1998, fourteen buildings in downtown Birmingham, Alabama, housed apartment dwellers, and six more conversions of commercial structures to dwellings were under way. For example, floors eight through nineteen of a twenty-one-story former bank building were being transformed into condominiums, and eleven floors of a seventeen-story office tower were being renovated as rental apartments. "There is no tradition of living in the city like you find in older, East Coast cities," commented a Birmingham leader. "We've found it's a niche market, but a bigger niche than most people anticipated, and a growing one."[53] Developers in Denver were likewise finding customers for downtown living among the niche market of young professionals. Chic LoDo was the focus of the hottest real-estate action. "LoDo has legitimacy, it has currency, it can't be cloned in the suburbs," remarked one real-estate broker. "When someone can live anywhere they want, and they choose to live in Lower Downtown, it's a statement about how the city is changing," observed an architect.[54] Similarly, Cleveland's downtown warehouse district was becoming a desirable place to live, boasting over one thousand apartments as well as trendy restaurants and bars by 2001.[55] In 2004 the *Columbus (Ohio) Dispatch* carried the headline "Demand for Downtown Living on Rise." Reporting on the opening of the sales office for his in-town project, a Columbus developer said: "We were inundated with people interested in urban living."[56]

In the 1990s, as in the 1980s, the young, childless, bohemian, artistic, and gay were the principal newcomers to the core, enjoying a lifestyle not available in Gwinnett County, Georgia, or Mesa, Arizona. One developer who had retrofitted former office space in Houston commented: "Sex is what sells the city. It's where the single people are, where you go to a bar to meet them. . . . In Houston there are few places for people to walk around and promenade—downtown is the exception."[57] A new condominium complex in midtown Atlanta appealed to prospective buyers by advertising: "Extremely hip shopping and dining is only an elevator ride away. Just press G—very cool stuff awaits you on the ground floor."[58] The *New York Times* reported that Denver's LoDo had "emerged as the city's gallery and restaurant center, with 18 galleries and about 100 bars and restaurants." A Coloradoan reinforced this image when he noted that LoDo was "going back to the old idea of Denver as the drinking capital for the hinterland."[59] Life in the core was for those who yearned for the sexy, the hip, and the bar scene, for a lifestyle far removed from Wal-Mart and McDonalds.

At the beginning of the twenty-first century, the rise in the core population brought hope to many central-city advocates. A Brookings Institution study titled "Downtown Rebound" found that in eighteen of twenty-four sample cities the downtown population had increased during the 1990s. Houston's downtown population soared 69 percent, Seattle's was up 67 percent, Denver's increased 51 percent, and Cleveland's rose 32 percent.[60] Responding to this good news from the 2000 census, *USA Today* carried the headline "Downtowns Make Cities Winners."[61]

Yet in absolute numbers, the downtown populations generally remained small, and the dramatic percentage increases reflected the very low base populations in 1990. In 2000 fewer than 12,000 Houston residents lived downtown out of a total city population of nearly 2 million. Cleveland's central business district had fewer than 10,000 inhabitants, and downtown Denver was home to 4,230 people, about enough to keep one small supermarket in business. Moreover, the redevelopment of downtown commercial structures for housing use was a sign as much of failure as of success. Traditionally, few people had lived downtown because real-estate values were so high in the core as to price housing out of the market. Only big department stores, major banks, and well-heeled corporations could afford core real estate. By the 1990s, however, the big spenders no longer wanted many downtown properties, making it economically feasible to rent them as housing. Birmingham's older skyscrapers were becoming dwelling units because they could no longer attract sufficient commercial tenants. This was true throughout the nation as older office space no longer commanded a market. In New York City, 45 Wall Street, an aging tower at the hub of the nation's premier financial district, became residences, and in Philadelphia the same fate awaited the old stock exchange building. Cincinnati's Shillito's Department Store building, once the center of the city's retailing, became ninety-eight dwelling units, and in Cleveland there were plans to renovate the grand old Statler Hotel as apartments after the converted hostelry had failed as an office structure.[62] Many cities, then, were making the best of a bad situation. Structures designed for more lucrative economic uses were being salvaged to play a modest role as housing. In 1945 the idea of wasting space on Wall Street for residences or using a city's largest department store for apartments was unthinkable. Wall Street and Shillito's were too valuable to hand over to apartment dwellers.

Despite all the rebound hype so commonplace among urban boosters since the 1950s, the news from the older central cities remained decidedly mixed. In many aging cities, the signs of decentralization were unavoidable, but nowhere were they more apparent than in Detroit. Detroit had created the automobiles responsible for the transformation of the city, and poetic justice seemed to dictate that it suffer the most from the consequences of the auto-borne flight from the core. In 1998 the giant J. L. Hudson Department Store building was finally imploded after fifteen years of standing vacant. For those seeking additional relics of the urban past, downtown Detroit offered a number of vacant office buildings, most notably the thirty-two-story David Broderick Tower. In the mid-1990s, an architectural historian pronounced the city's abandoned office structures "gray haunting monuments" and "the most depressing sight in urban America."[63] At the close of the century, the Motor City's thirty-three-story Book Cadillac Hotel, with over one thousand rooms and five floors of ballrooms, also survived as an empty hulk, having welcomed its final visitors in 1984. In February 2001, Detroit's last downtown movie theater closed, although the grand Fox Theater had been saved and renovated as a performing arts center. Meanwhile, many of the inner-city neighborhoods surrounding downtown had vanished or were in the process of disappearing. In 1995 there were 66,000 vacant lots in the city, and an urban observer noted that "vast parts of the city have reverted to prairie so lush that state game wardens export Detroit pheasants to the countryside to improve the rural gene pool."[64] "Detroit is reverting to a farm," concluded a former planning director of the city.[65]

Perhaps most insulting to the once grand Motor City was the proposal by the photographer and urban commentator Camilo Vergara that "a dozen city blocks of pre-Depression skyscrapers should be left standing as ruins: an American Acropolis." No longer the hub of southeastern Michigan, downtown Detroit should survive as a derelict relic of the American lifestyle destroyed by the metropolitan revolution of the second half of the twentieth century. For tourists, the Motor City downtown could evoke a lost past, an almost forgotten era of urban glory and grandeur. In 1995 Vergara found little but ruins left. "On the streets, wanderers and madmen sit on the sidewalks or push shopping carts," he reported. "Large numbers of skyscrapers that were planned to last for centuries are becoming derelict; a cluster of semi-abandoned structures rises like a vertical no-man's-land behind empty lots."[66]

Most central cities could take pride in the fact that at least they were not as bad off as Detroit. Yet the adverse signs of decentralization marked many other inner cities and downtowns. By the late 1990s, the urban renewal shopping mall that was intended to revive central New Haven was largely empty, Macy's having vacated its anchor store in 1993. In 2004 the downtown Lazarus Department Store in Columbus, Ohio, closed. Traditionally the city's preeminent emporium and the unchallenged mecca of Central Ohio shoppers in 1945, the downtown outlet could not survive in the decentralized world of the early twenty-first century. Along Nicollet Mall in downtown Minneapolis, a five-story retail center named the Conservatory opened with fanfare in 1987 but was demolished a decade later. In 2000 the retail space in downtown Minneapolis's giant mixed-use City Center was 25 percent vacant. At the beginning of the twenty-first century government offices occupied much of the retail space in Town Square mall in downtown Saint Paul, and the city's one remaining downtown department store was remodeling two of its five floors for offices.[67] In 1996 Mary Tyler Moore came to the Twin Cities for a book-signing appearance that took place not in downtown Minneapolis, the destination for her television journey in the 1970s, but in the outlying Mall of America, the nation's largest shopping mall. Television's Mary Richards might have made it after all in downtown Minneapolis, but if the real-life Mary Tyler Moore wanted to market her book she needed to head for the edgeless city along Interstate 494 where the Mall of America and twenty-three hotels with 5,500 rooms beckoned to the dollars of consuming Minnesotans and out-of-state travelers.[68]

Moreover, Detroit was not the only city with tracts of empty land and thousands of abandoned structures. In 2000 there were about twenty thousand vacant lots in Philadelphia and more than thirty thousand abandoned dwellings. The *Philadelphia Inquirer* claimed that "there is no market demand for most of [Philadelphia's] vacant land and buildings." A visitor to Saint Louis would find expanses of unused land equal to those in Philadelphia or Detroit. Much of central Saint Louis consisted of nodes of development separated by fields standing idle. The *Baltimore Sun* observed that forty thousand empty row houses in the Maryland metropolis had "spread blight, crime, and despair across wide swathes" of the city. Similarly, the New Orleans planning director reported thirty-seven thousand vacant dwelling units in her city.[69] Though abandonment was generally not proceeding at the devastating pace of the 1970s an inventory of unused and unwanted land and structures testified to the continuing plight of many older hubs.

Even in the lotus land of southern California, social commentators were painting a grim picture of the urban future. In a number of widely read works, critic Mike Davis most notably presented an apocalyptic vision of Los Angeles. "We live in 'fortress cities' brutally divided between 'fortified cells' of affluent society and 'places of terror' where the police battle the criminalized poor," Davis wrote. Focusing on the Los Angeles of gang conflict, police repression, social and economic inequities, and public warfare on the poor, Davis depicted the end-of the-century city as a place of fear and seething tension, an environment ready to explode and worthy of destruction. Davis posited the existence of a "new class war . . . at the level of the built environment," with Los Angeles as "an especially disquieting catalogue of the emergent liaisons between architecture and the American police state."[70] In other words, the glittering high-rise monuments to global capitalism so admired by many observers were actually stakes driven into the heart of the poor. The landmarks of wealth were also symbols of shame.

The social schisms of Los Angeles, the looming empty hulks of downtown Detroit, the fields of central Saint Louis, the young bar hoppers of LoDo, the Mall of America, the ubiquitous Wal-Marts and McDonalds, the gated communities, and the sprawling boomburbs all testified to the revolution that had swept across metropolitan America since 1945. The old notion of the city with a single dominant hub and a readily identifiable edge was as obsolete as the downtown department store. Americans had used their automobiles to escape the centripetal pull of the historic hub and had spread across the countryside. Throughout the latter half of the twentieth century, critics deplored this decentralization, identifying Levittown, shopping malls, big-box stores, and gated communities as symptoms and sources of societal decay, suburban neuroses, and environmental disaster. Yet most Americans seemed to disagree with these naysayers, investing in millions of suburban tract homes, filling outlying malls, and making Wal-Mart the world's largest retailer. Despite all the paeans to traditional neighborhoods, urbanity, and the enriching diversity of the core, Americans left the central city so admired by Jane Jacobs and her ilk and bought into the lifestyle sold by William Levitt and Sam Walton. Many of those who remained in the central cities retrofitted the old buildings and old neighborhoods to suit their own needs. They created gay ghettos and Yuppie havens, displacing working-class taverns with restaurants and bars deemed "hip" or trendy. Thus in both the historic core and the emerging edgeless city, diverse groups mapped out sectors of the metropolitan turf and made them their own.

The result was not the uniform, banal sprawl that unperceptive critics deplored. Instead, metropolitan America became a vast, centerless, edgeless expanse with diverse zones adapted to various uses and lifestyles.

Golden prewar suburbs such as Beverly Hills and Scarsdale survived, as did more modest postwar developments such as Levittown and Park Forest. Suburban Chinatowns were a short drive from Latino barrios, and southern California could boast of both homosexual West Hollywood and Leisure Worlds for retirees. Gentrification created communities of historic but renovated townhouses, art galleries, and expensive eateries. The jarring mix, the cacophony of communities, might not have appealed to planners and pundits, who seemed to believe that the good life required a set formula of front porches and busy sidewalks. But it accommodated the varied American population, and there seemed to be little desire among most Americans to return to the automobile-less, one-bathroom, un-air-conditioned, central-city apartment lifestyle that so many had endured in 1945. They had exploited unprecedented mobility, prosperity, and freedom to spread outward and fragment. Taking advantage of the ever-growing mass of automobiles, Social Security and government-guaranteed mortgages, liberation from age-based, gender, and sexual preference conventions as well as reduced barriers to immigration, they created a new metropolitan world far different from the constrained single-center city of the past. In response to changing lifestyle preferences, attitudes, and technology, a revolution had transformed metropolitan America. The city as conceived in 1945 no longer existed.

Notes

Introduction

1. Henry S. Churchill, *The City Is the People* (New York: Harcourt, Brace, 1945), p. 1.

1. 1945

1. Cleveland Rodgers, *New York Plans for the Future* (New York: Harper, 1943), p. 18.

2. Cited in Jan Morris, *Manhattan '45* (New York: Oxford University Press, 1987), pp. 7–8.

3. George J. Eberle, "The Business District," in *Los Angeles: Preface to a Master Plan*, ed. George W. Robbins and L. Deming Tilton (Los Angeles: Pacific Southwest Academy, 1941), pp. 129, 143.

4. Bureau of the Census, *Statistical Abstract of the United States, 1950* (Washington, D.C.: Government Printing Office, 1950), p. 514.

5. Harold M. Mayer, "Moving People and Goods in Tomorrow's Cities," *Annals of the American Academy of Political and Social Science* 242 (1945): 121.

6. *New York Times*, 30 September 1945, sec. 4, p. 10; Morris, *Manhattan '45*, pp. 43–44.

7. *New York Times*, 25 September 1945, pp. 1, 14–15; 30 September 1945, sec. 1, pp. 1–2, sec. 4, p. 2.

8. *New York Times*, 25 September 1945, p. 15.

9. Kathryn Bishop Eckert, *Buildings of Michigan* (New York: Oxford University Press, 1993), p. 68.

10. Richard J. Seltzer, *Proposals for Downtown Philadelphia* (Chicago: Urban Land Institute, 1942), pp. 15, 17.

11. Lloyd Wendt and Herman Kogan, *Give the Lady What She Wants! The Story of Marshall Field and Company* (Chicago: Rand McNally, 1952).

12. Mary Schauffler, *The Suburbs of Cleveland: A Field Study of the Metropolitan District Outside the Administrative Area of the City* (Chicago: University of Chicago, 1945), pp. 381–82.

13. Wendt and Kogan, *Give the Lady What She Wants!* p. 376.

14. *New York Times*, 8 December 1945, p. 22.

15. Zula McCauley, *The First Fifty Years* (Dallas: Neiman-Marcus, 1957), p. 36.

16. Charles S. Johnson, *Patterns of Negro Segregation* (New York: Harper, 1943), p. 66.

17. Ibid., p. 291.

18. Jessie Parkhurst Guzman, ed., *Negro Year Book: A Review of Events Affecting Negro Life, 1941–1946* (Tuskegee, Ala.: Department of Records and Research, Tuskegee Institute, 1947), p. 151.

19. St. Clair Drake and Horace R. Cayton, *Black Metropolis: A Study of Negro Life in a Northern City*, rev. ed., 2 vols. (New York: Harper & Row, 1962), vol. 1, p. 300.

20. Wendt and Kogan, *Give the Lady What She Wants!* pp. 312–13.

21. David D. Van Tassel and John J. Grabowski, eds., *The Encyclopedia of Cleveland History* (Bloomington: Indiana University Press, 1987), pp. 66, 483.

22. "Suburban Branch Stores in the New York Metropolitan Region," *Regional Plan Bulletin*, no. 78 (December 1951): 1–8.

23. *New York Times*, 15 September 1945, p. 26; 4 October 1945, p. 29.

24. *New York Times*, 16 January 1946, p. 28.

25. McCauley, *First Fifty Years*, p. 37.

26. Alan Balfour, *Rockefeller Center: Architecture as Theater* (New York: McGraw-Hill, 1978), p. 92.

27. Van Tassel and Grabowski, eds., *Encyclopedia of Cleveland History*, pp. 18–19, 486–87, 737–38, 750, 771–72, 923–24.

28. Eckert, *Buildings of Michigan*, pp. 72–73.

29. *Chicago Tribune*, 16 September 1945, sec. 6, pp. 2, 8; 30 September 1945, sec. 6, p. 8; 14 October 1945, sec. 6, p. 7.

30. *Chicago Tribune*, 14 October 1945, sec. 6, p. 7.

31. Seltzer, *Proposals for Downtown Philadelphia*, p. 38.

32. Carl S. Wells, *Proposals for Downtown Detroit* (Washington, D.C.: Urban Land Institute, 1942), p. 7.

33. Jon C. Teaford, *The Rough Road to Renaissance: Urban Revitalization in America, 1940–1985* (Baltimore: Johns Hopkins University Press, 1990), p. 19.

34. Jon C. Teaford, *City and Suburb: The Political Fragmentation of Metropolitan America, 1850–1970* (Baltimore: Johns Hopkins University Press, 1979), p. 77. For

all 140 metropolitan districts in the United States in 1940, the central city population constituted 68 percent of the total metropolitan population (Bureau of the Census, *Sixteenth Census of the United States: 1940*, vol. 1, *Population* [Washington, D.C.: Government Printing Office, 1942], p. 61).

35. Guzman, ed., *Negro Year Book*, pp. 8–9.

36. Ibid., pp. 9, 134; Drake and Cayton, *Black Metropolis*, 1:9; *Race Relations in Chicago* (Chicago: Mayor's Committee on Race Relations, 1944), p. 2; *Home Front Unity: Proceedings of the Chicago Conference on Home Front Unity* (Chicago: Mayor's Committee on Race Relations, 1945), p. 8.

37. Johnson, *Patterns of Negro Segregation*, pp. 28–29.

38. Ibid., p. 34.

39. Ibid., p. 35.

40. Ibid., pp. 56, 59.

41. Ibid., pp. 32, 42, 74–75.

42. Drake and Cayton, *Black Metropolis*, pp. 102, 106–7.

43. Florence Murray, ed., *The Negro Handbook 1944* (New York: Current Reference Publications, 1944), pp. 9, 222.

44. Ibid., p. 219.

45. Johnson, *Patterns of Negro Segregation*, p. 58.

46. Kenesaw M. Landis, *Segregation in Washington: A Report of the National Committee on Segregation in the Nation's Capital* (Chicago: National Committee on Segregation in the Nation's Capital, 1948), p. 16.

47. Murray, ed., *Negro Handbook*, p. 220.

48. Landis, *Segregation in Washington*, p. 50.

49. Ibid., p. 76.

50. Clement E. Vose, *Caucasians Only: The Supreme Court, the NAACP, and the Restrictive Covenant Cases*, 2d printing (Berkeley: University of California Press, 1967), pp. 75–76.

51. Herman H. Long and Charles S. Johnson, *People vs. Property: Race Restrictive Covenants in Housing* (Nashville: Fisk University Press, 1947), p. 49.

52. Robert C. Weaver, *The Negro Ghetto* (New York: Harcourt, Brace, 1948), p. 250.

53. Vose, *Caucasians Only*, p. 57.

54. Long and Johnson, *People vs. Property*, p. 53.

55. Thomas J. Sugrue, *The Origins of the Urban Crisis: Race and Inequality in Postwar Detroit* (Princeton, N.J.: Princeton University Press, 1996), pp. 73–74; Weaver, *Negro Ghetto*, p. 94. See also Dominic J. Capeci Jr., *Race Relations in Wartime Detroit: The Sojourner Truth Housing Controversy of 1942* (Philadelphia: Temple University Press, 1984).

56. Sugrue, *Origins of the Urban Crisis*, pp. 76, 80.

57. Kathryn Close, "New Homes with Insurance Dollars," *Survey Graphic*, November 1948, p. 487; Cleveland Rodgers and Rebecca B. Rankin, *New York: The World's Capital City* (New York: Harper, 1948), p. 300; A. Scott Henderson, *Housing and the Democratic Ideal: The Life and Thought of Charles Abrams* (New York: Columbia University Press, 2000), pp. 132–35.

58. Sugrue, *Origins of the Urban Crisis*, p. 42.

59. Guzman, ed., *Negro Year Book*, p. 215.

60. Long and Johnson, *People vs. Property*, p. 37.

61. John Gunther, *Inside U.S.A.* (New York: Harper, 1946), pp. 384, 574.

62. Robert C. Weaver, *Negro Labor: A National Problem* (New York: Harcourt, Brace, 1946), pp. 79–80; Weaver, *Negro Ghetto*, p. 78.

63. Weaver, *Negro Labor*, p. 81.

64. Weaver, *Negro Ghetto*, p. 81.

65. Weaver, *Negro Labor*, pp. 78–79; Weaver, *Negro Ghetto*, p. 78.

66. Weaver, *Negro Ghetto*, p. 78.

67. Weaver, *Negro Labor*, pp. 155–70.

68. Ibid., pp. 173–74.

69. Allen Cronenberg, "World War II Years," in *Mobile: The New History of Alabama's First City*, ed. Michael V. R. Thomason (Tuscaloosa: University of Alabama Press, 2001), pp. 223–24; Murray, ed., *Negro Handbook*, p. 219.

70. Murray, ed., *Negro Handbook*, pp. 219, 221.

71. Alfred McClung Lee and Norman Daymond Humphrey, *Race Riot* (New York: Dryden, 1943); Guzman, ed., *Negro Year Book*, p. 237.

72. Lee and Humphrey, *Race Riot*, p. 80.

73. Ibid., p. 100.

74. Arnold R. Hirsch, *Making the Second Ghetto: Race and Housing in Chicago, 1940–1960* (Cambridge: Cambridge University Press, 1983), p. 43.

75. Ibid., pp. 49–50.

76. Ibid., p. 42.

77. Guzman, ed., *Negro Year Book*, pp. 226–27.

78. *Race Relations in Chicago*, p. 1.

79. Ibid., p. 15; *Home Front Unity*, p. 6.

80. Guzman, ed., *Negro Year Book*, pp. 221–23.

81. Drake and Cayton, *Black Metropolis*, 1:213.

82. Teaford, *City and Suburb*, p. 77.

83. Harry Hansen, *Scarsdale: From Colonial Manor to Modern Community* (New York: Harper, 1954), p. 5.

84. Ibid., pp. 310–11.

85. Ibid., pp. 179–80.

86. Carol A. O'Connor, *A Sort of Utopia: Scarsdale, 1891–1981* (Albany: State University of New York Press, 1983), p. 160.

87. Ibid., p. 84; Hansen, *Scarsdale*, pp. 265, 269.

88. Hansen, *Scarsdale*, p. 241.

89. *Annual Report of the Incorporated Village of Garden City, New York, 1946* (Garden City: Village of Garden City, 1946), pp. 11–13; Jon C. Teaford, *Post-Suburbia: Government and Politics in the Edge Cities* (Baltimore: Johns Hopkins University Press, 1997), pp. 21, 23.

90. Paul H. Mattingly, "Politics and Ideology in a Metropolitan Suburb," in *Contested Terrain: Power, Politics, and Participation in Suburbia*, ed. Marc L. Silver and Martin Melkonian (Westport, Conn.: Greenwood, 1995), pp. 107–8.

91. Hansen, *Scarsdale*, p. 112.

92. Federal Writers' Project, *Shorewood* (Shorewood, Wis.: Village of Shorewood, 1939), pp. 11–12, 57–60. See also Jon C. Teaford, *Cities of the Heartland: The Rise and Fall of the Industrial Midwest* (Bloomington: Indiana University Press, 1993), pp. 207–8.

93. Arthur Evans Wood, *Hamtramck Then and Now* (New York: Bookman Associates, 1955), pp. 23, 25.

94. Ibid., pp. 131–32.

95. Ibid., p. 139.

96. Ibid., p. 165.

97. Becky M. Nicolaides, *My Blue Heaven: Life and Politics in the Working-Class Suburb of Los Angeles, 1920–1965* (Chicago: University of Chicago Press, 2002), pp. 25, 41.

98. Teaford, *Rough Road to Renaissance*, p. 25.

99. Andrew Wiese, "Places of Our Own: Suburban Black Towns Before 1960," *Journal of Urban History* 19 (1993): 46.

100. Johnson, *Patterns of Negro Segregation*, p. 60.

101. Harland Bartholomew, "The American City: Disintegration Is Taking Place," *Vital Speeches* 7 (1 November 1940): 61; *Urban Land Institute News Bulletin*, no. 2 (14 November 1941): 2; Teaford, *Rough Road to Renaissance*, p. 13.

102. Robert M. Fogelson, *Downtown: Its Rise and Fall, 1880–1950* (New Haven, Conn.: Yale University Press, 2001), pp. 229, 232, 238.

103. Boyden Sparkes, "Can the Cities Come Back?" *Saturday Evening Post*, 4 November 1944, p. 42.

104. Fogelson, *Downtown*, pp. 348–49.

105. Henry S. Churchill, *The City Is the People* (New York: Harcourt, Brace, 1945), p. 147.

106. Joseph D. McGoldrick, "The Super-Block Instead of Slums," *New York Times Magazine*, 19 November 1944, p. 10.

107. Joseph D. McGoldrick, "City Building and Renewal," *Annals of the American Academy of Political and Social Science* 242 (1945): 99.

108. Rebecca B. Rankin, ed., *New York Advancing* (New York: Municipal Reference Library, 1945), p. 105. See also Teaford, *Rough Road to Renaissance*, p. 37.

109. Sparkes, "Can the Cities Come Back?" p. 28.

110. Teaford, *Rough Road to Renaissance*, pp. 37–38.

111. Robert B. Fairbanks, "Metropolitan Planning and Downtown Redevelopment: The Cincinnati and Dallas Experiences, 1940–60," *Planning Perspectives* 2 (1987): 241.

112. Mel Scott, *The San Francisco Bay Area: A Metropolis in Perspective* (Berkeley: University of California Press, 1959), p. 264.

113. *City Planning in Philadelphia* (Philadelphia: Citizens' Council on City Planning, 1944), pp. 11, 14.

114. Fairbanks, "Metropolitan Planning and Downtown Redevelopment," p. 239.

115. Teaford, *Rough Road to Renaissance*, pp. 40–41.

116. Mark I. Gelfand, *A Nation of Cities: The Federal Government and Urban America, 1933–1965* (New York: Oxford University Press, 1975), p. 137.

117. Robert E. Alexander and Drayton S. Bryant, *Rebuilding a City: A Study of Redevelopment Problems in Los Angeles* (Los Angeles: Haynes Foundation, 1951), pp. 36–37.

118. Fogelson, *Downtown*, p. 221.

119. Seltzer, *Proposals for Downtown Philadelphia*, p. 5.

120. Wells, *Proposals for Downtown Detroit*, p. 15.

121. Fogelson, *Downtown*, pp. 235–36.

122. Teaford, *Rough Road to Renaissance*, p. 19.

123. Fogelson, *Downtown*, p. 226.

124. Ibid., p. 235.

125. Ibid., p. 236.

126. Ibid., p. 249.

127. *Christian Science Monitor*, 11 June 1940, pp. 1, 12. See also Teaford, *Rough Road to Renaissance*, p. 30.

128. Fogelson, *Downtown*, p. 273.

129. Rodgers, *New York Plans for the Future*, p. 216.

130. Seward H. Mott and Max S. Wehrly, eds., *Automobile Parking in Central Business Districts* (Washington, D.C.: Urban Land Institute, 1946), p. 10.

131. Ibid., p. 5.

132. Teaford, *Rough Road to Renaissance*, p. 84.

133. Frank Lloyd Wright, *When Democracy Builds* (Chicago: University of Chicago Press, 1945), pp. 9, 40, 43, 67, 113.

134. Ibid., pp. 60, 66, 70, 93–94.

2. Reinforcing the Status Quo

1. Victor Gruen and Associates, *A Greater Fort Worth Tomorrow* (Fort Worth: Greater Fort Worth Planning Committee, 1956), p. 3.

2. George Sessions Perry, "Pittsburgh," *Saturday Evening Post*, 3 August 1946, p. 15. See also Jon C. Teaford, *The Rough Road to Renaissance: Urban Revitalization in America, 1940–1985* (Baltimore: Johns Hopkins University Press, 1990), p. 84.

3. F. E. Schuchman, "Pittsburgh—'Smokeless City,'" *National Municipal Review* 39 (1950): 489.

4. *The Allegheny Conference on Community Development Presents Pittsburgh and Allegheny County: An Era of Progress and Accomplishment* (Pittsburgh: Allegheny Conference on Community Development, 1956), p. 9.

5. Ibid., p. 5.

6. "Pittsburgh Comes Out of the Smog," *Newsweek*, 26 September 1949, p. 25.

7. "Pittsburgh Renascent," *Architectural Forum*, November 1949, p. 59.

8. *Washington Post*, 3 February 1952, p. 1B

9. Herbert Kubly, "Pittsburgh: The City that Quick-Changed from Unbeliev-

able Ugliness to Shining Beauty in Less than Half a Generation," *Holiday*, March 1959, p. 80.

10. *Report on Urban Renewal in Cleveland* (Cleveland: Cleveland Advertising Club, 1955), p. 3. See also Teaford *Rough Road to Renaissance*, p. 48.

11. Katharine Lyall, "A Bicycle Built for Two: Public-Private Partnership in Baltimore," in *Public–Private Partnership in American Cities*, ed. R. Scott Fosler and Renee A. Berger (Lexington, Mass.: Heath, 1982), p. 29.

12. *St. Louis Post-Dispatch*, 5 March 1950, p. 1C.

13. Robert M. Fogelson, *Downtown: Its Rise and Fall, 1880–1950* (New Haven, Conn.: Yale University Press, 2001), p. 381.

14. *Washington Post*, 27 January 1952, p. 1B; 15 February 1952, p. 1.

15. Mel Scott, foreword to *Cities Are for People: The Los Angeles Region Plans for Living* (Los Angeles: Pacific Southwest Academy, 1942); "Our Changing Cities," *Newsweek*, 2 September 1957, p. 65.

16. *Detroit Free Press*, 2 November 1949, p. 2. See also Teaford, *Rough Road to Renaissance*, p. 95.

17. *The Master Plan for Kansas City* (Kansas City, Mo.: City Plan Commission, 1947), pp. 6–8, 20, 23–24; Mark H. Rose, *Interstate: Express Highway Politics, 1939–1989*, rev. ed. (Knoxville: University of Tennessee Press, 1990), p. 65.

18. Thomas H. O'Connor, *Building a New Boston: Politics and Urban Renewal, 1950–1970* (Boston: Northeastern University Press, 1993), pp. 82–88.

19. John W. Stamper, "Making the Mile Magnificent," *Chicago History* 30 (2001): 19.

20. "Our Changing Cities," p. 65; Leo Adde, *Nine Cities: The Anatomy of Downtown Renewal* (Washington, D.C.: Urban Land Institute, 1969), p. 29.

21. "Can the Big Cities Come Back?" *U.S. News & World Report*, 19 July 1957, p. 80.

22. Robert B. Fairbanks, "Metropolitan Planning and Downtown Redevelopment: The Cincinnati and Dallas Experiences, 1940–60," *Planning Perspectives* 2 (1987): 247.

23. Adde, *Nine Cities*, pp. 171, 173.

24. Ric Burns and James Sanders, *New York: An Illustrated History*, expanded ed. (New York: Knopf, 2003), p. 486.

25. "Can the Big Cities Come Back?" pp. 78–79

26. Zula McCauley, *The First Fifty Years* (Dallas: Neiman-Marcus, 1957), p. 44; Lloyd Wendt and Herman Kogan, *Give the Lady What She Wants! The Story of Marshall Field and Company* (Chicago: Rand McNally, 1952), p. 370; Fogelson, *Downtown*, p. 382.

27. C. T. Jonassen, *The Shopping Center Versus Downtown: A Motivation Research on Shopping Habits and Attitudes in Three Cities* (Columbus: Bureau of Business Research, Ohio State University, 1955), pp. 39–40.

28. Michael Johns, *Moment of Grace: The American City in the 1950s* (Berkeley: University of California Press, 2003), p. 12; William B. Dickinson, *This Is Greater Philadelphia* (Philadelphia: Bulletin Company, 1954), p. 25.

29. Martin Anderson, *The Federal Bulldozer: A Critical Analysis of Urban Renewal, 1949–1962* (Cambridge, Mass.: MIT Press, 1964), p. 98.

30. Rose, *Interstate*, p. 65; "Can the Big Cities Come Back?" p. 77.

31. Teaford, *Rough Road to Renaissance*, p. 112.

32. Adde, *Nine Cities*, p. 222.

33. Robert E. Alexander and Drayton S. Bryant, *Rebuilding a City: A Study of Redevelopment Problems in Los Angeles* (Los Angeles: Haynes Foundation, 1951), pp. 34–35, 39, 44–45; Dana Cuff, *The Provisional City: Los Angeles Stories of Architecture and Urbanism* (Cambridge, Mass.: MIT Press, 2000), pp. 303–4; Mel Scott, *The San Francisco Bay Area: A Metropolis in Perspective* (Berkeley: University of California Press, 1959), pp. 288–90.

34. Andrew S. Dolkart, *Morningside Heights: A History of Its Architecture and Development* (New York: Columbia University Press, 1998), pp. 328–32.

35. Muriel Beadle, *The Hyde Park–Kenwood Urban Renewal Years* (Chicago: self-published, 1964), p. 18. See also Jon C. Teaford, "Urban Renewal and Its Aftermath," *Housing Policy Debate* 11 (2000): 454.

36. Raymond Murphy and James Vance, "A Comparative Study of Nine Central Business Districts," *Economic Geography* 30 (1954): 301; Johns, *Moment of Grace*, p. 7.

37. Earl Spangler, *The Negro in Minnesota* (Minneapolis: Denison, 1961), pp. 132–33.

38. Thomas J. Sugrue, *The Origins of the Urban Crisis: Race and Inequality in Postwar Detroit* (Princeton, N.J.: Princeton University Press, 1996), pp. 209, 216, 218.

39. Charles Abrams, *Forbidden Neighbors: A Study in Prejudice in Housing* (New York: Harper, 1955), p. 156.

40. Ibid., p. 243.

41. See, for example, *Washington Post*, 1 May 1952, p. 11B; *Indianapolis Star*, 1 May 1952, p. 39.

42. Sugrue, *Origins of the Urban Crisis*, pp. 222, 248.

43. Christopher Silver and John V. Moeser, *The Separate City: Black Communities in the Urban South, 1940–1968* (Lexington: University Press of Kentucky, 1995), p. 133.

44. Abrams, *Forbidden Neighbors*, p. 185.

45. Clement E. Vose, *Caucasians Only: The Supreme Court, The NAACP, and the Restrictive Covenant Cases*, 2d printing (Berkeley: University of California Press, 1967), pp. 244–45.

46. Ronald H. Bayor, *Race and the Shaping of Twentieth-Century Atlanta* (Chapel Hill: University of North Carolina Press, 1996), p. 63. See also Silver and Moeser, *Separate City*, pp. 136–44.

47. Bayor, *Race and the Shaping of Twentieth-Century Atlanta*, p. 83.

48. Sugrue, *Origins of the Urban Crisis*, pp. 84–85.

49. William D. Jenkins, "Before Downtown: Cleveland, Ohio, and Urban Renewal, 1949–1958," *Journal of Urban History* 27 (2001): 488–89.

50. Arnold R. Hirsch, *Making the Second Ghetto: Race and Housing in Chicago, 1940–1960* (Cambridge: Cambridge University Press, 1983), p. 240.

51. John F. Bauman, *Public Housing, Race, and Renewal: Urban Planning in Philadelphia, 1920–1974* (Philadelphia: Temple University Press, 1987), p. 169.

52. John Barlow Martin, "Incident at Fernwood," *Harper's Magazine*, October 1949, p. 89.

53. Ibid., p. 95.

54. Hirsch, *Making the Second Ghetto*, pp. 55, 58–59.

55. Ibid., p. 77.

56. Abrams, *Forbidden Neighbors*, p. 118.

57. St. Clair Drake and Horace R. Cayton, *Black Metropolis: A Study of Negro Life in a Northern City*, rev. ed., 2 vols. (New York: Harper & Row, 1962), vol. 1, p. lii.

58. Abrams, *Forbidden Neighbors*, pp. 103, 105.

59. Sugrue, *Origins of the Urban Crisis*, p. 240.

60. Abrams, *Forbidden Neighbors*, pp. 85–87.

61. Ibid., p. 127.

62. Sherry Lamb Shirmer, *A City Divided: The Racial Landscape of Kansas City, 1900–1960* (Columbia: University of Missouri Press, 2002), p. 224.

63. Constance McLaughlin Green, *The Secret City: A History of Race Relations in the Nation's Capital* (Princeton, N.J.: Princeton University Press, 1967), p. 314.

64. Albert S. Broussard, *Black San Francisco: The Struggle for Racial Equality in the West, 1900–1954* (Lawrence: University Press of Kansas, 1993), p. 214.

65. Sugrue, *Origins of the Urban Crisis*, p. 113.

66. Ibid., pp. 94, 105.

67. Bayor, *Race and the Shaping of Twentieth-Century Atlanta*, p. 177.

68. Spangler, *Negro in Minnesota*, p. 136.

69. Broussard, *Black San Francisco*, p. 208.

70. Shirmer, *City Divided*, pp. 215–17.

71. Green, *Secret City*, pp. 297, 301, 326.

72. Bayor, *Race and the Shaping of Twentieth-Century Atlanta*, pp. 224–27.

73. Gregory C. Randall, *America's Original GI Town: Park Forest, Illinois* (Baltimore: Johns Hopkins University Press, 2000), p. 1.

74. Ibid., p. 3; Kenneth T. Jackson, *Crabgrass Frontier: The Suburbanization of the United States* (New York: Oxford University Press, 1985), p. 240.

75. "The Lush New Suburban Market," *Fortune*, November 1953, p. 128.

76. "Man, Oh Man!" *Time*, 1 February 1954, p. 66.

77. "The Rush to the Suburbs," *U.S. News & World Report*, 25 November 1955, pp. 44–45.

78. "Up from the Potato Fields," *Time*, 3 July 1950, p. 67.

79. *New York Times*, 5 February 1950, sec. 8, p. 3.

80. "Up from the Potato Fields," p. 68.

81. *New York Times*, 7 March 1949, p. 21; "The Line at Levitt's," *Newsweek*, 21 March 1949, p. 66.

82. Margaret Lundrigan Ferrer and Tova Navarra, *Levittown: The First Fifty Years* (Dover, N.H.: Arcadia, 1997), p. 17.

83. Penn Kimball, "'Dream Town'—Large Economy Size," *New York Times Magazine*, 14 December 1952, p. 40.

84. William M. Dobriner, *Class in Suburbia* (Englewood Cliffs, N.J.: Prentice Hall, 1963), p. 93.

85. Harry Henderson, "The Mass-Produced Suburbs, I. How People Live in America's Newest Towns," *Harper's Magazine*, November 1953, p. 29.

86. "Up from the Potato Fields," p. 69.

87. Dobriner, *Class in Suburbia*, pp. 89, 94, 109.

88. "Up from the Potato Fields," p. 69.

89. "The Industry Capitalism Forgot," *Fortune*, August 1947, p. 168.

90. "Up from the Potato Fields," p. 70.

91. *New York Times*, 30 September 1957, p. 33.

92. Ibid.

93. *Newsday*, 30 September 1957; *New York Herald Tribune*, 22 September 1957, sec. 7, p. 6; Jon C. Teaford, *Post-Suburbia: Government and Politics in Edge Cities* (Baltimore: Johns Hopkins University Press, 1997), p. 49.

94. Teaford, *Post-Suburbia*, p. 49; *New York Times*, 30 September 1957, p. 33.

95. Harry Henderson, "Rugged American Collectivism: The Mass-Produced Suburbs, Part II," *Harper's Magazine*, December 1953, p. 85.

96. William N. Leonard, "Schools in Crisis," *Nassau-Suffolk Business Conditions*, February 1955, p. 10. See also Harold L. Wattel, "Levittown: A Suburban Community," in *The Suburban Community*, ed. William M. Dobriner (New York: Putnam, 1958), p. 306, and Teaford, *Post-Suburbia*, pp. 49–50.

97. Dobriner, *Class in Suburbia*, p. 114.

98. Rosalyn Baxandall and Elizabeth Ewen, *Picture Windows: How the Suburbs Happened* (New York: Basic Books, 2000), p. 156.

99. Teaford, *Post-Suburbia*, p. 50.

100. Dobriner, *Class in Suburbia*, pp. 115, 118–20; Wattel, "Levittown," p. 309.

101. Jackson, *Crabgrass Frontier*, p. 241.

102. *New York Times*, 12 March 1949, p. 19; 19 March 1949, p. 12.

103. *New York Times*, 15 August 1957, p. 14; 16 August 1957, p. 10; 17 August 1957, p. 7; 20 August 1957, p. 29; 19 September 1957, p. 22; 25 September 1957, p. 19.

104. *New York Times*, 29 January 1950, sec. 8, p. 5. See also Baxandall and Ewen, *Picture Windows*, p. 178.

105. Randall, *America's Original GI Town*, p. 157.

106. Philip M. Klutznick with Sidney Hyman, *Angles of Vision: A Memoir of My Lives* (Chicago: Dee, 1991), pp. 141, 143.

107. William H. Whyte Jr., *The Organization Man* (New York: Simon and Schuster, 1956), p. 283. See also Randall, *America's Original GI Town*, p. 128.

108. Henderson, "Mass-Produced Suburbs," p. 29.

109. Randall, *America's Original GI Town*, p. 132.

110. *New York Times*, 17 February 1952, sec. 8, p. 1.

111. Greg Hise, *Magnetic Los Angeles: Planning the Twentieth-Century Metropolis* (Baltimore: Johns Hopkins University Press, 1997), p. 3.

112. *New York Times*, 5 February 1950, sec. 8, p. 3.

113. Ibid., p. 2.

114. *New York Times*, 1 January 1950, sec. 8, p. 2.

115. *New York Times*, 21 September 1947, sec. 8, p. 1.

116. Carol A. O'Connor, *A Sort of Utopia: Scarsdale, 1891–1981* (Albany: State University of New York Press, 1983), p. 164.

117. Jonassen, *Shopping Center Versus Downtown*, p. 48.

118. O'Connor, *Sort of Utopia*, pp. 175–85.

119. Henderson, "Mass-Produced Suburbs," p. 29.

120. Jonassen, *Shopping Center Versus Downtown*, p. 49.

121. Gary J. Miller, *Cities by Contract: The Politics of Municipal Incorporation* (Cambridge, Mass.: MIT Press, 1981), p. 105.

122. "Suburbia: Its Taxes Ache," *Business Work*, 18 July 1953, p. 146.

123. John Keats, *The Crack in the Picture Window* (Boston: Houghton Mifflin, 1956), pp. xi–xii, 193.

124. David Riesman, "The Suburban Sadness," in *Suburban Community*, ed. Dobriner, pp. 375–77, 386.

125. Frederick Lewis Allen, "The Big Change in Suburbia, Part I," *Harper's Magazine*, June 1954, p. 22.

126. Sidonie M. Gruenberg, "Homogenized Children of New Suburbia," *New York Times Magazine*, 19 September 1954, pp. 14, 42.

127. Gibson Winter, "The Church in Suburban Captivity," *Christian Century*, 28 September 1955, pp. 1112, 1114.

128. Phyllis McGinley, "Suburbia: Of Thee I Sing," *Harper's Magazine*, December 1949, p. 79.

129. Ibid.

130. Dobriner, *Class in Suburbia*, p. 110.

131. Barbara M. Kelly, *Expanding the American Dream: Building and Rebuilding Levittown* (Albany: State University of New York Press, 1993), p. 80.

3. Coming Apart

1. Jon C. Teaford, *The Rough Road to Renaissance: Urban Revitalization in America, 1940–1985* (Baltimore: Johns Hopkins University Press, 1990), p. 130.

2. *New York Times*, 17 February 1957, sec. 3, pp. 1, 8.

3. *New York Times*, 16 June 1957, p. 58; *A Plan for Pittsburgh's Golden Triangle* (Pittsburgh: Pittsburgh Regional Planning Association, 1962), p. 40; Teaford, *Rough Road to Renaissance*, pp. 129–30.

4. *Plan for Golden Triangle*, p. 39; Teaford, *Rough Road to Renaissance*, p. 131.

5. Jon C. Teaford, *The Twentieth-Century American City: Problem, Promise, and Reality* (Baltimore: Johns Hopkins University Press, 1986), p. 106.

6. David D. Van Tassel and John J. Grabowski, eds., *The Encyclopedia of Cleveland History* (Bloomington: Indiana University Press, 1987), pp. 66, 502, 667, 1052.

7. *Cleveland Plain Dealer*, 15 February 1962, pp. 1, 4. See also Teaford, *Rough Road to Renaissance*, p. 130.

8. Walter Guzzardi Jr., "An Architect of Environments," *Fortune*, January 1962, pp. 80, 134.

9. John E. Kleber, ed., *The Encyclopedia of Louisville* (Lexington: University Press of Kentucky, 2001), p. 816.

10. "Too Many Shopping Centers?" *Business Week*, 17 November 1956, p. 136.

11. "Pleasure-Domes with Parking," *Time*, 15 October 1956, p. 96.

12. Guzzardi, "Architect of Environments," p. 134.

13. "Brisk Business for a Bright Shopping Center," *Fortune*, February 1957, pp. 141, 143.

14. Edward T. Thompson, "The Suburb that Macy's Built," *Fortune*, February 1960, pp. 195–96.

15. Nicholas Dagen Bloom, *Merchant of Illusion: James Rouse, America's Salesman of the Businessman's Utopia* (Columbus: Ohio State University Press, 2004), p. 110.

16. George Sternlieb, "The Future of Retailing in the Downtown Core," in *Downtown Revitalization*, ed. Howard A. Schretter (Athens: Institute of Community and Area Development, University of Georgia, 1967), p. 95. See also Teaford, *Rough Road to Renaissance*, p. 129.

17. Victor Gruen and Larry Smith, *Shopping Towns USA: The Planning of Shopping Centers* (New York: Reinhold, 1960), p. 244.

18. Guzzardi, "Architect of Environments," p. 77.

19. "Brisk Business for a Bright Shopping Center," p. 141.

20. Gruen and Smith, *Shopping Towns USA*, p. 258.

21. Lizabeth Cohen, *A Consumers' Republic: The Politics of Mass Consumption in Postwar America* (New York: Knopf, 2003), p. 279.

22. Gruen and Smith, *Shopping Towns USA*, p. 263.

23. Ibid., p. 264.

24. Ibid.

25. "Brisk Business for a Bright Shopping Center," p. 143.

26. "Too Many Shopping Centers?" p. 144.

27. "Pleasure-Domes with Parking," p. 97.

28. Gruen and Smith, *Shopping Towns USA*, p. 264.

29. Thompson, "Suburb that Macy's Built," p. 196; see also p. 200.

30. "The New Breed," *Newsweek*, 1 April 1957, p. 36.

31. R. L. Duffus, "The Two States of California," *New York Times Magazine*, 18 December 1955, p. 63.

32. Gruen and Smith, *Shopping Towns USA*, pp. 23–24.

33. "Pleasure-Domes with Parking," p. 98.

34. Jon C. Teaford, *Post-Suburbia: Government and Politics in the Edge Cities* (Baltimore: Johns Hopkins University Press, 1997), p. 87; see also pp. 89–92.

35. John M. Findlay, *Magic Lands: Western Cityscapes and American Culture After 1940* (Berkeley: University of California Press, 1992), p. 137.

36. Louise A. Mozingo, "The Corporate Estate in USA, 1954–64: 'Thoroughly Modern in Concept, but . . . Down to Earth and Rugged,'" *Studies in the History of Garden and Designed Landscapes* 20 (2000): 29–30.

37. Ibid., pp. 32, 36. See also Louise A. Mozingo, "Campus, Estate, and Park: Lawn Culture Comes to the Corporation," in *Everyday America: Cultural Landscape Studies After J. B. Jackson*, ed. Chris Wilson and Paul Groth (Berkeley: University of California Press, 2003), pp. 255–74.

38. Ray Kroc with Robert Anderson, *Grinding It Out: The Making of McDonald's* (New York: St. Martin's, 1987), p. 115; John Mariani, *America Eats Out* (New York: Morrow, 1991), p. 169; John A. Jakle and Keith A. Sculle, *Fast Food: Roadside Restaurants in the Automobile Age* (Baltimore: Johns Hopkins University Press, 1999), p. 154.

39. Kroc with Anderson, *Grinding It Out*, p. 84.

40. Jakle and Sculle, *Fast Food*, p. 140.

41. Ibid., p. 117.

42. Mariani, *America Eats Out*, p. 172.

43. Teaford, *Twentieth-Century American City*, p. 113.

44. John A. Jakle, Keith A. Sculle, and Jefferson S. Rogers, *The Motel in America* (Baltimore: Johns Hopkins University Press, 1996), p. 263.

45. Ibid., p. 274.

46. *New York Times*, 23 December 1957, p. 14. See also Charles E. Stonier, "Long Island's Transportation," in *Developing Long Island*, ed. Harold L. Wattel (Hempstead, N.Y.: Bureau of Business and Community Research, 1959), pp. 38–39, and Teaford, *Post-Suburbia*, p. 57.

47. William M. Dobriner, *Class in Suburbia* (Englewood Cliffs, N.J.: Prentice Hall, 1963), p. 110.

48. Teaford, *Post-Suburbia*, p. 57.

49. Frances FitzGerald, *Cities on a Hill: A Journey Through Contemporary American Cultures* (New York: Simon and Schuster, 1986), p. 206; Findlay, *Magic Lands*, p. 165.

50. "Life Begins at 50," *Time*, 10 March 1961, p. 89.

51. Findlay, *Magic Lands*, p. 174.

52. "Life Begins at 50," p. 89.

53. FitzGerald, *Cities on a Hill*, p. 214.

54. "New Towns—Answer to Urban Sprawl?" *U.S. News & World Report*, 14 February 1966, p. 116.

55. Findlay, *Magic Lands*, p. 176.

56. "Life Begins at 50," p. 89.

57. Findlay, *Magic Lands*, pp. 177, 180.

58. "Life Begins at 50," p. 89.

59. Findlay, *Magic Lands*, p. 179.

60. "Life Begins at 50," p. 90.

61. Findlay, *Magic Lands*, pp. 199, 202–3.

62. Ibid., p. 207; James H. Andrew, "Leisure Power," *Planning*, November 1999, pp. 4, 6–7.

63. Guian A. McKee, "Liberal Ends Through Illiberal Means: Race, Urban Renewal, and Community in the Eastwick Section of Philadelphia, 1949–1990," *Journal of Urban History* 27 (2001): 556–57.

64. *Chicago Tribune*, 14 February 1961, pt. 1, p. 7. See also George Rosen, *Decision-Making Chicago-Style: The Genesis of a University of Illinois Campus* (Urbana: University of Illinois Press, 1980), pp. 114–15, 118, and "The Siting of the University of Illinois at Chicago Circle: A Struggle of the 1950s and 1960s," *Chicago History* 9 (1980–1981): 231.

65. Ronald P. Formisano, *Boston Against Busing: Race, Class, and Ethnicity in the 1960s and 1970s* (Chapel Hill: University of North Carolina Press, 1991), pp. 121, 122; Thomas H. O'Connor, *Building a New Boston: Politics and Urban Renewal, 1950–1970* (Boston: Northeastern University Press, 1993), p. 219.

66. O'Connor, *Building a New Boston*, pp. 220–21.

67. Joseph A. Rodriguez, *City Against Suburb: The Culture Wars in an American Metropolis* (Westport, Conn.: Praeger, 1999), pp. 24, 26.

68. Ibid., p. 26.

69. Ibid., p. 37.

70. Raymond A. Mohl, "Planned Destruction: The Interstates and Central City Housing," in *From Tenements to the Taylor Homes: In Search of an Urban Housing Policy in Twentieth-Century America*, ed. John F. Bauman, Roger Biles, and Kristin M. Szylvian (University Park: Pennsylvania State University Press, 2000), pp. 236, 238.

71. Bernard J. Frieden and Lynne B. Sagalyn, *Downtown, Inc.: How America Rebuilds Cities* (Cambridge, Mass.: MIT Press, 1989), pp. 28–29. See also Alan A. Altshuler, *The City Planning Process: A Political Analysis* (Ithaca, N.Y.: Cornell University Press, 1965), p. 61.

72. Howard Gillette Jr., *Between Justice and Beauty: Race, Planning, and the Failure of Urban Policy in Washington, D.C.* (Baltimore: Johns Hopkins University Press, 1995), p. 163.

73. Robert Kersten, *Politics and Growth in Twentieth-Century Tampa* (Gainesville: University Press of Florida, 2001), p. 140.

74. Robert O. Self, *American Babylon: Race and the Struggle for Postwar Oakland* (Princeton, N.J.: Princeton University Press, 2003), pp. 139, 143, 147, 151.

75. Janet R. Daly-Bednarek, *The Changing Image of the City: Planning for Downtown Omaha, 1945–1973* (Lincoln: University of Nebraska Press, 1992), pp. 140–43, 154–55.

76. Robert D. Thomas and Robert W. Murray, *Progrowth Politics: Change and Governance in Houston* (Berkeley, Calif.: Institute of Governmental Studies, 1991), p. 286.

77. Leo Adde, *Nine Cities: The Anatomy of Downtown Renewal* (Washington, D.C.: Urban Land Institute, 1969), p. 89.

78. Carl Abbott, *The Metropolitan Frontier: Cities in the Modern American West* (Tucson: University of Arizona Press, 1993), p. 45.

79. Adde, *Nine Cities*, p. 181.

80. Chester Hartman, "The Housing of Relocated Families," in *Urban Renewal: The Record and the Controversy*, ed. James Q. Wilson (Cambridge, Mass.: MIT Press, 1966), p. 306.

81. Marc Fried, "Grieving for a Lost Home: Psychological Costs of Relocation," in *Urban Renewal*, ed. Wilson, p. 360.

82. Wolf Von Eckardt, "Bulldozers and Bureaucrats," *New Republic*, 14 September 1963, p. 15.

83. Martin Anderson, *The Federal Bulldozer: A Critical Analysis of Urban Renewal, 1949–1962* (Cambridge, Mass.: MIT Press, 1964), pp. 54–55.

84. Herbert J. Gans, "The Failure of Urban Renewal," in *Urban Renewal*, ed. Wilson, p. 541.

85. Gillette, *Between Justice and Beauty*, p. 165.

86. Hartman, "Housing of Relocated Families," pp. 305, 310, 318–20.

87. Anderson, *Federal Bulldozer*, pp. 68–69.

88. Basil Zimmer, "The Small Businessman and Relocation," in *Urban Renewal*, ed. Wilson, p. 382.

89. Frieden and Sagalyn, *Downtown, Inc.*, p. 35.

90. Anderson, *Federal Bulldozer*, p. 70.

91. Ibid., pp. 73, 90.

92. *New York Times*, 4 August 1963, p. 52; 18 June 1964, p. 32.

93. Teaford, *Rough Road to Renaissance*, p. 156; Neil Kraus, *Race, Neighborhoods, and Community Power: Buffalo Politics, 1934–1997* (Albany: State University of New York Press, 2000), p. 113.

94. Anderson, *Federal Bulldozer*, p. 102.

95. Jeanne R. Lowe, *Cities in a Race with Time: Progress and Poverty in America's Renewing Cities* (New York: Random House, 1967), p. 451.

96. Ibid., pp. 192–93.

97. *New York Times*, 27 February 1961, p. 29; 4 March 1961, p. 11.

98. J. Clarence Davies III, *Neighborhood Groups and Urban Renewal* (New York: Columbia University Press, 1966), p. 88.

99. Ibid., p. 94.

100. *New York Times*, 19 October 1961, p. 1.

101. Davies, *Neighborhood Groups and Urban Renewal*, p. 104.

102. *New York Times*, 7 December 1962, p. 32.

103. Jane Jacobs, *The Death and Life of Great American Cities* (New York: Random House, 1961), p. 4.

104. Ibid., pp. 9–10.

105. Ibid., p. 50.

4. The Debacle

1. "Can the Big Cities Ever Come Back?" *U.S. News & World Report*, 4 September 1967, pp. 28, 31.

2. Robert A. Beauregard, *Voices of Decline: The Postwar Fate of US Cities* (Oxford: Blackwell, 1993), p. 201.

3. *New York Times*, 14 November 1978, p. B3.

4. George Sternlieb and James W. Hughes, "New Dimensions of the Urban Crisis," in *Cities Under Stress: The Fiscal Crises of Urban America*, ed. Robert W. Burchell and David Listokin (Piscataway, N.J.: Center for Urban Policy Research, Rutgers University, 1981), pp. 60, 64, 69.

5. Jon C. Teaford, *The Rough Road to Renaissance: Urban Revitalization in America, 1940–1985* (Baltimore: Johns Hopkins University Press, 1990), p. 208.

6. *Washington Post*, 24 December 1976, p. C5; 22 January 1977, pp. C8–C9.

7. *Washington Post*, 4 February 1977, p. D7; 22 October 1977, p. E7.

8. *The Suburbanization of Retail Trade: A Study of Retail Trade Dispersion in Major U.S. Markets, 1958–1967* (New York: Columbia Broadcasting System, 1970), p. 10.

9. *Chicago Tribune*, 3 February 1975, sec. 2, p. 4.

10. *Chicago Tribune*, 26 January 1975, sec. 1, p. 1.

11. *Chicago Tribune*, 11 September 1977, sec. 6, pp. 4, 6.

12. *New York Times*, 12 August 1972, p. 22.

13. *New York Times*, 13 August 1972, sec. 2, p. 1.

14. *New York Times*, 14 November 1978, p. B6.

15. Teaford, *Rough Road to Renaissance*, p. 213.

16. Wolfgang Quante, *The Exodus of Corporate Headquarters from New York City* (New York: Praeger, 1976), pp. 43, 49.

17. *New York Times*, 11 February 1967, pp. 1, 19; 12 February 1967, p. 66; 16 February 1967, pp. 1, 25; 17 February 1967, p. 40; 19 February 1967, p. 1.

18. *New York Times*, 17 February 1967, p. 40.

19. *New York Times*, 16 February 1967, p. 25; 14 February 1967, p. 42.

20. John A. Jakle and David Wilson, *Derelict Landscapes: The Wasting of America's Built Environment* (Savage, Md.: Rowman and Littlefield, 1992), p. 176.

21. George Sternlieb and Robert Burchell, *Residential Abandonment: The Tenement Landlord Revisited* (New Brunswick, N.J.: Center for Urban Policy Research, Rutgers University, 1973), p. 276.

22. Carol Poh Miller and Robert Wheeler, *Cleveland: A Concise History, 1796–1990* (Bloomington: Indiana University Press, 1990), p. 171.

23. Winston Moore, Charles P. Livermore, and George F. Galland Jr., "Woodlawn: The Zone of Destruction," *Public Interest*, no. 30 (1973): 41, 45.

24. Sternlieb and Burchell, *Residential Abandonment*, p. 276.

25. Larry Bennett, *Fragments of Cities: The New American Downtowns and Neighborhoods* (Columbus: Ohio State University Press, 1990), p. 66.

26. Jakle and Wilson, *Derelict Landscapes*, p. 176.

27. Jill Jonnes, *We're Still Here: The Rise, Fall, and Resurrection of the South Bronx* (Boston: Atlantic Monthly Press, 1986), p. 265.

28. Ibid., p. 317. See also Eugenie Ladner Birch, "From Flames to Flowers: The Role of Planning in Re-imaging the South Bronx," in *Imaging the City: Continuing Struggles and New Directions*, ed. Lawrence J. Vale and Sam Bass Warner Jr. (New

Brunswick, N.J.: Center for Urban Policy Research, Rutgers University, 2001), p. 58.

29. Moore, Livermore, and Galland, "Woodlawn," p. 42.

30. Frances Fox Piven and Richard A. Cloward, *Regulating the Poor: The Functions of Public Welfare* (New York: Vintage, 1972), pp. 183, 186–87, 190.

31. Fred Siegel, *The Future Once Happened Here: New York, D.C., L.A., and the Fate of America's Big Cities* (New York: Free Press, 1997), pp. 56–57.

32. James Q. Wilson, *Thinking About Crime* (New York: Basic Books, 1975), pp. 5–6, 17.

33. *Washington Post*, 27 May 1973, p. A12.

34. *Washington Post*, 29 May 1973, p. A8.

35. *Washington Post*, 27 May 1973, p. A1.

36. Wilson, *Thinking About Crime*, pp. 7–8, 15.

37. *Chicago Tribune*, 13 October 1975, sec. 1, p. 7.

38. *Chicago Tribune*, 14 October 1975, sec. 1, pp. 1, 10.

39. *Washington Post*, 27 May 1973, p. A12.

40. Ibid.

41. Roger E. Alcaly and Helen Bodian, "New York's Fiscal Crisis and the Economy," in *The Fiscal Crisis of American Cities: Essays on the Political Economy of Urban America with Special Reference to New York*, ed. Roger E. Alcaly and David Mermelstein (New York: Vintage, 1977), p. 33.

42. Jason Epstein, "The Last Days of New York," in *Fiscal Crisis of American Cities*, ed. Alcaly and Mermelstein, p. 63.

43. Robert Zevin, "New York City Crisis: First Act in a New Age of Reaction," in *Fiscal Crisis of American Cities*, ed. Alcaly and Mermelstein, p. 11.

44. Roger Starr, "Making New York Smaller," *New York Times Magazine*, 14 November 1976, p. 106.

45. Charles R. Morris, *The Cost of Good Intentions: New York City and the Liberal Experiment, 1960–1975* (New York: McGraw-Hill, 1981), p. 234; Epstein, "Last Days of New York," p. 75.

46. Teaford, *Rough Road to Renaissance*, p. 228.

47. *New York Times*, 28 October 1974, p. 33.

48. *New York Times*, 13 November 1978, p. A1.

49. "Negro Cities, White Suburbs—It's the Prospect for Year 2000," *U.S. News & World Report*, 21 February 1966, pp. 72–73.

50. Chester W. Hartman, *Housing and Social Policy* (Englewood Cliffs, N.J.: Prentice Hall, 1975), p. 124. See also Henry J. Aaron, *Shelter and Subsidies: Who Benefits from Federal Housing Policies?* (Washington, D.C.: Brookings Institution, 1972), pp. 116–17, and Devereux Bowly Jr., *The Poorhouse: Subsidized Housing in Chicago, 1895–1976* (Carbondale: Southern Illinois University Press, 1978), p. 222.

51. Eugene J. Meehan, *Public Housing Policy: Convention Versus Reality* (New Brunswick, N.J.: Center for Urban Research, Rutgers University, 1975), pp. 39, 154.

52. Lawrence M. Friedman, *Government and Slum Housing: A Century of Frustration* (Chicago: Rand McNally, 1968), p. 142.

53. Arthur E. Hippler, *Hunter's Point: A Black Ghetto* (New York: Basic Books, 1974), p. 15.

54. David D. Van Tassel and John J. Grabowski, eds., *The Encyclopedia of Cleveland History* (Bloomington: Indiana University Press, 1987), p. 640.

55. For an account of the New York City riots of 1964, see Fred C. Shapiro and James W. Sullivan, *Race Riots, New York, 1964* (New York: Crowell, 1964).

56. Josh Sides, *L.A. City Limits: African American Los Angeles from the Great Depression to the Present* (Berkeley: University of California Press, 2003), p. 175.

57. William McCord, John Howard, Bernard Friedberg, and Edwin Harwood, *Life Styles in the Black Ghetto* (New York: Norton, 1969), p. 60. For accounts of the Watts riots, see also Gerald Horne, *Fire This Time: The Watts Uprising and the 1960s* (Charlottesville: University Press of Virginia, 1995), and David O. Sears and John B. McConahay, *The Politics of Violence: The New Urban Blacks and the Watts Riot* (Boston: Houghton Mifflin, 1973).

58. *Report of the National Advisory Commission on Civil Disorders* (New York: Bantam, 1968), p. 39.

59. Hippler, *Hunter's Point*, p. 206.

60. *Report of Commission on Civil Disorders*, p. 40.

61. Ibid., pp. 69, 164.

62. Sidney Fine, *Violence in the Model City: The Cavanagh Administration, Race Relations, and the Detroit Riot of 1967* (Ann Arbor: University of Michigan Press, 1989), p. 160.

63. *Report of Commission on Civil Disorders*, p. 89; Fine, *Violence in the Model City*, p. 169.

64. *Report of Commission on Civil Disorders*, p. 107; Fine, *Violence in the Model City*, pp. 341–42.

65. *Report of Commission on Civil Disorders*, pp. 106–7, 115, 164.

66. Ibid., pp. 1, 407.

67. Ibid., pp. 134, 177.

68. Piven and Cloward, *Regulating the Poor*, p. 269.

69. Ralph M. Kramer, *Participation of the Poor: Comparative Community Case Studies in the War on Poverty* (Englewood Cliffs, N.J.: Prentice Hall, 1969), pp. 25, 31.

70. Daniel P. Moynihan, *Maximum Feasible Misunderstanding: Community Action in the War on Poverty* (New York: Free Press, 1970), p. 156.

71. Kramer, *Participation of the Poor*, p. 53.

72. Estelle Zannes, *Checkmate in Cleveland: The Rhetoric of Confrontation During the Stokes Years* (Cleveland: Press of Case Western Reserve University, 1972), p. 49.

73. William E. Nelson Jr. and Philip J. Meranto, *Electing Black Mayors: Political Action in the Black Community* (Columbus: Ohio State University Press, 1977), p. 159.

74. Ibid., pp. 245, 301; Alex Poinsett, *Black Power Gary Style: The Making of Richard Gordon Hatcher* (Chicago: Johnson, 1970), p. 78.

75. For analyses of the election returns, see Nelson and Meranto, *Electing Black Mayors*, pp. 162, 317–18, and Poinsett, *Black Power Gary Style*, p. 94.

76. *New York Times*, 9 June 1970, p. 30.

77. *New York Times*, 18 June 1970, p. 51.

78. Jon C. Teaford, *The Twentieth-Century American City: Problem, Promise, and Reality* (Baltimore: Johns Hopkins University Press, 1986), p. 148. See also Wilbur C. Rich, *Coleman Young and Detroit Politics: From Social Activist to Power Broker* (Detroit: Wayne State University Press, 1989), pp. 103–6.

79. Bradley R. Rice, "If Dixie Were Atlanta," in *Sunbelt Cities: Politics and Growth Since World War II*, ed. Richard M. Bernard and Bradley R. Rice (Austin: University of Texas Press, 1983), p. 51.

80. Peter K. Eisinger, *The Politics of Displacement: Racial and Ethnic Transition in Three American Cities* (New York: Academic Press, 1980), pp. 161, 164.

81. Maurice R. Berube and Marilyn Gittell, *Confrontation at Ocean Hill–Brownsville: The New York School Strikes of 1968* (New York: Praeger, 1969), pp. 165–68.

82. Ibid., p. 174. For more on the Ocean Hill–Brownsville controversy, see Wendell Pritchett, *Brownsville, Brooklyn: Blacks, Jews, and the Changing Face of the Ghetto* (Chicago: University of Chicago Press, 2002).

83. J. Harvie Wilkinson III, *From Brown to Bakke: The Supreme Court and School Integration, 1954–1978* (New York: Oxford University Press, 1979), p. 230.

84. Ronald P. Formisano, *Boston Against Busing: Race, Class, and Ethnicity in the 1960s and 1970s* (Chapel Hill: University of North Carolina Press, 1991), p. 47.

85. Ibid., p. 56.

86. "Southie Fights On," *Time*, 23 September 1974, pp. 29–30.

87. Formisano, *Boston Against Busing*, p. 119.

88. "Southie Fights On," p. 29.

89. Peter Irons, *Jim Crow's Children: The Broken Promise of the Brown Decision* (New York: Penguin, 2004), pp. 240–41.

90. *Milliken v. Bradley*, 418 U.S. 741, 745.

91. Nicholas Dagen Bloom, *Suburban Alchemy: 1960s New Towns and the Transformation of the American Dream* (Columbus: Ohio State University Press, 2001), p. 21.

92. Ibid., pp. 154–55.

93. *Washington Post*, 9 August 1976, p. A22.

94. Gurney Breckenfeld, *Columbia and the New Cities* (New York: Ives Washburn, 1971), pp. 172, 175.

95. Ibid., pp. 175–76, 181.

96. Bloom, *Suburban Alchemy*, p. 155.

97. For accounts of Irvine, see ibid., pp. 53–67, and Martin J. Schiesl, "Designing the Model Community: The Irvine Company and Suburban Development, 1950–88," in *Postsuburban California: The Transformation of Orange County Since World War II*, ed. Rob Kling, Spencer Olin, and Mark Poster (Berkeley: University of California Press, 1991), pp. 55–91.

98. *New Communities: Problems and Potential* (Washington, D.C.: New Communities Administration, Department of Housing and Urban Development, 1976), p. 3.

99. Ibid., p. 62; *Washington Post*, 15 January 1975, p. A4. For additional material on Jonathan, see *Washington Post*, 24 July 1976, pp. D1–D2; 31 July 1976, pp. D1, D10.

100. *Washington Post*, 15 January 1975, p. A4; 16 January 1975, p. A4.

101. *New Communities*, pp. 71–72.

102. George T. Morgan Jr. and John O. King, *The Woodlands: New Community Development, 1964–1983* (College Station: Texas A&M University Press, 1987), p. 51.

103. *Washington Post*, 12 January 1975, p. A12.

104. *New Communities*, p. 4.

105. Frederick Steiner, *The Politics of New Town Planning: The Newfields, Ohio Story* (Athens: Ohio University Press, 1981), p. 214.

106. *New Communities*, pp. 59, 65.

107. Ibid., p. 71; Andre F. Shashaty, "HUD Terminating Its New Communities Program," *Urban Land*, June 1983, p. 7.

108. *New Communities*, p. 63.

109. *Washington Post*, 14 January 1975, p. A13; 15 January 1975, pp. A1, A4.

110. *New Communities*, p. 61. See also Shashaty, "HUD Terminating Its New Communities Program," p. 7.

111. *Washington Post*, 12 January 1975, p A12.

112. *Washington Post*, 11 January 1975, p. A9.

113. *New Communities*, pp. 4–5, 82.

114. *Washington Post*, 12 January 1975, p. A12.

115. Raymond J. Burby III and Shirley F. Weiss, *New Communities U.S.A.* (Lexington, Mass.: Heath, 1976), p. 418.

116. Nicholas Bloom, "The Federal Icarus: The Public Rejection of 1970s National Suburban Planning," *Journal of Urban History* 28 (2001): 65, and *Merchant of Illusion: James Rouse, America's Salesman of the Businessman's Utopia* (Columbus: Ohio State University Press, 2004), pp. 144–45.

117. *Washington Post*, 12 January 1975, p. A12.

118. Morgan and King, *The Woodlands*, pp. 104–8.

5. The New Metropolitan World

1. "Why More and More People Are Coming Back to Cities," *U.S. News & World Report*, 8 August 1977, pp. 69–71.

2. Horace Sutton, "America Falls in Love with Its Cities—Again," *Saturday Review*, August 1978, pp. 16, 18.

3. T. D. Allman, "The Urban Crisis Leaves Town," *Harper's Magazine*, December 1978, pp. 41–56.

4. "A City Revival?" *Newsweek*, 15 January 1979, p. 28.

5. Charlene Prost, "Comeback City," *Planning*, October 1985, pp. 4–10; Robert Price, "The Good News About New York City," *New York Times Magazine*, 28 September 1986, pp. 30–32, 49–50, 54, 58–60; M. Gottdiener, ed., "Symposium: Whatever Happened to the Urban Crisis?" *Urban Affairs Quarterly* 20 (1985): 421–86.

6. Alexander Ganz, "Where Has the Urban Crisis Gone?" *Urban Affairs Quarterly* 20 (1985): 457.

7. Ibid.

8. Jon C. Teaford, *The Rough Road to Renaissance: Urban Revitalization in America, 1940–1985* (Baltimore: Johns Hopkins University Press, 1990), pp. 288, 294.

9. Rachelle L. Levitt, ed., *Cities Reborn* (Washington, D.C.: Urban Land Institute, 1987), p. 18.

10. Jeffrey R. Henig, *Gentrification in Adams Morgan: Political and Commercial Consequences of Neighborhood Change* (Washington, D.C.: Center for Washington Area Studies, George Washington University, 1982), pp. 19, 22, 26.

11. "Why More and More People Are Coming Back to Cities," p. 69.

12. "Barry's New Capital," *Newsweek*, 15 January 1979, p. 30.

13. Daphne Spain, "Been-Heres Versus Come-Heres: Negotiating Conflicting Community Identities," *Journal of the American Planning Association* 59 (1993): 169.

14. "City Revival?" p. 29.

15. Paul R. Levy and Roman A. Cybriwsky, "The Hidden Dimensions of Culture and Class: Philadelphia," in *Back to the City: Issues in Neighborhood Renovation*, ed. Shirley Bradway Laska and Daphne Spain (New York: Pergamon, 1980), p. 148.

16. *Chicago Tribune*, 6 June 1984, sec. 8, pp. 4, 6, 47.

17. Larry Bennett, *Fragments of Cities: The New American Downtowns and Neighborhoods* (Columbus: Ohio State University Press, 1990), p. 64.

18. *Chicago Tribune*, 6 June 1984, sec. 8, p. 12.

19. Levitt, ed., *Cities Reborn*, p. 97.

20. Ibid., p. 172.

21. David C. Hodge, "Inner-City Revitalization as a Challenge to Diversity? Seattle," in *Back to the City*, ed. Laska and Spain, pp. 193–94.

22. Ibid., p. 196.

23. Henig, *Gentrification in Adams Morgan*, p. 19.

24. *Chicago Tribune*, 6 June 1984, sec. 8, p. 3.

25. James R. Hudson, *The Unanticipated City: Loft Conversion in Lower Manhattan* (Amherst: University of Massachusetts Press, 1987), p. 60; see also p. 105.

26. William Zimmer, "Still Funky But Oh So Chic SoHo," *Art News*, November 1980, p. 90.

27. Hudson, *Unanticipated City*, p. 61.

28. Ibid., p. 63. For the making and influence of SoHo, see also Roberta Brandes Gratz and Norman Mintz, *Cities Back from the Edge: New Life for Downtown* (New York: Wiley, 1998), pp. 295–323.

29. Brian J. Godfrey, *Neighborhoods in Transition: The Making of San Francisco's Ethnic and Nonconformist Communities* (Berkeley: University of California Press, 1988), pp. 172, 184–85, 187, 190–91.

30. Ibid., p. 192.

31. Levy and Cybriwsky, "Hidden Dimensions of Culture and Class," p. 150.

32. Hodge, "Inner-City Revitalization," p. 198.

33. *Washington Post*, 22 October 1990, p. D5.

34. *Revitalization, Gentrification, and the Low-Income Housing Crisis: Hearing Before a Subcommittee of the Committee on Government Operations, House of Representatives* (Washington, D.C.: Government Printing Office, 1986), p. 100.

35. Ibid., pp. 3, 7.

36. John King, "Protecting Industry from Yuppies and Other Invaders," *Planning*, June 1988, p. 4. See also Robert Giloth and John Betancur, "Where Downtown Meets Neighborhood: Industrial Displacement in Chicago, 1978–1987," *Journal of the American Planning Association* 54 (1988): 287.

37. Christopher Mele, *Selling the Lower East Side: Culture, Real Estate, and Resistance in New York City* (Minneapolis: University of Minnesota Press, 2000), pp. 227, 230, 242; William Sites, *Remaking New York: Primitive Globalization and the Politics of Urban Community* (Minneapolis: University of Minnesota Press, 2003), p. 83.

38. Mele, *Selling the Lower East Side*, p. 257; Sites, *Remaking New York*, p. 113.

39. Mele, *Selling the Lower East Side*, p. 264.

40. W. Anderson Barnes, "Ghirardelli Square: Keeping a First First," *Urban Land*, May 1986, p. 7.

41. Gurney Breckenfeld, "Jim Rouse Shows How to Give Downtown Retailing New Life," *Fortune*, 10 April 1978, p. 91.

42. Nicholas Dagen Bloom, *Merchant of Illusion: James Rouse, America's Salesman of the Businessman's Utopia* (Columbus: Ohio State University Press, 2004), pp. 154–55.

43. Breckenfeld, "Jim Rouse Shows How to Give Downtown Retailing New Life," p. 90.

44. Jane Davison, "Bringing Life to Market," *New York Times Magazine*, 10 October 1976, p. 74.

45. Sutton, "America Falls in Love with Its Cities," p. 21.

46. *Washington Post*, 5 July 1980, p. B3.

47. Joseph D. Steller Jr., "A MXD Takes Off: Baltimore's Inner Harbor," *Urban Land*, March 1982, p. 14.

48. *Washington Post*, 3 July 1980, p. E1.

49. "He Digs Downtown," *Time*, 24 August 1981, p. 42.

50. Breckenfeld, "Jim Rouse Shows How to Give Downtown Retailing New Life," p. 91.

51. Gurney Breckenfeld, "The Rouse Show Goes National," *Fortune*, 27 July 1981, pp. 50–51.

52. John T. Metzger, "The Failed Promise of a Festival Marketplace: South Street Seaport in Lower Manhattan," *Planning Perspectives* 16 (2001): 25–46.

53. William Fulton, "The Robin Hood of Real Estate," *Planning*, May 1985, p. 7.

54. *New York Times*, 11 June 1989, sec. 1, p. 26; 16 June 1989, p. A3.

55. Bernard J. Frieden and Lynne B. Sagalyn, *Downtown, Inc.: How America Rebuilds Cities* (Cambridge, Mass.: MIT Press, 1989), 179–80.

56. Nicole Achs, "Putting the Fun(ds) Back in Downtown," *American City and County*, June 1991, p. 75; "Jim Rouse May Be Losing His Touch," *Business Week*, 4 April 1988, p. 33.

57. "Jim Rouse May Be Losing His Touch," p. 34; Jim Morrison, "Norfolk Takes Back Its Heart," *Planning*, June 2004, p. 7.

58. *New York Times*, 16 August 1986, p. 6.

59. John Pastier, "Uncommon Market," *Historic Preservation*, February 1996, p. 103.

60. Frances FitzGerald, *Cities on a Hill: A Journey Through Contemporary American Cultures* (New York: Simon and Schuster, 1986), p. 48. See also Godfrey, *Neighborhoods in Transition*, pp. 117, 121.

61. FitzGerald, *Cities on a Hill*, p. 34.

62. Godfrey, *Neighborhoods in Transition*, p. 119.

63. FitzGerald, *Cities on a Hill*, pp. 27–29.

64. Ibid., p. 61.

65. Richard Edward DeLeon, *Left Coast City: Progressive Politics in San Francisco, 1975–1991* (Lawrence: University Press of Kansas, 1992), p. 50. For more on Harvey Milk, see Randy Shilts, *The Mayor of Castro Street: The Life and Times of Harvey Milk* (New York: St. Martin's, 1982).

66. *New York Times*, 23 May 1979, p. A18.

67. DeLeon, *Left Coast City*, p. 30.

68. *Chicago Tribune*, 4 March 1983, sec. 5, pp. 1, 7.

69. *Chicago Tribune*, 27 June 1983, sec. 1, p. 7.

70. *Chicago Tribune*, 7 July 1985, sec. 5, p. 3.

71. Gary L. Atkins, *Gay Seattle: Stories of Exile and Belonging* (Seattle: University of Washington Press, 2003), pp. 263, 270.

72. Andrew Kopkind, "Once Upon a Time in the West," *Nation*, 1 June 1985, p. 672.

73. "A Gay City on the Hill?" *Newsweek*, 5 November 1984, p. 46; *New York Times*, 19 March 1985, p. A16.

74. *New York Times*, 19 March 1985, p. A16.

75. "In West Hollywood: Exotic Mix," *Time*, 16 December 1985, p. 7. For more on West Hollywood, see Simon LeVay and Elisabeth Nonas, *City of Friends: A Portrait of the Gay and Lesbian Community in America* (Cambridge, Mass.: MIT Press, 1995), pp. 125–36.

76. William Fulton, "Office in the Dell," *Planning*, July 1986, p. 14.

77. "Back to the Suburbs," *Newsweek*, 21 April 1986, p. 61.

78. Alex Schwartz, "The Geography of Corporate Services: A Case Study of the New York Urban Region," *Urban Geography* 13 (1992): 6–7, 14.

79. Joel Garreau, *Edge City: Life on the New Frontier* (New York: Doubleday, 1991), p. 439.

80. Susan Hanson and Ibipo Johnston, "Gender Differences in Work-Trip Length: Explanations and Implications," *Urban Geography* 6 (1985): 193–219; Orna Blumen, "Gender Differences in the Journey to Work," *Urban Geography* 15 (1994): 223–45.

81. Garreau, *Edge City*, p. 112.

82. Robert Fishman, "America's New City: Megalopolis Unbound," *Wilson Quarterly* 14 (1990): 41.

83. For a list of names given to the new metropolitan form, see Robert E. Lang, *Edgeless Cities: Exploring the Elusive Metropolis* (Washington, D.C.: Brookings Institution Press, 2003), p. 31.

84. Garreau, *Edge City*, pp. 3, 6; see also pp. 7, 426–38.

85. Fulton, "Office in the Dell," p. 16.

86. Thomas J. Baerwald, "The Evolution of Suburban Downtowns in Midwestern Metropolises," in *Suburbia Re-examined*, ed. Barbara M. Kelly (New York: Greenwood, 1989), pp. 46–48.

87. Christopher B. Leinberger and Charles Lockwood, "How Business Is Reshaping America," *Atlantic Monthly*, October 1986, p. 44.

88. Jane Holtz Kay, "Building a *There* There," *Planning*, January 1991, p. 4.

89. Gary Pivo, "The Net of Mixed Beads: Suburban Office Development in Six Metropolitan Regions," *Journal of the American Planning Association* 56 (1990): 461, 466.

90. Kay, "Building a *There* There," p. 8.

91. Fulton, "Office in the Dell," p. 16.

92. *Washington Post*, 8 March 1987, p. A27.

93. Truman A. Hartshorn and Peter O. Muller, "Suburban Downtowns and the Transformation of Metropolitan Atlanta's Business Landscape," *Urban Geography* 10 (1989): 384, 386–87; Thomas J. Baerwald, "Changing Sales Patterns in Major American Metropolises, 1963–1982," *Urban Geography* 10 (1989): 373–74.

94. Baerwald, "Changing Sales Patterns," pp. 373–74.

95. "The Boom Towns," *Time*, 15 June 1987, p. 16.

96. *New York Times*, 11 December 1988, sec. 2, p. 32.

97. Leinberger and Lockwood, "How Business Is Reshaping America," p. 48.

98. Michael H. Ebner, "Experiencing Megalopolis in Princeton," *Journal of Urban History* 19 (1993): 37.

99. Peter O. Muller, *Contemporary Suburban America* (Englewood Cliffs, N.J.: Prentice Hall, 1981), p. 169.

100. *Washington Post*, 8 March 1987, p. A27; Richard Ward, "Planning for Growth in Arlington County, Virginia," *Urban Land*, January 1991, pp. 2–6; Richard Miller, "Joint Development at Ballston Metro Center," *Urban Land*, June 1993, pp. 23–24.

101. *Washington Post*, 8 March 1987, p. A27; Christopher B. Leinberger, "Urban Cores: Development Trends and Real Estate Opportunities in the 1990s," *Urban Land*, December 1990, p. 9.

102. David Dillon, "Los Colinas Revisited," *Planning*, December 1989, pp. 6–11.

103. Leinberger and Lockwood, "How Business Its Reshaping America," p. 46. See also Hartshorn and Muller, "Suburban Downtowns," pp. 384, 388–93.

104. Robert Fishman, *Bourgeois Utopias: The Rise and Fall of Suburbia* (New York: Basic Books, 1987), p. 185.

105. Robert Cervero, "Jobs–Housing Balancing and Regional Mobility," *Journal of the American Planning Association* 55 (1989): 136.

106. "Back to the Suburbs," p. 61.

107. "Boom Towns," p. 16.

108. *Newsday*, 12 September 1985, p. 7, cited in Jon C. Teaford, *Post-Suburbia: Government and Politics in the Edge Cities* (Baltimore: Johns Hopkins University Press, 1997), p. 181.

109. "Back to the Suburbs," p. 61.

110. *Washington Post*, 8 March 1987, p. A26.

111. *Washington Post*, 9 December 1986, p. B1.

112. Ibid., p. B5.

113. *Washington Post*, 11 December 1986, p. C7.

114. *Washington Post*, 9 December 1986, p. B5.

115. *Washington Post*, 11 December 1986, pp. C1, C7.

116. *Washington Post*, 29 December 1986, p. B6.

117. *Washington Post*, 5 November 1987, p. A40.

118. Ibid., p. A41.

119. *Washington Post*, 31 December 1987, p. Va3.

120. *Chicago Tribune*, 26 July 1988, sec. 1, pp. 1–2.

121. *Chicago Tribune*, 28 November 1986, sec. 1, p. 11. See also *Chicago Tribune*, 27 August 1986, sec. 2, p. 2; 5 November 1986, sec. 1, p. 4; 6 November 1986, sec. 2, p. 7.

122. *San Francisco Examiner*, 15 October 1989, p. B8.

123. Fulton, "Office in the Dell," p. 15.

124. Dan Walters, *The New California: Facing the Twenty-First Century*, 2d ed. (Sacramento: California Journal Press, 1992), p. 90.

125. Teaford, *Post-Suburbia*, p. 174.

126. Walters, *New California*, p. 47.

127. John Landis and Cynthia Kroll, "The Southern California Growth War," in *California Policy Choices*, ed. John J. Kirlin and Donald R. Winkler (Los Angeles: University of Southern California School of Public Administration, 1989), vol. 5, p. 160.

6. Beyond the Black–White City

1. *Report of the National Advisory Commission on Civil Disorders* (New York: Bantam, 1968), p. 1.

2. Bureau of the Census, *Statistical Abstract of the United States: 1970* (Washington, D.C.: Government Printing Office, 1970), p. 93.

3. Bureau of the Census, *Statistical Abstract of the United States: 2003* (Washington, D.C.: Government Printing Office, 2003), p. 11.

4. Ibid., p. 10.

5. Ibid., p. 51.

6. Thomas D. Boswell and James R. Curtis, *The Cuban-American Experience: Cultural, Images, and Perspectives* (Totowa, N.J.: Rowman and Allanheld, 1984), pp. 41–43.

7. Herbert Burkholz, "The Latinization of Miami," *New York Times Magazine*, 21 September 1980, p. 45.

8. "Hispanics: A Visible Presence," *Time*, 8 July 1985, p. 37.

9. Joan Didion, *Miami* (New York: Simon and Schuster, 1987), p. 52.

10. Raymond A. Mohl, "Miami: New Immigrant City," in *Searching for the Sunbelt: Historical Perspective on a Region*, ed. Raymond A. Mohl (Knoxville: University of Tennessee Press, 1990), p. 160.

11. Census Bureau, *Statistical Abstract: 2003*, p. 58.

12. Boswell and Curtis, *Cuban-American Experience*, pp. 79, 82.

13. Ibid., p. 87.

14. Guillermo J. Grenier and Max J. Castro, "Triadic Politics: Ethnicity, Race, and Politics in Miami, 1959–1998," *Pacific Historical Review* 68 (1999): 281.

15. Burkholz, "Latinization of Miami," p. 46.

16. Alex Stepick, Guillermo Grenier, Max Castro, and Marvin Dunn, *This Land Is Our Land: Immigrants and Power in Miami* (Berkeley: University of California Press, 2003), p. 38.

17. Ibid., p. 34.

18. Grenier and Castro, "Triadic Politics," p. 282.

19. Census Bureau, *Statistical Abstract: 2003*, p. 11; Bureau of the Census, *Statistical Abstract of the United States: 2002* (Washington, D.C.: Government Printing Office, 2001), p. 45.

20. Vilma Ortiz, "The Mexican-Origin Population: Permanent Working Class or Emerging Middle Class?" in *Ethnic Los Angeles*, ed. Roger Waldinger and Mehdi Bozorgmehr (New York: Russell Sage Foundation, 1996), p. 247.

21. Andrew A. Beveridge and Susan Weber, "Race and Class in the Developing New York and Los Angeles Metropolises, 1940–2000," in *New York and Los Angeles: Politics, Society, and Culture*, ed. David Halle (Chicago: University of Chicago Press, 2003), pp. 71, 76.

22. Peter Skerry, *Mexican Americans: The Ambivalent Minority* (New York: Free Press, 1993), pp. 61, 65.

23. Peter A. Morrison and Ira S. Lowry, "A Riot of Color: The Demographic Setting," in *The Los Angeles Riots: Lessons for the Urban Future*, ed. Mark Baldassare (Boulder, Colo.: Westview, 1994), p. 30.

24. David Halle, Robert Gedeon, and Andrew A. Beveridge, "Residential Separation and Segregation, Racial and Latino Identity, and the Racial Composition of Each City," in *New York and Los Angeles*, ed. Halle, p. 182.

25. Dominic A. Pacyga and Ellen Skerrett, *Chicago: City of Neighborhoods* (Chicago: Loyola University Press, 1986), pp. 250–53, 255, 258, 261, 266.

26. Census Bureau, *Statistical Abstract: 2002*, p. 45.

27. Arun Peter Lobo, Ronald J. O. Flores, and Joseph J. Salvo, "The Impact of Hispanic Growth on the Racial/Ethnic Composition of New York City Neighborhoods," *Urban Affairs Review* 37 (2002): 719–20.

28. Beveridge and Weber, "Race and Class in New York and Los Angeles," p. 76.

29. David E. Lopez, Eric Popkin, and Edward Telles, "Central Americans: At the Bottom, Struggling to Get Ahead," in *Ethnic Los Angeles*, ed. Waldinger and Bozorgmehr, p. 289.

30. Deidre A. Gaquin and Katherine A. DeBrandt, eds., *County and City Extra: Special Decennial Census Edition* (Lanham, Md.: Bernan, 2002), pp. 57, 537.

31. Lucie Cheng and Philip Q. Yang, "Asians: The 'Model Minority' Deconstructed," in *Ethnic Los Angeles*, ed. Waldinger and Bozorgmehr, pp. 314, 317, 319.

32. "Immigrants," *Time*, 8 July 1985, p. 25; "Asians: An Influx of Skills," *Time*, 8 July 1985, p. 44.

33. *Chicago Tribune*, 21 February 1991, sec. 2D, p. 2; 20 May 1993, sec. 7, p. 1.

34. Min Zhou and Rebecca Kim, "A Tale of Two Metropolises: New Immigrant Chinese Communities in New York and Los Angeles," in *New York and Los Angeles*, ed. Halle, p. 127.

35. Wei Li, "Building Ethnoburbia: The Emergence and Manifestation of the Chinese Ethnoburb in Los Angeles' San Gabriel Valley," *Journal of Asian American Studies* 2 (1999): 5; John Horton, *The Politics of Diversity: Immigration, Resistance, and Change in Monterey Park, California* (Philadelphia: Temple University Press, 1995), pp. 10–11; Timothy P. Fong, "Economic and Ethnic Politics in Monterey Park," in *New Visions in Asian American Studies: Diversity, Community, Power*, ed. Franklin Ng, Judy Yung, Stephen S. Fugita, and Elaine H. Kim (Pullman: Washington State University Press, 1994), p. 18.

36. Fong, "Economic and Ethnic Politics," p. 21; Yen-Fen Tseng, "Chinese Ethnic Economy: San Gabriel Valley, Los Angeles County," *Journal of Urban Affairs* 16 (1994): 172.

37. Fong, "Economic and Ethnic Politics," p. 21.

38. Horton, *Politics of Diversity*, pp. 29–30.

39. Timothy P. Fong, "A New and Dynamic Community: The Case of Monterey Park, California," in *Asian and Latino Immigrants in a Restructuring Economy: The Metamorphosis of Southern California*, ed. Marta Lopez-Garza and David R. Diaz (Stanford, Calif.: Stanford University Press, 2001), p. 317.

40. Horton, *Politics of Diversity*, p. 28. See also Fong, "New and Dynamic Community," p. 316.

41. Tseng, "Chinese Ethnic Economy," p. 178.

42. Li, "Building Ethnoburbia," pp. 14–15.

43. Horton, *Politics of Diversity*, p. 10.

44. For Chinese immigrants in New York City, see Hsiang-shui Chen, *Chinatown No More: Taiwan Immigrants in Contemporary New York* (Ithaca, N.Y.: Cornell University Press, 1992), and Jan Lin, *Reconstructing Chinatown: Ethnic Enclave, Global Change* (Minneapolis: University of Minnesota Press, 1998).

45. Pyong Gap Min, *Changes and Conflicts: Korean Immigrant Families in New York* (Boston: Allyn and Bacon, 1998), pp. 10–11; Census Bureau, *Statistical Abstract: 2003*, p. 11.

46. Min, *Changes and Conflicts*, pp. 16–17; Pyong Gap Min, *Caught in the Middle: Korean Merchants in America's Multiethnic Cities* (Berkeley: University of California Press, 1996), pp. 47–49.

47. "Asians: An Influx of Skills," p. 45.

48. Min, *Changes and Conflicts*, p. 19; Min, *Caught in the Middle*, pp. 53–55.

49. "Asians: An Influx of Skills," p. 45.

50. Min, *Caught in the Middle*, pp. 66–67.

51. Bert Eljera, "Filipinos Find Home in Daly City," in *Asian Americans: Experiences and Perspectives*, ed. Timothy P. Fong and Larry H. Shinagawa (Upper Saddle River, N.J.: Prentice Hall, 2000), pp. 110–11.

52. Madhulika S. Khandelwal, *Becoming American, Being Indian: An Immigrant Community in New York City* (Ithaca, N.Y.: Cornell University Press, 2002), pp. 19, 21, 23.

53. Johanna Lessinger, *From the Ganges to the Hudson: Indian Immigrants in New York City* (Boston: Allyn and Bacon, 1995), p. 13.

54. Chor-Swang Ngin, "The Acculturation Pattern of Orange County's Southeast Asian Refugees," in *Asian Americans*, ed. Fong and Shinagawa, pp. 90, 95. See also Jacqueline Desbarats, "Indochinese Settlement Patterns in Orange County," *Amerasia Journal* 10 (1983): 23–46, and Raymond Lou, "The Vietnamese Business Community of San Jose," in *Frontiers of Asian American Studies*, ed. Gail Nomura, Russell Endo, Stephen H. Sumida, and Russell C. Leong (Pullman: Washington State University Press, 1989), pp. 98–112.

55. Roger Sanjek, *The Future of Us All: Race and Neighborhood Politics in New York City* (Ithaca, N.Y.: Cornell University Press, 1998), pp. 223, 225, 227.

56. James P. Allen and Eugene Turner, "The Most Ethnically Diverse Urban Places in the United States," *Urban Geography* 10 (1989): 537.

57. "'New Brooklyns' Replace White Suburbs," *USA Today*, 19 May 2003, pp. 1A–2A.

58. Raymond A. Mohl, "Ethnic Politics in Miami, 1960–1986," in *Shades of the Sunbelt: Essays on Ethnicity, Race, and the Urban South*, ed. Randall M. Miller and George E. Pozzetta (Boca Raton: Florida Atlantic University Press, 1989), p. 152.

59. Raymond Arsenault and Gary R. Mormino, "From Dixie to Dreamland: Demographic and Cultural Change in Florida, 1880–1980," in *Shades of the Sunbelt*, ed. Miller and Pozzetta, p. 132.

60. Burkholz, "Latinization of Miami," p. 84.

61. Mohl, "Ethnic Politics in Miami," p. 152.

62. Didion, *Miami*, p. 67.

63. Timothy P. Fong, *The First Suburban Chinatown: The Remaking of Monterey Park, California* (Philadelphia: Temple University Press, 1994), pp. 110–11.

64. Ibid., pp. 113–14.

65. Tseng, "Chinese Ethnic Economy," p. 184.

66. "English Spoken Here, O.K.?" *Time*, 25 August 1986, p. 27.

67. *New York Times*, 10 November 1986, p. A22.

68. "English Spoken Here," p. 27.

69. Margot Hornblower Lamont, "Making and Breaking Law," *Time*, 21 November 1994, p. 73.

70. Pacyga and Skerrett, *Chicago*, p. 250.

71. Ngin, "Acculturation Pattern of Orange County's Southeast Asian Refugees," p. 94.

72. David Rieff, *Going to Miami: Exiles, Tourists, and Refugees in the New America* (Boston: Little, Brown, 1987), p. 177.

73. Nicolas C. Vaca, *The Presumed Alliance: The Unspoken Conflict Between Latinos and Blacks and What It Means for America* (New York: HarperCollins, 2004), p. 115.

74. Stepick et al., *This Land Is Our Land*, p. 78.

75. Burkholz, "Latinization of Miami," p. 86.

76. Alejandro Portes and Alex Stepick, *City on the Edge: The Transformation of Miami* (Berkeley: University of California Press, 1993), p. 183.

77. Grenier and Castro, "Triadic Politics," p. 284.

78. Burkholz, "Latinization of Miami," p. 84.

79. Vaca, *Presumed Alliance*, p. 108.

80. Rieff, *Going to Miami*, p. 174; Grenier and Castro, "Triadic Politics," p. 286.

81. Grenier and Castro, "Triadic Politics," p. 286.

82. Portes and Stepick, *City on the Edge*, p. 49.

83. Vaca, *Presumed Alliance*, p. 110.

84. Ibid., pp. 121–22.

85. Jack Miles, "Blacks vs. Browns," *Atlantic Monthly*, October 1992, pp. 52, 54.

86. Paul Ong and Abel Valenzuela Jr., "The Labor Market: Immigrant Effects and Racial Disparities," in *Ethnic Los Angeles*, ed. Waldinger and Bozorgmehr, p. 178.

87. Edward T. Chang, "New Urban Crisis: Korean–African American Relations," in *Koreans in the Hood: Conflict with African Americans*, ed. Kwang Chung Kim (Baltimore: Johns Hopkins University Press, 1999), p. 42; Armando Navarro, "The South Central Los Angeles Eruption: A Latino Perspective," in *Los Angeles— Struggles Toward Multiethnic Community: Asian American, African American, and Latino Perspectives*, ed. Edward T. Chang and Russell C. Leong (Seattle: University of Washington Press, 1994), p. 79.

88. Vaca, *Presumed Alliance*, pp. 132, 138, 140.

89. *New York Times*, 1 November 1994, p. A21.

90. Vaca, *Presumed Alliance*, p. 187.

91. Patrick D. Joyce, *No Fire Next Time: Black–Korean Conflicts and the Future of America's Cities* (Ithaca, N.Y.: Cornell University Press, 2003), pp. 12, 16–17.

92. *Chicago Tribune*, 10 July 1990, sec. 2C, pp. 1, 6.

93. Joyce, *No Fire Next Time*, pp. 67–68.

94. *New York Times*, 19 January 1985, p. 1.

95. Joyce, *No Fire Next Time*, p. 90.

96. Ibid., pp. 92, 95–96, 109.

97. Ibid., p. 145. See also Karen Umemoto, "Blacks and Koreans in Los Angeles: The Case of La Tasha Harlins and Soon Ja Du," in *Blacks, Latinos, and Asians in Urban America: Status and Prospects for Politics and Activism*, ed. James Jennings (Westport, Conn.: Praeger, 1994), pp. 95–117.

98. Jeff Chang, "Race, Class, Conflict, and Empowerment: On Ice Cube's 'Black Korea,'" in *Los Angeles—Struggles Toward Multiethnic Community*, ed. Chang and Leong, pp. 87–88.

99. Ibid., p. 94.

100. Paul Ong and Suzanne Hee, *Losses in the Los Angeles Civil Unrest, April 29–May 1, 1992* (Los Angeles: Center for Pacific Rim Studies, University of California, Los Angeles, 1993), pp. 7, 9–10, 12; Joyce, *No Fire Next Time*, p. 150.

101. Chang, "New Urban Crisis," p. 47.

102. Min, *Caught in the Middle*, pp. 93–94.

103. Kyeyoung Park, "The Morality of a Commodity: A Case Study of 'Rebuilding L.A. Without Liquor Stores,'" *Amerasia Journal* 21 (1995–1996): 9.

104. Joyce, *No Fire Next Time*, p. 160. See also Raphael J. Sonenshein, "The Battle over Liquor Stores in South Central Los Angeles: The Management of an Interminority Conflict," *Urban Affairs Review* 31 (1996): 710–37.

105. Sanjek, *Future of Us All*, p. 228.

7. After the Revolution

1. Haya El Nasser, "Metro's Suburbs Make Name for Themselves," *USA Today*, 22 July 2003, p. 3A.

2. Robert E. Lang, *Edgeless Cities: Exploring the Elusive Metropolis* (Washington, D.C.: Brookings Institution Press, 2003), pp. 1–2.

3. "Paved Paradise," *Newsweek*, 15 May 1995, p. 42. See also Robert E. Lang and Patrick A. Simmons, "'Boomburbs': The Emergence of Large Fast-Growing Suburban Cities," in *Redefining Urban and Suburban America: Evidence from the Census 2000*, ed. Bruce Katz and Robert E. Lang (Washington, D.C.: Brookings Institution Press, 2003), vol. 1, pp. 101–15.

4. "Supersuburbs," *Planning*, January 1989, p. 7. See also Suzanne Weiss, "Aurora: Denver's Neighbor Catches Up," *Planning*, January 1989, p. 14.

5. David Dillon, "Arlington: Betwixt and Between," *Planning*, January 1989, p. 9.

6. William H. Hudnut III, *Halfway to Everywhere: A Portrait of America's First-Tier Suburbs* (Washington, D.C.: Urban Land Institute, 2003), p. 163.

7. Ibid., pp. 163, 166; see also pp. 164–65.

8. Richard Lacayo, "The Brawl over Sprawl," *Time*, 22 March 1999, p. 45.

9. David Dillon, "Fortress America," *Planning*, June 1994, p. 8; Setha Low, *Behind the Gates: Life, Security, and the Pursuit of Happiness in Fortress America* (New York: Routledge, 2003), p. 15.

10. Edward J. Blakely and Mary Gail Snyder, *Fortress America: Gated Communities in the United States* (Washington, D.C.: Brookings Institution Press, 1997), pp. 75, 111.

11. Dillon, "Fortress America," p. 8.

12. Blakely and Snyder, *Fortress America*, pp. 77, 113.

13. Dillon, "Fortress America," pp. 8, 12.

14. "State of the Industry," *Chain Store Age*, August 2001, pp. 4A–5A; "Global Retailing," *Chain Store Age*, December 2001, p. 90.

15. Laura Rowley, *On Target: How the World's Hottest Retailer Hit a Bull's Eye* (Hoboken, N.J.: Wiley, 2003), p. 9.

16. Ibid., pp. 6, 9.

17. *Chicago Tribune*, 29 July 2003, sec. 3, p. 1; 24 May 2004, sec. 1, p. 18.

18. *Chicago Tribune*, 13 May 2004, sec. 1, p. 27; 23 May 2004, sec. 1, p. 17. See also *Chicago Tribune*, 26 March 2004, sec. 1, pp. 1, 26; 4 May 2004, sec. 1, pp. 1, 20.

19. Philip Langdon, *A Better Place to Live: Reshaping the American Suburb* (Amherst: University of Massachusetts Press, 1994), p. 1.

20. James Howard Kunstler, *The Geography of Nowhere: The Rise and Decline of America's Man-Made Landscape* (New York: Simon and Schuster, Touchstone, 1994), p. 10.

21. Lacayo, "Brawl over Sprawl," p. 46.

22. Daniel Pedersen, Vern E. Smith, and Jerry Adler, "Sprawling, Sprawling . . . ," *Newsweek*, 19 July 1999, pp. 23, 25.

23. Donald C. Williams, *Urban Sprawl: A Reference Handbook* (Santa Barbara, Calif.: ABC-CLIO, 2000), p. 1.

24. James Howard Kunstler, *The City in Mind: Notes on the Urban Condition* (New York: Free Press, 2001), p. 43.

25. Phillip J. Langman, "American Gridlock," *U.S. News & World Report*, 28 May 2001, p. 19.

26. Kunstler, *City in Mind*, p. 41.

27. Michelle Cottle, "House Arrest," *New Republic*, 6 August 2001, p. 18.

28. John G. Mitchell, "Urban Sprawl," *National Geographic*, July 2001, p. 71.

29. Lacayo, "Brawl over Sprawl," p. 45; Randal O'Toole, *The Vanishing Automobile and Other Urban Myths* (Brandon, Ore.: Thoreau Institute, 2001), p. 32; Bruce Katz, "The Permanent Campaign," *Urban Land*, May 2003, p. 49.

30. Lacayo, "Brawl over Sprawl," p. 46.

31. Williams, *Urban Sprawl*, pp. 21, 47–48; Katz, "Permanent Campaign," p. 49.

32. Lacayo, "Brawl over Sprawl," p. 47.

33. Kunstler, *Geography of Nowhere*, pp. 201, 206.

34. Andres Duany, Elizabeth Plater-Zyberk, and Jeff Speck, *Suburban Nation: The Rise of Sprawl and the Decline of the American Dream* (New York: North Point, 2000), p. 243.

35. O'Toole, *Vanishing Automobile*, pp. 7–8, 41.

36. Pedersen, Smith, and Adler, "Sprawling, Sprawling," p. 26.

37. Greg Easterbrook, "Suburban Myth," *New Republic*, 15 March 1999, p. 20.

38. Ibid., p. 21.

39. Pedersen, Smith, and Adler, "Sprawling, Sprawling," p. 26.

40. Patrick A. Simmons and Robert E. Lang, "The Urban Turnaround," in *Redefining Urban and Suburban America*, ed. Katz and Lang, pp. 51–61.

41. Lynn W. Bachelor, "Stadiums as Solution Sets: Baseball, Football, and Downtown Development," in *The Economics and Politics of Sports Facilities*, ed. Wilbur C. Rich (Westport, Conn.: Quorum, 2000), p. 133.

42. Jay Weiner, *Stadium Games: Fifty Years of Big League Greed and Bush League Boondoggles* (Minneapolis: University of Minnesota Press, 2000), p. 475.

43. Edward I. Sidlow and Beth M. Henschen, "Building Ballparks: The Public-Policy Dimensions of Keeping the Game in Town," in *Economics and Politics of Sports Facilities*, ed. Rich, p. 163.

44. Bachelor, "Stadiums as Solution Sets," p. 132.

45. Robert A. Baade and Allen R. Sanderson, "Bearing Down in Chicago: Location, Location, Location," in *Sports, Jobs, and Taxes: The Economic Impact of Sports Teams and Stadiums*, ed. Roger G. Noll and Andrew Zimbalist (Washington, D.C.: Brookings Institution Press, 1997), pp. 324–54.

46. Bachelor, "Stadiums as Solution Sets," pp. 127, 139.

47. Ziona Austrian and Mark S. Rosentraub, "Cleveland's Gateway to the Future," in *Sports, Jobs, and Taxes*, ed. Noll and Zimbalist, pp. 355–84.

48. Ibid., p. 381.

49. Kevin Riordan, "Camden Rebound," *Planning*, February 2002, p. 16.

50. Dennis R. Judd, "Constructing the Tourist Bubble," in *The Tourist City*, ed. Dennis R. Judd and Susan S. Fainstein (New Haven, Conn.: Yale University Press, 1999), pp. 40–44.

51. David Barringer, "The New Urban Gamble," *American Prospect*, September–October 1997, pp. 28–34; Harold Henderson, "Luck Be a Lady in Gary," *Planning*, November 1999, pp. 8–12.

52. Henderson. "Luck Be a Lady," pp. 8, 12.

53. *New York Times*, 13 December 1998, sec. 11, p. 9.

54. *New York Times*, 29 December 1998, p. A10.

55. Ann Breen and Dick Rigby, *Intown Living: A Different American Dream* (Westport, Conn.: Praeger, 2004), pp. 243–44.

56. *Columbus (Ohio) Dispatch*, 11 October 2004, pp. B1, B3.

57. Joel Kotkin, *The New Geography: How the Digital Revolution Is Reshaping the American Landscape* (New York: Random House, 2000), p. 57.

58. Breen and Rigby, *Intown Living*, p. 49.

59. *New York Times*, 29 December 1998, p. A10.

60. Rebecca R. Sohmer and Robert E. Lang, "Downtown Rebound," in *Redefining Urban and Suburban America*, ed. Katz and Lang, p. 68.

61. Eugenie Ladner Birch, "Having a Longer View on Downtown Living," *Journal of the American Planning Association* 68 (2002): 5.

62. Ibid., p. 12.

63. Camilo Jose Vergara, *The New American Ghetto* (New Brunswick, N.J.: Rutgers University Press, 1995), p. 221.

64. Steve Belmont, *Cities in Full: Recognizing and Realizing the Great Potential of Urban America* (Chicago: Planners, 2002), p. 102.

65. Vergara, *New American Ghetto*, p. 211.

66. Ibid., pp. 211, 215.

67. Belmont, *Cities in Full*, pp. 90–91.

68. Ibid., pp. 93, 98.

69. Ibid., pp. 103–4.

70. Mike Davis, *City of Quartz: Excavating the Future in Los Angeles* (New York: Vintage, 1992), pp. 224, 228. See also Mike Davis, *Beyond Blade Runner: Urban Control and the Ecology of Fear*, *Open Magazine* Pamphlet Series, no. 23 (Westfield, N.J.: Open Media, 1992), and *Ecology of Fear: Los Angeles and the Imagination of Disaster* (New York: Holt, 1998); and Edward W. Soja, *Postmetropolis: Critical Studies of Cities and Regions* (Malden, Mass.: Blackwell, 2000), pp. 298–322.

Index